Praise for *Gardening at the Dragon's Gate*

"Flower and fruit of a lifetime's horticultural experience, this masterwork goes far beyond the practical gardening advice it offers in abundance. *Gardening at the Dragon's Gate* is full of profound meditations on the chemistry and poetry of botany, geology, and natural history, all rendered in Wendy's unmistakably rich voice. An instant classic."

—Norman Fischer, teacher and founder, Everyday Zen Foundation; author of *Taking Our Places: The Buddhist Path to Truly Growing Up*

"If Earth took a human voice, it would be Wendy's: wry, fierce, passionately attentive to detail, and so startling in its wild freedom it's almost scary. . . . This book is a tonic to the soul. I dare anyone to read it and not be shaken into a fuller, gladder life."

—Joanna Macy, author of World as Lover, *World as Self*

GARDENING
AT THE
DRAGON'S
GATE

At Work in the Wild and
Cultivated World

Wendy Johnson

Illustrations by Davis Te Selle

BANTAM BOOKS

GARDENING AT THE DRAGON'S GATE

Published by
Bantam Dell
A Division of Random House, Inc.
New York, New York

Book design by David Bullen

ISBN 978-0-553-37803-0

Printed in the United States of America

This book is dedicated to the garden,
a field far beyond form and emptiness.

And to Peter, for a lifetime of love and work.

CONTENTS

CONTENTS

INTO
THE
TANGLE

WHEN I WAS A BRAND-NEW GARDENER, I PLANTED MY FIRST bed of sweet corn at Tassajara Zen Mountain Center, San Francisco Zen Center's training monastery deep in the Ventana wilderness east of Big Sur in central California. I was working by myself in the upper garden, rapt with concentration. I stretched a string line the full length of the sixty-five-foot row where I was planting the corn, and just under this line I scratched out a three-inch-deep furrow. The string showed me where to plant and kept me straight. I filled my fist with dry, shriveled kernels of 'Bantam' sweet corn, and every two inches or so I dropped a kernel of corn into the furrow. I wasn't sure that I would have enough seed so I left the furrow uncovered until the entire line was planted. I was working on my hands and knees. Head down and deep under the spell of the ancient ritual of planting seed, I imagined green blades of corn rising up out of the black skirt of the ground.

Finally the line was sown and I looked up from my supplicant's crouch. A rotund Steller's jay was at the bottom of my corn furrow, hopping fearlessly down the line, gobbling up each of my carefully sown kernels of sweet corn. The bold, zaftig bird paused for a moment, fixed me with her bright eye, and continued to feast. And my life as a gardener cracked open and took root.

What I realized that summer day was fundamental. Gardening is about awareness and relationship—*consequential* relationship. It's also about taking a stand, and standing by your principles. At the same time, it's about giving up control and learning from your mistakes. This hasn't been an easy lesson for me. When I recovered from my stunned shock in the Tassajara corn furrow I leapt to my feet, bellowing war cries at the retreating backside of the fat, corn-fed jay. Muttering under my breath, I redistributed the remaining corn seed in the row and stamped closed the furrow. Today, thirty-odd years later, I'm still pursuing blue jays and they are still pursuing me.

After two years at Tassajara I moved in 1975 to another branch of the San Francisco Zen Center, Green Gulch Farm in Marin County just north of San Francisco. I lived and gardened at Green Gulch Farm for twenty-five years, settling my life, practicing Zen, and deepening my understanding of the earth under my fingernails.

Green Gulch has a second name, one woven out of poetry and meditation practice: Soryu-ji, or Green Dragon Zen Temple. I love this name that so deftly describes the sinuous valley of Green Gulch, which uncoils between high, dry hills like an ancient green dragon with its tail stirring the sea and its fire-breathing head held high in the mysterious clouds that rise like primordial vapor from the coastal mountains. I now make my primary garden at my home a scant mile north of Green Gulch, almost where the dragon's tail lashes the sea.

In the East the dragon represents wisdom and transformation. A dangerously fiery being, the green dragon sleeps in the cool bowels of the earth or in dark pools of water, until upon awakening it unfolds its huge, scaly wings and takes to the air, breathing molten fire to ignite an incandescent sky.

Like the dragon, meditation practice and gardening are not tame or obedient, but burn with an old fire that will not be extinguished. In these times of record global climate change caused by human activity, a fierce response is required. Gardening at the dragon's gate summons the four great elements: earth, air, water, and fire, all changeable and functioning as one dynamic whole. Their true nature is dragon-like and paradoxical, for just as meditation and gardening settle down into the deep core of the present moment, they also shift shape and take on the world in fresh form, never seen before.

The daily meditation I practice, zazen, is quite simple. It comes out of the Zen Buddhist tradition of sitting down in the center of your life, not moving or speaking, and connecting with the rhythm of your breath. For the last thirty-five years I have practiced this meditation—with a community of about fifty other Zen students in the converted hayloft meditation hall at Green Gulch Farm; with environmental activists gathered in the high mountains of northern New Mexico and central Vermont; and alone, by darkened windows of dawn, while the garden all around me comes into light.

Meditation practice is grounded in wisdom and compassion for myself and others, qualities that arise naturally with wholehearted practice. On my simple altar at home I have a small figure of the bodhisattva Kuan-Yin, the awakened transformation of compassion. Her dark robes billow with wind as she stands on the back of a fierce dragon whose scaly tail is fused to Kuan-Yin's robes as they negotiate the high seas of birth and death together.

Meditation takes gumption but it is not fussy. The gate is open to all beings and the practice does not depend on bells, drums, or intricate philosophy. Meditation is larger than all of this, grounded in simple curiosity and in the determination to know your heart and mind inside out and in the present moment. To do this you go directly into the tangle of your life, sit down in the middle of it, and allow the steady stream of your breath to carry you home.

Working in the garden is also meditation, though not in the conventional sense of calming down, moving slowly and deliberately, and dwelling in stillness. On the contrary, I am often most alert and settled in the garden when I am working hard, hip-deep in a succulent snarl of spring weeds. My body and mind drop away then, far below wild radish and bull thistle, and I live in the rhythmic pulse of the long green throat of my work.

This book is about gardening at the dragon's gate, where every leaf, every big-eyed bug, every rusty wheelbarrow is both utterly familiar and strangely new at the same time. I wrote this book longhand. It took me more than ten years, and I continued to meditate and garden like a Fury while I wrote. Each time I went off the path of my work, meditation and the garden brought me back, reminding me to just continue under all circumstances. Gardening at the dragon's gate is fundamental work that permeates your entire life. It demands your energy and heart, and it gives you back great treasures as well, like a fortified sense of humor, an appreciation for paradox, and a huge harvest of 'Dinosaur' kale and tiny red potatoes.

Gardening is all about picking and choosing and following your passion. Some very basic principles inform how I garden. They come out of my love for gardening and for the world. Today I count seven principles. Tomorrow there may be eight or nine, because they arise out of an untame rootstock from below the bottom of time.

    • My first principle is to learn gardening from the wilderness outside the garden gate. As I work to keep the links alive between wild land and the cultivated row, I get my clearest gardening instruction from listening to the voice of the watershed that surrounds our garden. I know that January is the time to prune our Japanese 'Elephant Heart' plum in the garden, but just *when* in January is always linked to noticing when the first white blossoms appear on the wild plum tree. I mark it on my calendar and sharpen my red pruning shears, because in two weeks the 'Elephant Heart' plum will flower in turn.

There is very little true wilderness remaining in the modern world. And yet when Thoreau says, "In wildness is the preservation of the world," he reminds me that wildness, at least, persists. It endures underneath the paved-over pathways of our cities as well as on the fringe of urban farmland. It persists in patches, sumps, and wallows, in weedy tangles everywhere on earth. Staying in relationship to the uncultivated world is a primary principle for me as I garden domesticated land.

In honor of wildness inside and outside the garden gate, every spring I leave a random corner of our garden untended. I let it go into a neglected tangle. Throughout the growing season I pass by this fallow spit of wilderness and it feeds my somewhat fierce soul. In early autumn, when I am obsessed with our latest harvest of slim, white-stockinged leeks and golden beets, I look across the ordered rows of the garden to that far tangle of seedy cow parsnip and dry skunkweed and my wild roots stir back to life.

◆ My second principle is to garden organically, always within the ample embrace of nature, without relying on chemical fertilizers, pesticides, or herbicides. Organic gardening and ecological farming is rooted in and encourages local stewardship and protection of land and water resources; it works in harmony with natural ecosystems to sustain diversity, complexity, and real health in the garden and in the wider community. Even now when organic gardening is no longer considered a marginal endeavor, it is essential to support organic farms and farmers in order to assure food security and safety over the long haul. Growing food organically and eating conscientiously are political acts that help to establish and ensure social, economic, and ecological justice.

◆ My third principle is to know the soil where I work in every way. Composed of clouds of countless, invisible microorganisms digesting the land and running it through their intestines, soil is feces, and within the body of soil, all beings garden. Remembering as I work that there are more microorganisms in one cup of fertile garden soil than there are human beings on planet Earth, I have a fresh view of my own scale and context in the life of the garden.

To know your soil is to work with your land and to let the land work you as well. How you cultivate your ground depends on you—maybe you will dig down deep like a joyous, unleashed dog and mound up your garden as we love to do at Green Gulch, or perhaps you will choose to create a long-term, slow-pulsed permaculture garden with soil that is hardly moved at all. What matters most is that you are in *relationship* with your land and listening to the soil as you work, finding your true place in the body of your garden.

◆ My fourth principle is to feed the soil and to work to build fertile land, not just to grow crops. An old Japanese proverb says a poor farmer grows weeds, a mediocre farmer grows crops, and a good farmer grows soil. Organic gardeners "grow soil" by planting a green mantle of cover crops on the ground to build fertility year round. We also cultivate deep-rooted crops like burdock and American sweet clover, which break up hardpan and consolidate minerals and nitrogen in their roots. Sometimes we help build fertile soil by stepping back and fallowing land, letting it rest for a season or two. But most of all, we build soil by making compost piles and celebrating decay. "Life into death into life" is the organic gardener's motto for the work happening in every compost pile built out of raw garbage and layered straw. This work is so fundamental to our gardening tradition at Green Gulch that we often joke that even though we don't proselytize about Zen we certainly do preach the gospel of hot compost.

• My fifth gardening principle is to welcome diversity into the garden. I have a passion for preserving and culturing biological diversity in the plant kindom—without a "king," all plants are kin—for growing a wide range of plants from seed and for supporting small seed companies that make a special effort to protect heritage varieties. Eighty percent of all the vegetable varieties that were available in the United States in 1900 have now disappeared, due to a huge centralization of the seed trade in the hands of a very few multinational corporations. Even while I inveigh against the erosion of genetic diversity and the unmonitored modification of crops, I also remember that agriculture is fifteen thousand years old, grounded in biological diversity and fueled by the determination of gardeners worldwide to protect and encourage this diversity.

• My sixth gardening principle is to slow down and invite the unknown, the unwelcome, and the failed into the life of the garden. When you garden at the dragon's gate you have no other choice *but* to do this, so you might as well be gracious and willing to be undone. At Green Gulch and the school and public urban plots where I garden, I work with all kinds of people. I have learned to trust and to garden with whoever shows up. We are never in control of the garden, anyway, so why not yield to the mystery of transformation? I have seen a sixty-three-year-old woman with pneumonia come back to health dead-heading white cosmos hour after hour to provide fresh flowers for the zendo altar. And I've witnessed an unhappy six-year-old hellion become a gallant angel by rescuing and caring for a newt about to be mangled by the garden lawn mower.

We live in a non-repeating universe, a world where we learn as much from failure as from success. Corn-gobbling blue jays and other garden pests serve as fine teachers and so do failed 'Easter Egg' radishes, crimson, white, and dark purple, laid out in worm-eaten decrepitude on a chipped platter. "Life is one continuous mistake," Shunryu Suzuki Roshi, the founder of San Francisco Zen Center, used to remind his students. When he shopped he sought out the rattiest vegetables at market, all the discarded and maimed culls, and his meditation grew strong, nourished by the continuous mistakes of human life.

 ◆ My seventh principle is generosity with the harvest. In the biblical book of Leviticus, one of the laws of Jewish life was not to cut the corners of the fields after the main harvest but to leave them standing so there would be food to be gleaned by the hungry, the lonely, and the stranger. I treasure this old admonition to share the bounty of the garden harvest with all beings; it reminds me not to cut corners and to garden wholeheartedly for the benefit of both the visible and the invisible hungry world.

✦   ✦   ✦

This book loosely follows these principles in and out of the dragon's gate. It begins by encouraging you to become intimate with the wildness and deep rhythms of the place where you live, and to listen to the particular, distinct voice of your watershed.

I get my bearings in the rich green world from particular plants that serve as North Star guides for me. They orient me to what I love and trust, and always surprise me with their wordless lives. In the second chapter of this book, I introduce you to basic botany for gardeners and a few plants that have helped to stabilize and locate me in the body of the garden.

Then we come to chapters on the craft of gardening, grounded in three primary practices. The soil must be cared for first, by cultivating the ground and by building fertility. Next is tending the garden, which includes irrigating, weeding, pruning, and recognizing and ministering to plant disease as well as to beneficial and harmful garden insects. Gardening would not be complete without renewal, so we turn to propagating plants, both from seed and by asexual propagation.

The following chapters place these plants in the landscape, in gardens designed with a common love for plants and people. To make the design more intimate I include the history of a few gardens I love and know well. The book closes with the harvest, not only in the garden but also in the kitchen and around the dinner table. The bounty grown and gathered from the heart of the garden is shared with children, family, friends, and invited and uninvited beings, far too numerous to count.

When the Buddha first began to teach, a magical deity visited him in the night and asked this question:

> The inner tangle and the outer tangle—
> This generation is entangled in a tangle.
> So I ask you,
> Who succeeds in untangling this tangle?

The Buddha's answer was simple and direct: the one who sits down in the middle of his or her life and looks with attention, calm and resolute, has a chance to untangle the tangle and to relieve suffering. This does not mean that oversimplifying or setting up strict rules and regulations is the answer. Gardens are far stronger than any notions about them. They elude the richest vows and principles and bend away from all ideas. In the presence of the twining vines of our huge Chinese wisteria, which daily engulfs the once-sturdy garden fence that surrounds my home, it would be a simplistic conceit to plot the untangling of this vast, fragrant being. Instead, I prefer to go *into* the tangle and to join the knot of entwined life.

GARDENING
AT THE
DRAGON'S
GATE

VALLEY
OF THE
ANCESTORS

The Voice of the Watershed

I N CHINESE THERE IS AN OLD WORD FOR LANDSCAPE, COMPOSED OF two root characters: *shan* (mountains) and *shui* (water). For the last thirty-some years I have been gardening, meditating, and teaching in both a mountain and a water landscape on the edge of the San Andreas Fault line in the Bay Area of northern California. I lived for much of that time at Green Gulch Farm, a Zen Buddhist meditation and retreat center with a working organic farm and garden. Green Gulch Farm is located on the western margin of North America, about a half-hour's drive north of San Francisco, at Muir Beach in Marin County. Now I live nearby, still in the deep bottomland of Muir Beach on that delicate seamline where solid earth floats, buckling and shifting without notice.

Green Gulch Valley is a very old place. The soil was formed under the

3

Pacific Ocean, the deepest and largest ocean in the world, which now breaks at its edge. Green Gulch soil is really compressed ocean bottom, heaved up millennia ago to become dry land. Made of the intensely folded and faulted rocks of the Franciscan complex, this bottomland soil includes Mesozoic marine sandstone and shale, chert, seafloor volcanic rock, and rare metamorphic rock interlaced with compressed marine fossils. When I look deeply I see that we are growing lettuce on the bottom of the ocean.

Mount Tamalpais, the sacred mountain of the native Ohlone tribes of the Bay Area, rises abruptly from the steep ocean cliffs at Muir Beach, climbing two thousand five hundred feet to its summit. Diaz Ridge, the foot ridge of Mount Tamalpais, defines the northwestern boundary of Green Gulch Farm, while Coyote Ridge, another part of the Coast Ranges, marks the southeastern margin of our watershed. In between these craggy coastal mountains, the green dragon snakes out to the sea.

Brush and ink paintings of Chinese landscapes show endless misty mountains molded by running water, or still lakes reflecting raggedly clouded peaks. These landscapes are never solid, never static. Always in motion, they move just below the rolling fog. The great thirteenth-century Zen master Eihei Dogen writes in his "Mountains and Rivers Sutra" that the green mountains are always walking and that they travel on water as well as across land. The mountains and rivers of this time and place are also never only what they seem to be.

I first read the "Mountains and Rivers Sutra" in 1975 at Tassajara Zen Mountain Center. Tassajara is a seasonal monastery and retreat center in the Ventana Wilderness of the Los Padres National Forest that, like Green Gulch Farm, is a branch of the San Francisco Zen Center. I copied the sutra out by hand and still reread it every year. "Although mountains belong to the nation," wrote Dogen, "mountains belong to people who love them." Gardeners are mountain-and-river pilgrims. We commit ourselves to the landscapes we know and love, traveling over their jagged terrain step by step. When I slow down and read the "Mountains and Rivers Sutra" carefully, or when I step up close to a Chinese

4

scroll, I always find a tiny human figure tucked between the folded canyons of the green mountains, meandering with the aid of a crooked pilgrim's staff through the shallow backwaters of rivers without end.

The first time I saw Green Gulch Farm I was on foot, and feeling like that tiny pilgrim lost in a Chinese landscape painting. When Peter Rudnick, not yet my husband, and I decided to leave the mountain wilderness of Tassajara in the autumn of 1975 to help San Francisco Zen Center establish a small organic farm at the edge of the Pacific Ocean, we decided to make the pilgrimage to Green Gulch on foot.

I had been working in the garden at Tassajara and I did not want to leave, but Peter was eager for the move. He loved change. So, in high spirits, he led our hike out, while I dragged along like a reluctant exile. The Tassajara tomatoes were just coming into color, and I was walking out. The dark opal Japanese eggplants were finally growing plump and ready to harvest, and I was walking out. The work positions at a Zen monastery are rotated every year, which is supposed to keep Zen students from becoming attached to one job or one identity. But it was too late for me, far too late. I had already dedicated countless hours of precious Zen meditation to plotting the layout of the Tassajara garden: 'Touchon' carrots sowed in early April in the lower garden would follow the winter crop of Chinese cabbage. By late July the carrots would be pulled and followed by a sowing of rhubarb chard for next autumn's kitchen. A blood sample taken from any part of my body would have confirmed the bitter truth: I carried in every corpuscle the incurable obsession of gardening.

It took us three full days to walk out of the wild and geologically young mountains, the age of the Himalayas and just about as sheer. Eventually I picked up my pace, the call of the coast pulling me now through the Ventana Wilderness. It was almost dark on the third day when Peter and I finally pushed out of the chaparral underbrush into the dark redwood canyons of the coast above the Big Sur River. We smelled of the loneliness of walking for hours on unmarked trails. Woodsmoke from our nightly fires filled our hair. I was repeating lines from the "Mountains and Rivers Sutra" to myself as we walked, as a magical incantation so that I would never forget Tassajara. "If you doubt mountains walking, you do not know your own walking; it is not that you do not walk, but that you do not know or understand your own walking . . . at this moment, do not doubt the green mountains' walking."

I remember the cool winds coming up from the redwoods of the Sur River canyon as we headed northwest to the coast. We heard the thick blood of the river pumping through the granite veins of the canyon. Far in the distance white shorebirds circled in slow hypnotic gyres below us, calling and sailing on the updrafts, the ocean a scant five miles away. It was almost dark by the time we finished our descent to the river canyon. We made a fire of broken redwood branches and oak leaf duff and cooked the last of our carrots and potatoes into a stew. We had a little hard bread left over and a heel of leathery Parmesan cheese. We ate without speaking, too tired to talk. I lay down and watched the stars appear at the top of the ancient redwoods. Peter rolled out our sleeping bags while I tracked the appearance of the North Star in the dome of the night.

In the closing hours of the night, when the coals of the stars were banked in the soft gray ash of dawn, we were wakened by the thunderous sound of a redwood tree falling in a steep side canyon of the river. We heard the tree creak and break, fifteen or sixteen loud reports like cannon fire, and then the long downward surge of the falling giant. The sound went on forever as the tree crashed down through other redwoods and finally fell on the thick duff litter of the forest floor.

Silent, we leaned together against a redwood tree until the sun began to burn red and yellow along the jagged tip-line of the Sur canyon conifers. I remember our walk along the steep sea meadows of Partington Ridge and the final vertical drop down to the ocean not far from Sea Lion Cove. The mountains and rivers of the Ventana Wilderness were behind us.

We hitchhiked to Carmel along the coast road and from there we caught a bus to San Francisco and hitched again to Marin County, along Highway One where the ocean spread out before us. I was a stranger here. I didn't know the coastal plants under my boots. All of our possessions were on our backs in our old, smoky, ripped Kelty packs. At the top of the crooked road leading down to Green Gulch Valley we stopped under the shelter of towering eucalyptus trees to look over the lowlands. Below the coastal hills seared brown by the fiery oven of Indian summer was a lush brocade of irrigated crops.

Peter was looking off to the west where the sea thudded on the edge of the land. We could hear the waves booming on the beach. The sky hung huge over us, pale blue and pressing down on the soft swell of the sea. The tail of the green dragon stirred the sea with autumn languor. Green was alive in the stepped scales of the valley, iridescent sea-foam green and durable hunter's green, all intertwined in the cells of the crops. We started down the long road to our new life.

✦   ✦   ✦

Since walking down that eucalyptus-lined road over thirty years ago, I have learned a lot about meditation and a lot about gardening. Meditation practice is not for the faint of heart. Neither is gardening. Both take gumption and commitment and a steady willingness for the world as you know it to come apart and be reorganized. Gardening and meditation intersect for me in the subtle, deep work of getting to know my home place inside out, a tricky pursuit in a meditation tradition that values the importance of being an *unsui*—a home-leaver. *Unsui* is a Japanese word for monk, literally meaning "cloud and water wanderer," since the practice of the *unsui* is to travel unfettered across the face of the deep mountains, like clouds and water.

I practice as a lay teacher and householder, long married to Peter, who worked for more than a decade as the field manager of the nine-acre organic vegetable production area at Green Gulch Farm and then moved on to organic urban farming: with prisoners at the San Francisco County jail, with community groups on land leased from the public utilities commission, and with a homeless shelter that has a small, massively productive garden. If we are *unsui* at all, then we are thundercloud and roaring water *unsui*. The culture of our Zen practice life includes the whole works: from formal Tang Dynasty sitting robes to battered digging spades.

Poet and Zen practitioner Gary Snyder has a simple, radical suggestion for citizens of this millennium:

 Don't move. Stay still. Once you find a place that feels halfway right, and it seems time, settle down with a vow not to move any more. Take a look at one place on earth, one circle of people, one realm of beings over time.

"Not moving" does not mean that you do not grow. On the contrary. Settling deeply down on one spot of earth demands that you grow and change constantly just to keep up with the pulse and will of your place.

The word "place" is both a noun and a verb. There are more than one thousand place nouns in the natural world, from "holler" to "talus" to "strand." Wherever you are, you place yourself on your home place and learn as much as you can about the spot of earth that is your home. Whether you own the land you work or rent a little house with a tiny alleyway of backyard makes no difference at all. Don't move until you know as much about that place as possible. When Henry David Thoreau walked the wooded thickets of his home landscape in Concord, Massachusetts, he mused that it was possible in one's lifetime to know and cover a range of about twenty square miles. Step by step, timeless hours of mindfulness are dedicated to knowing, inside out, the life and character of those twenty miles.

In our inner cities and in the corridors of suburbia there is a renaissance of interest in getting to know our home neighborhoods. Streams are being freed from their asphalt and concrete channels in East Palo Alto, old cobblestone streets in the South Bronx are being discovered and reclaimed below the cracked modern pavement, and community gardens are sending out their green tendrils from Fort Mason on the San Francisco Bay to Albion, Maine.

How does a gardener go about learning the raw truth of place? Every spot has a voice, a particular taste, a breath of wind unique to itself, a shadow, a presence. The best gardeners I know slow way down in order to receive the tidings of the land they are bound to work. We notice where the prevailing wind comes from and how strong it is, learning from the sculptured listing of bent trees. We notice when the sunlight comes up in the morning in every season of the year and where and when it fades red in the west at night. We track rainfall, the first and last frost dates, snowfall and sleet, and how long it takes the land to dry out after winter ends. We pay minute attention to the grit of our living mantle of soil. We taste the waters of home with discernment and unearned pride.

All this is second nature to gardeners. What is less native for us is to read the wider map of the watershed where our garden is located. I live in a land-scape that is rain-free from late May through November. In early December the dry creeks and freshets, the underground streams and old seeps of our rugged coastal range come alive as ribbons of cold rain unfurl down every sleeping watercourse. The dry hills snort out loud as bristle-backed ridges of Muir Beach shed their new sheen of rain, reminding me what is upriver, what is down. Land that was firm puddles and oozes, and the earth slumps and finds its place as water carves and resettles the soft edges of the solid world.

In the beginning of February I help to organize a yearly walk and spend one entire day slowly pacing the margins of the Redwood Creek watershed. When we climb up the steep-shinned flanks of Mount Tamalpais and reach the coastal meadows just below Druid Heights, the voices of the tributary waters of Redwood Creek burst forth. Some years on our watershed walk we are deafened by the roar of these creeks. Then we stand together above the multiple cascades pouring off the Dipsea Trail and call at top volume their given names: Fern Creek, Kent Creek, Spikebuck Creek, we shout, Rattlesnake Creek, Green Gulch Creek!

When Redwood Creek is at its height in the winter season, it is the southernmost spawning ground of the ancient silver salmon, members of the coho salmon line, a fish more primitive even than the prehistoric redwood trees that shelter their ancestral breeding grounds.

Salmon can only live where the waters are cool and fresh, and full of debris. Secret, unharnessed rivers are their ancestral home. As recently as the early 1900s, when salmon entered the great estuary of the San Francisco Bay to journey up the Sacramento River and spawn, they clogged the neck of the Carquinez Strait leading into the river. "There were so many salmon you could cross the strait on their backs," bragged old residents of that area. Now the salmon numbers are far less and the short, seven-mile run at Redwood Creek is one of the last unstocked winter river courses for coho silver salmon in the world.

The silver salmon live at sea for two years before coming home to their exact natal estuary to spawn and die. Salmon navigate with the aid of an inner magnetic map and a keen sense of day length, so any given fish knows approximately where it is in relation to its home watershed at all times. As spawning season nears, the salmon develop a heightened sense of smell and may actually locate their home stream by tasting and smelling the familiar waters where they were born.

It makes perfect sense to me that salmon would know home by the taste of their natal streams. I am convinced that each particular place where we garden and set down roots has its own distinct scent and taste. When I come home from a long journey away from Muir Beach, I like to go down to the garden and smell a handful of moist soil to get the real news of what's been happening while I was away. This soil is heavy and wet: the memory of its sea-bottom history is held in every fog-clogged pore of the land. This soil has grown the food I eat and has supported my life for decades, so it is no surprise that we recognize and pay heed to each other.

Chester Aaron, a writer and garlic grower gardening about fifty miles north of Green Gulch in Sonoma County, grows garlic because he cannot live without it. A Sonoma gardening friend told me that early in his garlic career Chester was given a variety of heritage garlic cloves by Seed Savers Exchange. He grew them all, but to the delight of his gardening mentors he kept selecting the same garlic variety, time after time, as the absolute best.

The Seed Savers keyed out the garlic and found it was from the Republic of Georgia. "It's from Tochli—a—Tochlia—" "Not Tochliavari?" interrupted Chester, suddenly full of life. "Yeah, that's it—Tochliavari," they answered, surprised at Chester's animation. It turned out that although Chester was born and raised in New York City, all of his people, from his father to his grand-father and great-grandfather before him, hailed from the small, remote region of Tochliavari in the Republic of Georgia.

Red garlic from Tochliavari woke up Chester Aaron. For each of us it will be a different taste or sound, distinct and particular to our own bloodlines. Much depends on staying in one place long enough for the voice of the watershed where you live to claim you in its own tongue. This happened to me one night years ago when I stood on the edge of Redwood Creek, swollen with winter rain, and watched it break free of the sandbar into the ocean at Muir Beach.

Every year in late winter the Pacific Ocean deposits huge drifts of black sea sand up against the wide shoreline cove of Muir Beach. As the land dries out after the winter storms, these sand deposits seal off the flow of Redwood Creek, which drops down underground, deep into the beach sand, and the mouth of the creek is barred closed. This sandbar dams back the fresh waters of Redwood Creek until the rains of the next winter season flood the creek again and burst out the bar.

Only that once was I lucky enough to be at the sucking mouth of the river as it rushed into the sea. Sweet and salt water mingled in the dark, and the voice of the watershed where I live became my own. That winter the rains had come early. It must have been close to Thanksgiving because we were still bringing in our groaning squash harvest at Green Gulch. I had been working alone in the rain all afternoon, cutting the soggy vines of the dense, flat-headed French 'Cinderella' pumpkin, 'Potiron Rouge vif d'Etampes,' and carrying the heavy pumpkins to the edge of the road where they would cure for a few days before going into the dark cellar beneath the zendo where we stored winter vegetables. I remember the gleam of vermilion squash in the cold rain. They were almost red in the storm light, the same color as the living embers at the base of the bonfire we build every New Year's Eve to welcome the fresh year.

The pumpkin field that year was the last field before the beach. It was almost dark when I finished the harvest. I was wet, all the way through my heavy yellow oilskin slicker. I wiped my muddy knife on the matted grass and laid it across the glowing 'Potiron' squash and let the call of the thick sea pull me out to the beach.

I stood on the edge of the ocean at the mouth of the swirling torrent of Redwood Creek, the river boiling black and surly in its chute. The wolf ocean gnawed at the narrow bone of sandbar that separates salt water from sweet. Cold needles of rain pocked the slate-dark sea. High above, on the cliffs overhanging the ocean, the lamps of evening were being lit in the homes of Muir Beach. The reflection of these lights shook yellow and deep on the thick waves, like warm, golden pumpkins themselves bobbing on the black sea. I watched with my back to the rain, and when the river broke through the bar with a soft, heavy sigh and thousands of gallons of water mingled at the mouth, I walked home alone in the dark.

Getting Down to Bedrock

TO KNOW HOW TO GARDEN THE SPOT OF LAND WHERE YOU LIVE, IT is helpful to learn the history of your local bedrock. The 1989 Loma Prieta earthquake that shook northern California from stem to stern gave me a personal tutorial on impermanence and local soil geology. The earthquake happened on October 17, 1989, at 5:04 in the afternoon, during the World Series. The two Bay Area baseball teams were playing against each other in San Francisco's Candlestick Park. Our twelve-year-old son, Jesse, was hooked on baseball, so we were all listening to the World Series on the radio. The game was about to start when our house began to quiver and vibrate. Jesse's clock fell off his shelf. We ran outside, my infant daughter in my arms. The garden around our house was buckling, undulating up and down, writhing as if a prehistoric dinosaur had woken up underneath the wrinkled mantle of a skin that no longer fit and was trying to shake the fleas of the twentieth century off his scaly hide. I was mesmerized by the buckling, rippled earth. All the different bells around Green Gulch began to sway and ring. The water sloshed out of the ancient swimming pool that we use for a fire reservoir. Our hayloft zendo sighed, shook, and shimmied in place. And I lost forever my faith in solid ground.

It is easy to remember that all land is alive and changing when you live in a Buddhist practice place perched on the edge of the fractured San Andreas Fault line. Quaking earth only reinforces the fundamental teachings of Buddhism. In these teachings there are three basic characteristics that all phenomena share: suffering exists; nothing is permanent; and there is no separate, unchanging self to hold on to. Depressing? Not to those who live close to the land, and on the edge where even the ground itself is stamped and printed with these three marks.

California is the product of a head-on collision of the leading western edge of the North American continent with the floor of the Pacific Ocean. From this collision we know that continents are really rafts of light rocks floating but embedded in the heavier black rocks of the earth's mantle. As long as the continents ride along on the mantle, there is very little geologic action. However, about two hundred million years ago the North American continent and the mantle of the Pacific Plate came unhitched, and California was created.

When the moving mantle of the ocean floor was pushed beneath the overriding edge of the North American continental plate, thick deposits of mud and sediment near the shoreline were crushed together under the grinding pressure of the moving plates. It is likely that the rocks of the coastal range of mountains were stuffed into a deep marginal offshore trench that was being pulled down as the seafloor sank beneath it. And, since nothing is permanent, about one hundred million years later this trench floated up and the crumpled, folded Franciscan rocks of the coastal range and the present Green Gulch bottomland broke in a contorted mass out of the cold ocean water.

On the crest of Diaz Ridge, three miles north of Green Gulch and almost two thousand feet above the garden, we still occasionally discover fossilized sea creatures that once lived miles under the ocean. Green Gulch is a valley of ancestors: rock ancestors from the Mesozoic era, and plant, animal, and human ancestors whispering from prehistoric crevices and the watery rills of the living landscape.

In the gardens of Green Gulch Farm the soil is heavy sea-bottom adobe. When we first began to work the land we could only penetrate about four inches deep into the earth with the tines of our heaviest digging forks. The first team of us who began double-digging in 1976 in the upper field had to open the earth with pickaxes, so tight was the folded coastal soil of our unstable home. Year by year, though, our forks went a little deeper in as we drew culture up out of the faulted mantle of the earth.

Digging the soil of the Gulch I regularly encounter the heavy clay that is the parent soil of Green Gulch Valley, dark and cold clay without a breath of air that comes from those deep-sea layers of sediment and primeval mud that were swept together in the marine trench and compacted millennia ago by the rubbing together of the floating tectonic plates.

Just six miles to the southeast of Green Gulch, though, the slumped bottomland of Tennessee Valley, on the far side of Coyote Ridge, is utterly different. That valley is an intact plain from the ocean floor, land that was never subjected to the intense faulting and pressure that formed Green Gulch Valley. The difference is there in the soil itself, in the distinctly different plants of the two separate landscapes, and in the ways water percolates over the surface of each place. It is wise to remember that this delicate skin of the earth that we spend our life cultivating will also one day sink down and become a thin stripe in the stacks of time.

❖ ❖ ❖

In the Green Gulch meditation hall there is a relic from a giant prehistoric mammal, a triangular hunk of rock about ten inches high and heavy as iron. The fossil was discovered by a particularly observant and slow-moving Zen student as he walked along the edge of the upper streambed of the Green Gulch Creek on his day off. He hauled the relic to Harry Roberts, our Native American naturalist teacher and farm advisor. Harry looked at the rock long and hard, turning it over again and again in his gnarled paws. He even licked the ribbed surface of the stone. "It's a mastodon's tooth," he finally proclaimed. The relic was sent to the Department of Paleontology at the University of California, Berkeley, where Harry's proclamation was corroborated. The fossil was the top third of the tusk of an ancient mastodon that had wandered over the folded terrain of our valley of ancestors in the early Pliocene epoch.

Green Gulch was much warmer then. In the vicinity of San Francisco is one of the most continuous sequences of Pliocene floras in the world. In the beginning of this epoch, approximately thirteen million years ago, there were vast inland seas bordered by towering swamp cypress and tupelo. Green Gulch was a tropical world then with fan palms and magnolias, huanchals, and ancient equisetum horsetail ferns towering 150 feet above the warm seas. The remains of these forests contribute to the ancestral soil that we cultivate in our fields today.

By the time of the four-toed mastodon the climate had begun to cool but it was still warmer than in modern times. Poplar and willow marked the stream courses of our ancestral watershed and mountain mahogany grew thick among the first live oaks and glossy sumac. The vegetation indicated that the land was drying out and cooling down. This flora fed the flat-headed mastodons until they became extinct some eight thousand years ago. But in our modern compact clay soil I still feel the weight of the hyaenoid dogs and dire wolves who stalked Green Gulch Valley long ago.

In the early spring when I walk down to the garden the bristly heads of present-day equisetum, or horsetail fern, are pushing up through the dense March soil on the edge of the Green Gulch Creek. These three-foot-high silica-rich primitive plants are living relatives of the giant tree species of equisetum of the Pliocene, close continuous descendants in our valley of ancestors.

15

One March morning in the late 1970s Peter was disking the back of the third field with the Green Gulch team of Percheron horses, Snip and Jerry. The disk cut swaths of horsetail and hedge nettle as Peter and the team made a wide arc at the margin of each cultivated row of heavy, bottomland soil. A glint of black fire caught Peter's eye as he made a turn. He pulled the team to a halt and climbed down to check the shiny spark of stone. It was a razor-sharp obsidian knife, flaked and fashioned by the native Miwok people who inhabited this land a mere two hundred years ago.

Obsidian is not native to our Franciscan formation of Greywacke bedrock. The nearest source is the volcanic magma furnaces of Lake County, one hundred miles north of Green Gulch. Valued for its strength and its ability to form sharp flaked edges, obsidian of the northern tribes was traded all along the north-central coast of California. When the Lake County Miwok came south to trade with the Coast Miwok, they brought their mirror-bright black knives and arrowheads. The light that reflected off each lustrous tool fashioned of volcanic glass was the same light that stopped Peter. Now this obsidian knife joins the mastodon's tooth in the old barn that houses the Green Gulch Zendo.

When you go down deep enough into your ground you find your true place in that valley of ancestors that inhabits every backyard. The soil of Green Gulch Valley is made of the discarded skeletons and feces of countless microorganisms and the well-worn rock of ages, rubbed raw by subducted sea bottom pushing up to form the coastal ranges of the Redwood Creek watershed. Cultured by countless visible and invisible organisms and swept together by a monstrous magnetism, this valley of ancestors is my home. It has been shaped by wind and water erosion, by the butting tusks of prehistoric mastodons, by the primitive spores of ancient horsetail ferns, and by flaked black glass tools in the hands of native Miwok people. And it has also been shaped and assembled by the work of modern hands.

❖ ❖ ❖

The shadowy and sunlit folds of Green Gulch Valley have been cultivated for many generations, their story checkered with dark and light patterns of use and abuse. Cattle ranching began here in 1838 in a huge land grant that included the valley. Portuguese ranchers from the Azores Islands ran the cattle that would inhabit the coastal range for a hundred years. By 1898 Constantino Bello, a descendant of the original Portuguese ranchers, had purchased all the land of Muir Beach suitable for dairy farming. By the 1930s the ranch land of the coast was being more broadly colonized. A tavern was built at Muir Beach near the mouth of Green Gulch Valley, and during Prohibition illegal alcohol distilled in San Francisco was rowed ashore and sold at the rowdy Muir Beach Tavern.

All this changed during World War II, when a coastal artillery installation was built three miles north of the valley. Observation bunkers were chiseled out of the soft stone of the ocean-facing cliffs above Muir Beach and soldiers keeping watch in these bunkers were housed with civilian families in the community. Almost overnight, the boisterous tavern outpost grew as quiet as the long-fingered fog that shook out its cold, arthritic knuckles and stretched into the lonely canyons of the coastal headlands.

At the close of the war George Wheelwright, the cofounder of the Polaroid Corporation, came with his new bride, Hope, to the remote Marin County coast, and purchased Green Gulch Valley for $66 an acre. Wheelwright, a passionately curious person, dreamed of breeding prize Hereford cattle on his ranch. George knew that he had to reclaim the neglected hillsides in order to raise livestock, so when the county extension service suggested he "clean up" the coastal brush, George leased a plane to aerial-spray the native headlands above Green Gulch with 2, 4-D, the newest chemical recommended by the UC farm advisory board. "We went after blackberries and poison oak and we got them," he boasted, "only now I doubt that I'd use those chemicals again."

George also secured a huge bulldozer to "shape" the valley and fit it for cattle ranching. He straightened the sinuous creek, forcing it into a concrete flume that he gouged out along the northern margin of the gulch. At the same time he excavated above- and belowground reservoirs to hold rainwater for the cattle and for irrigating the pastureland during the arid California summers.

After he straightened the creek and chemically cleared the headlands, George set to work reseeding his acreage. The native grasses of northern California clearly could not sustain the heavy tread and appetite of his bovine herd, so in 1948 George introduced into California a mixture of grassland pasture seed that he selected from the Massey Range of New Zealand, where the climate was similar to the coastal climate of the gulch. These bunch grasses were fierce rooters. George exulted in this fact as he spread their seed heavily from the cockpit of a helicopter that he chartered to seed the disturbed bottomland of the valley.

Even though George shaped and reshaped the face of Green Gulch to suit his own plans, he also held a maverick attitude when it came to land ownership. "My father taught me that no one ever really *owns* the land," George would often muse. "We're only custodians, caretakers of land. I suppose if I can be said to have any strong religious belief, that would be it."

In 1965 George Wheelwright was the first large rancher in northern California to sign over his land under the federal Williamson Act, which offered him tax reductions in exchange for a ten-year pledge to preserve the agricultural status of the place. This agreement was termed a "covenant running with the land" and it was George's greatest pride and delight.

A few years later Hope died of cancer and George found it impossible to remain on the farm that they had created together. At the same time, he desperately wanted his work to continue. So, to the amazement and undisguised horror of family, friends, and community, George made arrangements in 1972 to sell his beloved 115-acre coastal headland and bottomland acreage of Green Gulch Farm to the San Francisco Zen Center for a very modest sum.

George Wheelwright wanted the legal and deeply personal covenant that ran with the land to continue. "I was raised Unitarian, and a strict Unitarian," he explained to his shocked colleagues, "and I do not consider myself a Zen convert. But I am attracted to Buddhism as one of the few religions that doesn't make war on nonbelievers."

During these same years the Golden Gate National Recreation Area was being established in the Marin Headlands, protecting a vast acreage of coastal and urban land. Green Gulch Farm is a privately owned parcel within this park, a unique arrangement that depends on the Zen Center's agreement to farm the Green Gulch Valley and to keep it open to the public, while not developing the Gulch beyond its ecological carrying capacity. And so the original spirit of the covenant signed by Mr. Wheelwright in 1965 continues to run with the land.

When the Zen Center assumed responsibility for Green Gulch Farm, George was living a few miles away, but his heart was still at the Gulch. He visited us weekly with advice and a huge flood of stories. He would walk all around the property pointing out maintenance work for us to do. On stormy nights when the ocean roared and lashed at the cliffs above Muir Beach, Mr. Wheelwright, as we always called him, would telephone Peter at two a.m. advising him to lower the dam boards or to check the flow of the water through the upper Spring Valley culvert. He was still very much in charge.

In the late 1980s Mr. Wheelwright returned to live at Green Gulch Farm in our guest housing, with a rotating crew of senior Zen students assigned to take care of him. He was still physically strong, but his mental clarity was fading. Often in the middle of a rich episode from his colorful past he would pause and drift, his sparkling eyes facing back into the long mists of the past. One of my favorite jobs was to accompany him home through the fog to the track of his tale, and walk next to him through the landscape of his stories.

Mr. Wheelwright was like a grandfather to me and a great-grandfather to our children. He came to our house every morning at 7:45 a.m. sharp, rapping on the door with his cane and calling out in his deep baritone voice, "Anybody home?" We would be ready for him, with a comfortable chair pulled up to the table and hot tea, freshly brewed. While we got Jesse ready for school, Mr. Wheelwright played with the baby, who loved to pull off his glasses or thump his gnarled walking cane while she sat on his lap, drooling slow, intent baby concentrate onto his tweed trousers.

Mr. Wheelwright's return to the Gulch was sweet but brief. After about a year it was clear that he needed more extensive care, so he moved on to a local nursing home where he lived as the toast of the facility and a great favorite of the nursing staff until his death at age ninety-seven. Shortly after his death I walked up by myself to Hope's Cottage, the "sky cabin" high on a coastal bluff overlooking Green Gulch, where George and Hope Wheelwright's ashes are interred. The wind from the sea was so fierce that it was difficult to stand. "Hey, Mr. Wheelwright!" I yelled at the top of my lungs into the hammer of the wind and the empty sky. "Look at that messy Gulch down there. I'm still picking up after you, Mr. Wheelwright!" Far below me, red-tailed hawks circled silently, riding the thermals in a widening gyre.

Getting down to bedrock in your garden means learning from your mistakes as well as from your successes. It means becoming familiar with and learning to love and depend on the many beings who have worked the soil you now inherit to garden. And it means getting familiar with the contradictions in your own character and nature, because if there is one thing that I have learned from George Wheelwright and from my own gardening experience it is that most gardeners have a split personality: developer and conservationist are wound together indivisibly in us.

It is a good thing that these traits can never be unraveled, because gardeners need both qualities. In their peculiar unity is our craft and trademark. If I did

not dig into and alter the land with my sharp spade in order to grow butter lettuce and quartered roses, I would never know how vital it is to protect the fragile soil of endangered farmland. Practicing in the heart of contradiction, each time I dig into the Green Gulch soil I sign with my life a fresh covenant that runs with the land.

A Forest Thicket

A COMMUNITY OF PRACTITIONERS WHO GATHER TOGETHER TO study the Buddha Way in long meditation retreats is known as a *sorin* community, a forest thicket, from a Japanese word for a gathering of many different plant species growing in one area. A varied assembly comes together with a common intention and somehow the thicket develops a life and culture of its own.

When I began practicing Zen meditation in 1971, I did not feel drawn to Zen philosophy and the spare Zen life. I considered myself a political activist and a rabid protector of the natural world, not a meditator. But no matter, I got hooked just the same. I was living in Jerusalem, a graduate student in comparative religion at Hebrew University. A friend introduced me to an elegant, older woman, a rigorous hatha yoga teacher who had escaped from Nazi Germany as a young woman and immigrated to Israel after the war. I went to Hannah's yoga class, and afterward she drew me aside and said that while she was ready to teach me yoga she could tell that it was not my true path. I marveled at her bluntness. It disarmed me. She offered to introduce me to her primary practice, Zen meditation. *Spare me!* I thought to myself, but nevertheless I showed up at her house the next day at five-thirty a.m. Hannah took me with her to a modest house on the crest of the Mount of Olives in East Jerusalem, where she introduced me to her Japanese Zen meditation teacher, Dokyu Nakagawa, a disciple of Zen master Soen Nakagawa. I began going up to do *zazen*, literally "seated Zen," with Dokyu-san's small, ardent community every day and I have continued ever since that winter morning more than three decades ago.

I still ask myself what grabbed me. I want to understand, but what I know isn't logical or rational. It has a gravity of its own. What I do know now is that in all her years of teaching yoga in Jerusalem, Hannah never mentioned her Zen practice to anyone but me. I remember walking into the Mount of Olives zendo with her for the first time and sitting in that empty room overlooking the Judean desert and the expanse of the Dead Sea. There was a small altar in the room with a vase of dry wheat stalks, a brush painting of a sumi circle, and a turquoise-blue bowl of clear water. Nothing else.

Dokyu-san let me come every day for two and a half weeks before he showed me how to sit zazen. Some mornings I would be the only meditator in the room with him. It didn't matter. I didn't look around. I rode the bus up the mountain from the Arab Old City just before daybreak. At sunrise the muezzin would call devout Muslims to prayer. For two years I sat in silence in that solitary zendo filled with light. Beyond the Mount of Olives, the huge bellows of Middle Eastern conflict pumped and blew fuel on hundreds of wildfire flare-ups. We sat still through them all, season after season.

My introduction to Zen may seem exotic, but for me it was absolutely ordinary. When contemporaries of the Buddha asked him what he taught, how he practiced, and what his philosophical beliefs were, all the Buddha said was, "Come and see." That's what I did, I came and saw, without any ideas and without any special interest. What held me from the first was the silent, wide-awake, undecorated truth of zazen, sitting meditation that somehow faced the world and deepened my life as an activist.

Eventually, Dokyu-san gave me two Zen texts to study: *The Zen Teaching of Huang Po* and *Zen Mind, Beginner's Mind* by Shunryu Suzuki Roshi, the founder of San Francisco Zen Center and Tassajara. The simplicity of *Zen Mind, Beginner's Mind* worked on me. Already I knew from my daily meditation that I was running away from my life as an American. The war in Vietnam was raging while I was living in Israel as an expatriate. Suzuki Roshi's words called my bluff.

From the first moment, Zen practice was a field of action for me, never a safe haven from the world. It drew me home to North America, determined to discover how this field of Zen meditation could be engaged in relieving the suffering of our torn world. Having begun my practice of Zen in the Muslim section of East Jerusalem with a traditional Rinzai Japanese monk as my guide, I wondered what the American face of Zen Buddhism might look like. Suzuki Roshi had come to the West in 1959, and a few years later had founded San Francisco Zen Center because he felt that Zen was dying in the Far East. American students were eager and fresh. We had beginner's mind, the mind that is open to new ways of investigating the original teachings of Buddhism. Suzuki Roshi had died almost two years prior to my arrival at Tassajara and the community was in the throes of grief and reorganization. At the helm of the Zen Center ship was the new American abbot, a thirty-five-year-old student and dharma heir of Suzuki Roshi, Zentatsu Richard Baker.

Suzuki Roshi had emphasized the necessity of having a place to practice zazen in the midst of our busy urban lives. This was the Beginner's Mind Temple, San Francisco Zen Center, located in a rundown neighborhood of San Francisco's Western Addition. Then, of primary importance in balancing the stress of everyday life, there was the monastery, Tassajara, where Zen students could go for intensive three-month-long periods of meditation and Zen training. Somewhere in between these two extremes was a dream of finding a rural center where students could continue their meditation practice after training at the monastery. This rural center would be close enough to the city to offer zazen practice to urban residents and also be far enough away to provide respite from hectic urban life. Ideally the rural center would have land where food could be raised and where families interested in continuing their Zen practice could live, work, and teach. This farm would also be a place of healing. It was just after Suzuki Roshi's death that the Zen center realized this dream with the purchase of Green Gulch Farm, seventeen miles north of San Francisco.

❊   ❊   ❊

On the northern edge of Green Gulch Farm, just under the lip of a rugged coastal meadow, hangs a huge bronze bell about four feet long and two and a half feet wide. The bell is suspended from a gnarled cypress tree and is rung every day at dawn and dusk. This bell was cast in Japan and sent to North America to be the "temple voice" of Green Gulch Valley. In Japan every Buddhist temple has a bell; in one sense the temple *is* the bell. The Green Gulch bell is decorated with entwined dragons in honor of the center's temple name, Green Dragon Zen Temple, and on its side is a poem by Zentatsu Richard Baker.

> Awakened
> by this Japanese bell
> The sky-headed sea-tailed
> Green Gulch dragon
> Stirs the fine mists and rains
> of right Dharma
> for East and West.
> Farming and greeting guests
> The pre-voice voice of this old bell
> Is not hindered by the wind.

Zen practice comes out of everyday life. Since the autumn day in 1975 when Peter and I walked into Green Gulch Valley, my practice has ripened in both garden and meditation hall. Both the meditator and the gardener in me are encouraged by the inscription on the Green Dragon Zen Temple bell and by the silence and sound of this old bell. I confess that on some mornings during zazen I am too tired from the previous day's pruning of the tangled thicket of gallica roses to even hear the bell. It takes all my concentration just to stay upright, poised on the brink of sleep. But on other mornings, when the garden has been kinder to me, the sound of the bell booms through to me during zazen. Sitting drops a notch then, and tiny vanguard roots spread out from the base of my sitting bones into the dark ground.

The zendo meditation hall at Green Gulch Farm is the heart of the place, an old hay barn transformed to hold about two hundred people. When we first came to Green Gulch there were creaky trapdoors in the mud-encrusted floor of the ground-level hayloft. Hay had been thrown down through these chutes to the cattle, stanchioned below in the lower barn.

Our first job was to scrape this mud off the hayloft floor and to create a place to sit in meditation. Those assigned to this task worked for days. Often I thought of Heracles laboring in the Augean stables. Next we cleared old harness and rusty hand plows, broken window frames and hoops of baling wire out of the barn that adjoined the hayloft. We uncovered a catacomb of old box stalls underneath the piles of equipment. So we built up the walls of these horse stalls and made primitive rooms for student housing. I lived in one of these rooms with Peter when we first came to Green Gulch. The walls were so thin we could hear Jerome next door turning the pages of his book at night after zazen.

There were almost seventy of us living at Green Gulch in those days. There weren't enough rooms, so the newly arrived men slept in the zendo at night. We built raised platforms or *tans* for zazen and overflow sleeping, and one year we dried our squash and pumpkin harvest under those sturdy platforms. If there was to be enlightenment in the Green Gulch zendo the pumpkins would have their share in it, too. Uchiyama Roshi, the head teacher at Antaiji monastery in Japan, wrote that in zazen we practice to save all beings. We sit like individual pumpkins in a vast field, aglow with our vow. Yet we are connected by a common vine that runs between us, a vine that sustains our shared life even when we forget our connections to one another. Underneath our sitting platform in the Green Gulch zendo as the field squash cured and ripened, I heard Uchiyama Roshi encourage us: "Pumpkins! Sit zazen!"

And sit zazen we did. We practiced meditation together every day from four a.m. until six a.m. and then again at five-fifteen p.m., just before dinner, and

at the close of the day, from seven-thirty until nine p.m. Everyone followed the same schedule in those days. Most of us were in our early twenties. We were building Green Gulch Farm to fit our dream. We expanded the family kitchen of the old Wheelwright ranch, added on to the dining room to seat a large population of seventy residents, and built a small guest facility and conference center. At the same time we were cultivating the heavy bottomland soil of the Gulch and establishing the farm and garden.

We were quite idealistic and determined to grow our own food. We also didn't know much, especially about the rugged climate of the north Pacific Coast. Our first year we tried growing scores of crops, fencing off a quarter acre and planting like mad. We sowed lettuce and paste tomatoes, pickling cucumbers, and wild radishes, dibbled in lines of snow peas and rows of dry beans, and even planted some hills of peanuts. And then we hunkered down to watch what happened.

The plants grew furiously, especially with their heavy complement of aged cow manure gathered from the lower barn. A silent communal work period was added to our schedule right after morning zazen, before breakfast. Lou Hartman, a senior Zen priest and a great cook, would bake us fresh zucchini bread and serve it hot from the oven to tide us over on frosty mornings as we went down to work in the fields.

Zen practice honors work. "A day of no work is a day of no eating" is an old Zen proverb. We worked hard in those first years to establish the farm and to learn the lay of the land, teachers and students working together. Dainin Katagiri Roshi visited us periodically from his meditation center in Minneapo-

Lou's Zucchini Bread

3 eggs
1 cup oil
1½ cups sugar
3 cups grated zucchini
1 tablespoon vanilla

3 cups sifted flour
1 teaspoon salt
1 teaspoon baking soda
1 tablespoon cinnamon
¼ teaspoon baking
  powder

baking powder. Add to egg mixture, and mix until blended. The batter will be stiff. The liquid in the zucchini comes out in the baking.

* Divide batter into two greased loaf pans (9" x 5"). Bake at 325°F for about an hour. Cool on wire rack. Cut into generous slabs and serve while still warm.

* It helps to eat zucchini bread on foggy, cool mornings, dreaming of the garden that is stirring to life, just beyond the edge of your appetite.

* Beat eggs until light and foamy. Add oil, sugar, zucchini, and vanilla. Mix lightly but well. Sift together flour, salt, baking soda, cinnamon, and

lis, and did communal work in his meditation robes, tying up his voluminous Tang dynasty sleeves and scrubbing out pigweed with a rusty hula-hoe.

In the renegade collection of old junk that filled the outer barn we discovered a rickety cart that was spiffed up and hauled out to Tam Junction, the crossroads where the Green Gulch coast road meets the main road. From the back of this cart Darlene sold fresh vegetables and flowers and homemade bread to our neighbors and visitors.

Even though we were exhausted, life was good. But as we developed our practice and presence at Green Gulch, trouble cropped up in paradise. Babies began to be born, guests began to visit and want to practice with us, farming began to take on a life of its own. We now kept chickens and a dairy cow named Daisy. Thorny issues pricked at the smooth, taut skin of our practice. Who was going to milk Daisy at five a.m. during zazen? What did we do with our old chickens after we had enjoyed their eggs for four or five seasons? And were we really meant to leave our sleeping infants at home at four a.m. and *all* sit zazen together in the zendo? A fellow Zen resident summed up these dilemmas by asking a simple question: "How do grown-ups practice Zen?"

What I have appreciated most about Zen practice is that it welcomes a core question like this one, meeting the world squarely without smoothing over prickly concerns that threaten the calm surface of the mind. Grown-ups practice Zen by sending our feeder roots deep into the bedrock of modern culture, fierce in the commitment to face the real issues and dangers of our times, remembering that "every excellent endeavor turns from within toward the world," as Goethe wrote.

At Green Gulch Farm we have been lucky. Our covenant that allows us to be landholders within the Golden Gate National Recreation Area requires that we turn toward the world. If from prolonged meditation we get too misty-eyed about the ultimate reality of the moon shining in a single dewdrop, hikers passing through our preserve bring us back to earth by asking for directions to the nearest bathroom. And when the mad frenzy of harvesting more than a hundred boxes of fresh organic produce for market threatens the rhythm of daily life and obscures the dire situation of the world, the same guests passing through our fields restore us to our true work. "I can't tell you how much it means to me," they often say as we crouch, exhausted, over our huge market crop of Romanian speckled lettuce, "that this beautiful food is grown here at Green Gulch by people who meditate every day."

Now, almost forty years since its founding, Green Gulch Farm Zen Center continues to fulfill both sides of its name. Although primarily a place for the study and practice of Zen meditation, this practice is deepened by the pressure of our lively organic farm, the oldest such farm in Marin County. Many young students come to Green Gulch to enrich the *sorin* forest thicket of practitioners committed to the mutual cultivation of Zen meditation and organic gardening.

I am deeply grateful for my three decades of intensive Zen training, especially these days now that I am engaged in the wider community of nonprofit service. I practice as a lay dharma teacher at work in the world. A few days a week I teach the principles of organic gardening at the Edible Schoolyard, a nonprofit program at Martin Luther King, Jr. Middle School in Berkeley, California. I am mentor and advisor to teachers, staff, and nine hundred dynamic public school students at this innovative and inspiring program supported by the Chez Panisse Foundation established by Alice Waters. I teach meditation and gardening at Green Gulch Farm and Tassajara Zen Mountain Center and throughout the San Francisco Bay Area, and nationally I teach meditation and the dharma to dedicated groups of frontline environmental leaders and activists.

Over the coming years we have crucial work to do together. Our world faces unprecedented ecological destruction and soil disintegration that includes a massive dying-off of species; degradation of air, land, and water purity; and a loss of soil health and biological diversity—issues all bound together by the stark reality of global climate change. We have no choice but to work together. This means getting into the traces with unlikely partners and pulling to reverse the tide of human greed and ignorance. The human race is five million years old, one of my close dharma teachers reminds me, and it is time to act our age and fulfill our inheritance as human beings by responding to the cries of a world in trouble.

I have great faith and confidence in our ability to wake up, to pierce the veil of drowsy denial, and to draw on the strength of our collective human thicket of intertwined roots. Despair is lifted by facing the truth of our situation and sustaining the gaze as we turn toward the world. Inscribed on the face of the wooden sounding block that calls us to meditation every day are these simple words of reminder:

> Listen everyone!
> Great is the matter of life and death
> Awake, each one—
> Don't waste time.

Gardening for Five Hundred Years

I HAVE HAD TWO GREAT GARDENING TEACHERS IN MY LIFE, HARRY Roberts and Alan Chadwick, both of them raw and ragged prophets, both of them now long dead. I say that they are dead, but sometimes I wonder—even though I helped bury their bones and ashes. In January when I am thinning the crowded spurs of the espalier apples alone in the orchard, I still hear Alan hiss over my right shoulder, "Not that spur, sausage! Take that whizziky one growing into the core of the tree. Obey the apples!"

I am not the kind of person who seeks a teacher to complete myself or to learn a craft or to deepen my knowledge. Quite the opposite. I run away from teachers: the more they know, the faster I sprint. I smell them from a good mile off, catch their seductive whiff, especially when they pour out their unctuous syrup of distilled truth to lure the hungry and eager to their table.

Harry and Alan never taught me anything, never gave me anything. They were not prospecting for students and yet each showed me, unabashedly, and in his own distinct ways, a fierce love and uncompromised passion for the natural world. In spite of myself, and with a full battery of questions, I followed them in through the garden gate.

I first met Harry Roberts not long after Peter and I moved to Green Gulch.

Harry was a craggy beast of a man who walked with aluminum crutches. He had fallen forty feet from a eucalyptus tree and broken his back when he was a young man. He also had bursitis of the hip that he said he caught from digging bare-handed in earth laced with live pig manure. Parasites from the manure claimed his health, permanently inflaming the joints of his hips.

In the late 1920s Harry had run cattle for the ranchers of West Marin. When we started to work together, Harry told me that when he first saw Green Gulch Valley in 1927 with the unchanneled creek meandering in slow serpentine loops along the valley floor he thought it was one of the most beautiful places he had ever seen in his life.

Harry was raised about 250 miles north of Green Gulch at the mouth of the Klamath River, in the tiny village of Rekwoi. He was part Native American, part Irish. His father ran a fish cannery on the Klamath and Harry worked with his father, learning the fishing trade, but early in his life he was adopted by Robert Spott, a high medicine man of Yurok culture who became Harry's "uncle," or main teacher. Harry's primary lineage ran with the blood of the Yurok nation.

Harry was well trained in the Yurok tradition, a hardworking man with a passion for the plants and animals of northern California. He was a master fisherman and lumberjack, a trained horticulturist and nurseryman who helped establish the native plant section of the UC botanical garden in Berkeley, California. Harry was also a welder and a machinist, a rumrunner and a turquoise trader, a cowboy and an inventor, and a person with equal passions for cooking and for embroidering fine tea towels. During World War II Harry collected spiderwebs to be used in the creation of precision instruments and gun sights. He was also once Ginger Rogers's dance partner, or so I am told.

Harry's main role at Green Gulch was to help us slow down enough to see the land that we were farming and gardening. He taught us with his whole body, crippled and crumpled though it was, and with his keen, lively mind. Harry had no tolerance for philosophical speculation or theorizing. He was interested in passing on what he had learned from his actual training in Yurok medicine culture, and he was intent on helping us develop practical, worldly skills, especially as they related to the craft of farming and gardening.

"Whenever you do something, anything at all," Harry used to say with an old hand-rolled Drum tobacco cigarette dangling from the corner of his mouth, "make sure you ask yourself these three questions: What do I want? How much does it cost? and, Am I willing to pay the price? Once you can answer these questions, get to work."

Harry was willing to show anyone at all what he knew. And he was a rare teacher because he knew how to learn from his students. In fact, he depended on us. He let us take care of him and through this intimacy, he came to know us inside out. One of the strictest and kindest people I ever met, Harry played to the unknown, delighting in surprise. If a student was cavalier and carelessly confident Harry would be fierce, demanding that the student pay minute attention to every single nit-picking detail of the gardening process. But with someone like me, who tends to be overly reverential and superstitious, Harry delighted in being both gentle and brash. Once when I asked for exact directions before planting Belgian endive he snorted out, full volume, "Oh, just stuff it in the hole!"

Every Sunday afternoon for years we held a long garden seminar session with Harry. He would stump out to the garden with us and begin to explore a topic in precise detail, like the difference between white rocks and black rocks, or how to catch a sockeye salmon with your bare hands. At first I wondered what any of this had to do with the craft of horticulture or Zen practice, but soon I was hooked. I saw that Harry was asking us to know the real nature of the place we were tending, to listen to the original voice of our home terrain as it whispered and bellowed out its truth.

In his shaman training with Spott, Harry had been pushed to the edge of what he knew time and time again. Spott had chosen his students by a simple method. He asked them to bring him five plants that they had never seen before. Most of his avid candidates for study would then fan out over the boundaries of the Klamath watershed searching for original plant material. But Spott always chose those few dolts who stood stock-still and looked down at their feet for five unknown treasures. Like the warrior Gideon of the Old Testament, Spott chose his shamanic army from the ranks of simpletons.

Harry could be maddening in his insistence that we take our time, look long and deep, and believe what we saw. Almost every Sunday for close to a year, Harry had us look north during our seminar class, across the well-watered beds of the vegetable garden and beyond to study the steep, blank wall of the coastal meadow that rose up just outside the garden gate. "What do you see?" he would ask us time and again. The eight or ten of us gathered around him for the class would answer, "The trail of a deer disappearing to the west," or "Signs of ripening in the purple needlegrass." Late one Sunday afternoon in early September I pointed out a faint trace of green under the dry brown grass of the parched meadow. Harry exploded with delight, knocking over his camp chair and leaping to his unsteady feet, poking the still, hot air of that Indian summer afternoon with his jabbing crutch. "That's it!" he bellowed. "You saw it! You got it! Now go mark that spot and we'll direct you from down here."

Mystified, I climbed the hill with a long, sharpened bamboo stake in one hand and a sledgehammer in the other. Steve and Ginny yelled to me through cupped hands, directing my steps: "A little to the west—uphill a bit. There— you got it!" Harry was undone with a crackling delight that lasted for weeks, and we all thought he had lost his mind. From that Sunday on until early January the meadow-observation exercise ceased entirely. But in January when we were getting ready to plant out our first hillside apple orchard, Harry's interest returned to the steep coastal prairie. He chose a strong maiden whip of 'King David' apple for my marked meadow spot. He even stumped up onto that rough and barren hillside to supervise the planting, grunting with enthusiasm throughout the entire process.

Now, almost twenty-five years later, the 'King David' apple tree is the sole surviving plant of that coastal prairie orchard. The rest of the trees have been ring barked by voles or chomped down by browsing black-tailed deer. All the trees were weakened by drought and fierce ocean wind. 'King David' alone has its roots in the rich black water of a seep spring, which Harry waited eight months for one of us to detect from a faint glint of green at the base of the bone-dry hill.

Over his years at Green Gulch, Harry taught us how to weld and how to repair harness, how to weave a winnowing basket out of butterscotch-yellow willows, and how to sow a fine seedbed by mixing dust-size seed with white river sand. He gave me lessons in planting black cottonwood trees and collecting native lilies, but most of all he taught me how to see my home place and how to dream deep dreams of gardening the Green Gulch Valley. "Remember in your thinking," Harry once said to me, "that this is a Buddhist community. And we are trying to live like one. Buddhism is forever. It's not a crash program for the next five weeks. We are looking at things from the perspective of five hundred years. Buddhism is not a religion. It is a way of life. If we make it for five hundred years we will make it for five thousand. We are building for the far future."

On the last Arbor Day that Harry Roberts attended in February of 1981 he was too weak to deliver his address. Harry was dying of bronchial pneumonia. Yvonne Rand, a good friend of his and one of the main teachers of San Francisco Zen Center's early years, read his speech while Harry sat on his old brown camp chair by the huge pile of cottonwood whips that we had collected from his native Rekwoi to begin an arboretum of Northwest Coast native trees. "When you plant a single tree," Harry wheezed to me under his faltering breath just before the planting began, "remember that you are planting an entire ecosystem."

One of the last things we did together was to sow the seeds of *Cryptomeria japonica* gathered for us by the Japanese natural farmer Masanobu Fukuoka. This cryptomeria is a blood relative of the shallow-rooted coast redwood, which had once blanketed north-facing canyons of the Green Gulch watershed. But unlike their North American relatives, the Japanese cryptomeria have deep roots that help culture soil. Harry and Fukuoka dreamed that these redwood cousins from Japan might help rebuild the depleted soil of the Northwest Coast and act as a shelterbelt of nurse trees for our shallow-rooted native redwoods.

Ginny and Yvonne and I planted the seeds of the cryptomeria trees in a deep box of soil that was perched on the edge of Harry's sickbed. He directed us throughout the entire planting process. I did the seeding work, Yvonne was the scribe for his instructions, and Ginny ministered to Harry. The seed was ripe and vital, collected by Fukuoka from a virgin stand of cryptomeria growing in the Koji preserve of Japan. "You know," Harry said to us quite clearly when the sowing was complete, "You know, the seed of these trees takes seventy-five years to ripen. You won't harvest it in your lifetime or in the lifetime of your children. These trees are for your grandchildren and for their grandchildren."

Harry died in mid-March of 1981. A few weeks later the cryptomeria seed-lings germinated mightily in their seed box and two years later we planted them exactly where we had sited them with Harry before he died. Now these trees are almost twenty feet high and thriving.

We buried Harry's ashes under an outcropping of native stone jutting out over that steep meadow where the 'King David' apple tree is planted. I like to go up to sit by myself at Harry's ashes site. From the mounded crest of his stony grave I squint and look out into the light. Far below me billows the unstoppable flood of garden crops. But from up here, I am slowed down enough to also notice a soft smudge of green under the dry meadow grass. "Tell me the landscape in which you live," wrote José Ortega y Gassett, "and I will tell you who you are." Looking out, I imagine a swell of apple trees sprouting up out of the secret sockets of hidden meadow springs running under bone-dry grass. I take my place in this landscape, the work of a lifetime holding me here, now, and for the next five hundred years.

❖   ❖   ❖

The first time I met Alan Chadwick was in the mid-1970s, a few years before I began to work with Harry Roberts. Although it was early in my life as a gardener, I was seasoned enough to recognize my future teacher from that single encounter. The legend of Alan Chadwick preceded the man to Green Gulch Farm that Sunday morning in early June when I first met him. Alan had started the original gardens at Green Gulch in 1972 and now he was the horticultural director of a huge garden in Covelo, California. He had agreed to make a rare journey back to Green Gulch to present a lecture to the community. The talk was to be at three p.m. sharp, but I was up well before dawn with the garden crew preparing the garden for the visit of this distinguished horticultural master. To our horror, Alan Chadwick arrived a few minutes before eight a.m.

As was his custom, Alan was dressed in pure white, wearing long Bermuda shorts and a tailored, well-pressed white shirt. Almost seventy years old, he was an imposing man, quite regal, really, with a shock of wavy silver hair that topped his six-foot-three angular frame. On this day he was shadowed by two attendants who followed behind their teacher at a respectful distance, bearing a bottle of crystal cold springwater for Alan to drink and a beautiful gift basket of fresh strawberries and plump black currants from the Covelo garden. Registering my unmasked shock at their early arrival, Alan addressed me as I stood thigh-deep in plant debris. "We *are* a bit early," he conceded, in imperial fashion, "but one can never be too sure about possible motor traffic delay."

Then his excuses ceased entirely and disordered with delight he marched straight past me, leaning his wiry body into that giant stride of his that spanned heaven and earth. He stopped in front of one of our prize roses, a young tea rose named 'Sunny June.' "What a perfectly beautiful rose," he cooed. "What an exquisite creature!" He towered over that demure rose just coming into her first flush of bloom. Her buds were pale custard yellow, suffused with an undertone blush of warm peach. She quivered in the wind of Alan's gaze. Then slowly, with great theatrical poise, the gaunt and kingly man lowered himself to his knees before 'Sunny June.' He went down with all the gangly grace and hauteur of an ancient dromedary, that great ship of the desert, lowering itself to the floor of the Sahara. On his knees, Alan paid unabashed homage to the guileless rose. Flustered, we all looked away.

Born in 1909 in the fashionable seaside resort of St. Leonards-on-Sea in southern England, Alan Chadwick was the son of a barrister at Oxford and a pianist mother with Theosophical yearnings. He was raised as a vegetarian and a pacifist in an environment alive with occult speculation, and surprised his prosperous parents early in his life by entering into a series of horticultural apprenticeships that led him from England to France and back again. He developed a parallel love for the stage and the garden. Throughout the 1930s, repertory theater and the study and performance of Shakespearean drama were Alan's lifeblood.

During World War II Alan was stationed in Bombay, India, and in the 1950s he continued to travel, serving as the head gardener of the Admiralty House in Simon's Town, South Africa. He gardened in South Africa until the beginning of the 1960s, when he first came to the United States and tended several grand estate gardens on Long Island. The severe climate of the Northeast was difficult for Alan and so in the spring of 1967 he joined his friend and guide Countess Freya von Moltke on the grounds of the new campus of the University of California, Santa Cruz, where Alan agreed to establish a garden.

Alan Chadwick was fifty-eight years old when he began his first California garden. He chose for the garden site an almost vertical four-acre hillside poised at the entrance to the Santa Cruz campus and solidly infested with poison oak, dark thickets of stinging nettle, and blackberry brambles. Friends and students who were at Santa Cruz during those years still talk about Alan Chadwick. He never solicited permission to cultivate the ragged slope he had chosen. Instead, he worked by himself seven days a week seemingly without rest, from sunup to sundown. Two years later, all four acres of that uncouth Santa Cruz hillside pulsed and swelled with fertility and culture. Birds never seen before on the campus called and cooed from the thick shrub borders of the garden. Sweeping cascades of Old World and modern roses from 'Sombreuil' to apple-scented eglantines festooned the garden arbors. Vines of the green-fleshed Malta winter melon cascaded across the path twining toward raised hills of 'Rose Fir Apple' fingerling potatoes. A groaning abundance of food spilled forth from this garden, free to all for the taking.

Alan Chadwick no longer worked alone. His fierce dedication had attracted dozens of curious apprentices to his side. For the first time in his life Alan was teaching the young, giving back to eager students who were thoroughly new to horticulture the rigor and passion of his own classical training. He was a tempestuous and often tyrannical taskmaster. Although he demanded of himself the same high standards and discipline that he drew out of his students, Alan was far from beneficent.

Alan Chadwick burned with a single-minded mission to offset the numbing dehumanization of the technological and materialistic postwar era. He strove to accomplish this task by kindling a revitalized love and comprehension of the natural world in all who worked with him or visited his gardens. Many were seared by the fire of Alan's Old Testament rage and passion, and yet we continued to study with him. Perhaps we were hypnotized by Alan's prophecy: "You enter the garden because you love creation. Imagination is required right from the start and in this spark of imagination kindled among beautiful places and people there will be a fire of orchards, vegetables, flowers, and plants of every kind."

Santa Cruz was the flintstone for this fire, but in 1970 Alan was asked by the university administration to move on, perhaps because so many students defected from proper university studies to the lair of the eccentric gardening wizard, perhaps because of his unpredictably savage tongue. In any case, Alan Chadwick's wildfire vision could never be contained within university walls, so after Santa Cruz Alan began a decade-long pilgrimage following the spine of California's coast, moving north and leaving in his considerable wake a trail of glorious gardens.

When Alan came to Green Gulch in 1972 he chose a somewhat tamer site to garden than that at Santa Cruz, a lonely coastal meadow with a southwestern exposure. Peter lived in San Francisco in those years and he told me later about notices luring Zen students out to Green Gulch for an afternoon of weeding with the famous British horticultural master Alan Chadwick. When the innocent ones arrived they were given huge field mattocks and sent to join Alan on the windswept garden site. There they set about "weeding" out twelve- to fifteen-foot-high eucalyptus tree seedlings to help clear the land.

Wherever he went, Alan Chadwick was trailed by a coterie of dedicated garden apprentices. We all worked like the Furies to prepare land and to plant the "raiment of the archangels," that cloak of garden plants that fanned out in a vast brocade cape across every garden that Alan Chadwick ever cultivated. Alan grew hundreds of species of herbs and flowers and heritage vegetables in each garden he began, yet I also remember him pausing above a modest, small sweep of fragrant woodland violets just outside the Green Gulch laundry room. "This simple violet flower," he said just under his breath, "has the ability to strike mercy in the heart of the most heinous criminal."

Alan's techniques were theatrical, rough, and memorably vivid. One moment he upbraided us by quoting long passages of reverent plant tribute drawn from his memory of Shakespeare, and in the next, he strangled and strung up a marauding blue jay whom he caught bare-handed while the brassy bird was pecking apart flats of newly sown 'Ailsa Craig' tomatoes. Alan hung the murdered bird at the entrance gate to our peaceful Zen meditation center as a macabre and ominous warning to all transgressors of the true Garden Way.

After less than a year it was clear that Alan Chadwick could not fully develop his vision of Eden at Green Gulch. He wailed at top volume each time the wooden sounding block was struck for meditation and faithful Zen students mindfully put down their tools and headed calmly for the meditation hall. "Look at this—look at this!" Alan ranted and seethed. "Perfectly able-bodied young men and women running to the atavistic sound of wood beating on wood. Running without shame, and leaving an old man like me to work alone in the garden!"

Nevertheless, the seeds of earthly paradise had been sown and Alan's passionate spirit had lodged itself in the hearts and minds of some of the Green Gulch community. He exhorted us to do better, to push against our own limits and to work wholeheartedly. He never relented. The garden had its own rules, its own time, and its own laws, he reminded us regularly. "We only believe today what can be absolutely proved. Only the visible. Yet everything that is absolutely true is invisible."

We were not to live and practice with Alan Chadwick again until eight years later when he returned to Green Gulch at the end of his life. Yet after meeting Alan that first time in the presence of 'Sunny June' I felt my life as a gardener expand. It was a physical sensation. The garden got bigger around me and in me. I saw plants differently. And I handled them differently, as well, not so nonchalantly. Suddenly plants had greater weight, a dense gravity all their own. I remember cutting a long spray of regal lilies the day after Alan left to return to Covelo. Tiny ants were crawling over the moist stigma of the bloom and into the inner chalice of the flower. I saw the old image of the angel of God announcing the birth of Christ to Mary by presenting her with an outstretched lily, just opening into bloom. When I finally cut the regal lily in our garden, it felt strangely dense, as if the burden and presence of every lily ever sown throughout the ages was now in my hand.

Alan returned to Green Gulch in 1979, just before the winter solstice, ravaged by prostate cancer. Behind him loomed the still and haunted shades of two more great gardens after Green Gulch: his master-piece, the Covelo Garden at Round Valley, and his final garden, Carmel-in-the-Valley in New Market, Virginia. This last garden had just been snatched from Alan's grasp when the project own-ers fell into arrears on their land payments, leaving Alan without a garden.

Despite the unrelenting grip of his illness, Alan continued to rage against the dying of the light. He greeted me, the head gardener of Green Gulch Farm, formally and elegantly as I entered his guest room to welcome him back. At the same time, he looked at me like a startled warhorse caught in a tight box stall, fully ready to bolt. I saw live fire lick-ing around the edge of his eyes. He announced with dignity, "I intend to be in the garden tomorrow." "We will welcome you," I murmured, backing out of his stable.

Alan never made it to the garden. Instead, we brought the garden to him. I cut armloads of fresh flowers for him every few days, winter jonquils and Korean lilac, windblown anemones and stiff coral quince that Alan recognized from his original gardens at Green Gulch, and a single bloodred poppy grown from seed gathered from the World War II battlefields of Flanders. During these months the garden itself upwelled with a rare treasure trove of bloom and Alan drank long draughts from the bottomless pool of flowers.

He implored us to use him well while we might. Every week during the last months of his life, seven or eight of us gathered at his bed-side for a garden study class. Alan was mortified to be abed. He had always taught in the sanctuary of the living garden. When we came to his bedside each time, he turned to the wall and began the class in a thin frail voice from under a pile of blankets, but after fifteen minutes or so he slowly turned toward us, awakened by the beauty of *Angelica archangelica* or by the creak of a woodland bower heavy with pale yellow tresses of fragrant clematis. "Not even a single moment in the garden is reiterated," he whispered to us from his sickbed, "not a single moment."

My position during these studies was a delicate torture. The horticultural master painted a huge sweep on the divine canvas of the garden but relied always on the minute specifics of each plant to give soul and character to his words. He required the specific names of plants, as a painter requires paint. But his memory of the vast classification of Latin binomials was blurred by pain. So in mid-sentence, and always without warning, Alan would heave up from his bedcovers and demand of me, the cowering head gardener, "What is the name of that plant?" I fell into a faint of terror every time this occurred, until the pale silhouette of the rose that Alan had summoned might show me the slim outline of her ankle and then, with this sighting, warm blood would pump again into my frozen brain and I would squeak out, "That would be *Rosa noisette*, wouldn't it, Alan—variety 'Jaune Desprez'?" and he would sink back into his bank of pillows, whispering, "Quite."

I brought my teacher a spring bouquet of his most trea- sured anemone flowers not long before his death. These flowers, known since classic times as "the daughters of the wind" or the biblical "lilies of the field," remained on the bedside table until long after their midnight-blue pollen had dusted the turned-down white linen borders on Alan's sheets. When I brought him fresh flowers then to replace the fallen anemones Alan raised his bony hand to ward me off, flower-bearing infidel. "Please!" he commanded in a whisper, "Leave me to the daughters of the wind. They are still releasing their secrets."

Alan died a few weeks later on Pentecostal Sunday in his sunny bedroom at Green Gulch Farm. On the wall near his bed hung Shakespeare's fifteenth sonnet and on either side of the doorway leading into his room, we placed Alan's spade and digging fork. As visitors and students, apprentices and old friends alike came for days to pay their final respects to Alan Chadwick they strewed the hallway and outer pathways leading to his chamber with cascades of fresh flowers, gathered from all of Alan's gardens.

When I consider every thing that grows
Holds in perfection but a little moment,
That this huge stage presenteth nought but shows
Whereon the stars in secret influence comment;
When I perceive that men as plants increase,
Cheered and cheque'd even by the self-same sky,
Vaunt in their youthful sap, at height decrease,
And wear their brave state out of memory;
Then the conceit of this inconstant stay
Sets you most rich in youth before my sight,
Where wasteful Time debateth with Decay,
To change your day of youth to sullied night;
And all in war with Time for love of you,
As he takes from you, I engraft you new.

Shakespeare's Fifteenth Sonnet

I know nothing of gardening in general. I only know the specifics of the fine art of horticulture as I have learned them from the living garden and from my particular gardening teachers. I heard my mentors rant and preach what they believed in with wholehearted conviction and I got up and went to work with them. Mostly I believed what I saw when I gardened with Alan and Harry and I believed what I tasted from that harvest of plenty that we brought to the table from our common ground. It never troubled me for one moment that their teachings diverged not only in emphasis but also in content. I noticed that even when each man was adamant and precise in his instructions about how to gather the wild native strawberries or "stray-berry" of the shadowed flanks of Coyote Ridge, or how to plant the exquisite royal sovereign strawberry of old England, each changed his procedural law ever so slightly with every repetition. This "wobble" in their compass needle that indicated the true north of garden technique interested me almost as much as their specific teachings. True, I learned how to listen and how to obey with Alan and Harry. But I also learned how to trust my own wild, wobbling, and foolish self.

Root Teacher

MY PRIMARY ZEN TEACHERS, MY ROOT ZEN TEACHERS OVER THE last thirty years, have been Japanese, Vietnamese, and American. I like these words—"root teacher"—they are grounded words, strong and true. "Root teacher" summons the gnarled roots of an ancient apple tree pushing down through bedrock and deeper still, splitting stone into raw chips of rock, and sucking up black water from the floor of the ground. I know this root country. So does poet Charles Olson when he writes:

> Whatever you have to say, leave
> the roots on, let them
> dangle

> And the dirt
> just to make clear
> where they come from.

Zen teaching is like this, rooted in a face-to-face lineage of ragtag characters pumping with real blood and living fire. Many teachers throughout your life may help sustain you, serving as fine feeder roots, pulling mist out of dry soil and carrying you through lean times, or fanning out like the fibrous root system of massive clumps of seventy-five-year-old Japanese iris, steadying your life, and stabilizing the banks of your practice. This relationship is not always civil, not always nice. You cut no bargains with your root teacher. You bind yourself to the unknown and often you get more than you have bargained for, way more, for just when you are sure that you have gone plenty deep and well beyond your limit, your root teacher drops another notch, pulling you down.

My first Zen guide and original root teacher was Soen Nakagawa Roshi, the primary teacher of Dokyu-san, my first Zen instructor with whom I practiced zazen meditation for two years in Israel. Zen master Soen came to Jerusalem in 1972 to lead a seven-day *sesshin*, a silent meditation retreat, at a small Trappist monastery where the resident monks welcomed pilgrims like us from other traditions. Soen Roshi was a fierce Zen teacher trained in Japan in the tradition of Lin-Chi, a Tang Dynasty Chinese Zen monk from the ninth century. A monk and meditator for more than fifty years, Soen Roshi was abbot of a prestigious Zen temple, Ryutakuji, or Dragon Swamp Zen Temple, as well as a poet and an accomplished calligrapher.

In the Zen world, Soen was considered a wily rascal. He hated the stink of the Zen establishment and pointed underneath the formal layers and skirts of traditional Zen trappings to the bare bones of the teaching. Soen carried a mercilessly sharp sword that was often invisible but when unsheathed packed a memorable sting. "If you want to know who Buddha is," he advised us during our sesshin retreat, "ask a three-month-old baby. But hurry, before she forgets."

Soen taught seamless Zen, coaxing light and shadow, sameness and difference, to come together and merge for one fleeting moment. He connected me back to the natural world, speaking of no vacancy in the entire universe and of the impossibility of water ever being polluted. "Water, by nature, is pure. Pollutants can be *added* to water but the true, original nature of water is never destroyed, never polluted."

Another time, late at night and toward the close of the sesshin, Soen Roshi came into the zendo and herded our mangy group out of the shelter of the meditation hall and into the stone-black hills that surrounded the monastery, hills that stood with their shaggy rumps turned toward Jerusalem. We gathered on those low mountains, under a starless sky, bellowing in full voice, "*Mu!*", the Japanese syllable for "complete emptiness, nothing holy," until all the dogs hidden in the dark folds of the hills of Judah returned our baying cry.

"Exhaust your words and empty your thoughts," insisted Soen again and again. "There is a girl trapped at the bottom of a well. Without a rope, bring her up." For the entire seven days of our Jerusalem sesshin we worked on this group koan, each person endeavoring to solve the mystery using the tools of our own life experience.

I only practiced with Soen Roshi once in my life, in that brief seven-day sesshin on the outskirts of Jerusalem, in a time of war and grief, when I was twenty-five years old. Yet from this encounter I got back my own life. I looked down into the well and saw that the girl at the bottom of the shaft was me. "I'll pull you up with despair and my own loneliness, nothing holy," I vowed to myself and to the girl. "I don't have any other rope." I vowed to work for peace and justice and to dedicate my practice to what Soen Roshi called "endless dimensions universal life."

To continue I needed the help of what the Buddha named the three jewels, or refuges—an awakened heart and mind, regular exposure to the truth of the old teachings, and a community of practitioners to work and meditate with, shoulder to shoulder, every day. I went directly to northern California. Soen Roshi had influenced this move by something he said during a farewell tea for him in Jerusalem. I asked the roshi for guidance about leaving the Middle East and returning to North America. He lifted his small cup of green tea to the light that was streaming in through the windows of the Mount Olive Zendo and, in a mixture of Zen toast and grand proclamation, he boomed out, "Deep in the mountains of California there is a little *tasse* of *hara* [a cup of the belly of Zen, mixing French and Japanese]. Please investigate!"

And so in the early autumn of 1973 I found my way down the long and narrow dirt road that dropped more than 3,500 feet in elevation through the Ventana Wilderness of central California to arrive at that "little tasse of hara." At Tassajara Zen Mountain Center I deepened my roots in the fundamentals of the Zen tradition. We were encouraged not to be obsessed with enlightenment, but to practice meditation wholeheartedly, as if to save our heads from fire. I felt uneasy at first in the formality of the practice at Tassajara and was plagued by wondering if by walking around in black robes, bowing to everyone, and chanting lustily in Japanese I was copping out of active political engagement. But the craggy, unwashed terrain of the Ventana Wilderness and my own desperation kept me there. At night, after meditation, I walked along the rocky banks of the Tassajara Creek, straining to see into the thick darkness of my mind, which seemed to hover just above the water. Whenever there was a day off from the rigorous Zen training schedule I spent it by myself, disappearing into the steep mountains. I met rattlesnakes on the path, pungent black sage, and fire ants, as well as my own wild mind, cocked awry and brimful of scorn and righteousness.

The first time I saw Zentatsu Richard Baker, already the lead teacher at Tassajara and the San Francisco Zen Center, was in the dim lamplight of the Tassajara meditation hall. I blinked in surprise. He stood tall, swathed in ink-dark robes, with a shiny, shaved head and a thick, raccoon-mask of mischievous intensity around his eyes. He looked like the devil trickster to me. And somehow, this was a relief.

Here was an American Zen teacher only ten years older than me, a product of the Berkeley Free Speech Movement and of radical discontent. Now I could hear Zen taught in the vernacular, in forceful English. Every time I sat down on my meditation cushion, blunt questions rose up out of the quiet: What does sitting still have to do with the Great Matter of birth and death? What is the connection between meditation practice and the war going on in Vietnam and in me? I did not want to be reassured. I wanted to be met.

I practiced closely with Baker Roshi for ten years. His teaching was inspired

and smart, bringing a long, vivid lineage of Zen philosophy and practice into modern, Western life. He often spoke of Zen practice and meditation itself as "a non-repeating universe," fresh and new every day.

Baker Roshi saw my dual interest in meditation and ecological activism clearly and supported me in cultivating this common ground. Most Zen Center students rotated their jobs every two years, but I worked in the Zen Center gardens at Tassajara and at Green Gulch Farm for more than two decades. While many of my peers were pursuing a path of priest ordination and Zen teaching, or helping to establish and run a wide range of Zen businesses, my focus was on socially engaged lay life and on developing the garden as a true practice place of productivity, beauty, and inspiration.

Then, in the early 1980s came a new and painful issue within the San Francisco Zen Center community. Our center was becoming famous and even trendy, and so was our articulate and savvy teacher. Worse even than this was my realization that I had come to believe and bask in our Zen Center's fame.

In the early years after Suzuki Roshi's death, Baker Roshi had often spoken about recognizing the "dark at the base of the lighthouse," but by the early 1980s Richard Baker's Zen beacon was so dominant that it was difficult to see and attend to the weeds growing in the lengthening shadows. I hid in the blinding light, content to practice rigorous Zen meditation, work in the Green Gulch garden, and raise Peter's and my young son. This was an unspoken and ultimately costly covenant, as I realized in the spring of 1983 when Richard Baker fell from leadership and the Zen Center came tumbling after. Accused of sexual involvement with several of his students and of abuse of power, money, and authority, Baker Roshi's descent at San Francisco Zen Center was steep and bitter.

When I was a child I used to love to play horse. I was a wild-eyed steed and a rider at once—an energetic centaur. My pumping legs were all thoroughbred filly down to the tips of my flashing hooves, while the top part of my body was the calm, courageous rider who knew exactly where she was going. I snorted, pawed the ground, and cantered off at full speed through the New England forests of my childhood, calling out orders to my true horse nature.

I kept this legacy of freedom and playfulness throughout my troubled wandering in the Jerusalem desert, but I had given some of it up in my early years of practice at Zen Center. The "Samyuktagama Sutra" describes four kinds of horses: the supreme steed follows the driver's will without assistance; the good horse trots at the shadow of the whip; the poor horse moves only with the sting of the whip; while the bad horse must be thrashed soundly before it responds. I had become the good horse, domesticated and eager to serve my teacher and community, but sacrificing my own unbridled nature in exchange for a well-appointed stable.

The leadership crisis at Zen Center shook me awake. Horse and rider merged once again and I saw that in a non-repeating universe even a fallen teacher continues to teach. Refusing to sever that root that had nourished my primary Zen practice, I stayed in connection with Richard Baker while I continued practicing and gardening within the Zen Center community. I learned to continue steadfastly, "under all circumstances," as the Zen tradition encourages.

Shortly thereafter I began to study with Zen master Thich Nhat Hanh, whom I met in the early summer of 1982 when Peter and I were in New York City for a huge international peace march. Close to one million people had assembled on the streets of New York that day. In an electric spirit of revival meeting and Independence Day parade, a surge of humanity roared for peace all along the avenues of Manhattan. Thich Nhat Hanh, born in 1926 in south central Vietnam and a Zen monk since the age of sixteen, stood quietly in the streets with a throng of peace activists and Zen students gathered around him. He was still and somber, somewhat grave and watchful. Silently we joined hands and began to walk, with excruciatingly slow steps.

Thich Nhat Hanh's Buddhist practice was forged during long years of colonial rule, war, and political upheaval in Vietnam, so he knew exactly what he was doing that day in New York City. "To really make peace you must first slow down," he said to us, very softly. "Be aware of your every step. You moved through my country with great haste. We failed to slow you down. Today, be mindful of your walking. Life depends on your peaceful steps."

Behind us the crowd backed up for blocks. People called out in irritation and impatience. Thich Nhat Hanh moved with sovereignty, unfazed and measured in his pace. We walked with him. Baker Roshi described this slight, brown-robed Zen monk as a cross between a tractor and a cloud. Angry peace marchers, annoyed at our slow pace, thronged about us, gesturing and blowing, red-faced, on shrill whistles. Undistracted, adamantine, the Zen group inched on, pressing peace with every step into the heat-softened pavement of New York City. Slowing down my steps, I felt the deep grief I carried in my body and mind for the world. Awareness of war, both in myself and in the world, had been the reason I began to study Zen, in 1971, but in the frenzy of my Zen Center practice and work life over the following decade I had buried this source under piles of well-cultivated, fragrant earth. Now the spring of awareness was bubbling up and I bent down and tasted its sharp, bittersweet water with gratitude and relief.

During the fighting in Vietnam, Thich Nhat Hanh had refused to choose sides in the war. Instead, he practiced for the peaceful resolution of conflict by reminding his students and coworkers that the fate of each country, of each army, is always linked to the fate of the other side. "During any conflict," he repeatedly taught, "we need people who can understand the suffering of all sides, and go to each side to wage peace. We need links. We need communication."

Shortly after the New York peace march Thich Nhat Hanh visited us at Green Gulch Farm. He taught us outdoor walking meditation, and he taught the gift of taking our practice out of the meditation hall and into the streets, the wards of prisons and hospitals, and into the corridors of corporate America. At first I was startled by Thich Nhat Hanh's style. He was bold, curious, and experimental. When I first met him he asked me if there could be a Zen center without Zen and without a center. "Too many people distinguish between the inner work of our mind and the world outside," he said. "But these worlds are not separate. They belong to the same reality."

I continued to live and practice at Green Gulch Farm while studying with Thich Nhat Hanh. This meant traveling to Plum Village, Thich Nhat Hanh's exile community in rural southwestern France, and joining him on his North American retreats held with veterans of the Vietnam War, peace activists, artists, and frontline environmentalists as well as fellow Zen students. Throughout this time I grounded my practice in the garden and deepened my Zen meditation roots even as I turned toward the world. In 1991 during the first Gulf War, I was ordained as a lay Buddhist teacher by Thich Nhat Hanh.

During these years, three aspects of Thich Nhat Hanh's teaching were primary for me: the importance of lively, present-moment Zen mindfulness; the awareness of what he called "interbeing," the interconnectedness of life; and the steady practice of extending the field of meditation into engagement with the life of the world.

The Chinese ideogram for mindfulness is composed of two characters: "heart and mind together" and "in the present moment." Mindfulness is a way of life, not a magic spell. Mindfulness clears, shapes, and liberates the mind. It needs to be practiced where you live, not on some solitary, lofty peak, for mindfulness is always mindfulness of something: of the breath, of the life pulse that runs up and down the stem of a Russian sunflower, of hunger and loneliness in the refugee camps bordering the Gaza Strip.

Interbeing is the awareness that arises out of mindfulness practice, the fruit of mindfulness. When I look in mindfulness at broccoli and beet plants growing in the winter garden, I know that my own life is intertwined with theirs. Thich Nhat Hanh holds up a sheet of paper and calls us to see in it the logger, the rain clouds, and the misty sunlight. When I keep looking, I also see the cut-over forest and the polluted thread of river running through hacked-off stumps of trees, and I see the logger's wife and children.

I also see that I am included in this thin sheet of paper, that I am part of the paper. "You cannot point to a single thing on earth that does not have a relationship with this sheet of paper," Thich Nhat Hanh once said to me. So, paper is made up of non-paper elements because when I return all the elements of the paper—the cloud, the logger, the polluted river—to their source, then the paper is empty. Empty of what? Empty of a separate, isolated, and independent existence. With that awareness I awaken to the vastness of life and the vastness of human ignorance, and I do not turn away from what I see: suffering and liberation in a single sheet of paper, in myself, and in all things.

I do Zen practice to be in touch with the world and to be in touch with my own mind. When I lose myself in the pain and suffering of our times, the one yellow cottonwood leaf floating on the black face of the garden pond brings me back; when I am swept away by the perfumed wind exhaled by Persian roses in the warmth of May, I look up to see a red-tailed hawk flying above the garden with a writhing garter snake in her talons.

Our son, Jesse, was eight years old when we first met Thich Nhat Hanh and Jesse had almost never been in the Green Gulch Farm meditation hall where I sat zazen every day of my life. "Why do you keep your children from the meditation hall?" a perplexed Thich Nhat Hanh asked a group of Zen Center parents. We looked at him in disbelief. What naivete! Then we looked at each other in knowing solidarity. "Because they can't sit still for thirty seconds," said one truthful parent. Rising to the challenge, Thich Nhat Hanh offered to take our children into the meditation hall during a period of sitting and to meditate with them. We were skeptical and nervous. They were sure to reveal our slim skill as parents by their barbaric, unruly behavior. But we agreed.

The children surprised us. They were grateful to be taken seriously. They loved Thich Nhat Hanh and they sat with him like little Buddhas, alert and curious and very still for about twenty minutes, and then filed out quietly to play when they grew restless.

Practicing with Thich Nhat Hanh and my other root teachers, I see that what I am really searching for is true satisfaction beyond labels and categories. I mean the kind of happiness I feel after a day of digging new beds for snow peas all by myself in the spring garden. I am tired and happy, well-used and alertly mindful. Horse and rider are one, and neither is particularly tame or obedient. The practice of Zen mindfulness and interbeing is a lifetime work, one that lives and grows in the heart of the world and depends on my own satisfaction and curiosity.

But satisfaction, like meditation and gardening, is never a safe field. Your roots may be strong, yes, but in order to keep growing strong, old roots must also die off and feed raw ground, yielding to new roots in every season. Remember to let these roots dangle—don't hide them and don't sever them, just make clear what you are made of and where you come from.

These days my Zen practice takes a different path from that of my root teachers. Although he continues to teach worldwide, I see that Thich Nhat Hanh's primary emphasis is now directed toward the monastic training of the community of mostly Vietnamese ordained disciples with whom he works and practices every day.

The monastic path is not my way. Instead, grateful for the teachings I have received, I negotiate a thin, unmarked garden track through the dragon's gate and out into the world. In the last decade or so I have been privileged to train many young gardeners in the craft of organic horticulture and meditation. Several times a year I lead weeklong retreats for a wide range of exhausted environmental leaders and policy makers. And in the early summer of 2006, I completed my formal Zen Center training by receiving lay teaching recognition and entrustment at Green Gulch Farm from my longtime dharma sister and abbess of San Francisco Zen Center, Jiko Linda Cutts.

Sometimes I walk in mindfulness, sometimes I do not. My hands carry garden plants and wild seed sutras, and my heart is full of bittersweet gratitude. Although I sit still in Zen meditation almost every day and lead retreats for activists of all stripes, if you ask me for my lineage credentials you might get splashed in the face with cold water from the bottom of a ropeless well, or be handed a clutch of weeds pulled from the dark base of an abandoned lighthouse. You might be offered a single piece of paper stained with hope and disappointment pressed together into the very fiber of the sheet. But really, I can't be sure what you'll get, since my entwined Zen roots are still growing down into bottomless, uncultivated ground.

THE GARDEN MAKES THE GARDENER

The Blue in Beets

WHEN I FIRST MOVED TO GREEN GULCH IN 1975 WE REGULARLY welcomed groups of inner-city schoolchildren out to tour the farm. I remember one group in particular of very active kindergartners from the Hunters' Point neighborhood of San Francisco, many of whom had never been out of the city before.

I was waiting for them in the garden, braced, weeding a large planting of brilliant, crimson Oriental poppies in full bloom. It was late May, windless and a little hot. The kids pelted down to the garden at full speed, drinking in their unaccustomed freedom in short, staccato gulps as they ran. I motioned to them and they skidded to a stop near the poppy bed and came over. One little boy who was just about at eye level with the poppies grabbed his teacher's hand and stood on tiptoe, staring down into the immense, throbbing chalice of a poppy. "Do they bite?" he asked me in a terrified whisper.

The child and his question have stayed with me over the years. This little boy saw the exposed nerve of the poppies and startled me with his question. "Nobody sees a flower—really," Georgia O'Keeffe commented in 1939. "We haven't time and to see takes time like to have a friend takes time." She painted what she and the boy from Hunters' Point saw—giant, flesh-eating poppies, with red velvet throats lined with black, razor-sharp stamens.

Alan Chadwick loved to remind those of us who worked with him that it is always the garden that makes the gardener, never the other way around. I have known this since I was a child absorbed in Frances Hodgson Burnett's classic book, *The Secret Garden*. From the first of my many readings I related most strongly not to the gardener of Misselthwaite Manor nor to the complex children of the story, but to the abandoned garden itself, which claimed my imagination with its old, secret code.

On some days the garden is dangerously vivid for me. My hemoglobin turns chloroplast green and I am transported across the invisible membrane that separates plants from people. Yet although I fancy such shape-shifting, my deepest practice is simply to work in the garden every day with the actual plants, not my fantasies of them, but the living beings themselves as they grow and come apart all around me.

In my early years of gardening at Green Gulch I studied one of Harry

Roberts's favorite books, a simple botany text, *How Plants Grow*, written for children in 1877 by Asa Gray, a founder of the science of plant geography and botanical exploration. I had a simple goal: to learn to see the plants in front of me in the garden, without diminishing or enlarging them. Simple perhaps, but not easy.

In his botany lessons Asa Gray encouraged his young readers to choose a pattern plant that would clearly show the botanical sequence of how plants grow from seed to seed. Without hesitation I chose the poppy and immersed myself in the study of this ancient medicinal plant.

The word "pattern" is derived from the Old French and medieval Latin *patrōnus*, meaning something to be imitated. Pattern also refers to an archetype, to an ideal worthy of appreciation, and to a design of natural or accidental origin. It soon became clear to me that by studying the life cycle of the poppy my perception and appreciation of other plants in the garden was deepening and widening.

Basic botany, the study of plants and how they grow, arises out of wanting to see and know the plants you love. Plants are the only living beings, along with some algae and blue-green bacteria, that can produce their own food as well as the nourishment necessary to sustain various forms of animal life. The potential is in each ripe seed. When a poppy seed germinates it sends its radicle root tapping down into dark soil, opening up pathways for the absorption of water and dissolved soil minerals. This vanguard root pushes and burrows its way into rocky soil with a protective sheath over its root tip. As the root descends it often exudes a mucilaginous gel that lubricates its journey

down through rough ground. This muscular root opens stiff soil for the later penetration of fine feeder roots that will nourish the growing plant.

Aboveground, the caulicle, the visible green shoot of the poppy, climbs toward the light. As the stem vigorously seeks sunlight the distance between buds and leaves increases, assuring the leaves' maximum exposure to light.

All green leaves of plants share the extraordinary ability to capture and hold sunlight in their nets of chlorophyll pigment. Plants harvest sunlight, harnessing the energy of the sun to rearrange molecules of water and carbon dioxide. In this process of photosynthesis, literally "putting together by light," oxygen is diffused into the atmosphere and simple sugars are created. The plants do this for their own sake, for food and growing tissue, and we animals are their beneficiaries as we harvest them for food and medicine.

The roots and shoots of every plant are linked by an internal vascular system. This plumbing system has two tasks: to carry water and dissolved mineral food up from the roots and out to the leaves, and to move nourishment down through the plant. To accomplish this all plants have two types of thin conduit veins that run just inside their skin, or bark. The xylem veins conduct water and dissolved minerals up through the plant's system and out through the leaves while the phloem veins transport nutrients down from the leaves and throughout the plant.

At a certain point in the life of a plant the sugars produced by photosynthesis and enriched by mineral salts drawn up from the soil go toward making a new kind of organ: the flower. The function of flowers is to produce fertile seed, and from this seed to provide for the next generation of plants. However, grounding this technical definition of the function of a flower is the pattern of a bloodred pool of poppies, their snapping stamens sweeping the inner well of every bloom.

When the first simple flower blossomed more than one hundred million years ago it influenced the entire world. And when the Buddha held up a single flower in his hand and chose his successor by his disciple Maha Kasyapa's smile of recognition that, too, influenced the world. What was seen in that single, tender blossom? Perhaps birth and death, arising and coming apart, all contained and revealed in the open heart of a single flower.

The first true angiosperms, or "encased-seed" flowers such as the poppy, grew seeds in the inner core of their blossoms that ripened into fully endowed embryonic plants. Biologist Loren Eiseley points out how these first flowers changed the face of the world by their unique ability to produce concentrated food from three distinct sources, all originating within the reproductive system of flowers. The first source of food is the rich protein- and carbohydrate-packed stores of pollen and nectar; the second, a swollen, fertilized ovary or fruit with seeds encased within sweet fruit pulp, and last of all, the seeds themselves that provide food to nourish the unborn, embryonic plant.

There is a delicate chemical balance at work in every living plant, a balance of nitrogen and water for growth, and carbohydrates (starch and sugar) for flower and seed production. When water and nitrogen are plentiful, green plants grow leaves, branches, and new shoots. Once this nutrient supply diminishes, the plant transmits hormone messages and the growing parts begin to draw on the carbohydrate reserves of the plant, causing flowers to develop and seed to ripen.

Seeing a Flower Really

The outer whorl, or cup, of a flower is called the *calyx* with its protective bud leaves, or *sepals*, that surround the inner flower before it opens. Moving toward the center of the flower, the next whorl is the *corolla*, or ring of true flower *petals*. Inside this whorl of petals is the ring of male sexual organs, or *stamen*. The male stamen is made up of two parts, a *filament* stalk holding up a swollen *anther* containing male *pollen*. Finally, the innermost whorl in a perfect flower is the female ring, or *pistil*, of the bloom. The pistil is divided into three sections: at the top is the *stigma*, or sticky surface, to which male pollen adheres; an elevated *style*, or stem, that supports the stigma; and at the base of the style there is an *ovary* that ultimately becomes a fruit containing one or more undeveloped seeds, or *ovules*.

Pollen may come from the same plant to fertilize the female ovary (*self-pollination*) or from a different plant (*cross-pollination*), but sexual reproduction by seed can only occur between plants of the same species. Self-pollinated plants like the poppy usually have "perfect flowers," or flowers with functional male and female sexual organs within the same blossom. In these flowers pollination occurs within each individual flower and does not generally depend on insect transfer or wind pollination.

Cross-pollination occurs on the plants that produce separate male and female flowers. All these plants rely on outside help to transfer pollen from flower to flower, and by so doing, to produce viable seed. Insects, wind, bats, and the occasional reverent gardener all help to distribute pollen from ripe blossom to blossom. Most of the pollen on these "imperfect flowers" ripens in a loose spiral pattern rather than in the concentric-whorl pattern that distinguishes perfect flowers.

One of the simplest lessons of Asa Gray's botany textbook summarizes the pattern of this process beautifully. All plant life consists of two processes: assimilation and growth. To assimilate is to make similar, to turn raw matter into substance. This is what happens in every upturned poppy leaf as air, water, soil minerals, and sunlight are assimilated to become simple sugars, starch, and cellulose and to manifest as a living plant. "Green sun," writes my root teacher, Thich Nhat Hanh, "Green sun in a basket of vegetables." And in the unfolding stem of a single poppy flower.

Growth is the increase of a living plant in length and girth. Plants grow by a multiplication of cells, stimulated by the assimilation of raw elements. Plants grow and purify the air, they clean toxins out of polluted soil, they make food and medicine that support all animal life, and they supply the world with fuel, clothing, tools, shelter, warmth, and beauty from their growth and metabolism.

Growth includes all change, not only increase but reproduction, ripening and death as well. Botany for gardeners reveals patterns that connect us to this ancient cycle. We assimilate life and death in every moment as we garden, particularly when we take the time to see a flower really, one never seen before.

❖   ❖   ❖

When we first began to sell Green Gulch Farm produce to the public we transported bulging crates of vegetables to the old Alemany produce market on the south edge of San Francisco. It was 1975, long before outdoor farmers' markets became popular, but at the Alemany market produce buyers, wholesalers, and hungry citizens in search of a bargain lined up in droves at our packed stall.

Zen vegetables were popular from the first. They shone in their battered crates, exhaling the foggy breath of their native seaside soil. Harvested by meditators, the Green Gulch vegetables clearly had their own healthy meditation practice, amply revealed whenever we went to market. Even though we loaded our truck full with crops on produce day we never seemed to have enough, and early one morning to my horror two burly produce buyers got into a screaming, pushing fight over our last crate of 'Bloomsdale' spinach. I cringed behind the farm truck while they had at it.

Another time when I was on market duty with Peter four beautiful Indian women, dressed in patterned silk gauze saris and wearing silver bangles, showed up at our stand. They consulted with one another behind perfumed hands and then advanced and proceeded to pick through our groaning harvest baskets, plucking out all of the yellow beans, leaving the purple and green snap beans behind. Then, as one rhythmic, swaying body, they turned to our beets.

Green Gulch beets were a legend at the market: Zen beets, with almost obscenely huge bloodred globes, flecked with crumbly, black soil. The Indian women chose twenty or so bunches of these beets, three fat beets to a bunch, and then snapped off all of the beautiful burgundy globes and tossed them onto the ground at their feet. They paid us and went off chattering, their prize beet greens stuffed into their plastic sacks.

This was a seminal event for me. Up until that day I had labored under the assumption that we were growing beet *globes* for sale, even though the Green Gulch kitchen has always served beet greens as well as beet roots. What the Indian women showed me was how much I see the garden from my own perspective. When living plants become "produce," beets are a *root* crop, and kale is a leafy green. Now and then I see the whole plant if, as Georgia O'Keeffe reminds me, I take the time to see the pattern within the pattern. But what about the beets, I began to wonder as I picked up the discarded roots from the ground, what is a beet, really?

> Watching gardeners label their plants
> I vow with all beings
> to practice the old horticulture
> and let the plants label me.
>
> *Meditation verse by Robert Aitken Roshi*

When my daughter was very young one of her favorite musical groups was the Banana Slug String Band, a rowdy group who drew their tunes from the heart of the natural world. The Slugs sang a ditty called "Six Plant Parts," which taught children to see and know garden plants from underground up. "Roots, stems, leaves, flowers, fruits, and seeds," strummed the chorus, "Six plant parts are all I need!"

Every plant relies on all of these six plant parts to live and thrive. In their fullness plants define and claim their gardeners since we are made of each other. Still, it is in our human nature to differentiate and to pick and choose, emphasizing the virtue and value of one or two distinct plant parts: beets for their roots (and also for their healthy leaves), poppies for their spellbinding flowers, apples for their succulent fruit.

Botany for gardeners calls on an older, innate capacity to see not only the pattern of assimilation, growth, and decay revealed in a single poppy but also to perceive that deeper pattern of the total, dynamic working of all plant parts together, as one coordinated body. Of particular importance here is seeing the intertwined function of roots and shoots, the underworld and aboveworld realm of plants.

Plant roots have three primary functions: The first is to anchor the plant in the soil, either with a fibrous root system like that of the vast grain family, or with a singular, hefty tap-rooting system like that of the beet or poppy. Roots also absorb water and minerals, the web of fibrous roots consolidating surface moisture, while singular taproots plumb the depths. Last of all, roots store in their organs surplus food for future needs. Had our Indian women of old come out to harvest their prized beet greens from the plants growing in the field, the stored nutrients in the underground beet roots would have pumped out new beet shoot tops in the fullness of time.

All aboveground shoots of garden plants have their origin in the apical meristem, a dynamic knot of rapidly dividing cells found at the tip of every green caulicle shoot. Underground radicle root tips also have such a meristem system for pushing into the depths. As above, so below, although the apical meristem of aboveground shoots is decidedly more complex in function than its underground counterpart since it initiates and directs the growth of stems, leaves, flowers, fruits, and seeds.

When I work in the garden and slow down enough to practice the old horticulture of seeing plants in totality, the garden comes alive in a fresh way. Not only do I see and perceive the six vital parts of the plant, I also experience in root and shoot patterns the life force of the four elements—earth, water, air, and fire—moving through the body of each garden plant.

Plants were described by botanists of antiquity as fourfold in nature. It is not difficult to sense the earth element, solid and dense, teeming with microscopic life, manifest in the roots of plants. Water flows through the stems and leaves of every plant, pulled up by osmosis and transpired back to the atmosphere as the exhaled breath of water vapor. The element of air is conveyed in the flowers of the plant world, blooming and communicating in the soft summer wind. And the fire element is consolidated in the fruit and seed of certain plants since fruit and seed, those "inward seeds of fire," are both ripened and cured by the heat of the sun.

Gardening practice is enhanced by tasting the elemental nature of the six plant parts that compose every healthy garden. When you nourish yourself with the roots, stems, leaves, flowers, fruits, and seeds of the many plants you love and culture in the garden, and when you perceive their natural resonance with the four great elements, they become your best teachers. Yet the truest gardening guide I know has always been the complex garden itself, alive in all of its patterns and richness.

Walking with *The Metamorphosis of Plants*

When he was a young man Goethe made a walking pilgrimage through the Italian Alps, with the intention of observing plants. His journal of this pilgrimage is a slim volume entitled *The Metamorphosis of Plants*. In this journal Goethe challenged himself to *really* see the alpine plants. "All is new and always old," he reminded himself as he walked through the mountains. "When we observe all organic forces," he wrote in another of his intuitive nature studies, "we find nowhere something continuing, nowhere something at rest, but that all is in continuous, fluctuating movement."

The poet saw that plants grow by expansion and contraction and that the history of this process is revealed in the morphology of the plants themselves. Accordingly, a seed is the contracted or essential nature of a plant that expands with water and good soil to the vegetative growth of stem and leaf, contracting again in the calyx, or outer protective cup of the flower bud. Expansion occurs again when the petals of the corolla expand and the flower opens into bloom, and the pistil and stamen expand to produce the fertilized ovary, or fruit, of the plant within which is the completion of the cycle, the contraction of the seed.

The Blue in Beets

The blue in beets
comes and goes
sometimes a shadow
of the weeds
where beets grow
or of their towering leaves
other times a suggestion
of what the beets
might have been:
blue birds
blue stones
blue fish
blue whales
blue water.
If blue isn't here
it's there
If it's not there
it's coming
If you have just seen it
it will be back,
If you have never seen it,
you will.

Erica Funkhouser

North Star Plants

THE ESSENCE OF MEDITATION PRACTICE IS AWAKENING. WITH confidence and sincerity, you wake up to your heart and mind's inmost request. In many Asian languages the words for heart and mind are one, and in the practice of meditation this oneness comes alive. You discover how to know your heart and mind, shape your heart and mind, and free your heart and mind.

In so many ways meditation practice is like gardening. Every garden comes alive in the mind of the gardener. By investigating your land, and the plants you love and know so well in your garden, you come to know the heart and mind of your place, and your own heart and mind as well. When you select your favorite tools and begin to shape the ground, in this digging and cultivating, the garden shapes you. Eventually, you free your heart and mind from what you think you know and prefer, and in this work you also free the true heart and mind of your garden.

I am not speaking of gardening as a metaphor for meditation or for waking up to your true life. Not at all! I have never met, nor hope to meet, a metaphorical garden or a symbolic plant. Gardens and plants are unmanageably alive, speaking with long grass-green tongues in their distinct language woven out of blank sunlight and matted roots. "Leaves are the verbs that conjugate the seasons," writes gardener and author Gretel Ehrlich. Plants and gardens alike speak in complex sentences, uniting garden and gardener with their every utterance.

To know your heart and mind and the true nature of the land that you are gardening, plants and the land must speak for themselves while you listen without moving or saying a word, even if only for five or ten minutes at a time. This was the instruction Katagiri Roshi gave me years ago for basic meditation and everyday life:

> Settle your self on your self—
> and let the flower
> of your life force bloom.

When I am unsettled there are always certain North Star plants that call me home, give me my bearings, and reorient me to the true north of my life. These plants uncover the lay of the land and help me settle while the garden all around me comes to life.

When Peter and I first moved to Green Gulch from Tassajara a huge, wild red rose growing on the crest of the Marin Headlands became just such a North Star plant for me. Until I discovered this rose I had not found my place at the Gulch. I missed the Tassajara landscape and the rugged plants of the Ventana Wilderness. Green Gulch was unfamiliar and cold. I couldn't settle, my mind was restless, and the land was hidden to me. I did not know where I was.

I went for a walk alone on the blustery headlands above the ocean. It was late summer and a stiff west wind was blowing across the Pacific, burning the tips of the coastal grasses a pale ash gray. I followed an overgrown spur path off the main trail and toward the sea cliffs, the abandoned path matching the rutted loneliness of my mind.

The spur ended abruptly at a deserted enclosure filled with a chest-high snarl of weedy poison oak and stinging nettle. From the center of this tangle, a vast red rosebush lifted its battered crown above the fray.

I stood, stunned, before this massive, solitary rose. Although it clearly had not been pruned for years, this old rose grew thick with arched canes bent beneath the weight of carmine-red flowers too numerous to count.

This exotic cultivated rose somehow planted on the lonely headlands above Green Gulch helped me know the mind of my new place more fully than any natural history guide could ever have done. It reminded me that I was on well-loved land. Perhaps a homesick cattle rider from the Azores Islands had planted this rose to remember his native land. Perhaps the rose marked a grave. I will never know and it hardly matters now since the headland rose has become a North Star guide for me, settling my heart and mind in the awareness that everything I love and know is also of the nature to change and come apart, even my own loneliness and estrangement.

❖   ❖   ❖

Shaping your heart and mind and your garden follows on the heels of knowing your mind. "You are fine just as you are," Suzuki Roshi used to say, "and you could use a little improvement." Shaping the mind works in this landscape of duality, calling gardener and meditator alike to pause before acting, and then to gather yourself into service, all the while living fully in the present moment.

This is not easy. In fact, it takes a lifetime of work and practice even to get close. Cultivating, shaping, and freeing the mind demands diligence as well as relinquishing what you think you know and what you think needs shaping. I learned this firsthand in my early years of gardening and Zen training when a poisonous weed reshaped my notion of what medicine was.

On Thanksgiving Day at Green Gulch Farm we always make a harvest offering in the meditation hall, the spare Zen altar yielding to baskets of 'Yellow Finn' potatoes and crisp 'Snow White' apples, braids of red Italian garlic, and gigantic bunches of 'Dinosaur' kale mixed with purple Osaka mustard, underpinned with a voluptuous assortment of large, pink banana squash, and 'Blue Hubbards' that cover the zendo floor. Instinctively, I complete the harvest tribute with one last, essential offering from the shadow realm of weeds. Sometimes I bring matted bindweed or cape ivy, sometimes a few oily branches of poison oak or the tenacious rhizomes of Bermuda grass. But my prize offering is poison hemlock, for without these uninvited guests gardening life loses its punch and drifts into the sleepy, sun-dappled backwater of predictable routine.

Poison hemlock is known as the executioner of philosophers and kings and is sometimes called Socrates' friend, for the swift and fatal dose of hemlock that the Greek philosopher was condemned to drink twenty-four centuries ago by his political enemies. The outer skin of the hollow-stemmed hemlock plant is flecked with red stains that are called the "blood of Socrates." They are also believed to represent the indelible brand that marked Cain's brow after the murder of his brother.

I live in cautious détente with poison hemlock, respecting its dangerous strength. An acquaintance once accidentally ate poison hemlock. Lost in the maze of an unmarked forest for a few days, she came on a stand of poison hemlock growing in a small clearing, and in the wan light she mistook the foliage for that of its distant cousin the domesticated carrot. The famished woman pulled and swallowed the limp albino roots of hemlock, where the essential poison of the plant is most concentrated. Almost immediately a chill numbness began to spread from her weakened legs into her groin. She realized that she had been poisoned and that if the poison reached her heart, she would die. This was her last coherent thought as the hemlock seized her stomach and reversed its course. She retched and collapsed from nausea and numbing vertigo, to be discovered a day or so later still in a delirious stupor.

The botanical name for poison hemlock, *Conium maculatum*, is from the Greek word *konas*, to spin about, like the ancient whirling dervishes of Kona, Turkey. A potent nerve poison, when ingested in full dose poison hemlock induces an extreme dizziness and numbness that culminates in death. Whenever I work too long grubbing this plant out of the borderlands of the garden I grow woozy from the stale yellow stench of Socrates's friend.

Despite the danger of poison hemlock, I cannot imagine my gardening life without its fetid presence. Hemlock shapes my gardener's mind. When the cloying sweetness of French lilac and zephyr lilies makes me bilious with their perfume, I can always rely on the stink of poison hemlock to snap me back to my senses, reminding me that potent poison taken in proper dosage can be medicine and that the wounder also heals.

Although it was understood from the Middle Ages onward to be a deadly poison, hemlock was also invited into the pharmacopoeia of the early tenth century. It was administered in minute dosage as a mild narcotic sedative for cramping, nervous excitability, and even for epilepsy. Mixed with betony and ripe fennel seed, hemlock was reputed to cure the bite of a mad dog and to relieve the wrack of chronic bronchitis and whooping cough.

Gardening without a salutary medicinal dosage of poisonous plants and a pinch of green treachery is inconceivable. Even in their malevolence, poisonous plants are North Star guides for me. Their danger shapes me and calls me to my senses. I raise a cautious welcome to those I dread and fear, to the dervish executioner of philosophers and kings and to that single, unnamed noxious weed at the edge of the cultivated world that broods alone in baneful silence. You strengthen and shape the mind of the garden.

✦　✦　✦

When it comes to freeing the mind, classic meditation traditions praise the virtue of detachment from the busy world, of finding an "inner distance from things," if only for a brief period of sitting or walking meditation or for an hour of quiet weeding beneath your favorite planting of pale pink lotus dahlias. This inner distance can be invaluable for freeing your mind.

Liberation also calls for insight into what is difficult to accept: suffering in the world, impermanence and change, and the lack of an abiding self that is separate from suffering and change. Fortunately, the vast, green world shows me that liberation can come just as readily from a plant I despise as from one of my cherished darlings.

There is a certain plant, *Euryops viridis*, a perennial flowering shrub of the vast family Compositae, that I have always disliked and shunned. It is an innocent and cheery enough plant festooned in a common, everyday shawl of bright yellow daisies floating above finely cut bright-green foliage, but when I encounter this indestructible shrub I avert my gaze, hiss a little, and pray for pestilence to strike it down.

I should not be so proud of my prejudice, especially since euryops was one of my mother's favorite plants. "Oh look," she would say whenever she visited me in California, "there's my precious yellow daisy plant again." She always ignored my wooden silence and raved repeatedly in the presence of every euryops we encountered.

The name "euryops" comes from the Greek meaning "wide eyes" or "wide, full countenance," which I sorely lacked and withheld in the presence of this plant until I met nine-year-old Marissa, who briefly became my unintended gardening and mind-liberation teacher. Marissa lives next door to a good friend of mine in Berkeley. One night last summer, my friend Lennis showed me a little potted euryops that was not merely scrawny but truly decrepit.

Lennis asked my advice. It was startling to see *any* problem on the immortal euryops, let alone be consulted about aiding my least favorite plant. I was tempted to offer cheap, inscrutable Zen wisdom like, "Ah! Everything changes, just sit with your plant and release it to the great beyond," but instead I recommended the obvious: replant the root-bound little bugger, which was still in its original minuscule nursery pot, and give it a good shot of water followed by benign neglect.

The next day young Marissa visited Lennis and offered to help her garden. Together they took the suffering euryops out of its pot, noticing that the roots of the plant had already broken out of the bottom in a desperate search for water and real soil. Lovingly they repotted the plant and snipped off all of its dead foliage and wilted flowers. Then Marissa watered the patient euryops for a good fifteen minutes, singing to the plant as she worked. Before going home the child announced, "This is the best day of my summer because we saved the life of a plant," and suggested that when the euryops had five new flowers on it they plant it in the garden and have a lunch party at Lennis's house to celebrate.

And so in a few weeks' time when the euryops plant quite naturally returned to life, Marissa's handwritten invitation to the plant lunch party arrived and, resignedly, off I went. To my surprise quite a few people attended the gathering in Lennis's backyard, where there was potluck food and a beautiful peach rose as a favor for each guest. We fed ourselves and each person offered a bit of rich compost to the now hale and hardy euryops plant. We folded peace cranes to bless the party plant. To close, we were served homemade cake decorated by Marissa with a gigantic yellow flower made out of colored icing in honor of new life for the euryops.

I am no pushover when it comes to abandoning my opinions. But I confess that it was good to spend that timeless afternoon in Lennis's garden honoring an enemy plant that would never have been a chosen North Star guide for me.

At the end of the party I spent a little time alone with the celebrated euryops, breathing with it in the summer afternoon. The euryops shone with new life in its garden home, draped with peace cranes and bearing one fully opened yellow daisy flower with five fat flower buds surrounding it. Did my own countenance grow wider in this encounter? Probably not, especially since what is true north today on the plant compass can shift in an instant and vanish in a flash. To know the mind of the garden, and to shape and be freed by it, is the work of a lifetime.

The Three Sisters

I AM THE ELDEST OF THREE SISTERS BRAIDED INTO A BRIGHT ROPE of destiny that will never be undone, wound together with the strong cords of love and pride for one another, and the remnants of pale green jealousy and competition almost half a century old. We are a fierce lot, having endured the bitter death of our parents within three months of each other, and an ample array of marriage and divorce, terminal disease, the joys of birth, and the loss of unborn children, not to mention screaming fights over the precise whereabouts of various irreplaceable two-piece swimsuits, coveted eyelash curlers, and misplaced party shoes.

In honor of this sibling lineage, and to celebrate affinity and kinship in the plant world, every year for the past decade I have planted the three-sister crop trio of the New World—corn, beans, and squash, or *Dio-He-Ko*, "those who sustain us." Grown together since the dawn of agriculture in Mesoamerican gardens, these ancient ones were considered by the Iroquois to form a three-in-one goddess, growing together to nourish body, mind, and spirit.

Corn is the world's second most productive staple food crop, after rice. First domesticated eight thousand years ago from wild teosinte grasses growing in northern Mexico, corn is a prolific and adaptable plant measured by some Midwestern farmers to grow up to four inches a day. Known as the Old Woman Who Never Dies by traditional native farmers of the Mandan and Hidatsa nations, corn is a revered crop as well as a mystery, for unlike any other plant, the flowers and seed kernels of corn grow separately on the same stalk. Because of its readiness to receive and accept corn pollen from many different sources, traditional strains of native-grown corn are in grave danger of genetic pollution from modern laboratory-raised varieties of genetically modified corn.

Also called *ta'a*, the "seed of seeds," corn is sacred to its native people. They have evolved together over the ages. In most corn-based traditional societies the gardening year is ordered by ceremonies honoring and blessing the life of corn. From the first planting of the "seed of seeds," to the opening of slim water channels for thirsty corn roots, to the hoeing and hilling of the plant and the first harvest of green corn in early August, up to the autumnal feasts celebrating the main harvest and distribution of ripe corn, and closing with the final braiding together of the stems of the best ears of corn, as seed for future gardens, corn is central to the life of its people.

Beans grow along with the Old Woman Who Never Dies, often planted in the same raised hills as corn seed and trained to climb up the green ladder of the corn mother for support. Beans were first cultivated almost eight thousand years ago in Mesoamerica, and bean images have long appeared in prehistoric art. The seed of the bean plant was used as a color-coded means of ornament and communication, and in the ancient Inca empire, long-distance runners raced with bean seed along sophisticated roadways that ran for hundreds of miles, carrying world news conveyed in a handful of colorful beans.

Squash is the eldest of the triple-treasure sisters, dating back ten thousand years to scattered remnants found in the prehistoric caves of the Tamaulipas mountains of Mexico. Modern methods of DNA retrieval have uncovered genetic traces of squash remains from more than ten thousand years ago in the oldest *middens*, or garbage dumps, of Ecuador. Sorted into four species that span the ages and range from pumpkin to squash to bitter melon to gourd, squash plants cover the ground of time with their succulent vines and heavy burden of fruit. From one squash seed as many as 250 fruit of the vine are known to have grown. These ancient plants protect the skin of the earth at the base of their corn and bean sisters.

* * *

I have always loved the three-sister crops, each for its unique beauty and strength and collectively for the way these sisters amplify and support one another. These are origin plants surfacing from the well of time and tradition, and modern staples in the garden and at the table, as well.

For the last ten years or so we have planted special children's gardens at Green Gulch and at the Edible Schoolyard, gardens dedicated to the three sisters and reserved for the culinary and horticultural pleasure of young people and their families. In honor of the long and rich tradition of these New World crops we plant three-sister seed that is open-pollinated and close to its wild, unhybridized origins, convinced that these old plants have stories to tell within their braided culture.

For corn we plant 'Rainbow Inca' flint corn received more than a decade ago in a seed exchange held at the annual Ecological Farming Conference and grown at Full Belly Farm in the Capay Valley, a finger valley of the Sacramento Valley of north-central California. Those of us who received the Inca corn that first year pledged to bring fresh 'Rainbow Inca' corn seed back the next season to share with our organic farming friends, a renewable pledge that we have kept faithfully for years.

For beans, we grow dun-and-chestnut-speckled climbing beans from gardeners living in Kosovo, who were unable to grow these traditional Balkan beans because of war in their homeland. We have faithfully grown these beans in a network of children's gardens all over the country and kept the seed for years. In the summer of 2003 we were able to send bags of the Kosovo bean seed home to the Balkans. Luckily we had grown enough seed by then to also taste for ourselves these delicious, creamy beans.

For squash, we grow a beautiful, warty aqua-green midsize Guatemalan one given to me a few years ago as a birthday present. Seed from this single squash has provided the garden with a treasure trove of plump squash season after season.

In traditional gardening cultures all life existed in a circle with material and spiritual forms intermixed. In honor of this ancient pattern, we planted our original children's three-sister garden at Green Gulch in a circle pattern, following the native tradition of entrusting the most important plants both to the center of the circle and to the outer edge. The children drew a round print of their garden on the soft soil of the Gulch, with three concentric circles, and narrow walking paths between the beds.

The central, inner circle of the garden was kept as bare earth just for children to visit, their hub of refuge within the wheel of the surrounding garden. The next ring was host to the trinity of New World crops that have grown together for thousands of years. Corn seed was planted first, at two-foot centers. Next, the corn was surrounded with Kosovo beans so that this twining sister could be supported by the 'Rainbow Inca' corn, and the children poked a few Guatemalan blue squash seeds into the remaining soil and watered their circle garden well. All of this work was done in silence, out of respect for the ancient ones. Last of all the children planted sunflower and ornamental tobacco seeds on the outer circle ring for beauty, medicine, and protection.

By midsummer the children were lost in the thicket of their three-sister circle garden. Like some traditional native gardens of Mesoamerica, everything grew in a wild jumble of interdependence and productivity. The children were at home there, lying on their backs in the inner circle, sucking a sweet section of cornstalk, and looking up at the open sky. They reminded me of a passage from Thoreau: "There were times when I could not afford to sacrifice the bloom of the present moment to any work, whether of the head or hands. I love a broad margin to my life. Sometimes on a summer morning I sit in a sunny doorway from sunrise until noon. I grow in these seasons, like corn in the night."

My favorite time of all in this first three-sisters garden was at the cusp of its decline in late Indian summer, when all the crops were ripe and beginning to wane. The 'Rainbow Inca' corn stood a good nine feet high by then, bowed down by the weight of Kosovo bean vines that completely engulfed the cornstalks, their dry, brittle pods rattling in the late-season wind. At ground level the vines of the Guatemalan blue squash radiated out at least fifteen feet, reminding me of a field of soft sea-green soccer balls left out under the autumn sky. Not only were these crops prolific, they were also delicious. With the children we cooked up a mess of succotash made from the three sisters and ate our feast in the remnants of their Indian summer garden.

Around this same time in late October a toddler wandered through the Green Gulch garden with his mother. Joshua pushed his way through the thicket of the three sisters aiming for a beautiful Guatemalan squash growing at the edge of the charmed circle. His excitement in the presence of this one particular squash was infectious. Joshua pointed at the ancient sister and finally spat out, "Pum!" for the long lineage of squash.

We protected Joshua's "pum" long after the main harvest was complete. However, by mid-November the less respectful and ravenous rats and field mice of the garden had begun to sample his treasure. A small, rodent-size hole was gnawed through the thick blue hide of Joshua's prize squash.

Joshua noticed. He stood above his squash and contemplated the irrevocable

Three Sisters Succotash

1 cup cubed squash, uncooked
½ cup uncooked dried beans
¾ cup dried sweet corn (whole kernels),
    or 1½ cups fresh whole-kernel corn
2 tablespoons butter or margarine
¾ cup cold milk
2 tablespoons flour
1 teaspoon salt
⅛ teaspoon white pepper
½ teaspoon sugar

♦ Wash squash, dried beans, and corn separately, by rinsing each well in a strainer. Place the beans in a bowl with enough cold water to completely cover the contents, and let soak overnight.

♦ Next day, place each ingredient in a separate medium-size saucepan, add additional water to cover, bring to a boil, reduce heat, and simmer with lid on until tender. Dried corn will take thirty to forty-five minutes and fresh corn only about five minutes to cook; dried beans will take an hour or more; squash will take about twenty minutes.

♦ In a medium-large saucepan, melt the butter. Combine milk and flour until perfectly smooth. Add to butter in saucepan and cook over medium-high heat, beating constantly with a wire whisk, until mixture is thickened. Add salt, pepper, and sugar. Add cooked corn, squash, and beans.

♦ Blend succotash ingredients, heat through gently until hot, without boiling, and serve.

♦ This is a "winter" succotash, served at the end of the growing season. This recipe serves six to eight people.

Adapted from the book *Slumps, Grunts, and Snickerdoodles*, by Lila Perl.

truth of suffering and impermanence, pointing at the ominous rat hole. The puckered wound had begun to ooze and fester. Viscous squash sap drooled onto naked ground. Joshua patted the squash sympathetically, murmuring, "Ouwie."

By early December the blue squash had become a soft gray mound of mold. On his last visit to the site of feral language Joshua leaned over his decayed and mossy teacher, wrinkled his little nose at the foul stench, and proclaimed, "Dead-o," before walking home through the cold winter evening with his mother.

Not even the Buddha was as succinct as Joshua in his appraisal of the truth of temporal existence: "All conditioned things are of a nature to decay," the Buddha reminded his disciples. "Strive untiringly!" For me, "Pum, ouwie, dead-o" is a sufficient gardening and meditation mantra, one I recite under my breath when I plant three-sisters gardens. These New World crops stand together as true North Star plants, braided testimony to a persistent culture that is older than language or metaphysical thought.

Leave the Flowers to the Wind

EACH YEAR, WHEN THE BITTER LAND WIND FROM THE EAST UNRAVELS its long whip and begins to flay the winter gardens of Green Gulch, I know it is time to divide the Siberian iris. This wind rips off the scabbed surface of the winter soil and lays bare my gardener's nerves. Known as the *mistral* or "master wind" in southern France, that cold and dry northerly wind that blows in squalls across the Rhône valley toward the Mediterranean, this phantom causes schools to be closed and is responsible for unpredictable and violent human behavior. Because this wind blows from the northeast across the land in our watershed rather than from off the ocean, it carries the smell of snow and ice from the Sierra mountains. It is always a strong wind, torquing the garden in an unfamiliar direction. Branches snap and blow toward the sea, spinning away in the howl of the updraft.

In these cold winds it is easy to imagine that I am on the Russian steppe, hunching over huge clumps of beardless Siberian iris. These plants are best divided when they are dormant, although we joke that they only really go "dormant" in our mild, coastal climate for two or three hours a year. When the supple grass leaves of the Siberians are burned coppery bronze by the reverse wind, it is time to divide the plants. No calendar of garden procedures is as accurate a reminder of work to be done as the bitter east wind, insisting that I take out the serrated hand scimitars I use to harvest the lush spinach of summer and apply them to the Siberians' foliage. Then begins the division of the Siberians, one of the hardest tasks of the winter garden and one that must be done in season. Timing is everything in the garden, timing and response. "Otherwise, you always eat stale bread," said Alan.

As recently as two hundred years ago, native Miwok people ranged over the inlets and finger valleys of Green Gulch and the neighboring coastal canyons. Miwok women stripped the outer ribs of the California native iris and wove them into strong twine for trapping small birds, for making fishing nets, and for binding together their autumnal granaries where the acorn harvest was stored. Nomadic and seasonal, they followed a rhythm and order dictated by wind and flowers. Whenever I handle the tough, gritty foliage of the Siberian iris, which is botanically related to the California native iris, the Miwok people move like solemn clouds across this land I now call home.

In the first months of establishing the Green Gulch garden I divided an old block of huge Siberian irises with my gardening partner, Skip Kimura. We were innocent of their nature, these beasts that had grown undisturbed for years. We wanted to divide them and give them a prominent role as primary bones in the skeletal frame of the new garden.

Timing the Division of Perennial Plants

Climate and bioregion influence the season of division for perennial plants. In the northern and northeastern regions of the United States, as well as in the colder climates of the central U.S., hardy perennials must be divided and replanted before the hard frost of winter sets in, usually by late October or early November.

In the frost-free regions of the U.S., the Pacific maritime states and the Southeast, perennial division may be accomplished through mid-December, so the new divisions have time to root and establish themselves before flowering.

We were both slightly ill with a winter flu that lays waste most of northern California in the windy winter season. Skip was sicker than I. A pale green pallor rose and fell like the ocean tide beneath the surface of his skin. We walked around thick rings of Siberians, sunk into deep craters in the garden like fallen meteors burrowed into the buttocks of the land. The earth around them stood in wind-sculpted ridges, dusted with white frost.

Skip and I were thoroughly trained in classic procedure; we both knew what we had to do. We began lifting separate plants, though after ten or twelve deep probing strokes of our heavy forks we moved in resignation to the same clump of iris and worked together. It was going to be a big job. The wind muttered cold, phlegmy obscenities at our backs. During the entire procedure, which began in late morning and continued until after dark, we never spoke to each other except to say, "A little lower," or "Too much cover soil."

Iris, the flower of the gods of ancient Greece, traveled the Rainbow Bridge between Olympus and Earth in the hands of Hermes, the messenger, who bore the flower as an offering from the Gods to the world of humankind. The stem wand of the iris is slender, the original scepter. The three petals of the iris blossom typify faith, wisdom, and valor. Ours were 'Caesar's Brother,' a prize Siberian iris and a treasured gift originally given us by the founders of Western Hills Rare Plant Nursery. 'Caesar's Brother' flowers midnight purple and unforgettable. We wait all year for those brief three weeks in early spring when the Siberian irises uncurl their black silk buds, take a deep breath, and exhale into a glory of bloom.

Years ago in the Asian Art Museum of San Francisco I saw painted palace screens of fields of iris from medieval Japan. The backdrop of the screens was hammered gold leaf, while in the foreground waves of iris bloomed. Lavender, indigo, blue-black, and violet tides ran over an inland sea of soft green foliage.

I sought to summon those ancient screens for inspiration as I bent over the vast clumps of living Siberian iris that cold morning. We groaned under the sheer weight of the plants as we sucked them out of their frosty soil. At least one heavy-duty lifting fork from England snapped under the weight of the work. Shamelessly, I prayed for human relief, for assistance, but no one came along to spell us; we were totally alone, except for the banshee wind and the endless row of iris.

It never occurred to us in those hours just before nightfall to modify the lifting procedure and dig less deeply. We followed the order of the roots, and we obeyed the Siberians, digging up giant plants with matted root systems at least two and a half feet deep and wide. No clump of Siberians weighed less than twenty-five pounds. We dragged these frosty monsters onto the dirt farm road and pried our heavy forks back-to-back into the tangle, jumping on the bar of the fork to send the tines down into the cave of iris roots. As the forks descended and we pulled them apart, the Siberians tore with a soft hiss. White roots covered the road. One healthy clump yielded eight full-size divisions. Over us, the east wind whined and snarled, dragging in the dark by the throat.

❖   ❖   ❖

A decade later I helped Sukey, who followed me as head gardener at Green Gulch, divide and replant the Siberian irises. The plants had been established in the garden a good twelve years by then, divided faithfully every second year. Sukey was going to do it alone, as the wind bore down from the east, of course, crushing the spine of the garden. She asked me to review the procedure for dividing the Siberians. I stared at her perched on top of the huge plants. *She looks like a wiry winter wren*, I thought, *with a waist like Scarlett O'Hara*. Her cheerfulness nauseated me. "Let's just do it together," I said, with old dread. "I'll add my bulk to yours. I can't possibly describe how to do this one."

The sleeping soul of the Siberian iris awoke in me as we worked. I pulled off my wool hat, then my coat. The wind flicked them off the hedge, like dry cigarette butts. The tangle of old white roots pulled me down into its familiar den. The procedure and sequence of this classic division process rose up in me from out of the ball of roots and stood forth in clean, timeless lines. It takes forever to do this work well. We have that long to obey the details.

The great Japanese Zen master Eihei Dogen said, "Mind is beyond measure. Things given us are beyond measure. Leave the flowers to the wind, the birds to the seasons." In the young, New World Zen meditation halls rooting and dividing and flourishing across the continent, we still follow the guidelines for meditation set up in Dogen's time in his monastery on the rugged coast of northern Japan. And in the garden, the bloodline of tradition and obedience to the plants pumps in the arteries of every gardener. Do we ever leave anything alone? I wondered, stepping on my fork.

Many gardeners claim that you can't hurt Siberian irises, but they fail to say whether the iris can hurt you. They are so hardy, so vigorous, and so obstreperous. In their wild, native habitat they are never divided. Instead, they increase in broad, concentric rings, the center of each clump dying as the roots multiply and radiate outward. Only those of us gardening in fixed beds insist on directing their growth and increasing these iris by lifting and dividing them regularly. Some gardeners split their Siberians with a spade; others use an ax. I have even seen some gardeners divide them with pruning saws. Precisely because they are hardy and triumphant in the garden, because their mind is beyond measure, I meet their might with the discipline and order of the best tradition of handling grand herbaceous perennials.

In most places Siberian iris reach a height of three and a half or four feet, and they may need to be divided once every four or five years. In the mild climate and rich soil of Green Gulch they raise their midnight wands well over five feet above the earth. I stand at eye level to their penetrating black satin gaze every spring.

Shortcuts to save time and work have never held much weight in the dense presence of the Siberians. But sometimes a devil voice whispers to me: *Go ahead—cut the roots off at this level. No one is watching. You've gone deep enough for years and the plants can take it—you know they can take it.* Then I remember the night that I went into the Green Gulch meditation hall after dark to bring home my meditation cushion. The huge, carved wooden figure of the bodhisattva Manjusri was sitting in the core of the zendo, reminding each meditation student to look deeply at what is and to awaken the mind of insight and wisdom. I felt the continuity of this vow alive in the darkness. Whether seen or not, there was nowhere in the world to hide. Every action matters. I decided to obey the Siberians.

The Siberian iris are North Star plants, opening the gate into the garden for me. I am made of their stuff. I say that I follow their law, though it would be more truthful to say that I garden obeying the techniques I was taught, which are as specific and varied as the plants themselves. Most plants do not demand the kind of labor the Siberians call for. Hardly! Michaelmas asters are pulled apart in the hand and bearded iris want shallow soil with their top rhizomes revealed. Since climate influences plant division as well, no puny California peony grown in warm soil ever calls for the crowbars that are needed to lever a fifty-year-old and fifty-pound New England peony clump out of its September bed. Each plant demands a distinct form of obedience, precise and particular, born of relationship, in all seasons.

When I am as careful as I can be with the Siberians, and as unsentimental, they show me a standard to which every procedure in the garden is hitched. The iris are boundless, their lives beyond human calculation, yet exactly how I lift and divide these particular iris has mysterious resonance with the whole, true garden. When I leave the flowers to the wind, the gifts of the garden are beyond measure, entrusted to me for a brief season.

The Threshold Oak

FOR OUR FIRST TWENTY-FIVE YEARS AT GREEN GULCH FARM WE practiced in the shelter of a huge coast live oak tree growing in the center of the community, just off the main path leading to the meditation hall. Early in the morning, on the way to zazen, I occasionally stopped to greet this stately tree. Sometimes I would lean back against the rough bark of the trunk and look up to the crest of the sky where the last night stars were caught in the fine filigree net of interlaced oak branches.

The Green Gulch oak was one of a matched pair of seedlings started from acorns planted in the early 1950s by Andrew Singletary, a man from central Texas who worked for the Wheelwright family for years and nursed the young oaks into being. One of the pair succumbed to witch's broom fungus and died just about the same time as Andrew did, in the mid-1970s. George Wheelwright fashioned a bronze memorial plaque in honor of his beloved friend and affixed it to the remaining giant oak tree growing in the heart of Green Gulch.

This giant oak was a North Star tree for me. I shot my bearings in relationship to the oak no matter where I was at Green Gulch. I reckoned my place by this tree. It anchored and steadied me whenever I was within its range, and if I woke up anxious and restless at night, just imagining the solid coast live oak tree outside our house brought me back to myself.

Peter's and my wedding reception unfolded in the shade of this oak tree, our young son learned to climb in the wide embrace of its branches, and coming up from the fields at dusk, tired and dirty, I always felt a surge of strength when the rising crown of the coast live oak came into view.

In the early winter of 1992, after fierce winds and hard rain, a huge limb crashed onto the earth, ripping open the main stem of the tree. We bolted the split trunk back together and cabled the heavy primary scaffold branches to keep the oak from collapsing under its own weight.

The damaged oak continued to thrive in our midst, broken open but vigorous. Some community members wanted to take the plant out. "It's dangerous. It could fall and crush a guest," they predicted ominously. Others winced when they passed the wounded veteran. The oak tree was a steady reminder of our own mortal dilemma. "You're only keeping it alive with life-support systems," they chastised me. "It's unnatural." The more practical members of the community cited the expense of ministering to a damaged tree: the costs of pruning, cabling, bolting, and monitoring were all reviewed. But in the end, those of us who loved the tree with that old fierce fire and passion that oaks have always inspired, prevailed.

On a windy December night in 1995 a violent storm blowing with hurricane velocity out of the Gulf of Alaska ended all of our tedious oak debates with one savage roar. The trunk of the oak tree was slashed apart, the snapped cable lines swinging in the wind like thin silver threads. The heavy limbs crashed to the ground as if Zeus himself had pierced the chest of his totem tree with an unsheathed thunderbolt, laying bare the raw, red heart of the sacred oak.

Stunned, we let the giant tree lie in state for almost a month. No one wanted to buck up this fallen patriarch. It was menacingly alive even in death, exuding an acrid sap from its core. The storm that savaged our coast live oak also laid waste miles of Bay Area power line. We were without electricity or telephone service for over a week. Something in me celebrated this extended blackout. It matched the darkness I felt at the death of the oak.

On the day after the tree fell I went out in the storm at dusk, just as the wind dropped its pitch to a low, dark moan. I sat alone on the torn-open trunk in the rain. Night fell. Behind me, the black wind snarled and sucked raw marrow out of its fresh kill. No lights led me back home, but the scattered limbs of the oak tree reached all the way to my gate.

The Druids' alphabet was originally expressed by totem trees. The Celtic word for "oak" was *duir*, the letter "d" standing for door, just as it does in ancient Hebrew. The oak tree has long been a doorway between worlds, a threshold, an opening. When Junípero Serra, father of the California missions,

first arrived in the New World, he planted his original cross beneath a huge coast live oak, feeling the wind of raw spirit moving through the door, calling him into California. And the Maidu and Senal, native peoples of northern California who were never truly colonized by missionaries, still believe that fire runs from the core of the earth to rise up as sap in the arteries of every coast live oak growing on their land.

When you live next to certain plants, greet them every day, and depend on them for shelter, direction, food, warmth, inspiration, and relief, they become part of you. They fill your imagination. They hold on to you and also leave you profoundly alone to find your own way, steadied by their presence. This is how it is with me, at least. This is how plants work on me.

It's been over a decade since the Green Gulch oak blew down. The coastal meadow where the tree grew is mowed and swept by the prevailing winds that blow across the wrinkled brow of the Pacific and smooth out the land. Not a trace of the oak tree remains to the naked eye. Still, within nothingness there is a door, and on some mornings when I walk to zazen through the cold veils of fog, I feel that great, wild oak tree nearby. Like an amputee who still senses her lively phantom limb twitching at the end of a dead stump, the oak tree moves in me.

✦   ✦   ✦

There is a small altar in the Green Gulch glass greenhouse. Whenever I would go into this glasshouse to work I would follow the same ritual: open the air vents to let the young plants growing under glass breathe fresh air and then step up to the rustic altar and offer a stick of incense to begin the workday. On the glasshouse altar is an old, battered Buddha figure, made of white plaster painted a bilious sea green, an eight-inch model of the great, forty-foot-high bronze Kamakura Buddha crafted in thirteenth-century Japan. In the Japanese tea garden of the Golden Gate Park in San Francisco there is a ten-foot bronze copy of the Kamakura Buddha who sits steadily beneath the flowering cherry trees of spring and the naked branches of winter. When our son, Jesse, was a baby we laid him down in the huge folded hands of the

Golden Gate Buddha one day. Jesse looked perplexed but comfortable in his bronze cradle. As I light incense in the glasshouse day after day, I can still see the baby in the Buddha's hands.

Our plaster glasshouse Buddha is weathered and decomposing. Day by day, there is a little less of him; still, for the last thirty years, this Buddha has been a loyal garden mascot. For many years he sat outside, unprotected from the weather, keeping vigil in the dripping dawn fog of July and enduring the occasional fiery sun that sears the coastal garden in late May and early October. Alone in the dark, the garden Buddha has practiced upright sitting through long winter nights of driving rain.

A number of years ago a fast-moving jet in our farm irrigation system went awry and blasted the green Buddha in his face, blowing off his calm, round head. I found the head the next morning, facedown in the front border of 'Bloody Cranesbill' geraniums. The Buddha's nose had been sheared off by the water's sword and his face had a startled look. I put his head in his lap and remembered the ancient Gandharan Buddhas of Asia, defaced by bands of warriors more than a millennium ago. Although their stone noses were deliberately hacked off and their serene countenances deformed, these stone Buddhas maintained their sovereignty.

For several years after losing his head, our green Buddha sat unperturbed in the garden with his head in his folded hands. There was something strangely comforting for me about gardening next to a headless Buddha. He kept reminding me to stop thinking so much and to believe in the garden that is far older than thought, and in plants that are unthinkably determined and full of surprise, like the 'Hupeh' crabapples.

I received a handful of this wild crabapple seed from east-central China at just about the same time that we were building our new glasshouse. I had never sown tree seeds before and I was anxious about their life cycle. These particular crabapple trees have been cultivated for centuries for the fine tisane, or tea infusion, that is made from their tender leaves.

Sadly, the crabapple trees refused to germinate. I hovered over them for months, willing them to sprout. Finally I gave up in disgust, sure that the seeds were no longer viable. Still, I had waited for so long that I was reluctant to dump the whole flat entirely, so I took it outside, away from the incubating warmth of our old ramshackle greenhouse, and abandoned my tree experiment to the vagaries of uncontrolled weather. Instantly, the crabapples went out of my mind.

Months and months later I found this seed flat, pushed over on its side by the winter winds. The 'Hupeh' crabapple trees were four inches tall with three sets of glossy, true leaves. A white webwork of matted roots had split the bottom of the old redwood seed flat, and the tree roots fanned out, searching

84

for deep soil, like a hungry newborn rooting at night for its mother's nipple. Once the Chinese crabapples were finally planted in the garden, they took hold without a thought and made themselves at home.

Not long after the new glasshouse was completed in the autumn of 1993, the headless green Buddha finally moved inside. I sat him up on a fragrant round of oak sawed from one of the threshold oak's fallen branches. The new glass palace was dedicated with incense and flowers offered to the weather-pocked Buddha. Over the years since then, many Zen students have tried to repair him. Some clever ecologically inclined meditators have attempted to stick his head back on with a handmade plaster of clay and soil, mixed directly from the fields. Others have used melted candle wax from the altar. Some have even stooped to white glue repair.

It's hard to offer incense day after day to a headless Buddha. It's unsettling. But no re-capitation sticks, and the green Buddha is always headless again before very long. He stays put, his calm head resting in his lap, and tirelessly demonstrates the classic Zen admonition to "think non-thinking." Open your mind so wide it includes your thoughts, your wish not to be thinking so much, and the garden all around you, deepening your life as a gardener, while planted just outside the headless Buddha's glasshouse, the 'Hupeh' crabapple trees stand nine feet tall, unthinkable in their beauty and laden with tiny vermilion crabapples shot with gold.

THE LIVING SOIL

The Ground of Beginner's Mind

THE SOIL IS DARK, THE WIND IS RED, AND MY DREAMS ARE SNAKE green with long white roots. At the back of my mouth, way behind memory and longing, is the taste of the ground I garden every day, grit that lingers on my tongue and tells me who I am. Gardens come up out of the ground, surfacing from fissured rock, blank air, and moving water, all teeming with indivisible life. Every garden is stamped with the indelible and evolving signature of its home soil.

The Zen tradition speaks of cultivating an empty field. This is the field of our whole life, full of every possibility and empty only of a permanent, unchangeable identity, of one absolute way to be. It takes true grit to cultivate this empty field that, from the beginning, is vast and complete unto itself. This field includes all beings, animate and inanimate, in the folds of its ground.

Gardening unfolds from this empty field and from engaging with your home soil and getting to know it in every way. Even if your garden is composed of earth trucked in from miles away, as soon as this soil is deposited on your land and you put your hands into it, your work begins. You are cultivating your life as well as your garden.

The word "cultivate" comes from the Latin *colere*, to culture, to worship, to respect, to till, and to take care of, from the still older root *kwel*, which means to revolve around a center. When Shakyamuni Buddha gave his first sermon more than two thousand five hundred years ago, cultivating the ground of his teaching, he was said to be turning the Wheel of the Law. When a gardener picks up a tool and begins to cultivate the ground, the wheel of life continues to turn. And every gardener knows that a wheel turns only if it is "empty": the wheelbarrow moves because the hub of the guiding wheel turns around an axle passing through empty space at the center.

The ground that is cultivated in the garden is common ground, shared by many and host to multitudes. Every particle of soil, every atom of earth, is alive with mystery and potential all stirred up together. Every soil is a long winding story, told in the voices of water and inhaled and exhaled air, of the stone-slow cycle of rock itself becoming soil, and in the voices of the swarming masses of microorganisms feeding, breeding, and dying on fertile dust, creating new life out of their own bodies made from exploded stone.

✤ ✤ ✤

One of my favorite sights in the summer garden is the California quail taking leisurely dust baths in the endlessly cycling soil, on the dry margins of our irrigated fields. They bob and coo and hunker down, making nests of soft dust and cleaning themselves with dirt. Sometimes after a long day of work in the garden I have a mind to put down my digging spade and join the quail for a long, slow dust bath in the bottomless soil of our garden. After all these years of working the land, I am made of the soil and water of my home place. I have become these elements and they have become me. I may pretend that my work is growing red currants, long-stemmed noisette roses, and Greek oregano, but I know better. My real work is getting to know, inside out, my home ground.

Every garden is based on affinity for and knowledge of the ground, on true intimacy and kinship with your home soil that comes not only from cultivating the garden but also from sitting completely still on the earth that you garden, and walking aimlessly and mindfully about on this same ground. These practices are rooted in listening to your soil and in following your garden down to its source. Begin by sitting still and doing absolutely nothing. Make yourself very comfortable on the ground and then, don't move at all. Give your full attention to what is happening around you. Watch the shadows of the black mulberry leaves move like cirrus clouds across the face of your garden. Be ordered by the beat of the ruby-throated humming-bird pulling red nectar out of full-blown salvias. Sink down to earth and sit deep in the saddle of your home garden. Settle yourself on yourself and let the flower of your life force bloom.

In the first years of Green Gulch Farm, whenever a new Zen student came to work in the garden, he or she was sent out alone to spend the day sitting in meditation somewhere in the garden. When you slow down like this, the real garden is uncovered. And so is the real gardener. You unfold together. This takes time and a willingness to sit still past the moment when you get bored, or past the moment when you think of at least thirty worthy garden tasks that you need to accomplish immediately. Instead, give yourself all the time in the world, and don't move, even if by the clock you only have half an hour to be in the garden. This is radical cultivation, for out of this stillness, the real nature of your garden soil is exposed. The digger ants near the spot where you are sitting show you how to cultivate dry land. You learn tilling from the blue earthworms pulling rotted straw down into the subsoil around the quince tree. Pay attention to the jay pecking into the first apples, and to what she shows you about the ripening sequence of your fruit, and about the soil that grows good fruit. But beyond any particular lesson, sitting still on the earth restores you to yourself and to the freshness of the whole garden.

Sitting still is also risky business. In your core, you begin to "un-know" your garden. The unknown garden, the secret garden, waits inside the garden where you sit. Whenever I let myself sit down and get really quiet in the garden, I think of Shakyamuni Buddha finding his place more than two thousand five hundred years ago under a massive ficus tree in northeastern India. Frustrated in all his striving for enlightenment, he sat down and vowed not to move until he understood how to relieve suffering. Shakyamuni was challenged by Mara, the Great Tempter, who tried to unseat him by sending spooks, goblins, and violent storms, and when all that failed to dislodge him, Mara sent seductive beauties to lure the Buddha into moving off the ground at the center of his life. Resolute, the Buddha sat still under the tree of life. Finally, Mara sought to undermine Buddha's confidence and determination by challenging his right to be sitting on the ground. "Look at you," he said. "Who do you think you are, sitting there? Countless beings have attempted this task and failed. By what authority do you take this seat?" In response, Buddha extended his right hand and touched the earth, and the earth confirmed his presence with a great, resounding cry of affirmation. In the oldest of iconographic representations, the spirit of earth is pictured swimming up through channels of dark soil to hold her hand just beneath Buddha's hand as he sat absolutely still and fully awake.

The best gardeners I know continue to find time both to sit still and to walk the margins of their land. This walking is not to arrive anywhere in particular, and certainly not to plan what needs to be done in the garden. It is the walk of a mangy coyote exploring soft edges, the boundary line where garden and wilderness meet. This kind of margin-line walking is a matter of finding your true pace, your breath coordinated with your steps in mindful ease.

The most important thing is to relax and move through your garden in mindfulness, without trying to control your walking or your breathing. Let the earth carry you forward. Some days I walk really slowly, especially when I know there is a lot of work to be done. Breathing in, I take a step; breathing out, another step, moving slowly and steadily, like sugar maple sap rising in early spring sunshine. Other days I move a little faster—maybe three or four steps on the inhalation, four or five as I exhale. Often, when I walk this way, I feel the ground rising up to meet the sole of my foot. I know that this world and the garden are breathing all around me and that they are larger than I know. Walking in mindfulness settles me on this truth. So I open my eyes and really look at the world as I walk.

When I slow down sufficiently to actually *arrive* in the garden, I see that everything around me is constantly changing. Alan Chadwick, inspired by Heraclitus, pointed out that you never step into the same garden twice. And when I really slow down, I see that garden and gardener are changing too, ripening and decaying with every breath.

If I paid attention to what work needed to be done on these garden walks, I would go deaf from the shouting demands of all the plants. Plus, I would never return. I'd be eaten by the unpruned cherry tree and belched out next year as a tiny, dried pit. Walking in mindfulness, however, has no aim except to meet and know the life of the garden, the garden that is changing in every moment.

When Suzuki Roshi came to San Francisco he decided to stay on because he found that American Zen students were able to kindle the fire of beginner's mind in their practice, the mind that notices everything and questions without preconceptions and without fear. This is the mind that looks with confidence into the unknown and takes responsibility and action for what is difficult. Beginner's mind suffuses the mind of the gardener unafraid to come down to earth, to sit absolutely still on the ground, to walk without searching for a path, and, moment by moment, to know the unknowable life of the soil.

True Grit

AGAJA, AN OLD GARDEN FRIEND AND COLLEAGUE, WIELDS A FLASHING purple spade. It was fashioned by the Bulldog Tool Company of England and made to last, with a solid steel shank and a sharp and gleaming digging blade a foot long. Agaja sanded the ash-wood handle of his spade clean and painted it morning glory purple so that he would not lose his prize tool in the high grass of summer. Now, after more than two decades of digging, the blade of Agaja's spade is just seven and a half inches long. In every new bed he digs, this tool leaves a trail of glorious, well-lifted soil in its wake, laced throughout with fine metal filings from Agaja's diminishing spade.

Soil is true grit, so no wonder Agaja's spade is disappearing day by day from the rub of the garden furrow. All soil has a physical body, roughly 45 percent mineral matter, 5 percent organic matter, and 25 percent each of air and water. The cycle of rock crumbling into fertile soil and eventually becoming solid rock again in the depths of the earth's pressure is a long cycle that has its own rhythm, slower than the reptilian blink of a two-hundred-year-old tortoise awakening from a cold winter's sleep. "Why should I move?" asks the stone in Richard Wilbur's poem "Two Voices in a Meadow":

> To move
> befits a light desire.
> The sill of heaven would founder,
> Did such as I aspire

And yet, stone does move. It takes at least half a millennium to create one inch of fertile soil, a work of the ages that had its beginning about four and a half billion years ago when burning magma erupted from the core of the earth, oozing up through the broken crust of the land and thrusting volcanic mountains and blistered ridges of igneous rock up above the surface of the ground. For half a billion years the burning surface of the earth was too hot for life. Then, as the earth began to cool, water vapor condensed in a young atmosphere alive with carbon dioxide, cyanide, and formaldehyde while a slow, continuous rain that lasted for almost twelve thousand years began to fall. In the primordial seas formed during this long rain the first soil was mixed. "Stir the ocean with a broken stick," admonishes the Zen tradition. "Bring forth dragons and fishes!" And so it was millennia ago, only what came forth from the rich mineral deposits washed and stirred into the sea from the land was the gritty ancestor of soil.

In the Archean era three billion years ago the first claylike compounds were washed up on the shores of this land from out of the ocean. Stirred by a broken wand never since found again, the clay compounds began to magnetize and bond nutrients to themselves, eventually hosting the first cyanobacteria, which were, in turn, able to absorb sunlight, manufacture archetypal plant sugars, and excrete oxygen into the new air. Then began the dance of the ages: air giving life to soil, soil giving life to air, and death, decay, and change playing the rhythmic undertone of the old music.

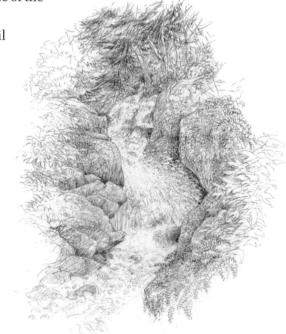

Matter cycles. The cycling of rock into living soil that eventually returns to mineral form is a cycle that always depends on the double dynamism of destruction and synthesis of new matter from old stone, an ancient process governed by the mechanical, chemical, and biological weathering of rock. The mechanical disintegration of rock caused by weathering and erosion affects the size of stone particles, not the fundamental composition of the rock. Weathering by chemical and biological factors, however, works on the fundamental nature of rock, decomposing and resynthesizing stone itself.

In the chemical weathering of rock, soluble minerals are released from exposed stone, a process that began when rain first carved the rocky land in the Archean era. In chemical weathering the softened constituents of stone are leached away by water, leaving a residue washed of its soluble base and ready for transformation. This residue is occupied by new silicates that recrystallize into oxidates of iron and aluminum, those elements responsible for the cloak of ruddy color thrown over the rump of the land.

Biological weathering also transforms rock. The primary biomass of the living world is composed of soil microorganisms. Core samples taken from solid rock three miles below the surface of the earth reveal scores of different microorganisms digesting raw stone. Where we once believed that no life could exist in the burning-hot magma chambers of the earth, modern research reveals that deep-sea vents spewing up fire from the center of the earth are alive with fiery heat-loving bacteria. Microscopic bacteria and vast fungal networks weather soil, and plants create and modify the ground as their roots colonize and split apart bedrock and open a trail in the rock for microorganisms to follow. The body of earth is full of life, and the stability and responsiveness of the earth depend upon the total dynamic working of these many living and dying organisms.

Soil is the resilient hide of the earth that we cling to like hungry fleas on the backside of a long-horned ox, yet soil can also bruise, for strong though it is, it can be as delicate as the blush on the surface of a ripe peach. This skin of the earth, breathing and protecting the greater body of the land, needs our close attention, especially now, as the body of earth faces multiple grave and growing threats from our human presence. The list is long and sobering, and to air and water pollution and depletion, overpopulation, deforestation and massive erosion, chemical and radioactive poisoning, we now add the threatening truth of global climate change.

"To forget how to tend the soil is to forget ourselves," warned Gandhi more than fifty years ago. The empty field outside our door calls us to remember who we are and what we are made of. Every molecule of soil calls to us, from the inside out, to develop true grit, to come down to earth and to get to work.

✦　✦　✦

This process of remembering yourself through knowing your soil begins with getting to know the physical properties of your garden earth. Is your soil buff-gold, flecked with tiny crystal chips of quartz and light-transmitting sand? Or is it dark sepia and heavy, almost oily, and ribboned with wet bands of steel-blue or ochre clay? Every soil has a distinct character and color, fitting into one of four common color groups—black, white, red, and blue-gray—each with a distinct origin and story. Although soils of the same color in different regions of the country may be very different, there are some overall similarities worth noting.

Black soils are colored by carbon-rich humus and usually indicate fertile ground. The soils of peat bogs and muck soils of wetlands are deep black. The soil of Green Gulch Farm is bitter-chocolate brown and heavy, rich with organic matter. But not all black soils are fertile; the soils of the southern Brazilian rain forest are also black with organic matter, but centuries of leaching from the high rainfall have left them acid and very low in soil health.

White soils startle me. I have seen bare white ground in the coastal pine forests of southern Florida where the top six to eight inches of the earth is pure white decomposing sandstone and organic rock. White earth indicates a mineralized soil, one composed of silica and traces of aluminum, in comparison to the black organic soil of bogs or clay deposits. If you garden a white soil you will probably need to enrich your mineral base with plenty of cured organic matter.

Red and yellow clay soils are dominant along the Atlantic Coast from southern Florida north to New Jersey and along the southern border of the United States, southwest to Texas. The red color in these soils indicates a very old ground, rich in iron oxide or hematite. It takes tens of thousands of years for the deep red stain of iron oxide to pervade soil. What I remember most vividly about the funeral of my ninety-two-year-old grandmother, Eva Comer Lathrop, in Birmingham, Alabama, was the heavy red clay soil of her grave. Above the city is a statue of Vulcan, the god of fire, at his forge, working molten iron into strong Birmingham steel. Vulcan stands on red clay earth, my ancestral homeground, pumping his bellows above the heavy iron soil of the South.

Blue-gray soils are clay soils that have been drowned in wetlands and then drained or heaved up into the air. Bacteria in these wet clay subsoils cannot get fresh air to breathe, so they resort to drawing oxygen from the iron oxide crystals in their parent soil. Consequently, red soils turn bluish gray under-water. Iron works in clay just as it does in the blood: in the presence of oxygen, clay soils are red; without air, clay soils have blue blood.

I have a close friend who is an artist and a master storyteller. Every winter solstice Ane Carla joins a lively group of us at Muir Woods National Monument to welcome hundreds of children and their families to the woods at dusk in celebration of the longest night of the year. Following a time-tested recipe from Leonardo da Vinci, Ane Carla prepares rich pastels colored with the different soils and ground-up stone of our home watershed. Surrounded and assisted by hordes of eager kids, my wild artist friend draws rufous-sided salmon, gold-ruffed coyotes, and sepia-toned otters on the well-worn paved paths leading into the winter woods.

Leonardo da Vinci's Pastels

Here is the five hundred-year-old recipe for earth pastels adapted to modern soils and ingredients by my beloved colleague Ane Carla Roveta.

- Take 3 tablespoons of soil or soft rock and hand-grind this material to a fine powder using a good mortar and pestle. Then sieve out the roughage using a fine tea strainer.
- Add 3 tablespoons kaolin clay to the soil mix. This ingredient is crystallized aluminum and silicon and it will make your pastels creamy and smooth. Kaolin clay is readily available from pottery supply stores or any good art store.

- Grate 3 ounces of hard castile soap (from the bar, not the liquid variety) into 12 ounces of water, letting a slurry form. This ingredient helps to bind the pastels.
- Mix the dry ingredients with enough soap slurry to form a pie-dough-like paste. Without overhandling the dough, pull off little sections and roll them into fat, cylindrical pastels. Let the pastels air-dry for 24 hours and then paint the world in earth tones.

This is an excellent project to do with children. (For more information see the resources for chapter 3.)

The soil reveals itself to your ears and fingers as well as to your eyes: listen to your ground, and touch it as you listen to it. Sift your soil between your fingers and hold it near your ear. Sandy soil is gritty and sharp; its angular particles grate at the ear and are abrasive to the touch. Sandy soil, like the mineral-rich ground of Tassajara, is often young and raw with minerals. Bare rock of sandstone, limestone, or granite, which contains quartz and feldspar, fractures to a soil that heats and cools dramatically and will be light to work. Carrots and other deep-rooting vegetables adore the open grit of sandy soil. In contrast, clay soil, like that of Green Gulch Farm, is smooth, worn down, and finely particled, quiet and heavy at the ear, and almost greasy to the touch. Heavy-lobed cauliflower and all other brassicas crave the rich fertility of a clay soil. Clay soil is ancient, fertile, and dense.

Bringing all your senses to bear, sniff and taste your home soil as well. Warm a pinch of it in your fingers and inhale its aroma. Every soil has a faint perfume that will linger in your nostrils. It is said that rice growers in Vietnam can tell precisely which river tributary rice was grown in just by sniffing the fragrant steam from rice cooking on the hearth.

Our son, Jesse, long before he could walk, would bury his face in the newly dug beds of the Green Gulch garden, lapping like a newborn mole at the soft garden soil. When we plucked him off the open earth, he would wail and mourn his separation from the black soil of home. You can tell worlds about your soil just by tasting it. All you have to do is to touch your tongue to your home ground. Acid soil is sharp and sour. It fizzes on your tongue. Clay soil lingers, thick and heavy on the roof of the mouth. The young, wild soils of alkaline rock are sweet and gritty, chalky to the tongue, laced with minerals. To taste garden earth is to also taste the raw life and breath of homeland soil, dark and rich and strong. Gardening with this taste as a guide, real appetite grows for knowing the land and for taking care of it in every way.

❖   ❖   ❖

To fully know the physical body of your soil it is essential to understand the texture and structure of your garden ground. Soil texture simply refers to the relative proportions of various mineral grain sizes in a soil. Gravel and sand are the coarsest and sharpest-edged components; then comes silt, which is finely broken-down sand; and finally the smallest particle of all, clay, reduced to microscopic size and rounded by weathering so it feels like old silk if you rub it between your fingers. Texture is what your soil is made of, and structure is how it behaves.

Your soil's texture determines how well it will absorb and hold water and organic matter. Large-pored sandy soils drain quickly, while fine-grained clay soils are heavy, and nutrient and moisture retentive. Most soils are a mixture of sand, silt, and clay. In fact, the ideal soil texture for a fertile garden is a blend of the three sizes of particles, containing 10 to 20 percent clay and about 40 percent each of sand and silt. Such a soil is classified as a true garden loam.

My favorite test for soil texture is the ribbon test, where you take a handful of moist soil (adding a sprinkle of water if your garden soil is dry), squeeze it into a ball in your fist, and examine it. If the ball falls apart immediately, you have a sandy soil. If the ball stays intact on the palm of your hand, try to squeeze it into a ribbon between your thumb and middle finger. No luck? Then your soil has a sandy texture, with a pinch of clay mixed in. If you can make a ribbon, see how long it can hold together, and measure its length. One to two inches long usually indicates a clay loam with some sand present. If your ribbon is longer than two inches, like the long-ribboned Green Gulch soil, then you have clay, probably with a little silt mixed in.

Soil structure defines the way soils hold together. Good garden soil clumps together in workable aggregates, much influenced by the results of organic decay. Soil is said to be in "good heart" or "good tilth" when the structure of the aggregates is open and porous, with crumbly, pea-size particles on the surface of the soil and larger, blocky clumps in the lower subsoil surface of the ground.

You can test both the texture and the structure of your soil easily by placing a small handful of garden earth in each of two glass jars and filling the jars slowly with tepid water. To test the texture shake one jar vigorously for two minutes or so, and then let the soil settle out over a day or more. Clay can remain in cloudy suspension for over a week, while sand settles out almost immediately. To test the structure, fill the jar but don't shake it. Watch what happens to the soil. Does the aggregate keep its shape? Good structure is stable, with large crumbs that keep their shape even underwater.

It is almost impossible to change the basic texture of your native soil—it will always be sandy, clay, or silty in nature—but there are many ways to guard and enhance soil structure. In order for good structure to develop, it is essential that there be plenty of organic matter present in your soil. Land in good heart holds up to twice as much water as soil with poor structure. This ability of soil to absorb and hold water and at the same time not to seize up and become stiff but rather to remain open with air depends on biological activity in the soil, on that furiously busy community of microscopic living beings that inhabit every healthy soil. In this biological community, decay is just as important as life. Gardeners know that by adding microbially rich organic matter such as aged manure, seasoned mulch, or ripe compost to the surface of the soil in the proper season, soil structure is improved.

Remember, soil is alive—it can burn and bruise, it can lose its breath or drown under too much water. So it is important to work the soil only when it is neither very wet nor very dry. Pick up a little handful of earth and form it into a round ball. If you can flick that ball apart easily with a quick ping of two fingers, then it is a good time to work your land. If soil is waterlogged when you work, you will cause compaction and seizing; if it is too dry, working the soil will turn it to dust.

Five centuries ago Leonardo da Vinci observed that we know more about the movement of celestial bodies than about the soil under our feet. We spend so much time scurrying around looking for meaning, seeking out the soul of the matter in whatever we do, while all the while the body of life is alive in the true grit right beneath our feet.

The Flow of Fertile Soil

SOIL CHEMISTRY IS A LIVELY SCIENCE, ALL ABOUT MOLECULAR attraction and the transformation of matter, and about its composition, structure, and properties. The root for the word "chemistry" comes from the Greek *kheo*, meaning to flow or to pour, referring to the ever-changing quality of chemical reactions, but when I think about soil chemistry I remember Alan Chadwick rearing up from his sickbed at the end of his life and defiantly stopping all flow. Someone had innocently questioned him about the different functions of nitrogen, phosphorous, and potassium in the life of the soil. "N, P, K are death itself!" the master thundered, collapsing back into his pillows and glowering menacingly at his deflated questioner.

Every garden grows best when the gardener encounters the pulsing, incorporated body of the soil in its entirety, Alan taught. This was where my teacher flowed with the ground itself, insisting that the body of earth is unique and different with every footstep, every passing hour. It cannot be captured by analysis, and so to dissect this vibrant body in order to measure its discrete chemical composition is blasphemy under heaven. Instead, Alan swore, an obedient gardener learns about garden soil by working the land and by following the instructions of the earth itself. But now my teacher is long since "death itself," and I disobediently follow the flow of nitrogen, phosphorus, and potassium in the life of our garden soil, along with other nutrient elements, the acid-alkaline balance, and the positive and negative ion-exchange capacity.

I used to shy away from investigating soil chemistry, which I confused with the world of synthetic fertilizers, pesticides, and herbicides. Synthetic or chemical agriculture signaled for me increased soil erosion, soil and water pollution, loss of biological diversity as well as loss of arable farmland, and increased loss of tilth through soil compaction. But the flow of fertility in every garden depends on a simple appreciation of the interplay of soil and plant chemistry, no matter what approach to growing you take. We have a neighbor, a third-generation Italian farmer, who asked me if growing organically was hard. "I don't know, Amadeo," I answered. "I've never gardened any other way." Then it was my turn: "What about farming with chemicals—is it hard?" And of course Amadeo gave me the same answer I'd given him.

❖   ❖   ❖

We need to know the terrain of basic soil chemistry to be more alert organic gardeners. Soil chemistry is about attraction, magnetism, and affinity in the living earth of the garden, a force that every attentive gardener feels as we walk the ground. Most chemical reactions in plants and the soil around them take place between particles that carry a positive or negative charge when they are dissolved in water. Negatively charged particles like nitrogen, carbon, phosphorus, and sulfur are called anions, while positively charged particles such as potassium, magnesium, and calcium are called cations.

In order to take up and absorb nutrients, the plant must remain electrically neutral. This means that the net positive and negative charges in the soil community must be balanced in order for plants to grow and thrive.

Soil anions, which form acids when they are in solution, are held in the living, organic part of garden soil and are released to plants through air and water as organic matter decays. Anions are the mutable building blocks of protein and carbohydrates that plants depend on for their vitality. A soil rich in these anion nutrients is a fertile soil.

Cation nutrients are more durably stable than soil anions, and slower in their work. Cations are the mineral, metallic element in garden soil and the primary components of soil enzymes so important for plant nutrition and growth. Attracted chemically to the negatively charged surface of clay particles and stored thereon, these positive soil cations dissolve into a basic or alkaline solution in water.

Most plant nutrients are bound tightly to particles of soil until the plants require the nutrients for growth. When the plant needs nutrients and the roots are in well-aerated and moist soil, then the plant roots slough off hydrogen ions in exchange for cation and anion nutrients, and the flow of fertility gains momentum and force.

The cation exchange capacity, or CEC, of soil measures the amount of positive cation nutrients a soil can hold on the negatively charged surface of its clay and humus particles. You can think of the CEC of garden soil as a kind of treasure store, a savings account of plant nutrients. As garden plants draw down the nutrient reserves in their home ground, these nutrients are replenished by healthy soil reserves as well as by organic fertilizers offered to plants from their doting gardeners.

Soils high in decomposed organic matter have the highest exchange capacity or CEC. This makes good common sense because the exchange capacity of every soil is based on the ability of that soil to hold and increase nutrients. Humus and decomposed organic matter cling to cation nutrients with every mighty particle of their negatively charged being. In contrast, anion nutrients are supplied to the garden through powdered rock dusts rich in phosphorus, through carbon and nitrogen-rich drifts of compost and in aged animal manure, and through other organically derived minerals applied to the soil.

✦   ✦   ✦

Carbon, oxygen, and hydrogen make up 98 percent of most plants, and these elements are derived directly from the atmosphere or from water, with carbon coming mainly from the carbon dioxide of the air. In addition to these three major elements, plants also need fourteen additional elements from living soil solids. Three of these elements are major nutrients, needed in large amounts: the famous (or infamous) NPK trio of nitrogen, phosphorus, and potassium. Calcium, magnesium, and sulfur are also needed in good amounts, and eight other elements are needed in much smaller amounts as trace minerals: chlorine, iron, manganese, boron, copper, zinc, molybdenum, and cobalt. A gardener does well to wonder at her or his place in this huge flow of soil nutrients, to question carefully how and when to intervene and change the life of the earth's thin skin.

The answer has to come out of the complete, integrated life of the soil itself and out of interpreting the flow of fertility in the soil underneath our feet. This is a subtle and challenging balancing act. When the Buddha began to teach twenty-five hundred years ago, he offered a Middle Way between the two extremes of greedy indulgence and nihilistic dismissal, and gardening is also a Middle Way path. This path is expressed chemically by a balanced soil pH, or potential hydrogen, which measures the concentration of hydrogen ions in a soil or other mixture of matter.

In every soil, plant nutrients cling to particles of humus and clay and each nutrient holds on with a different strength. Hydrogen holds on with the greatest force of all. If your soil is very acidic this means that all of the available clay and humus particles are covered with hydrogen ions, offering no room for other nutrients, while if your soil is too alkaline the available soil stations are all occupied with potassium, magnesium, calcium, or sodium.

In the soil the pH scale measures the acidity or alkalinity of your ground on a scale that runs from 0 to 14, with 0–7 indicating an acidic or sour soil and 7–14 indicating an alkaline or basic one. The most balanced pH in garden soil falls in the neutral zone, 6–7.5, where most cultivated crops love to grow. The pH of your soil is influenced by the bedrock mineral composition of your ground, by its vegetative history, and by the weather and climate of your bioregion. Wet soils tend to be more acidic, while arid soils are usually alkaline. In the span of a year garden soils fluctuate within a range of pHs depending on rainfall and drought and on the presence of organic matter in the soil. A humus-rich soil that has many stations on its surfaces for plant and microbe nutrients tends to hold that soil to a more neutral or balanced pH.

I take a soil sample and send it out to a local lab for analysis every two years or so. I always take the sample in the spring, before fertilizing the garden, and after the land has dried out from the long winter rains. I pay careful attention to what the lab report says about the pH reading of our ground, to the presence of macro- and micronutrients, to the measure of organic matter and the CEC index of our soil, and to the reading of overall salinity of the ground, since I garden next to the Pacific Ocean.

A full soil sample analysis gives a composite picture of your garden since you are mixing soils from a variety of garden sites. If I want to get a reading of just one specific area then I can carry some litmus paper and a bottle of distilled water to the site, mix the earth with the water, and check to see if it is running acid or sweet. Usually I have a pretty good idea before I even test just by observing the local plant cover—sorrel and bright green sour grass and yellow dock show me that the soil is running acid and is probably wet and boggy, while common garden weeds like chickweed and speedwell indicate an alkaline run of drier, sweet earth.

Thousands of chemical reactions occur simultaneously in each fraction of a second in one grain of lively earth. These changes occur in the body and mind of every alert gardener as well. So when a gardener of the Middle Way picks up a speck of dust or reads a laboratory analysis of his or her garden soil, it is clear that this report, this single dust mote, is just a snapshot of one moment in time and that this moment in time arises out of the whole history and rhythm of the garden.

In the Green Gulch garden office we keep a loose-leaf notebook where we file all our lab tests so we can see how the chemical life of our soil has developed over the years of garden culture. I treasure one test in particular because it always brings Harry Roberts back to life for me. In the center of the nitrogen analysis is a large cigarette burn, for when Harry saw how much the nitrogen level of the soil had increased from the previous season, he dropped his cigarette right onto the lab report in gape-mouthed delight.

The Web of Life

ONE CHILLY WINTER DAY THREE ROGUISH SEVENTH-GRADE BOYS and I wrestled a two-year-old anise-flavored French pear tree out of its temporary nursery bed in their public school garden project so that we could transplant the pear to the main school garden. The tree was anchored by a sinewy taproot, and we labored for almost an hour, seesawing the tree loose with our digging forks. As we eased it out of its hold, the soft soil at the bottom began to pucker and writhe and a huge, crumpled Jerusalem cricket was belched up and out of the spread-open seams of the cold ground.

The once-cool boys screamed in terror as the eyeless insect in its shellacked convict's suit of brown and black stripes scuttled across their designer sneakers and disappeared into the dark heart of the January garden. I was delighted, for although fearsome at first, the Jerusalem cricket is a good-luck omen in all gardens as well as a valuable predator of nasty pests. Variously called *Niña de la Tierra* and Old Bald Man, this insect was a vivid reminder of the vast hidden life of the underground soil community, for along with visible creatures like the Jerusalem cricket, garden soil is host to billions of microscopic life-forms digesting, defecating, decomposing, and dying underfoot. A close horticulturist friend pointed out to me that in the two-hundred-yard plot of our kitchen vegetable garden there are some twenty billion bacteria at work along with two hundred and fifty billion fungi, two hundred million single-celled protozoa at least, probably three million nematodes, thousands of minuscule mites, a sound two thousand earthworms, along with perhaps a good-luck clutch of Jerusalem crickets.

The biomass of the invisible soil community underfoot is equal in measure to the biomass of the mostly far larger creatures in the aboveground world, a truth that can be best imagined when you consider that there are more microorganisms in one cup of fertile soil from your garden than there are human beings on the entire planet. So many of these beings live and work close to the surface of the ground that it is said that the real wealth of all cultures depends on the top three inches of soil that cloak the earth. You can think of this teeming interconnected web of life beneath the ground as the *soil itself* rather than as the *inhabitants* of the soil. This extraordinary diversity of organisms creates a soil food web that plays a vital role in the circle dance of fertility, with each partner in the dance essential to and intertwined with every other. As the complexity and fertility of the underground web of life increases, so does the health of the plant world aboveground. Organisms of the underground dance take three main, and of course overlapping, roles—as energy producers, consumers, and decomposers.

As producers, soil microorganisms, like the nitrogen-fixing bacteria working in the root zone of a fertile row of black-eyed peas, create proteins and carbohydrates from simple nutrient elements. Green plants themselves are primary soil producers, capturing energy from sunlight by photosynthesis and feeding their roots.

All animal life and certain non-photosynthesizing microflora live by consuming what the producers create with their efforts. From simple protozoa to human beings, these consumers depend on the food produced by green plants for their nourishment and existence. The primary consumers eat plants directly, while secondary and tertiary consumers feed on other consumers, and of course green plants consume as well as produce.

The decomposers remind me of a line from a song by Bob Dylan: "What isn't busy being born is busy dying." The decomposers, primarily bacteria that inhabit grassland soils and fungi that pervade forest ecosystems, perform the

Soil Is Alive!

Our friend and farm advisor Amigo Bob Cantisano showed me a simple test to monitor the presence of microbes in our soil. This is a great test for those who do not fully believe that soil is alive.

First, Amigo selected a spoonful each of neglected and unworked earth, good garden soil, and well-decayed organic compost. Then he poured a capful of hydrogen peroxide—the same stuff we use to clean out and disinfect simple cuts and scratches—over each spoonful of soil. The poor soil fizzed meekly and grew quiet, the well-dressed garden soil bubbled up in a storm of bacteria, while the spoonful of fertile compost is still testifying in froth, foam, and furious fizz to the invisible host of microbes of which it is made.

Except for the fact that the microbes present in your garden soil sample get zapped by this hydrogen peroxide dunk, this is a wonderful way to believe what you cannot always see. And kids love this experiment and never forget its lesson.

critical function of dismantling dead organisms and capturing nitrogen in their bodies as they work. About two-thirds of total soil metabolism depends on microbial decomposers living for the most part in the liminal stratum at the soil's surface, who break open the structure of decaying organisms and rebuild soil life through their digestive processes.

In each grain of fertile soil, bacteria occur by the millions. In the natural world, grassland soils are predominantly cultured by legions of bacteria. Some bacteria are aerobic, requiring air in order to live, while others function anaerobically, without air. Together, the bacteria are responsible for three essential processes of nutrient cycling and transformation: nitrification, nitrogen fixation, and the oxidation of sulfur. Without the underground bacterial web, nitrogen and sulfur, as well as other plant nutrients, would return to the atmosphere as gas and be unavailable to plants.

Fungi are also essential to the web of underground life. In the natural world, forest soils are the richest in fungal networks since there is such a predominance of decayed organic matter in these soils. Molds, yeasts, and mushrooms are both consumers of energy and active decomposers. Vegetative fungi are distinguished by filaments, called mycelia, that spread through the soil and are critical to the decomposition of organic residues, helping to keep the decomposition process going long after bacteria cease to function. Although fungi cannot fix nitrogen or oxidize ammonia as bacteria can, they are able to transform and hold in their threadlike mycelial net a large amount of carbon and nitrogen. More than half of the substances decomposed by molds become fungal tissue, which is essential to the formation of soil humus.

Fungi form a living bridge spanning the soil world and the world of the green plant. Most plants have a symbiotic relationship with certain soil fungi called mycorrhizae or fungus-root organisms. In this relationship the fungi invade the roots of living plants, making possible the uptake of nutrients, particularly phosphorus. In exchange, these fungi absorb carbohydrates from plant roots.

Current research confirms that not only do different genera of plants have their own distinct fungal populations but even distinct species within each genus have their own particular fungus-root relationships. Without this "living bridge" provided by mycorrhizae, many plants fail to thrive. I have seen this repeatedly in my years of raising redwood trees from seed. After two or three years of growth the young redwood seedlings only continue to grow if I stir into their soil mix shovelsful of fungus-rich litter from our nearby old-growth redwood forest where the ripened redwood seed was gathered. Without the nourishment of this fungus-rich forest litter our seedling redwoods inevitably starve.

I include the roots of plants themselves in the underground soil community, for roots are active soil organisms. One November I was dividing perennials in the dormant winter garden, digging up a mass of Michaelmas asters. The tops of these asters were dead and decaying, so I cut the old bloom stalks down to the ground. But when I then lifted the heavy mass of roots out of the earth, I was startled by their brilliant crimson color. That mass of bloodred roots pulsing with life was a reminder that we are always handling raw life and death simultaneously.

No matter how careful I am when I lift and divide perennials, a portion of the roots always remains in the soil. These roots decay and add organic matter to the ground. At the same time, living roots condition the soil as they push down into its depths. Tiny channels in the earth are expanded by the network of root hairs that increase as the roots swell and grow in the ground. These roots draw up precious soil moisture and carry it into the green stems of plants. Roots also provide a mass of living organic material that helps stabilize soil aggregation.

Death is a home for life, and the sloughed-off remains of dead and decaying root tissue provide a feast for the green world. But the roots of higher plants do more than draw up water and offer dead tissue for the nutrition of soil microbes. In their lifetime plant roots influence the equilibrium of soil life. Roots contribute to the availability of nutrients in the soil. As roots withdraw proteins and amino acids directly from the soil to feed the growing plant, other amino acids, carbohydrates, sugars, and proteins particular to each species are formed and excreted at the tips of the root ends. Consequently, the numbers of soil organisms in the root zone, or rhizosphere, may be as much as one hundred times greater than elsewhere in the soil.

For the underground web of life to thrive it depends on what I call a 3-D world: a *deep diversity* of organisms and growing conditions; *death and decay* throughout, since nutrients are only released and recycled when bacteria and fungi themselves expire and fuel the underworld web; and last of all, the *dynamic balance* between life and death that is present in every fertile soil and stabilizes the heart and mind of every frontline gardener.

It is essential in the cycling of nutrients in the soil that it be a balanced process. If too great a volume of nutrients is released, the nutrients leach out of the soil, because they cannot be processed thoroughly enough, while too scarce a supply of these nutrients causes plants and soil microbes to die. When in balance, this cycling of nutrients in the soil food web is responsible for soil, water, air, and plant health.

Gardeners work this 3-D world not outside of the web of life, or merely in support of it, but from the inside out. We are made of each other—soil and gardener interact in a vast web that is both alive and dying in the same moment, marked with emptiness and full of surprise. Knowing this, we pick up our spades and get to work.

Groundwork

I AM A MAD GARDENER. I MUTTER AND RANT, AND AT NIGHT I SHAKE dry seeds out of my unruly mane of hair. The garden is in my bones, in my gut, and in my hands that pearl sweat at the first hint from the overturned soil of March that it is time to sow Cherokee beans again in the open ground. And although I am a civil person, I am at my best when left completely alone at nightfall to spread that last wheelbarrow of aged horse manure around the base of the budded-out black currant plants from England.

When I was a new gardener I first read *The Joy of Man's Desiring* by Jean Giono. The book begins with a farmer unable to sleep in the bright moonlight of a late spring night. Finally he yields to the pull of the moon and goes out to an unworked field in the dead of the night and begins to plow the ground with his team of horses. This moonlight farmer is my kin.

All groundwork begins with an awareness of the breath of the land and of the density of soil and moisture within the earth that you are gardening. What matters most in your relationship to the soil is your steady attention to the dynamic balance of its elements—mineral matter, air, water, and organic matter—and their connections to all the members of the garden community.

"When you cultivate the earth you are opening the ground to starlight," Alan Chadwick loved to remind us, "and inducing a capacity for breath in the land." This statement came out of the joy of man's desiring to culture a spot of land, and from Alan's study of the ancient Greeks, who noticed how alive soil was at the base of a landslide or avalanche. There, where the soil had been aerated by the slip of the land, huge plants towered over their scruffy neighbors growing nearby on undisturbed, hard ground.

Every growing season that we worked with Alan, before beginning our groundwork we walked the land surrounding the garden, sometimes by day and occasionally by night, opening to starlight and the breath of new awareness rising up from the ground underfoot. This was a good practice and one that makes sense no matter what method of soil cultivation you choose. Each garden and every gardener are intertwined, changing from day to day and from hour to hour along with the garden's microbial populations, chemical balance, thirst, and organic content and the gardener's efforts and expectations.

My own longing to go down into the ground comes from both my heart of hearts and my training. My hands itch to bury a well-oiled spade in the soft folds of the earth. Over the decades that I have been gardening I have dug beds in many different ways, most often in versions of the deep-digging methods I first learned in 1975 when I began to garden at the Gulch. I have also worked soil behind a huge, chestnut-brown draft horse, Joe, and I have even fired up a vintage Troy-Bilt rototiller and had it drag me down surging, one-hundred-fifty-foot-long rows of snowball cauliflower and pale blue borage interlaced with drifts of crimson flax in spring. I have also tried and been impressed by the techniques of the no-digging schools of gardening. I am sobered by their predictions of the damage caused by overzealous digging—oxidation of organic matter and damaged soil structure—but my daily, bread-and-water technique of cultivating the ground is deep digging with a spade in my hand.

When my daughter was in kindergarten I helped to set up a small organic vegetable garden at her public elementary school. We were given a rotten little spit of land between two school buildings, darkened by seasonal shade. Mischievous children were in the habit of throwing their old juice containers and empty sandwich bags into this abandoned alleyway of shadowy, scraped earth. But it was a great place for a garden, because it was what we had finally been given after torturously long PTA meetings, and because we could only improve from here, since this was some of the worst soil in the county.

I set to work immediately with a handful of ardent parents and their hefty kindergarten kids, but our enthusiasm cooled off fast as we tried to pry open the ironclad soil. We were working subsoil. *Sub* subsoil. I love a challenge and all soil is beautiful soil to me, so I kept on digging with Javier, a daddy cut from the same cloth as me. The less fanatic parents migrated to the one sunny corner of the rock-hard plot and held a whispered conference. After a short while they approached us with their proposal: let's build a box two feet deep, five feet wide, and fifty feet long and fill it with new and improved "good soil" and forget this backbreaking work. We want the kids to experience success, they insisted. We don't want them to be discouraged. And besides, this ground is harder than sin.

This was definitely foreign logic for me since my way to experience success is to work local soil and observe its almost miraculous transformation from punk subsoil into fertile loam. So I was given the chief booby prize plot, the outer margins of the garden where the soil was the worst and the most compacted. The modern, reasonable parents built their planting box in the center of the garden, and eventually back-filled it with black commercial fluff from the local garden center. "Soul-free soil," I haughtily called this stuff under my breath. Way outside their box, I threw myself into digging and cultivating the seized ground, forking in ample air and organic matter.

This original school garden has been growing strong now for a decade. The outer beds of local soil that I pickaxed open with Javier and the stoutest kids are home to a wild jumble of plants offering sweet nectar to butterflies and succulent leaves to feed their prolific larvae. At last sighting the vigorous escallonias and pale blue buddleias were climbing six feet up the shady school wall with a colorful tide of orange and gold milkweeds lapping vigorously at their knees.

I confess that the central fluff box has also done surprisingly well. The first season it produced a stunning, eight-foot-high thicket of sweet corn and scarlet runner beans that were ready to harvest for the annual back-to-school picnic. However, I am somewhat vindicated in my dire prophecies concerning commercial soil-filled planting boxes since this material functions pretty well for one or two seasons but must be dug out and replaced biennially in order to keep the wonder crops pumping.

Working with Commercial Soil Mixes

If you decide to use a commercial soil mix, you can make it work for you if you choose and tend it with care. Make sure that your mix is free of contaminants and chemical additives, especially if you are working with children. Many commercial mixes are also sterile and weed free. I am not an advocate of such sterile mixes since the presence of insects and weeds tells me that my soil mix is alive, hospitable, working. Like living garden soil, the best commercial mixes should be one-half mineral and one-quarter water, one-quarter air.

Avoid fluffy mixes since when they are dampened they shrink, sink, and compact, and check the particle size of whatever commercial mix you plan to use: chunks over ¼ inch are too big to be useful, while powder is too fine. "Soil free" mixes tend to be made of sphagnum peat moss, bark, reed sedge peat, and dry vermiculite, none of which contains nutrients. Add organic fertilizer to your mix, along with some true soil to help your ground retain nutrients. The soil will buffer the mix and hold on to the fertilizers you add.

Before you leap in and begin to dig your garden there are some fundamental considerations to remember, first and foremost of which is: don't hurry. Even if you are only going to be living in your home for one growing season, give yourself enough time to learn about your site before you start to dig and plant. This was already canonical advice in the first century BCE. As Virgil counsels in the *Georgics*: "Before you work an unfamiliar patch it is well to be informed about the winds, the variations in the sky, the native traits and habits of the place, what each locale permits and what denies." Cultivating an awareness of your place itself is the beginning of cultivating your soil.

Once you know the physical, chemical, and biological properties of the bedrock soil out of which your garden will grow, you will have a good sense of how to work your ground. One of the best ways to get this kind of information is by reading the plant cover that is growing wild on your soil. This "reading" means cultivating a lively familiarity with the local weeds and the native plants that are growing in your backyard. Many of these plants are primary soil cultivators because of their deep root systems or because of the root exudates that they release. Not just nuisances to be summarily yanked out, your weedy companions indicate particular soil problems and often act as remedies for those very difficulties, like the yellow dock that indicates a sour, acidic soil and also opens stiff, sour soil with its muscular taproot.

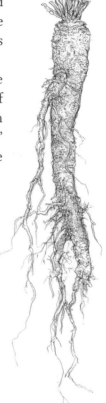

Before you begin to dig, find out as much as possible about your local weather patterns and the climate of your region, which affect how and when to cultivate your ground. Pay particular attention to the first and last frost dates, to wind velocity and direction, sun and shadow patterns throughout the seasons, to rainfall and snowfall, and to usual high and low temperatures.

Have a vision for your garden, but don't forget to include yourself in this vision. Factor in your available time and energy, and the possibility of developing a case of garden addiction or garden allergy, which can overpower your sense of balance. When you plot how to cultivate your garden it is prudent to know what your body can take. How's your back? How do you feel about machines? And what kind of soil culture do parsnips need, compared with lush beds of Peruvian lilies? Plan to cultivate only what you can manage and start smaller than you think you should. I have seen more gardens fail from overambitious ideas than from any other cause—blight, gophers, and natural disaster included. Start small and pay careful attention to feeding and culturing the soil you are digging so that your garden will be fertile for the long haul. You can always designate areas you plan to dig next season and pre-cultivate this land as we have done at Green Gulch by planting a good cover crop of legumes, grasses, and deep-rooted beneficial weeds and sweet clover that will begin your groundwork for you.

❖   ❖   ❖

Once you have made your plans, enter your ground. Whether you dig down or mound up, you open the soil to air and starlight. The result is loose, well-aerated soil that rises above the surrounding ground and allows air, moisture, nutrients, warmth, and deep roots to penetrate into the fertile ground. In this friable ground uninterrupted plant growth and nutrient flow abides.

In compacted soil plant roots cannot thrive. Not only does a transplanted plant suffer from the transition from the loose and friable soil of the seed flat or plant nursery, it suffers doubly if it is transferred into a tight soil in the garden. If the tender feeder roots of a transplanted seedling encounter tight or seized soil, the plant's overall growth is checked. It stops producing and developing protein, which is essential to healthy growth, and begins to produce carbohydrates instead, which makes the struggling plant attractive to insect populations and to disease.

Well-aerated soil or a loose planting medium reverses this process and allows a newly sown or transplanted seedling to grow uninterrupted, developing a healthy and balanced root and shoot system. The soil of a well-aerated garden bed will normally rise about ten to fifteen inches above the base level of your garden. This soil loft is simply the result of the incorporation of air to the cultivated earth of your garden.

All my gardening life I have primarily been a practitioner of double- and single-digging. I learned these practices from Alan Chadwick, from my gardening colleagues, and from working the soil of the Green Gulch garden for twenty-five years. The double-digging method evolved out of two forms of horticulture practiced in Europe during the 1800s and early 1900s: French intensive agriculture, practiced outside of Paris where land was scarce and plants were grown in deep beds fertilized with horse manure and spaced very closely, creating their own climate and living soil mulch; and biodynamic techniques developed by Austrian philosopher and educator Rudolf Steiner. Alan Chadwick used a combination of these two methods, in what was called the biodynamic, French Intensive method, a name that has now blessedly been shortened to the biointensive method.

Double-digging has traditionally been the primary soil cultivation method of biointensive agriculture. It involves a deep hand-tool cultivation of the ground that happens in three clear steps: digging soil out of your garden bed to the depth of one shovel blade or one foot's depth; using a garden fork to loosen the subsoil another foot's depth at the bottom of the dug-out trench; and replacing the top layer of soil. Single-digging is a simple process of digging soil to the depth of one shovel blade. I have largely shifted to single-digging because life is short and there are so many beds to dig, so much food to raise, so many plants and people to love.

Once your bed is dug you can tilth or break up the soil on the surface of the bed so that it has a fine, granular texture. First of all, spread a layer of organic rock powder and dry fertilizer on the soil. I use rock phosphate, kelp meal, and granite dust when we initially prepare our garden beds (see next chapter for full description of soil amendments). Next, spread one to two inches of well-decayed manure or compost on top of the powdered amendments. After this is done mix these ingredients into the bed by walking along the path with a tilling fork or smaller digging fork, inserting the tool into the bed at a sideways angle and lightly lifting the surface soil (about the first four to six inches of soil) into the air and

115

letting it fall back to place. This action incorporates the organic amendments into the bed and helps to condition the surface of the soil. It also incorporates additional air into the surface of the soil. If big clods rise to the surface as you tilth just invert your fork and give the clods a sharp smack with the back bar of the fork. I call this step "spanking the bed," and it is always a source of real pleasure for me.

When your bed is dressed and tilthed, give it some water. If your digging has been vigorous and deep, your bed will be puffed up with air. The shaping, amending, and watering help the soil exhale a bit and settle down. It is always a good idea to let your bed settle for one to two days before planting. You can also rake the surface of your bed now to smooth it out or use a heavy bar rake to break up any remaining clods. This also helps with settling the soil.

Another way to raise beds is to lower the paths between them. You can dig down about six inches to create a path and toss the soil up on the (cleared and opened) ground next to it. Alternatively, you can build up a raised bed with soil you bring in from another spot or with commercial "soil" as the school parents did.

Mounding up beds makes for lofty beds and clear, incised earthen paths, but if your area is prone to heavy rains and your soil fails to drain quickly, your garden may turn into a floating agricultural version of old Venice, without the gondolas, so do not excavate your paths too deeply. Remember that a mounded-up bed is formed not by digging into the ground of the bed but by

Mounded-Up Garden Beds

This is a fast and effective way to prepare a raised-bed garden.

- Mark out the beds of your garden and make the pathways wide so you have plenty of soil to spread onto the beds. Next, I like to open the ground of the proposed beds with a fork. This foot-deep loosening lets air into the ground and provides for better long-term drainage.
- Excavate the path soil between your new beds, digging no deeper than eight to twelve inches

and distributing this path soil directly onto the beds.

- Dress these new beds with compost or aged manure and rock minerals and other organic fertilizers lightly forked into the surface of the soil. It is also a good idea to spread dry straw or well-decayed leaves in the lowered pathways of your garden once your new beds are prepared.
- As in all groundwork, water your beds after they are shaped and let them settle for a day or so before planting.

lowering the paths of the garden *around* the bed and mounding up the path soil onto the beds.

Mounded beds are a simple, fast, and very effective way to create a garden. They are easier on the body than double- or single-digging, and their height makes them easy to tend. On the other hand, the soil may not be as consistently worked as in deep-dig beds and it will tend to dry out faster. Deeper cultivation (by single- or double-digging) will keep your beds productive over a longer period of time.

❖   ❖   ❖

I see the garden spade as the tool that cuts through and takes life and the fork as the wide-tined giver of life as it enters the earth and cultivates the soil. Together these tools make deep groundwork possible.

I am a digger so I teach digging as the prime way to cultivate garden soil. There are many approaches to groundwork, including working with machines or not opening the ground at all. The condition of your soil will guide you. When we began the present Green Gulch garden in 1983 we invited our small farm tractor onto the site to pull a deep cultivating bar called "the ripper" through the tight clay soil. This bar opened up the hardpan and following this initial mechanical procedure we worked the ground by hand.

Many gardeners elect to use a small cultivating tractor or rototiller on their land for the first cultivation and then proceed to cultivate by hand thereafter. If you choose this option, bear in mind that repeated rototilling can create a hardpan or "tiller pan," since the tines of the tiller consistently beat at the same depth and soil water often settles there. Rototilling is also dangerous to larger soil dwellers, especially to earthworms and other beneficial soil fauna. In

117

addition, rototilling can chop up and spread the roots of any noxious weeds present in your land.

If after all these cautionary words about rototilling, you still elect to rototill, follow these two general rules. First, make sure your ground is moist, neither too dry nor too wet, before you till. Second, use the rototiller infrequently and follow by adding ample organic matter to your garden.

You don't have to be a digger in order to garden well. A woman I know who gardened on the windy bluffs of Whidby Island in the Puget Sound region of Washington State prepared new beds by first laying thick sections of newspaper over the sea of living meadow grass behind her house. Then she covered the newspaper with mounds of old harvested grass and moldy hay that continued to decay aboveground. After about a month she dug down through this mulch and tucked healthy seedlings through the newspaper weed barrier into fertile ground below. The native grass underneath the newspaper had decayed by then and all she had to do was add a trowel-full of rich compost to each hole where she transplanted her seedlings.

This is a simple permaculture method, based on designing sustainable human habitats by following the patterns of the natural world. When it comes to gardening, the permacultured bed system is a no-dig, no-disturbance system that works very well on weedy grassland or other rough land. Although the permaculture bed involves minimal disturbance of the soil and is fast to create, my experience is that it does take a little longer for the soil to be ready to receive transplants.

Every gardener has distinct lineages that are anchored in our temperaments and in the home ground we are given to garden. While my Puget Sound friend cultivates her garden by raising mulched beds above undisturbed ground, I dig down into the heavy bottomland soil at Muir Beach, incorporating air and organic matter into the earth as I work.

Groundwork is always influenced by how and what you plan to plant. Most of our garden is transplanted from the greenhouse or cold frames out into the garden, so our bed preparation can be a little rougher than the more refined seed bed, which needs to be raked and shaped until it is quite even in order to receive the fine seed of vegetable and flower crops like baby carrots or salpiglossis, a flowering member of the nightshade tribe. But whether you are transplanting or seeding, the deep-bed digging cultivation is the same; only the surface of your bed is prepared differently according to how you plan to plant your crops.

I recommend that you experiment with cultivation. You will soon know whether you are a "digger-down" gardener, a "mounder-up" cultivator, or a patient permaculturist. Once you know how you are inclined, experiment. Try a sheet-compost bed if you never have before. Or if you are a fanatic no-dig gardener sneak out one moonlit night and locate a corner of one of your permaculture beds and dig it up with a fork and spade and see what happens in the light of day. The primary work of every gardener is to stay alert and playful within the heft and heart of your soil. In this way garden and gardener culture each other, well inoculated with surprise.

As you work, follow your affection and take your time. Let the garden itself and your love of the garden direct your groundwork. Remember that the terms of a lasting agriculture are never only human terms but nature's terms as well. Love these terms unconditionally, without trying to bargain with them, explain them, or make them behave. Trust the garden and your love of the garden and just continue, under all circumstances.

CHAPTER 4

LIFE INTO DEATH INTO LIFE

Nature's Round

FROM THE BEGINNING, THE FERTILITY OF THE GARDEN DEPENDS on the fertility of the gardener's imagination, on that wild mind that sees death as a gateway into life, a mind that turns with the same delight toward the toothless jaws of decay as toward the untwining, green shoot. Watching the things of the world come apart and recombine is core Zen work and the fundamental anchorage of every gardener's life.

Garden fertility comes out of the discarded waste of our lives. "Life into death into life," Alan Chadwick called it, when we collected long drifts of dry leaves, old piles of pulled cheeseweed and sow thistle, and barrels of kitchen waste to stack on the edge of the garden. For most of my life I have been mounding up raw "death" into huge humps of compost layered with oat straw and ripe horse manure or aged cow dung to feed soils and plants and offer the garden a well-balanced diet of nutrients released over an extended time.

In the Zen tradition true mind or the pure essence of each student is revealed in the simplest acts: contemplating a camellia bud about to push into flower, walking through the mountain forest in early autumn, encountering the teacher face-to-face in fiery dialogue. All these moments show and confirm Way-seeking mind. But for me, the true mind of my Zen colleagues shows clearest in how they respond to raw garbage slopped out onto the Green Gulch compost pile.

I watch the compost crew with a trained eye, aware that most of them avert their gaze from the putrid flow of old coffee grounds and dumped steel-cut oatmeal floating in a slurry of three-day-old burned lentil soup, and take little shallow gulps of air as they work. I can tell that these gardeners are counting their breaths until compost detail is over. Some few, however, turn toward the river of rot all around them with gusto. These are my tribe, a select band of slightly feral Zen students whose tool kit includes the short-handled Scottish manure fork as well as the plump zafu sitting meditation cushion.

Garden fertility is based on nature's round, on the wheel of life that turns to death and back to life again, and especially on the balance of the two primary processes of this wheel of life: growth and decay. Balance is the key point and this balance depends on the even growth and decay of the green plant and on the fertility of the ground that sustains this plant.

In the presence of sunshine plants capture floods of light in the green chlorophyll nets spread out within their leaves. Oxygen is expelled into the atmosphere in this process of photosynthesis, carbon dioxide is both breathed out and taken into the leaves, and water is drawn up from the soil. Sunlight is transformed in the growing body of the plant to sugars, carbohydrates, and simple proteins, all stored in the tissues of the green world. Eventually, plants die and are consumed by microscopic organisms and larger animals. This

122

process happens slowly in the natural world and is accelerated in the compost pile. Whatever the velocity, the soil is always hungry for life and for the coming apart of life; all of life depends on nature's ancient round of growth and decay.

My steadfast teacher of nature's round is the old-growth redwood forest that grows in Muir Woods a scant three miles north of my garden. Over the decades that I have gardened in northern California I have seen what was once a two-million-acre span of primordial redwood wilderness running along the spine of the California coast all the way to the Washington border be whittled down to less than 4 percent of its original size.

To be so close to a living remnant of this original forest is a great blessing. It makes me a fierce gardener. When the steady hum of all the entitled, short-legged plants I minister to daily bores into my skull, draining out my nerve and love of gardening, I walk beneath thousand-year-old *Sequoia sempervirens* and find my way back home. I go to the redwoods for a little breathing room; not to *escape* the garden, exactly, more to be able to see and hear it again, fresh. It is cool in the woods, and dark. The out-breath of the forest is thick with saturated oxygen. I take my place among the elders, a gnat on the hide of God. A virgin's bower clematis climbs a hundred feet up from the floor of the forest and tangles overhead in the cathedral-like arched branches of the redwoods, where a pair of ruby-crowned kinglets have built their nest.

The lessons of the forest anchor my life as a gardener. First and primary is the teaching of the rich diversity of fertile rot. Life loves to feed on decay: while seventeen hundred distinct organisms inhabit a single living redwood tree, at least four thousand are present and thriving on a dead log, and in just one cubic inch of fungus-rich forest soil is a mile's length of intertwined fungal mycelia. This network of life and death includes predator and prey and all their mingled shenanigans. I feel them rubbing up next to each other in the tan oak understory of the redwood forest, where the dusky-footed wood rat builds her nest so she can feed on tan oak acorns while northern spotted owls pluck their dinner from her pink-eyed litter.

The slow decay and renewal of old-growth forest is a growl that runs beneath the melody of wind and rain, owl and wood rat. Far above this deep drone, gardeners scurry about on the sunny surface of the land making compost and heating up the rhythm, piping into the blank air our wild, lilting tune.

The second gardening lesson of the forest is connected to the first: fertility is built in layers that age and ripen over time. Four hundred and sixty-five million years ago plants and fungi joined together and came onto land. Intertwined, they reveal that the basis of our biology is communal. To remember this all I need do is peel back the heavy duff that runs in knee-deep drifts throughout the old-growth forest. Layers of dry redwood needles and branches protect a moist understory of rotting leaf mold still discernible as fallen leaf litter from the overhead canopy. Underneath this layer runs a coal-black stratum of decayed soil, alive with mosaics of mycelial network. If you inject a single redwood tree with red vegetable dye a trace of this dye appears throughout the forest, carried in widening circles by the fungal network in the soil. This bottom layer of fungus-rich soil is the black gold of the forest, the old wealth of the woods.

A third lesson for the garden is the forest's reminder of how it stores water, sunlight, and living carbon in the body of its plants. The complex canopy provided by young and old-growth trees lets light into the forest irregularly. Mostly, sunlight is filtered through the trees while the deep litter of the forest retains moisture underground. But water is also conserved and held in the needles, bark, and stems of the huge trees themselves. Each of the seventy-five million or so needles in a full-size, old-growth redwood traps and holds fog, sieving the gray summer skies for water. A fifth of the annual rainfall of the forest comes from the fine mists of fog that envelop and are held in the canopy of the summer forest. When I walk through the woods in mid-July I remember Suzuki Roshi saying that Zen practice is like walking through fog—you go out at dusk and when you return in the dark your robes are thoroughly wet.

A fertile garden stores and releases water just as the forest does. You do not have to live next door to old-growth redwoods to observe this. Water is stored in the surface soil and protected from evaporation by drifts of mulch and by the green plant canopy. Fine films of water move slowly through this garden soil, pervading the layers of decomposing mulch. Fertile well-aerated soil stores and releases water, and any excess is absorbed by the subsoil. As nature's round continues to turn, stored soil water returns to the atmosphere by evaporation from the surface of the soil and by transpiration from the surface of plant leaves. Moisture enters the soil again through precipitation or irrigation.

Gardeners know that fertility depends on moisture and the best way to store and release water in the garden is to mimic the forest and create diversely planted beds covered with a living understory of green crop or deep mulch. Water is essential to garden fertility since it hydrates the microbiological population and transports nutrients and plant compounds in solution through the bodies of the living plants.

* * *

Grounded in these teachings of nature's round in the garden and the forest, gardeners work with patience and persistence, tolerance for rot and decay, and bottomless curiosity to keep our soils in "good heart." A soil in good heart is a healthy, fertile soil and one that is steadily being used up and replenished as nature's round turns from life into death into life again, never missing a beat. Keeping soil in good heart requires that gardeners have a well-developed sense of humus, the rich, ebony-dark decomposed organic matter on the floor of every undisturbed forest and every well-made compost pile.

Some old friends of mine live in the coastal hills of central California, above the city of Santa Cruz at the dead end of a country road, just where rural suburbia butts up against the wild scrub canyons of live oak and tangled honeysuckle of the Santa Cruz mountains. On their land is a very old compost pile, a ten-year-old heap of black duff that broods under the mottled shade of stately oaks. Recently Richard told me that he tucked a dead chicken that had just been killed by a patrol of raccoons into the folds of this black heap. "It's funny I did that," he mused, since he hadn't added any fresh material to his broody mound in years. The chicken was gone, totally picked clean, in less than two days. "Only her feet were left," Richard reported to me, under his breath, "her leathery feet, sticking out of the pile."

We have little awareness of the swarming biology of decomposers that can transform a dead chicken into fertile compost in two days, but these beings determine the course of our life on earth, for without this dark cloud of microscopic organisms that inhabit Richard's chicken-eating heap of humus we would drown in the flood of our own waste stream. Humus may appear to be a well-digested, black mass of fertile compost, but it is endlessly diverse. Each particle of humus is a unique, non-repeating universe, like a human fingerprint or each of a flurry of snowflakes falling on the Alaskan tundra.

The word "humus" has many deep, old roots and connections. In Latin *humus* means "earth," "ground," and "soil." But it also shares the root for humankind, humane, and exhume, words buried in earth roots. Humble, humiliate, and humorous derive as well from this same fertile root word, as do humid and hubris. I love this richness: it matches humus itself. Yet it is humiliating to know so little about this humid, moist, dark brown culture of humus that supports our life, this culture so humbling in its elasticity and mysterious nature, and so deeply deserving of humane attention.

Building and turning a hot compost pile, until it molders with age and finally settles down to become black gold, is to culture a sense of humus that is deep and abiding. And culture it is, because, like the yeast of all old cultures in the world of bread, wine, and cheese, humus itself is a culture that ferments and feeds on itself, creating new life.

When the yeasty culture of humus is worked into garden soils, those soils change. Humus joins molecules of clay, and the humus-clay compound and the soil it is in make a colloid. Colloids are mixtures where tiny particles of one substance are dispersed in another. The word itself comes from the Greek for "gluelike," since colloids hold their particles in a gluelike suspension. Mayonnaise is a colloid, as are marshmallows and cheese.

Colloids have a huge surface area in proportion to their weight and they are important chemically because every single colloidal particle carries an electric charge, and all the particles in a colloid carry the same charge, either positive or negative. The clay-humus particles in soil always carry a negative charge, and this is essential in building fertility because the negative charge attracts and holds on to positively charged soil nutrients such as potassium, calcium, and magnesium. When your soil is rich in humus it is also rich in the ability to hold on to nutrients, releasing them on demand to plants and to hungry microorganisms.

Stable and rich, with the fragrance of the deep woods after a summer rainstorm, humus retains almost 90 percent of its weight in moisture, making soils rich in humus considerably more drought-tolerant than soils that have not been composted. Humus also builds soil structure by allowing for ample air circulation in the ground and by holding soil particles together with microbial secretions that are released throughout the decomposition process. Humus also moderates the pH of garden soil, buffering it in the balanced 6.0–6.8 range that is ideal for most plant growth. In addition, humus has the ability to absorb and immobilize toxic heavy metals, protecting plants from their negative effects. As humus absorbs toxins it also creates a hospitable environment for beneficial microorganisms that aid in the creation of a healthy soil ecology.

All of these wondrous, fertility-enhancing properties of humus do not mean that the finished material behaves in an orderly fashion. Humus is an undomesticated culture; neither humble nor tame, it lays claim to your ground.

And not only your ground. Eventually humus gets underneath your fingernails, animates your imagination, and claims you. Because it is a culture, good humus spreads. From the garden, to the table, to your heart and mind, humus enfolds you in its rich ferment. Brewed from whispered relationships, rotten redwood forest duff and dead chickens, from dung and ooze and molted snake skins, humus raises life from out of the dead underworld. Organized, it disorganizes the world. Unstable, it stabilizes life.

The Breakdown Ball

COMPOST COOKS. EVERY WELL-BUILT AEROBIC COMPOST PILE generates heat as the invisible microbes that inhabit the pile initiate a hot process of metabolic decay that I like to think of as a steamy rock-and-roll party in the compost pile or the "breakdown ball" of decomposition. In the January garden I often find a line of feral cats sitting in a ragged row on top of our hottest compost pile warming their mangy backsides. These escaped housecats, the wild toms and their gaunt consorts, would stare at me hollow-eyed and rise up, hissing, on their bony haunches, reluctant to yield their hot seat. Over the years the transfixing warmth of the breakdown ball allowed us to bag a number of these feral cats and take them to our local vet for shots and neutering.

It is not only feral cats that are attracted to the warmth of a well-made compost pile. In the late autumn of 1975, soon after Peter and I first arrived at Green Gulch, we wanted to camp out near the beach and get to know the Gulch by night. We walked down through the chilly autumn fields at dusk carrying a tarp and our sleeping bags to

the last field just before the ocean. It was almost dark. There, a huge mound of composting hay and sweetgrass freshly mixed with field weeds caught our attention. Tiny jets of steam puffed up from the heart of the fresh grass pile into the cool, lowering night sky. We looked at each other and laughed out loud as we charged up the steep hay mountain, scrambling to the top of the seven-foot-high mound. We spread out our tarp, opened our sleeping bags, and fell asleep on the warmest and softest bed I can ever remember camping on. In the morning the four horses pastured in the field near our plush, heated bed snorted in surprise as we rose off the surface of their steaming sweetgrass pile and swept the last remnants of wispy hay out of our hair.

✤　✤　✤

The main compost ingredients that power the breakdown ball are all around us, and usually right under our feet. "All conditioned things are of a nature to decay," said the Buddha. Everything that is or was once alive will come apart in the compost pile and turn into black gold: kitchen scraps, lawn clippings, thick ropes of rank weeds, old potting soil, the prunings of your fruit trees and those rotten, windfall apples of late September, most animal manures and bones, dust and lint and human hair clippings, tear-moistened Kleenex, and old love letters. All these ingredients and many more can be stacked up to decay and ripen into humus in the compost pile.

I have entrusted my most precious materials to the compost pile, like my now-grown son Jesse's small blue-gray wool baby sweater that was tattered with wear, some of the locks from my daughter Alisa's first haircut, and the stained and creased photograph of the Dalai Lama that I found in the Goodwill box behind the used gloves. I want these ingredients to "live again" in the breakdown ball and to nourish the microbes and the garden with their unraveling boogie.

Although most decay is aerobic, stimulated and fed by air, decomposition can also happen anaerobically, or without the circulation of air, which is what occurs underwater in bogs of peat moss or in rough compost piles that are stacked up and never turned. This is a slow dance without any breath of wind.

These "cool rot" piles are stacked organic matter left for a year or more to rot without the steady incorporation of air, moisture, or fresh organic matter, so they decompose very slowly. I respect slow, cool rot, but I mainly practice and preach aerobic compost making: "hot rot" piles with intense heat generated from the steady metabolic digestion of billions of aerobic bacteria.

The first ingredient to consider when you begin to make compost is the most fundamental ingredient of all—air. Even at the beginning of anaerobic compost, or compost that does not depend on the lively circulation of oxygen, the process is initiated with a long, cool exhalation of breath before passing on to the domain of the anaerobic bacteria. "Wild air, world mothering air," invokes poet Gerard Manley Hopkins, and the bacteria of the breakdown ball echo his cry.

Aerobic compost depends on air to decompose and when good compost is mixed into the soil it aerates the earth in turn, building air pockets between fertile soil granules in the ground. The presence of lively, circulating air in well-composted soil helps to activate and build humus reserves, to maintain reserves of nitrogen in the soil, and to balance the carbon/nitrogen ratio. In addition, well-aerated soil enables plant roots to take up needed nutrients, especially phosphorus and potassium that are so important for the root and stem health of the plant community. Soil aeration assists in the formation of healthy fungus-root bridges as well, links that connect plant roots with vital soil nutrients. All plant roots and soil microorganisms breathe soil air that contains varying amounts of carbon dioxide and oxygen (although less than in atmospheric air). Then they use this soil oxygen to help break down stored starches, carbon dioxide, and water being returned to the atmosphere in the respiration that completes the cycle.

The next fundamental compost ingredient is water. If air is the fuel for life, then water gives all living beings body and substance. Water also serves as a flowing passageway for nutrients and microbes to travel along in the underground world. What plants most need and absorb from the soil is water, and water is essential to the life of the compost pile, too.

We say that good compost is as moist as a wrung-out sponge. Piles naturally dry out standing in the air and the heat of the pile speeds this drying process, so as you build your compost pile, be sure to keep it moist while you work. Liz, one of my colleagues at Tassajara Zen Mountain Center, surmised that compost ingredients themselves are mostly water. She recognized this from making compost every day, but in order to be sure she took some raw garbage and snuck into the Tassajara monastery kitchen after hours and weighed it. Liz then roasted this muck in a slow oven on a baking sheet well covered with sheets of parchment paper, simulating the heat of a compost pile, just to see what percentage of moisture would "bake off" as water vapor. She found that 83 percent of the weight of the garbage was water, and after her midnight experiment she composted the well-desiccated remains.

It is good to remember how much of your compost pile is water, since too little moisture stalls the breakdown ball and too much moisture forces the air out of your pile and causes the compost to become anaerobic. As ever, balance is the key.

After air and water, the primary constituents necessary for the breakdown ball in the compost pile are carbon and nitrogen, provided by garden and kitchen. Like carbohydrates in human nutrition, carbon is the primary energy food for decomposer microorganisms. Microbes digest carbon compounds and the heat in a compost pile comes from their metabolic oxidation as they "burn up" these carbon compounds. Microbes respire and give off carbon dioxide as they digest carbon-based organic matter, recycling it back into the atmosphere.

Carbon materials for the compost pile are usually dry and brown, shades of buff, tan, and pale gold. Think of dry straw, shredded paper, old sawdust or wood chips, sticks and dry stems of hefty and ripe garden plants like sunflowers and spent pea vines, raked-up leaves, plant husks and hulls, and you are thinking of the carbon components of your compost pile.

Nitrogen in the compost pile works much like protein in our diet. It is responsible for the growth of new plant tissue and for the growth and reproduction of the microbes themselves. Carbon molecules cannot be broken down or digested by microbes without some nitrogen. Nitrogen ingredients for the compost pile are wet and green. Think of fresh weeds, kitchen garbage, raw manure (even though it may be brown in color it is "green" in nature), grass

Compost needs more carbon (dry/brown) than nitrogen (wet/green)

30:1

clippings, fish scraps, animal urine, and sewage sludge, and you are thinking of some of the primary nitrogen sources for your compost pile.

In order for microorganisms to grow and function as active participants in the compost pile's breakdown ball, they must be fed a balanced diet of organic matter. Nitrogen in the pile is also like protein on our plate in being a concentrated food. The breakdown ball requires a far more modest helping of nitrogen than carbon, in a ratio of about thirty parts of carbon to one part of nitrogen. In the presence of air and adequate moisture, this carbon/nitrogen ratio will fire up the breakdown ball.

If a compost pile has too much carbon and not enough nitrogen, the growth processes slow down. The cause of most compost heap failures is a lack of nitrogen, with the composting microbes spending all their time trying to digest or chew up stiff drifts of woody carbon and lignin, a compound responsible for much of the rigidity in plant structures. A good dose of a quick nitrogen such as urine or thick manure tea will stimulate the growth of the decomposer microorganisms and bring the pile back to life.

When a pile has the opposite problem of too much nitrogen and not enough carbon, it gives off a strong stench of ammonia, because the bacteria cannot use all of the rich, wet nitrogen present in the pile and this nitrogen is "breathed off" into the atmosphere as ammonia. Carbon added to such a pile

Carbon and Nitrogen Sources for Compost-Making

All compost piles are composed of ingredients that are high in carbon (C) and usually dry, or brown, and ingredients that are high in nitrogen (N), and green, or wet. The ideal ratio for a healthy compost pile is about thirty parts of carbon to one part of nitrogen, a ratio nicely combined in well-rotted oat straw used for bedding in horse stables and saturated with nitrogen-rich equine urine. The following list shows compost ingredients with their C/N ratio included. A high C/N ratio is called a wide ratio (e.g., 500/1 for sawdust) while one that is more in balance for compost-making is shown as a narrow ratio (e.g., oat straw at 25/1).

Sawdust	500:1
Paper	200:1
Straw	40–80:1
Corn stalks (chipped)	60:1
Dry mulch mix	60:1
Dry leaves	60:1
Old hay or well-rotted litter straw	30:1
Wilted greens and garden weeds	20:1
Grass clippings	15:1
Legume hay (green)	15:1
Manure	15:1
Kitchen scraps	15:1
Blood meal	15:1

Adapted from Wolf Storl, *Culture and Horticulture*

in the form of old sawdust or other wide-ratio carbon ingredients will absorb the excess nitrogen and prevent the loss of this crucial nutrient.

Every aerobic compost pile is alive and changing, and goes through clear stages of decomposition in the breakdown ball. In the first stage the compost pile is colonized by legions of heat-loving bacteria, or thermophiles, which attack the drifts of nitrogen-rich garbage and weeds mixed up with carbonaceous layers of straw, leaves, and dry twigs, and begin to tear them apart. During this stage of decomposition tremendous heat is liberated by the metabolism of the thermophilic bacteria. Proteins are broken down into amino acids and, finally, ammonia. Carbohydrates are decomposed into simple sugars, organic acids, and, eventually, carbon dioxide.

If this initial breakdown stage of decomposition were to continue unchecked then inorganic substances such as free carbon dioxide, oxygen, hydrogen, nitrogen, and sulfur would be the end result. However, this does not happen in a healthy compost pile. Instead, the next stage of decomposition, the buildup stage, begins as soon as the heat-loving bacteria and microbes in your pile have completed their initial digestion of the raw organic material of your compost.

During the second stage of the breakdown ball actinomycetes and fungi come into play. Actinomycetes are microbes that function like a cross between bacteria and fungi. They are essential to the ripening of humus in the compost pile and in the home garden, for while they are decomposing organic matter, actinomycetes also liberate nitrogen, ammonia, and carbon and make it available in the pile. Actinomycetes also have the extraordinary ability to produce certain antibiotics that suppress the ability of bacteria to generate disease. The heat-loving bacteria in the compost pile form spores that fungi have predigested and made available for earthworms and actinomycetes to digest.

Simple fungi begin to colonize the compost pile along with the actinomycetes. Fungi lack the ability to make their own carbohydrates since they do not produce green chlorophyll. Therefore, fungi rely on dead or decomposing organic matter for energy. They soak up the gases given off by bacteria and build up protein in their own mycelia, taking up the free ammonia released by

the pulsing metabolism of the bacteria-generated breakdown ball and building amino acids.

In the third stage of decomposition larger organisms begin to colonize the
compost pile. At this point the main chemical processes of decomposition
are finished. These organisms continue the physical transformation of the
pile's ingredients as they inhabit and digest the ripening compost pile. These
physical decomposers, such as manure worms and pill bugs, springtails (an
order of primitive, wingless insects that jump using a tail-like appendage)
and centipedes, cannot live in the high temperatures of the early stages of
decomposition, so their presence is a clear indication of the cooling off and
mellowing of the compost pile. When these visible macroorganisms are present they are a signal that your compost is cool and ripe enough to be applied
to the garden.

The compost process is actually its own dynamic food chain.
In the earlier stages of decomposition, bacteria and fungi break
down raw organic matter. In turn, nematodes ingest these bacteria, and mites and springtails eat the fungi. Then predaceous
mites and pseudo-scorpions prey upon these same nematodes
as well as upon fly larvae and the mites and springtails. Without skipping a beat, consumers such as flatworms ingest the
predaceous mites and continue the decomposition process. And as compost
enters into its last, ripe stage, large birds and nocturnal mammals feed on the
earthworms and larvae in the finished pile.

Humus itself, the end product of the decomposition process, also ripens
in stages, and no two molecules of humus are ever alike because humus is
composed of vast decomposure. Early on, young, raw humus is wild and randy,
showing its constituents and wearing cords of partially decayed orange peels,
flakes of eggshell and half-digested skunkweed in its uncombed hair. But even
though raw humus is a little rank, it also improves soil aeration and offers
some soluble nutrients to plants and soil, leaving behind a generous reserve
of carbon dioxide as it continues to decompose.

Later on, as humus settles down and becomes ripe, it is most effective in
attracting and holding soil nutrients. Colloidal, effective humus is a mobile

force in the soil community, banking nutrient anions in an accessible form for plant roots to absorb when they are hungry. And as plants take up nutrients from effective humus this humus continues to release hormones, antibiotics, and vitamins into the soil community.

Stable humus, like the rich black humus of my friend's chicken-devouring compost heap, is the mysterious, wise chaperone of the garden and forest, not so much a plant food as the food's accompanist, a source of long-term nutrient storage. It is in this stable environment that toxins can be captured and disassembled, preventing them from entering the wider soil community.

The transformations of the breakdown ball offer a view into the heart of fertile life itself where all beings feed on one another, come apart, and are rearranged. And the humus-rich compost that emerges is the most balanced and complex fertilizer for your garden, feeding soil microbes, plants, and gardeners, until it finally becomes the living soil itself.

Arranging Garbage

IN THE ZEN MEDITATION TRADITION, EACH TORN CHERRY LEAF HAS value, each polished river stone, each pine needle pathway drenched with rain. There is a wonderful story of two monks making a traditional walking pilgrimage to a remote monastery deep in the mountains of southern China. The steep, rocky pathway to the monastery ran alongside a stream for much of the journey. After walking for hours one of the monks noticed a green mustard leaf floating by on the river current. He stopped in astonished disbelief. "How can we continue to this monastery?" he asked his pilgrimage partner. "No mustard leaf could escape the monastery kitchen unless the monks are careless with their food. We're turning back this instant!"

The older monk reasoned with his partner: it was late in the day, they had been walking for hours, and surely this was a rare accident. Reluctantly, the other pilgrim agreed to continue on, but not ten steps later another leaf floated by on the river. "That's it!" the first monk proclaimed. "We go no farther." The second monk agreed and they turned around. They had gone but a few hundred yards back down the darkening trail when a winded monk from the monastery overtook them on the path, carrying a long dipping net and quite out of breath. "Excuse me," he puffed, "have you seen two mustard leaves floating by on the river? I lost them while I was washing the greens for dinner."

Good composting, like good cooking, is anchored in an unabashed love of your ingredients, each and every one, and in a great, roaring appreciation of change and interbeing. Making compost is an art, the fine art of arranging garbage. It seems to me that it is because I love to arrange flowers—'Black Dragon' lilies mixed with the first slim-stemmed moss roses of mid-June—that I also love to arrange garbage. The two tasks fit snugly together, like a box and its lid. Wheelbarrows of rotten cabbage leaves, broken iris stems, and drifts of sheep sorrel and fire nettles, when arranged with oat straw and dried grass harvested from the coastal headlands, live again to nourish and become the following season's fertile lily and rose beds.

Cool, largely anaerobic decomposition occurs naturally in a forest ecosystem or deep in the layers of decaying grass and leaves decomposing on a windy prairie. Anaerobic composting systems mimic this process. They need very little maintenance and can be built or added to over a long time. The temperature of a cool anaerobic compost system never exceeds 120 degrees, so it spares the disease-suppressing microbes that are burned up in a hot compost system, and it conserves nitrogen since the decomposers do not require great sources of growth food to do their work. However, a cool pile is not hot enough to kill weed seeds or soil pathogens, and in the prolonged time it takes to produce finished compost there will be nutrient loss from extended exposure to the elements unless you protect and insulate your pile.

Long-term cool anaerobic compost piles are ideal for woody brush and debris, old stalks and blackberry canes as well as decayed grass, thick branches and stems, and pruned-back plant parts that come out of the heart of the established garden. It is best to stack this material in a shady spot, accessible to occasional watering and somewhere your anaerobic pile can decay over a one- to two-year period. The finished compost from the cool system may contain more undecomposed chunks of high-carbon materials such as wood or brush, but this fertile compost is excellent for the garden.

✤　✤　✤

One of my passions is arranging hot stacks of aerobic compost. Everything about this approach appeals to my already hot and zealous nature. Aerobic stacks are juicy, varied, willing to incorporate so many forms of life, and they produce finished compost relatively quickly, a great advantage if you have a garden with high fertility needs. The heat that results from accelerated decomposition keeps the pace of decay moving and also kills most weed seeds and pathogens. This method requires periodic turning of the compost pile to incorporate air and to mix the ingredients, so it is somewhat labor intensive, but it is not particularly demanding: you can choose to turn your stack just once or twice while it cooks, or you can turn it every few days to stimulate the process. It is best to have enough room in your garden both for restacking the pile as you turn it and for starting a second aerobic compost pile while your first one is decomposing, because it is best not to keep adding fresh raw material and garbage. Hot compost requires and consumes considerable nitrogen since the microbes in the pile need this fuel to accelerate their decomposition process.

Every compost pile has a unique signature, a hot, rotting charm all its own. Certain of our compost piles have even been named. One succulent pile, "Holy Shit" by name, was made of rich seams of rhubarb chard, hot horse manure, and truckload after truckload of 'Rose Fir Apple' potato greens layered in with blond oat straw and raw cow manure. This pile reached a noble 160 degrees in less than a week and decomposed completely in just under two months. I still remember spreading that dark, finished Holy Shit compost around our young pear and apple trees as the first winter storms rolled in from the north in early December. I felt like the wealthiest gardener on earth.

Making compost is an ancient craft whose every ingredient is precious. A written record of the practice of composting organic matter is preserved in cuneiform on a set of clay tablets from Mesopotamia a thousand years before Moses was born. Compost making was practiced in classical Greece, throughout the Fertile Crescent of the Middle East, in Rome and Asia, and wherever human beings have settled down, raised crops, and kept animals.

I prefer to make compost where everyone can see the artfully and neatly arranged homage to garbage. The compost piles at the Edible Schoolyard and at Green Gulch Farm have an intuitive appeal for visitors who can sense their fecund dynamism. Just last season when asking a graduating class of eighth graders leaving the Edible Schoolyard what they would remember most about their middle school garden experience one boy answered, "The steaming hot compost piles on a cold morning."

There are many methods, styles, and ingredients for making hot compost that will be ready to use in two to six months, and you can work out your own effective approach to stacking garbage as long as you take care of a few essential details. First of all, choose a good site for your pile and decide how large to make it. At both Green Gulch Farm and the Edible Schoolyard, our compost piles are made under the cover of stately coniferous trees where the shade keeps the compost from drying out in the hot California wind. This is a good way to use land that is otherwise not arable. While it is not essential to build compost piles in the shade if you have a more temperate climate than that of arid California, it is always a good idea to protect your compost from heat scorch or excessive rain and wind damage.

I always begin compost piles by forking open the ground below the site to improve drainage and so that soil micro- and macroorganisms can surface from the loosened ground and permeate the compost pile as it cooks. Check the site for weeds whose roots might invade your pile, and before forking open the ground, decide how large you want to build your pile. I find that a freestanding compost pile must be at least three-by-three-by-three feet in order to generate enough mass to effectively heat up and break down the ingredients. You may also need to allow for extra space to turn your piles and to stack up stored compost ingredients like manure, old hay and straw, and mounds of weeds.

If you find you really like composting, you might want to refine your process by using some accessories. A rod thermometer can be inserted to measure the aerobic heat of your pile, allowing you to follow the decomposition process more closely and time your pile turning most effectively. A record book to enter data about your piles will help you track and learn from your past successes and failures. Breathable compost covers made of polypropylene are excellent for protecting the pile from rain, snow, or even from excessive summer heat, if you don't want a simple thatch roof of straw.

If you want to accelerate the composting process you can shred your dry and wet ingredients, since the greater the surface area exposed to air, the speedier the decomposition. You can use a shredder or lay materials on the ground and run a mower over them to chop them up, or else use a sharp spade to cut your ingredients into pieces about three to six inches long before you incorporate them into your compost pile.

Many gardeners choose to build compost inside contained bins rather than creating freestanding piles as I do. There are many innovative designs for bins, from straw-bale-sided piles to well-fenced bins. If you are most concerned about screening *out* compost pests such as feral cats, raccoons, dogs, and rats it may be sufficient just to build a simple stake frame around your pile and wrap hogwire or chickenwire around this frame. This way, as you move your piles you can easily move your frames, too.

Once it is time to assemble your hot-rot compost pile you can be very creative. Begin by stacking your roughest, woodiest materials at the base of your pile: branches lopped off your neighbor's hedge, dried-out blackberry canes, broken sunflower stalks. This roughage helps with moisture drainage and aeration as you build your pile, and if these materials do not break down in the first round of the decomposition ball, they will be happy to dance again in the next round. Be careful not to use woody materials high in lignin such as huge branches or wood chip mulch since these materials are difficult for microbes to digest and may even cause disease in the garden.

As you proceed to arrange the layers of your compost pile be sure that you keep your ingredients moist. I like to stack compost in alternate, eight- to twelve-inch layers of green nitrogen source materials and brown carbon materials, reviewing all the materials that go into the pile as they are added. Be mindful that your nitrogen and carbon sources are balanced in a rough ratio of thirty parts by weight of carbon to one part of nitrogen. This ratio is

Composting with Earthworms

Charles Darwin referred to the earthworm as "the intestines of the earth" since the digestive system of an earthworm functions by grinding all digested materials and mixing them with enzymes that assist in the decomposition of organic matter. Earthworm casts or manure are a premier soil conditioner, rich in nitrogen, potassium, phosphorus, calcium, and magnesium. These casts help to neutralize any acidity in the soil while increasing the ability of garden soil to maintain a strong bank account of viable nutrients readily available to plants.

Every garden I have ever worked in has had a worm composting system. In the public schools vermiculture systems are both in the classroom and outdoors in larger garden bins.

For the home household a suitable size for an indoor worm bin is about two feet wide and long and about a foot deep. Make sure your container is well aerated to increase air and nutrient circulation and good drainage. If you are composting out-of-doors with worms your containers can be larger. For those living in a climate that freezes consider sinking your earthworm bins one to two feet in the ground with an open bottom to your bin. Always locate your vermiculture composting system in a cool, shady spot.

For earthworm bedding provide good drainage in the bottom of your bins by adding an equal measure of shredded newspaper, old leaves, hay, or dry grass clippings covered with a light mixture of friable garden soil and well-rotted compost. Make sure this material is cool before you add your earthworms. (*Lumbricus rubellus*, or red bait worms, and *Eisenia foetida*, or brandling worms, are best for composting systems.) Two pounds of worms will get you started—this is more than one thousand wriggling composters.

Spread your worms on top of your bedding and once they have burrowed in, give them kitchen left-overs, two to three pounds at a time, and cover their food with newspaper strips and straw. Every month or so add more bedding, fluffing up the bin materials at this time. Wait a few days after this disturbance to let your worms settle before feeding them again. Or you can also leave your bins alone as we do at the Edible Schoolyard, just adding food and bedding.

Every six months or so you can harvest earthworm castings by gently scraping off or scalping worm compost, working slowly so that the worms can get out of your way. This compost is more than 50 percent organic matter with at least ten trace minerals present. It is an excellent, concentrated garden fertilizer, appreciated by all plants.

best achieved with equal parts by volume of green and brown materials. If you are shredding your materials, they should be roughly equal in volume before you chop them up, not after.

On top of the brushy bottom layer I—or we, as stack-building is a wonderful thing to do with another person—pile a good source of carbon, such as old straw or dry grass. Then I spread kitchen waste on the dry layer and cover with a light layer of weeds and then another layer of carbon-rich straw or dry grass. As I construct the layers I also scatter old compost and a dusting of garden soil on top of each carbon layer. This helps to inoculate the new pile with the garden bacteria and microorganisms that are necessary for effective aerobic decomposition. You can stop when your compost pile is three feet high, or keep on until it is four or five feet tall. I love arranging a tall, stout compost pile. When the pile is finished I cap off my compost mountain with a thick layer of carbon to help discourage feral cats and other compost raiders from tearing up my work.

Once your pile is built you can let it rest for a week or so before you turn it. Green Gulch and Edible Schoolyard compost piles are gigantic, because we have so much raw material and such a steady need of finished compost. We turn these piles just two or three times during their lifetime, which is usually about six months long, including a full month's time for the compost to mellow before we apply it to the gardens.

Composting works best when the temperature inside your pile stays at about 140°F or higher. Bacteria go dormant and the breakdown ball slows to a crawl when the compost pile temperature falls below 60°F. When you turn your compost pile regularly you incorporate air and mix up the ingredients, stimulating the pulse of decomposition. In the height of the growing season you can have finished compost ready to feed garden soil and plants in two to three months' time, depending on the size of your compost pile and your willingness to aerate the pile by turning it.

Composting tends to move along smoothly, since decomposition is a pre-eminently natural process, but occasionally problems do come up. In his book *The Gift of Good Land*, poet and farmer Wendell Berry says, "In the presence of problems intelligence encounters details . . . it is in the presence of

141

problems that their solutions will be found." In arranging garbage, problems are as welcome as any other decomposable ingredient.

Most aerobic composting problems can be solved by simply turning your pile. The key remedies for problems are the same as the key ingredients that make up your compost pile—air, water, carbon, and nitrogen. Once you see and understand the symptoms of problems that may arise, you can easily remedy them.

If you have wet, foul, ammonia-smelling compost, perhaps with fly maggots in it, you have too much nitrogen in the pile. Aerate your compost by turning it and add a high source of absorbent carbon to soak up the excess nitrogen. If there has been a lot of rain in your area, cover your compost pile so that it

Hot, Fast Compost in 14–28 Days

Be careful to begin with a good balance of C and N ingredients, well layered. Your stack will be ready to turn for the first time when it reaches a temperature of about 120 degrees. This will probably take just a few days. Each time you turn your hot-rot compost, take all the material on the outer edges of the pile and put it into the center of your new pile, where it will rot fastest. Don't be put off that most of your materials will still be recognizable and a little smelly. The turning process allows you to rearrange your garbage as you restack your pile and to notice what is happening in the heart of the compost pile as you work. Following this first turning and aerating, your pile will heat up dramatically.

Two or three days after you first turn your compost pile, take the temperature of your pile again. When it is hotter than on the first days, about 130–135 degrees or higher, it is time to turn your pile again. The outer layer of the pile may have a gray powder, indicating that fungi are absorbing the free ammonia gases given off in the hot center of your pile and rebuilding the broken-down amino acids in the strong fiber of

their mycelia. As you turn your pile for the second time it is essential that you monitor moisture. If your compost feels at all dry add a light spray of water as you turn and restack it.

After three more days, the original material of your pile will be barely recognizable and your compost will reach its optimal breakdown temperature of 150–160 degrees. Now turn it again. If your pile is not this hot, fold in additional nitrogen sources—grass clippings, manure, or compost tea—to stimulate decomposition.

After the third turning of your compost pile, the temperature should rise up to 150–160 degrees once again. Wait a few days and the temperature will drop down to 110 degrees. You do not need to turn the pile again, and even if you were to turn your pile once more at this stage the temperature would not rise above 110 degrees, because all the easily digestible carbohydrates of the pile have been consumed. The C/N ratio is now around ten to one, and your compost is finished. Let it settle for a week or so and then apply it directly to your garden.

can dry out. And if you have a dry center in your compost without any heat or with musty white mildew present, there is too much carbon in your pile. By adding ingredients high in nitrogen, like grass clippings or fresh manure, your pile will be reactivated and will decompose fully.

When arranging garbage there are certain plants that it is best *not* to include in your compost pile. Whatever weeds or garden plants are especially invasive in your area and may not be killed by the heat of the pile are best omitted. Pernicious weeds, rhizomic grasses, and seedy shrubs, any plants sprayed with toxic chemicals, and dog, cat, or bird feces, all of which may carry pathogens or growth inhibitors for other plants, should be excluded.

When your garden produces an abundance of these problematic plants, you may want to make a special compost pile based around them. Take, for example, the needles of fir and pine trees. They are usually kept out of piles since they are very acidic and can lower the soil pH if they are added to the garden. But azaleas and rhododendron, and other ericaceous plants, love these acidic nutrients, so I sometimes collect the needles of conifers and make a special compost to feed acid-loving plants. In the presence of problems, garden intelligence feeds on acidic details.

At Green Gulch we have occasionally gone so far as to create special compost piles of noxious, poisonous, invasive, and troublesome plants such as bone-dry joints of cape ivy, limp bindweed, or field morning glory, comfrey, Michaelmas aster roots, and harding grass, all stacked up and composted with good hot manure.

When making a pernicious weed pile like this it is good to clap a skull-and-crossbones sign on the top to warn innocent or forgetful gardeners not to use this compost on the main garden, and then let it rot and decay for a few seasons at least before testing to see if the pestiferous weeds continue to prevail. So far, the strongest survivor of just such a skull-and-crossbones composting process that I experimented with years ago was comfrey. Returning again and again from the oven of 160 degree heat to sprout on the edge of a line of fruit trees where I tested this pernicious compost, also an old-world medicine plant, comfrey was the most persistent survivor.

If breeding your own skull-and-crossbones compost is not for you, a viable alternative is to use the modern services of curbside pickup for municipal composting systems. Their controlled and expert process can generate the heat needed over sufficient time to kill problem seeds, spores, and roots. Know the problem ingredients you are sending out of your garden and be mindful of their life force. Handle these materials respectfully before they pass on and out of your mind. Remember that they will "live again," since municipal composting systems sell their compost back to the community.

Once you begin experimenting with arranging garbage there is no limit to your field of action as you help it on its way to becoming a rose. Building fertility in the garden is a dynamic and ever-changing process of life into death into life, guided by your affection for the land you are called to work, for the plants you grow and minister to, and for the mystery of water and air, wind and raw garbage, forever intertwined with the lifelines of every garden and gardener.

✦ ✦ ✦

By Halloween on the north coast of California all the cover crop for the winter season and the tulips and narcissus, the frittilaria, and bloodred regal lily bulbs of spring must be planted. The hatchet falls on All Hallows' Eve, for after October 31 it is too late to plant. This is also the season of *Dia de los Muertos*— or the Day of the Dead, that day standing between Indian summer and black-eyed winter when the veil between worlds thins out and gardeners are called home to sleep in the long throat of rot.

Some years at Green Gulch we celebrate the Day of the Dead by making a huge, end-of-the-season compost heap in the middle of our autumn fields. No being escapes the yawning jaws of this Halloween compost pile, the last chance to scrape all broken and shattered crops off the empty field into one great steaming mound.

We work all day long clearing the land. In a solitary corner of the field I pull broken sunflower stalks out of the exhausted row. Often these stalks are ten feet long with thin, ghostlike necks at their summit, snapped by the weight of large, eyeless heads of Russian sunflowers. Heavy as the grave, I haul these stalks out of the earth and lay them down for the base of the Halloween heap.

Another Halloween pile builder pulls up cartloads of dry bean litter, laying out tangles of brittle vines on top of the sunflower stalks. The Vermont cranberry beans and 'Dragon Tongue' beans themselves were harvested weeks ago and now glow in their wide-rimmed burlap sacks in the seed cellar like burnished gems.

On top of the dry bean litter we stack armloads of cornhusks from the 'Rainbow Inca' and 'Blue Hopi' flint corn that will be ground up into meal in a few weeks for moist Thanksgiving bread. These dry husks and sheaves of Mother Corn are the pared-off leavings of a sacred crop eight thousand years old, the staple grain of the New World. But today, corn husks are fine fodder for the furnace of decay.

Our Halloween compost pile totters between six and seven feet high, already twenty-five feet long and growing, like a black, segmented dragon sloughing off its skin. Old Yeller, our farm truck, is backed up to the pile and two more revelers in decay hurl shovelsful of ripe green manure and moldy oat straw, drenched with still-warm horse piss, onto the pile.

For the last few hours we haven't spoken at all. Our work rhythm is synchronized with the old music that broods at the roots of the dark cypress trees that border the autumn field. And even though long-limbed summer still paces the field, I can't be wooed. I am tired of plump-kerneled corn and striped sunflowers, and I am tired of baskets brimming with crinkled 'Dinosaur' kale and burgundy chard. Gnawed out by death and decay, I am not hungry now. Our Day of the Dead compost pile is a fearsome being, with curved nails that have never been cut and long crone whiskers growing out of its nostrils. The pile already begins to steam in the cold evening air, as invisible hordes of microorganisms fall on the exposed jugular vein of the last crops of the season.

When our compost pile is finished it is almost dark. Night hovers, showing its yellow teeth, at the edge of the field. For a crowning touch we take our most fallen-in Halloween pumpkins and sit them in a crooked line on the crest of the pile. These sagging pumpkins with their collapsed, moldy grins summon me. My garden friends walk up to dinner, laughing, far ahead. I hear the gate swing open and clang shut behind them. High in the cypress windbreak a great horned owl opens and closes her wings. A November wind crosses the world. I put down my pitchfork, wipe my hands on the front of my overalls, and walk through the thin veil of steam that separates the worlds, into the bright, clean fire of decay.

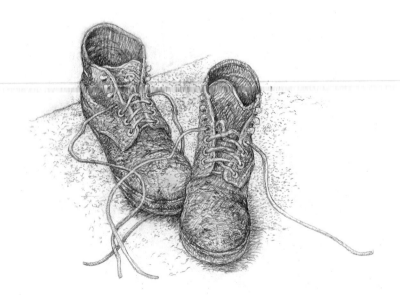

Spreading the Wealth

A FEW DAYS A WEEK MY HUSBAND PETER WORKS TWENTY-FIVE miles to the north of Muir Beach at a residential center for the homeless, Homeward Bound, where he manages an immensely productive 2,300-square-foot organic garden providing fresh food almost year-round for the eighty or so residents. At the back of this garden is a small yard where the residents make compost with Peter, spreading the wealth of their black-gold compost supplemented with truckloads of local manure, on their Homeward Bound garden every autumn and spring.

Spreading compost and working it into the ground is one of the simplest pleasures among all tasks in the garden. This work begins with investigating your compost pile and being sure that your materials are ripe and ready. When your array of good compost ingredients has been well and fully digested, your pile will be cool and friable with a sweet, woodsy scent.

As you dig into your compost pile, excavate any undigested stalks and roughage and set them aside for your next pile. Stir and break apart the largest lumps of finished compost, tilthing, or breaking up, these rougher sections of your pile before incorporating the compost into your garden beds. I like to tilth as I load compost into a wheelbarrow and then deliver the prepared fertilizer to the garden. Tilthing not only breaks the compost into a digestible size before it is added to the garden, it also helps to incorporate fresh air.

Every gardener has to decide how much compost to apply to various garden beds, and you have to take into account the nature and health of your soil and the crops you plan to grow. It is a process of mindful attention to discover how much fertile compost your crops need. If you are new to composting, you might begin by applying about eight cubic feet of compost per one hundred square feet of garden bed, or a generous two wheelbarrowfuls per bed.

Although almost all of the nutrients your garden needs are available in well-made organic compost, when it is time to prepare and dress a garden bed it is a good idea to apply a dusting of dry, organic fertilizers as well, to build a good nutrient base on your home soil. This supplement application is made once or twice a year along with the addition of good compost. Together these ingredients form the heart and soul of garden fertility and they work at the same time to break up clay, bind together granular soil, improve drainage, and retain moisture. Good garden fertility helps soil warm up and retain warmth and life and also keeps soil from overheating, while continuously releasing and feeding the microbiotic life of your garden ground.

Here the three groups of plant nutrients all need to be taken into account: the primary trio of nitrogen, phosphorus, and potassium, which Alan Chadwick called "death itself" when they were considered apart from their combined life and function in the soil; the secondary trio of calcium, sulfur, and magnesium; and the eight key trace elements that enhance microbial enzyme function in the soil. All of these nutrients serve plants best when they are offered in combination with one another. The best source of most of these nutrients is compost, but additional amendments are sometimes added to fertilize the soil for specific plant health.

It has been a long-standing goal for me as an organic gardener to use as few amendments imported from beyond the garden as possible. For students of meditation as well, the richness of wisdom emerges from a well-cultivated moment stimulated by just enough outside inspiration to keep the heart and mind open. Feeding plants and ministering to their well-being is intimately

Fertilizer or Amendment?

There is a simple distinction between these two terms: a fertilizer's primary purpose is to provide nutrients to plants, while a soil amendment is a material added to your garden to enhance soil physical qualities or microbial activity.

Compost itself is both a fertilizer and an amendment, so if you base your soil health program on well-decomposed compost you are offering a balanced fertilizer to your garden soil and your plants.

In choosing which soil amendments to add to your garden be sure to consider these questions:
- Is this amendment safe for me to handle?
- Will it affect the safety of the food I want to grow?

- What will it do to or for soil organisms? Here I appreciate the suggestion from the Necessary Trading Company that you ask the earthworm. By putting an amendment near earthworms you can easily see if the worms incorporate the product or wiggle away from it.
- What is the ecological tread of this product? Does its mining or manufacture harm the environment? Does it lead to air or water pollution? How energy intensive is it to make?

(For some reputable sources for organically derived soil fertilizers and amendments see the resource sections for chapters 3, 4, and 6.)

connected to taking care of garden ground and understanding how different fertilizers and amendments function in the soil. So when I spread rock phosphate mined from quarries in southern Florida, I know that the three-year slow release of phosphorus our garden receives from this fertilizer sweetens our heavy clay soil. I also know that I am borrowing from the bedrock fertility of the Southeast to grow fine cabbages and strong-stemmed lilies in our coastal California garden.

Nitrogen is usually considered the first of nutrients, since all soil life requires significant quantities of nitrogen to thrive. The primary natural source of nitrogen is the atmosphere, which is 78 percent nitrogen. Since plants cannot utilize nitrogen in this gaseous form it must be added to the garden as a natural amendment or "fixed" by soil microorganisms. All plants of the legume family serve as hosts to mycorrhizal populations of bacteria that consolidate nitrogen from the living atmosphere and "fix" it on the roots of the legumes in tiny pink pouches of protein.

Nitrogen is responsible for leaf and stem growth. When there is an excess of nitrogen in the bodies of plants this is indicated by a lush, rank growth of leaves and very little flavor or fruit-set. Insects begin to attack plants that exude excess nitrogen. Surplus nitrogen also promotes the growth of soil-borne disease like blight, scab, and powdery mildew, so be careful as you add nitrogen to your garden beds that you do not add too much.

There are many organic sources of nitrogen that can be applied to the soil, compost, and plant community to boost fertility. All aged or composted animal manure is an excellent source of nitrogen, particularly seasoned cow, horse, sheep, rabbit, and fowl manure. Feather; horn-and-hoof meal; blood meal; the seed meals such as cottonseed, linseed, and soybean meal; and fish scraps are also high sources of nitrogen.

Potassium, the second vital macronutrient, is called the Great Regulator of the green world since it has the unique function of regulating the metabolic processes in plants. In particular, potassium is involved in photosynthesis and protein synthesis in leaves and in the cellular structure of the stalks, and starch synthesis in the roots. When potassium is lacking in soil, root health is affected and deficient plants are prone to pest attack. Since potassium is not present in the soil itself it is an excellent practice to nourish your garden beds with natural sources of potassium.

soil ⟶

All animal manures and most plant residues, like hay and straw, are good potassium fertilizers. I like to apply potassium to the soil by mulching with manure and straw; I also apply granite dust, wood ash gathered after a slow-burning fire, bracken fern or greensand to the compost pile, from which it is eventually incorporated into the soil. Greensand is an undersea deposit, an iron-potassium silicate containing traces of all the minerals available in sea-water. Other good sources of potassium are rice hulls, well-decomposed banana peels, seaweed, cocoa bean hulls, corncobs, and molasses. I have mulched heavy clay soil with rice hulls and cocoa bean shells over the years to very good effect. In combination with well-digested compost, they seem to both lighten the soil and strengthen root growth.

Phosphorus has several functions in the plant, but its primary role is to encourage strong flower and seed formation and to assist in the transfer of energy from one point to another. While nitrogen is the most mobile of the soil nutrients, phosphorus is the least. In addition, phosphorus undergoes some of the most complex chemical interactions of all the soil fertility elements. Organic matter and biological activity are the two main keys to unlocking phosphorus in your soil. When phosphorus is released by decaying organisms, it is readily available for plant take-up. Fungi also pick up phosphorus and carry it through the soil. In addition, many soil organisms release organic acids as they metabolize and these acids help dissolve inorganic phosphorus. Good garden sources of phosphorus are colloidal rock phosphate (mined from Florida rock deposits), bone meal, bracken fern, buckwheat and clovers, and, in particular, compost enhanced with these ingredients.

Phosphorus and nitrogen have a strong complementary relationship and they also compete for take-up by plant roots. All three macronutrients work in concert, nitrogen affecting the green stems and leaves of plants, phosphorus influencing the formation of flowers and seeds, and potassium, the roots and leaves. Nitrogen is a primary component of proteins, potassium helps synthesize the proteins, and phosphorus determines whether those proteins are synthesized.

Both excess and deficiency of these nutrients are very hard on plants, and the plants will display symptoms you can use to diagnose the problem. But other problems like pests can produce the same symptoms, so you need to proceed judiciously and with a soft, open mind. Sometimes there is no disaster at all.

An old friend who is an excellent grower and advocate of ecological horticulture paused in horror at the edge of a Green Gulch bed of summer leeks one July morning. "What *happened*?" Richard asked in obvious distress, since the entire leek crop was a dusty purple red color. I laughed in delight, for this leek does not lack phosphorus in the least; instead, it is an old French heritage leek, 'Bleu de Solaize,' noted and prized for its striking reddish-purple color and a pride and joy of the farm. So be careful before you claim disaster.

The secondary macronutrients of good garden culture work in accord with the primary trio of N, P, K. Calcium is involved in the metabolism of both soil and plants. Alkaline soil, or soil made basic with calcium fertilizers, aids soil

Macronutrient Deficiencies

When nitrogen is deficient in the soil and plant community this deficiency is revealed first by the bottom leaves of plants. These leaves become yellowish and their growth is restricted. The older leaves above them turn orange, red, and a ghastly purple with chartreuse-yellow undertones. Eventually, the leaves wilt, droop, and fall off.

It is important to remember that there are other causes for these same symptoms, including low temperatures, drought, waterlogged soil, hardpan, a choke of weeds nearby, wireworms, potato eel worm, cutworms, and bark injury. So be sure to carefully check your soil culture before claiming nitrogen deficiency.

When potassium is deficient in plant roots the plant is stunted. This is particularly true of grains and trees. The leaves take on a bluish-green cast with yellow showing between their mid-rib veins. The tips of plant leaves grow brown and the leaf looks scorched, with prominent brown spots showing at the edges. Even though the symptoms of potassium deficiency are quite clear, frost, drought, wind, waterlogged soil, hardpan soil, aphids, root rots on beans and clover, botrytis on gooseberries, potato virus diseases, and bark injuries to trees all produce the same symptoms.

Lack of phosphorus is indicated by plants failing to thrive and mature. Their leaves grow reddish-purple and their seeds do not fill out. The same weather and pest-damage factors that parallel the symptoms of nitrogen and potassium deficiencies also mimic the signs of a lack of phosphorus. Be sure to really check for these other possible causes before deciding for a nutrient deficiency. Also check the pH of the soil, because if it is too far from neutral, the nutrient may be present in the soil but unavailable to the plants.

bacteria in the uptake and release of nitrogen. It also aids soil structure by opening up seized soil and neutralizing excess acids in the soil.

Natural, organic sources of calcium are plentiful and varied. Because of the high incidence of viral disease in cattle and my resistance to using by-products of the slaughter industry, I avoid one of the highest sources of natural calcium, bone meal. All rock minerals of dolomitic origin and some feldspars, calcites, and apatites contain good natural calcium, as does limestone, ground egg-shells, and oystershell meal. Gypsum, a mined calcium sulfate, also contains about 23 percent calcium. As in human nutrition, calcium gives tone and rigor to plants, and when it is lacking stems droop, plant growth wanes, new leaves curl and produce yellow spots, and the roots of the calcium-deprived plant are stunted and weak.

Sulfur in the soil changes the pH by acidifying the ground. Sulfur is generally available in most compost-enriched soils. It is a vital component of proteins and vitamins and is essential for fixing nitrogen on the roots of garden legumes. Gypsum is a good natural source of sulfur, as is compost and other organic matter. Elemental sulfur, called flowers of sulfur, is available as an industrial waste product from mining. It is almost pure sulfur, so it must be applied lightly. Sulfur deficiencies are indicated by older leaves growing yellow and lax, eventually falling off your plants, very much as in the case of nitrogen deficiency. Sulfur deficiency also causes plant stems to grow hard and thin, almost reedlike.

Magnesium in the soil aids in the germination of seeds and is also an essential component of green chlorophyll, which stimulates the production of sugars and starches in plants. Magnesium is available in rock dust from deposits rich in serpentine, mica, and dolomitic limestone. Magnesium deficiency is signaled by a yellowing of leaves followed by brilliant tints of color in the chlorophyll-starved leaves. Magnesium starvation also causes fruit to wither and drop.

The trace minerals or micronutrients, iron, zinc, boron, copper, manganese, molybdenum, chlorine, and cobalt, are also important sources of fertility essential for enhancing plant, animal, and microbial enzyme function. Micronutrients are best applied to the soil and plant community through regular applications of organic matter and rock minerals, rather than by special amendments.

Sir Albert Howard, a master composter and one of the founders of modern organic agriculture, insisted that a good farm or garden "manures itself." Especially when compost is generated from the vast banquet of ingredients provided by every healthy soil, and is then returned to the soil, spreading and increasing the wealth of the garden, this is so. You can always enhance the health of particular plants in your garden by fertilizing them with a complement of macro- or micronutrient ingredients or by adding trace elements, just as you boost your own health with supplements and vitamins. But the abiding health of the garden comes from compost, containing in its complexity all of the necessary nutrients for soil and plant health.

❖ ❖ ❖

Serving tea to a well-esteemed guest in a ceremonial and respectful way is a time-honored tradition in the Zen world. Bodhidharma, the original Zen master, sat in concentrated wall-gazing meditation in a cave in China for nine years before beginning to teach. It is said that during those years his meditation was often plagued by drowsiness, so one apocryphal tale claims that he ripped off his eyelids and tossed them over his shoulder rather than succumb to sleep. From Bodhidharma's eyelids sprang the first tea plant on Chinese soil.

Although compost and manure teas are not administered to plants to arouse the sleeping green world, they are respectfully offered in order to boost the plant's immune system, suppress foliar disease, and speed the breakdown of toxins in plants by serving them beneficial microbes and vital enzymes as well as nutrients in a soluble and readily accessible form. You can brew these teas for your plants anaerobically, by soaking your tea ingredients in water, or aerobically, by circulating air and water through your compost or manure source.

The easiest way to prepare tea is anaerobically, adding two to three cups of well-decomposed compost or live manure for each gallon of water and letting these ingredients "steep" for about three days. If you put your fertilizing source in a porous "tea bag" made out of muslin, burlap, or nylon there will be less rough material to filter out. Then you can scoop out or drain the water away from the compost or manure and side dress your garden plants or strain the water well through filters and spray it on your plants as a foliar feed.

The only difficulty with this method is that you have to be quick. After a few days of soaking, the air-loving or aerobic bacteria in the fertility source of the tea will absorb all the oxygen out of the water, leaving you a fetid and foul-smelling brew, so serve your compost or manure tea to your garden plants while it is still fresh.

Making aerobic tea depends on setting up a way to circulate air and water through your source of fertility. Peter created a slightly Rube Goldberg-esque but very effective compost tea system at Green Gulch many years ago by stacking two fifty-five-gallon drums on top of each other and circulating water with

Liquid Fertilizers for the Home Garden

Manure Tea

Tea made from animal manure decays faster than compost tea and delivers a strong dose of nitrogen, phosphorus, and potassium to your plants. Horse manure is especially high in these nutrients, while cow manure provides valuable humic acids that help plants ward off disease. Remember to use your manure tea quickly after it has steeped for a few days so that your plants receive the maximum benefit.

Compost Tea

Richer in humic acids and beneficial microbes, compost tea is enhanced by longer brewing times and by the incorporation of air in the tea-making process. Once your tea is rich and dark (after four to seven days) strain the tea and spray it in a dilution of one part tea, five parts of water on the top and underside of your plant leaves for enhanced disease protection. Repeat every month or so during the growing season.

Indigenous Microbe Tea

In recent gatherings of the Ecological Farming Association groundbreaking research has shown that by gathering native microbes from healthy garden or forest soil or from vigorous plants and fermenting these microbes, you can culture a local strain of inoculant for your garden plants, helping to increase soil and compost health.

Worm Tea

At the Edible Schoolyard we love to harvest ripe worm compost and steep a few cups of it for two days or so in a muslin bag immersed in a five-gallon bucket of cold water. The kids make sure not a single worm gets into this tea. After the brew is steeped we strain it through cheese-cloth and apply it by watering can to all of our kid-started greenhouse seedlings. Worm tea gives these young plants a dramatic boost, and we apply it once a month from spring to fall.

a small pump from drum to drum through a bag of finished compost until he had a wonderful brew of tea to serve our 150-foot-long rows of thirsty Zen vegetables. Many inventive, and far simpler, models of aerobic tea makers are now commercially available for the home gardener. But it is simplest of all to make good manure and compost teas in your backyard without any mechanical assistance at all.

✦   ✦   ✦

Of the many ways to feed and build garden soil, one of the simplest is to introduce a system of green manure cover cropping. Green manure plantings are crops grown and planted to build soil fertility and to increase organic matter directly in the garden. Green manures have multiple benefits. In the cold season they serve as an insulating blanket for naked winter soil while their roots push deep into the subsoil to pull up valuable minerals and nutrients, which are consolidated in the green stems and leaves of the plants. Green manure crops are also planted to condition soil as well as to protect the surface of the land from weeds and erosion, while those in the legume family also fix nitrogen.

When we first began to cultivate the soil of Green Gulch we encountered an impenetrable firmament, a hardpan barrier of compressed soil formed over millennia that allowed us to penetrate into the ground four inches deep at most. We became well-known in the local tool store as the "fork-busting Zen students," a testimony earned from the record number of splay-tined digging forks that we destroyed in our endeavor to open seized ground.

In those first years we nicked away at our soil, like mosquitoes biting an iron bull. But it was only by planting a green manure cover crop that we were finally able to work the soil. Of particular value in cultivating our seized earth was *Melilotus alba* or sweet white clover, a deep-rooting biennial green manure crop with fibrous, nitrogen-fixing roots that we saved for our tightest ground.

I will never forget the day we disked in that first sweet white clover field. The clover had been growing for more than a year, along with legions of other deep-rooting weeds. We were working with horses that season, our powerful team of black Percherons named Snip and Jerry. They pushed into this field with Peter behind them on the plow. The sweet clover, growing higher than the upper traces of the team's harness, shuddered as the horses entered. Snip and Jerry snatched at fat clover buds as they worked. They chewed and pulled, straining through the thick field. I stood in the shadow line of the cypress windbreak, staring at the black soil being turned over by the team and remembering a line of poetry from William Everson:

> Before my feet the ploughshare rolls the earth,
> Up and over,
> Splitting the loam with a soft tearing sound.

Many green manure plants have complex flowers rich in nectar and pollen that attract populations of beneficial insects to the garden. These insects feed on the plant nectar and prey on pestiferous insects. In turn, beneficial insects also serve as valuable natural pollinators in the garden ecosystem.

Once green manure crops begin to flower and set seed, it is time to harvest or incorporate them back into your soil. I usually harvest or dig in my green manure when it is about 15–20 percent in flower because once the seed of the cover crop begins to set and ripen, most of the nourishment of the plant is drawn up and into the seed, where it is consolidated. When the seed of green manure begins to ripen, the life cycle of the plant comes to a close. You also do not want the cover crop to reseed the plot on its own and become a weedy problem.

If you harvest your green manure from the surface of your garden bed and take all of that good, rich top growth to the compost pile, you will be able to replant your garden bed quite soon, whereas if you dig the green manure *into* your garden bed and let it decompose in place you will have to wait anywhere from one to several months before you can plant in the same soil.

If your green manure cover crop is a legume, you can cut the tops of the legumes and take this green material to the compost pile, leaving the roots so their stored nitrogen can be released into the soil to feed the soil microbial population and to serve as fertilizer for the roots of the next generation of plants. If you choose to incorporate your green manure directly into the bed where it was grown, it is a good idea to knock the crop down first with a grass whip or a small scythe and then to chop it into smaller pieces, to accelerate decomposition. While the green manure is decomposing it is not a good idea to replant your bed, because all of the soil microbes in the bed are tied up digesting the turned-in crop and will not be available to help establish and sustain new growth.

Whenever I garden I love to run a portion of the beds to cover crop throughout every season of the year. In the summer about 10 percent of a garden may be in summer cover, planted to nourish an overused bed, to suppress weeds on a new bed, or to serve as a source of pollen and nectar for hungry beneficial insects. Fast-growing crops can be seeded and dug back into the soil or taken to the compost pile within a two-month-long turnaround cycle. There is a great variety to choose from, each conveying special gifts. Buckwheat helps to smother weeds and is a fine accumulator of phosphorus, crimson flax fiberizes the soil with its extensive root system and has glorious clear red flowers, and fenugreek is a fast-growing legume, also with beautiful flowers. A mixture of brassicas, planted when the soil is still cool, is valuable as green manure food for beneficial insects. I favor wild or cultivated radish, bishop's weed, stock, black mustard, wild arugula, and a dash of 'Dame's Rocket' for extra beauty. You might plant a bed of sunflowers—an excellent choice for beneficial insects and a delight in the garden, although it is hard to dig these glorious plants in once they begin to flower. A bed of various peas and other legumes can be grown all in a jumble and allowed to fix nitrogen in the soil, flowering with an unforgettable array of fragrant blossoms.

In mild winter climates you can cover about one-third to one-half of your garden in cover crop to nourish the soil, protect the land from wind and water erosion, feed the beneficial insects, choke out weeds, and offer the soil an abundant source of organic matter. I like to green-manure with a mix of legumes to build up nitrogen reserves in the soil and grasses to fiberize the land with their thick mat of underground roots. Some of my favorites for our mild coastal winters (from early November until April) are rye, winter wheat, oats, or barley for grain and fibrous roots, to be cut and harvested before they set seed, and legumes like vetch, Austrian peas, bell beans, fava beans, and crimson clover and other varieties of clover.

If your soil is hungry for mineral wealth an excellent way to apply slow-releasing rock powder fertilizers, like rock phosphate, is to spread them in the compost heap or, easier still, on the ground when you sow your long-season green manure crops. Many green manure plants can access the otherwise unavailable nutrients in rock powders and make these fertilizers available to the plants that will follow the green manure cycle.

Another excellent way to spread the wealth of both organic and inorganic materials is by top-dressing your soil with mulch. The primary advantage of spreading organic mulch such as leaf mold, or rotted leaves, ground-up oyster shells, well-decomposed compost or manure, dry grass, hay, or straw on the surface of your soil is that these ingredients help to build soil humus, especially around perennial plants that can take up the slower release of surface nutrients more completely than fast-growing annuals.

Mulch helps to protect the surface of your soil from drying out by balancing against sudden swings in soil temperature, and by preventing soil saturation and nutrient leaching after heavy rains. Mulch also reduces wind and water erosion of your ground and reduces or even prevents certain soil-borne diseases by protecting your plants from rain splashing on naked soil. Organic mulch recycles lawn and garden waste while increasing retention and availability of nutrients and it feeds earthworms and other macro and micro soil organisms while it conditions soil.

158

All this said, I confess that I am not a heavy fan of mulching, except on perennial beds and in the orchard. In soggy Bay Area winters a heavy mulch can actually prevent the garden from breathing and drying out. I am also careful not to apply mulches that have a wide carbon ratio such as raw sawdust or wood chips, as they can tie up enough soil nitrogen in their decomposition to adversely affect plant nutrition, even though this problem can be remedied by spreading a rich source of nitrogenous manure or compost underneath the woody top mulch.

Inorganic mulches such as black plastic, landscape fabric, or gravel and other stone topdressings are excellent for warming soils, choking weeds, and retaining moisture. Because these materials do not supply nutrients to your soil you might underdress them with a few inches of good compost before applying them. Also, remember when you apply these mulches, especially those of stone, they are difficult to remove.

If you plan to use mulch, it is good to follow a seasonal approach. In cool spring climates rake back your thick winter mulch so that your soil can warm and breathe, and wait until your soil is in good heart before mulching heat-loving annuals. Choose light-colored summer mulches to reflect heat in hot climates, while in cool summers, mulch with darker materials, like the cocoa

Hot Shit

My favorite way to incorporate animal manure (from hot rabbit pellets to chicken manure, including sheep and goat manure and large-animal manure from horses and cows) is to run these nitrogen-rich manures through a hot compost pile.

However, another excellent way to add manure to your garden is to spread it directly on the ground in the winter before the land freezes so that it can be broken down by soil organisms to build strong reserves of soil humus. If you dust rock phosphate over your animal manure you will minimize nitrogen loss and enhance the biological availability of the phosphorus.

It is best to work with manure that you know the source of to avoid pesticide, antibiotic, or hormone contamination. Since fresh manure contains a high concentrate of soluble nitrates and phosphates, always be careful not to spread manure uphill from a drinking well or on land adjoining open surface water sources.

Fresh animal manure releases its nutrients to your soil over a long period of time. It is best not to plant root crops or potatoes on manured land for six months since the manure may burn these crops. It is also important not to add fresh manure to a leguminous crop since the soluble nitrates in the manure will suppress nitrogen fixation.

Quid de utilitate loquar stercorandi?
Oh, how may I extol the merit of manure?
Cato the Elder, 234–149 BCE

bean hulls that we use at the Edible Schoolyard. Not only will your garden smell like Charlie's chocolate factory, the plants will benefit from the heat conservation of their dark-hulled mulch. In the autumn it is wise to leave your soil bare as you prepare your fall garden for late-season plantings. Once your plants are established, tuck them in with a protective winter mulch to prevent soil erosion and nutrient leaching. In the winter a rich, deep layer of mulch insulates plants from alternating periods of frost and thaw. In cold climates wait until hard frost kills back your annual garden plants before applying mulch and in your cold climate perennial garden cut back all diseased plant parts and mulch well around the crowns of these plants.

In all seasons remember that rodents, slugs, and snails love to hide under thick drifts of mulch. Even though your garden is covered and protected, be sure to continue investigating your plants for potential pest and plant disease damage.

✢   ✢   ✢

In the excitement and energetic exchange that occurs as you spread the wealth of organic fertilizers on your soil it is also well to remember what Suzuki Roshi loved to call the nothingness of the ground. "Emptiness is the garden where you cannot see anything," he taught. "It is actually the mother of everything, from which everything will come."

Soil health and fertility are delicate matters, mysterious and changeable, like the composition of the living earth itself. In honor of this mystery, one of my favorite stories is the tale of van Helmont's seventeenth-century willow tree. Curious about what plants actually extracted from the soil in order to thrive, van Helmont did an experiment. He planted a five-pound willow sapling in a tub with two hundred pounds of healthy, humus-rich soil. For five years he fed his willow tree nothing but rainwater. At the end of this period van Helmont's willow weighed 169 pounds. And what about the soil? The soil weighed 200 pounds, minus 2 ounces.

Van Helmont's willow and his tub of earth are a living tribute to the mysterious nothingness of soil that Suzuki Roshi invoked. But van Helmont's willow is also a testimony to the power of curiosity, to the mind of the gardener who never leaves anything alone and always wants to try a new experiment, even if the experiment leads to a confounding surprise. Life into death into life, gardeners celebrate the nothingness of fertile soil enhanced with compost from the breakdown ball, soil that somehow transmutes rainwater, sunlight, two ounces of black earth, and long-rooted mystery into supple, green willow wands.

CHAPTER 5

TENDING THE GARDEN

Bare Noting

ONE OF MY FAVORITE TREATS IS TO WALK BY MYSELF IN THE garden late at night when the moon is full. I like to go out in late spring, before the cold fog of the Pacific Ocean lays claim to summer nights. Sometimes our cat, Blackjack, follows along behind me, at the outer edge of my moonlight shadow, his muscular tail held erect, the stealthy pads of his paws sending up little puffs of dust as we descend the thin ribbon of road unwinding into the heart of the night garden.

The land is altered after dark, at once more welcoming and more inhospitable. My habitual bearings fail me and my senses stretch to attention, seeking access between the folds of the dark, into that unmarked place where the slow, green exhalation of plants rises up into the mind of night.

At the edge of the garden, where the cultivated row slips into a jagged mosaic of stinging nettle and red-veined hemlock, the cat lies down under a stand of silver wormwood in spilled dregs of moonlight. Even during the day I am cautious in the presence of this ancient medicine plant. Wormwood, or *Artemisia absinthium*, is said to counteract the bite of the sea dragon and to steady the nerves. It has been taken for centuries to relieve gout and to treat wounds, bruises, and sprains, as well as to calm grievous pain. The dark green essential oil of wormwood contains a trace of narcotic poison if taken in excess, and it is the special ingredient in absinthe.

At night the garden drops below daylight language and murmurs in an older tongue, in voices of wormwood and rue, black cohosh and henbane, reminding me that the plants of the garden attend to me as well as allowing me to tend them. In the berry patches, orchards, and vegetable, herb, and flower beds that surround our homes, medicine, food, and poison abide together in a deep-rooted tangle.

All the Artemisia plants in the garden—wormwood, tarragon, southernwood, and mugwort—are under the dominion of Artemis, Greek goddess of the moon and of the hunt, and guardian of the sovereign chastity of those who choose to travel in her band of solitaries. The plants of Artemis all carry her unmistakable signature: finely cut silver foliage, acrid scent, and abidingly bitter taste. Technically, all Artemisias are classified as the "bitter herbs." Their medicine is strong and lasting, working on the procreative organs as well as on the mind. Some Artemisias cause contractions of the uterus and clear the womb, while others stimulate the menstrual cycle and bring vivid dreams of Eros. All light a path through the midnight copse, welcoming night hunters home to the garden.

✤   ✤   ✤

To tend a garden well and to practice meditation are both ways to cultivate attention. The word "attention" comes from the Old French *atendre*, meaning to stretch toward, or to extend. The Sanskrit word *tantra* is related to the French root, *tantra*, meaning to stretch out and weave together, like the pattern of Artemisia foliage interwoven with moonlight.

The garden helps me stretch my attention and extend myself toward what I may not always notice or even want to see, especially if I am hurried. Attention is active; moving deliberately, it settles on its object while keeping a wide view. In order to cultivate a mind that is stable, deliberate, and inclusive, and in order to see into the heart of the green world, a naked, unobstructed attention to what is right here is required. A practice from the time of the Buddha known as bare noting advocates just such an active attention, the foundation of mindful awareness.

Bare noting is grounded in bringing your senses to what is in front of you, and noticing—without judging, reacting, or responding to—what is already present. It is really not necessary to carry on an endless inner dialogue evaluating what you note. "Return to what is already there," advises one modern Buddhist teacher, "and rest."

This "resting" can be difficult, especially when the bare daylight noting of your garden reveals that a young deer has been sleeping in the thicket of Artemis's wormwood and has probably been sashaying out in the rosy-fingered dawn to sample the long rows of tender 'Ermosa' lettuce that is just sizing up. You never would have noticed the deer's trace at night, but in the daylight all is revealed. Everything in you will want to rush into the sacred wormwood tangle and prune back the plants, slashing down the deer's shelter with your sharp shears and unquiet mind.

But resist, at least for the duration of a few breaths. Restrain your mind and hands, return to what is already there in your garden, and rest. Receive the bare object of your attention, the slender, bent stalks of the silvery wormwood, and, bare of labeling or desire, note what is. Breathe in and out and rest. Mindfulness texts from shortly after the Buddha's time extol the virtue of bare noting or bare attention for its ability to help ardent mindfulness meditators know the mind, shape the mind, and free the mind. Just slowing down, breathing deeply, and noting what is right in front of you allows things to speak for themselves without interruption or interpretation.

"Silver branches, bent twigs." Stay with this bare noting for five or six breaths at least, and then note the changes that occur within your body and mind as your attention grows stable and quiet. At first you see the branches and twigs. Then the mind moves on and sees change: "Oh, these branches were bent by *something*. By what? By a deer, probably." Stay with this awareness. Stretch your attention toward the awareness of physical sensations and note what is occurring in you, even for a moment. "Oh, no! A deer . . . bad news for the lettuce." And underneath this worry, rest a breath's worth or so and note the change in your own body and mind. "Pounding heart, anxious mind." Then return to what is already there, and rest, breathing in and out, in the thicket of Artemis.

Slowing down and coordinating your breath with what you note and what you feel may give you a little breathing room in your life. The mind is shaped and freed by moments like this, by times of spaciousness and attention.

With the practice of bare noting, your garden deepens all around you. When you slow down and see what is actually going on, you may even find that you feel less victimized by and separate from the garden you love and from all of its creatures. Let whatever reminds you to pay attention also remind you to breathe deeply and look deeply; then, without judging or reacting, receive what is in front of you.

With the stability of mindfulness and the practice of bare noting, a clear perception of your garden arises in you quite naturally. Attention is made of stability and clarity, woven together and reaching out from your body and mind and into the heart of the living garden. Attention and clarity call each other up, like wormwood whispering to the moonlight, and Artemis summoning the shadows of the night forest to guide her hunter's steps.

Bare noting stabilizes your heart and mind and lets you receive what is; its companion, clear comprehension, allows you to respond, to act. At some point you get up, walk over to the wormwood patch in full daylight, and clearly see, without needing to rush into battle, that yes, a young deer *has* been sleeping in this very wormwood thicket. Clearly seeing what is going on calls for seeing that the garden you tend today as solid ground is actually in constant flux and change, groundless and boundless as well as green and growing. Bare noting and clear comprehension reveal this fundamental law, but how you respond depends on you. You may prune the thicket, not forgetting that pests like the lettuce-loving deer will always be with you no matter what, or you may choose to leave the thicket profoundly alone and stretch protective nylon netting above your lettuce bed instead, knowing that in this lifetime you will never fathom the mind or appetite of black-tailed deer.

No matter how you choose to respond, ground your action in bare noting and clear comprehension. And no matter how busy you are as you tend your garden, take some time to sit by the Artemisias at night and forget everything you know. Breathe in and out with the invisible plants of the garden, and receive the raw medicine of stability and change. Return to what is already there, green and growing in a mighty tangle all around you, and rest.

Water So the Soil Can Dry Out

I DIDN'T REALIZE HOW SICK MY FATHER-IN-LAW WAS AT THE END of his life until I began to dig up his beloved backyard garden a few days after his death. Charlie had been struggling with leukemia for almost seven years. He was a contender, fiercely bonded to life and to his family and community, who never took off his boxing gloves.

Preparing for the flood of family and friends we knew would come over to pay their final respects to him at the family home in Trenton, New Jersey, I noticed the grounds around the back of the house needed work. It was mid-August and the family had been with Charlie in and out of the hospital for weeks, so the garden was in a flat wilt. This was just the place for me, a backyard refuge, out of the way and bone dry.

I found an old shovel and a battered fork and began to dig. The soil was compacted dust, as if forty circus elephants had been tethered to that very spot for decades. I chipped away at the dry flanks of this abandoned garden and remembered Charlie years ago watering his riot of 'State Fair' zinnias and prize Jersey tomatoes in this very same spot.

It took me two solid days just to loosen the soil in his garden, going a few inches down at a time, coaxing the ground to accept small, tentative sips of water. Even though it is best not to cultivate soil when it is too dry or too wet, I had only this time and ground, so I pried open a shallow seam in the dirt and watched the water trickle into the dry earth. An hour or so later, when the soil was softer and more receptive, I pried deeper with fork and hose.

Slowly the garden began to take in moisture again like a dehydrated soldier crawling out on all fours to drink from a muddy puddle. The taste of water revived the garden's memory and it woke up my memory as well. As the earth began to suck long draughts of cool water down its parched throat, and Peter joined me in the garden, I remembered Charlie as he had been: a legendary baker in the Trenton area, where he and his wife, Kate, ran the Hermitage Pastry Shop for thirty-seven years. I thought of him kneading dark pumpernickel dough, his arms dusted with flour, as Peter worked alongside me folding old horse manure and decayed maple leaves into the earth of his father's garden.

Little by little the soil began to swell with new life, humming a slow, fat summer song. When it was time, we planted a beautiful white memorial rose, 'French Lace,' for Charlie in his garden. The earth was warm. A fragrance of yeast and sweet water, and of sorrow and delight, rose up around us in billows on the late-summer wind.

❖   ❖   ❖

Every garden is unique, quirky, distinct, and disobedient, just like every gardener, and no one can really tell you how to water your garden. Yet all well-watered gardens have a common song that greets you the moment you walk through the gate. Watering is a form of courtship rooted in affection and experience, and in the desire for garden and gardener to know each other inside out. Watering shows you the dry corners and boggy sumps of your land and the needs of the plants you sow, reap, and dream of at night. Careful watering also depends on raw intuition and on trusting that if you make a mistake with irrigation, the garden will forgive you and direct you toward the best remedy. Ride the swell and ebb of garden irrigation with a loose rein, and trust your garden to teach you how to navigate the way.

Many years ago Alan Chadwick gave us succinct instructions on watering: "Water so that the soil can dry out," he suggested, with a wicked twinkle in his eye. Good irrigation practice seeks that delicate equilibrium and balance between applying too much water and too little. Watch the surface of your soil shift and change in sudden hot wind or summer downpour, aim for the Middle Way between drought and deluge, and keep alert. Water so the soil can dry out, and when the garden is dry, water again.

Remember that life is animated water, as the Russian scientist Vladimir Vernadsky observed. Three-quarters of the body of the earth is covered by water, alive and circulating, while our own bodies are at least 60 percent water. "Chemically speaking," runs a passage from the 1846 *Farmers' Almanac*, "a human being is 45 pounds of carbon diffused through 5½ pails of water." From the depths of our cells, in the moisture of blood and sweat, tears and saliva, water speaks to water.

The ancient water cycle that animates all life turns as a huge gyre, a living wheel of precipitation, absorption, transpiration, evaporation, condensation—and more precipitation. In addition there is another water cycle that moves within the earth. Moisture travels through the soil by three distinct forces: downward by the pull of gravity, laterally by the force of attraction that charges every living particle in the soil matrix, and upward through the root system of plants by osmotic pressure and capillary action.

Water shifts the shape of land as well as its own shape, as it moves and as it changes from solid (ice), to liquid (water), and to gas (steam vapor). The atoms within the water molecule also shift endlessly and incredibly rapidly: the oxygen and hydrogen that make up a single molecule of water may change partners ten billion times a second! Because of its loose and ever-changing patterns of hydrogen bonding, water is the universal solvent, surrounding other atoms and molecules and hooking up with them at their various points of electrical charge.

Living water in garden soil is like a vast liquid net, constantly shifting shape while maintaining connection with the microbial and plant life. Now and then this underground web of water is revealed above the surface of the soil. Just as the sun begins to warm the ground, the gossamer trap nets of field spiders in the late autumn garden light up, shining with dew. The pores of the soil exhale stored warmth and water vapor and the moisture is captured momentarily in the spiders' webs. This glistening, aboveground web echoes the invisible network of water, soil, and air running just beneath the surface of the ground.

＊　　＊　　＊

In late autumn at Green Gulch Farm, after the season of the trap-net spiders, the fields are planted to a winter cover crop of bell beans and vetch, and gardeners pray for rain. Once the first precipitation of the season enters the soil, rain moves down through the finely textured surface ground, displacing air and filling the pores of the land with water.

Eventually all of the soil pores in the upper horizon of the garden are filled and there is a continual downward movement of water into unsaturated earth. When this downward motion ceases, the ground is said to be at its field capacity. Water oozes out of the macropores of the soil and is replaced with air, while the fine capillary tubes or micropores in the ground remain filled with water. Once field capacity is reached this soil water is actively available to plants.

The living web of water that links plant roots with soil microbes and soil nutrients is always moving, responding to weather and climate, to soil conditions, and to the thirst of plants. In a well-cultivated and adequately hydrated soil this web of water flows across the membranes of the fine feeder roots of thirsty plants and is drawn up by these root hairs into the body of the plant. Roots are continuously being drained of their contents by the upward pull and pump of osmosis and by capillary action. In fact, in order for the pump to work at all and for water to climb up the green stems of plants, root hairs must be partially empty.

Once soil water enters the green tubes of a plant, it moves as a river of moisture up through the roots, stems, and leaves and back out to the atmosphere through the surface stomata (a Greek word meaning "tongue") that line the undersides of leaves. As water transpires or is breathed out through the stomata, it escapes as a cool vapor, stimulating the plant to pump up more water from the depths of the soil. As water moves through plants it holds them upright and turgid, it delivers soil-based nutrients to them, and it contributes to photosynthesis, where carbon dioxide and water are broken down in the presence of sunlight to create sugars, starches, and proteins in the body of plants. As a by-product of photosynthesis plants release oxygen and water vapor back out to the atmosphere and the cycle continues to turn.

The Art and Practice of Watering the Garden

I confess that I am a hand-waterer by preference, taught that way by my gardening teachers, and I always return to this practice even though I also water with drip irrigation, overhead oscillation, and occasional deep furrow watering. Hand-watering and weeding are meditations for me, times when I slow down and see the garden and listen to its voice with fresh attention. I am most alert with a hose or a hoe in my hand.

A number of years ago we hosted a conference at Green Gulch about the lively, healing practice of horticultural therapy, especially for people who have experienced grave trauma, illness, or personal loss. Ida Cousino came to address this conference from her project of gardening with war veterans at the VA medical center in Los Angeles, California. She told us that three practices stood out as beneficial above all others: having the vets drive the tractor out on the field, inviting them to take their vegetables and flowers to the local farmers' markets, and encouraging them to water the garden by

171

hand. "Watering was especially good," Ida emphasized. "It brought the guys back down to earth."

When I hold a hose in my hand and water the soil of a newly sown bed of French haricots verts interplanted with seeds of the 'Easter Egg' radish, I am happy and free, even though the indignant garden may be shrilling at me from every corner of its domain about all the work I need to do. I focus my breathing on the curve of the water and follow the soft line of the raised bed as the water falls in an arc of gentle rain onto the surface of the soil. I know that this fine mist absorbs beneficial airborne nutrients and brings them down into the ground, and that this gentle hand-watering will prevent a hard-baked skin of soil from forming on the surface of the bed. I am linked to the heart of the world as I water, and refreshed as the new legume and radish seeds stir to life in the moist garden soil.

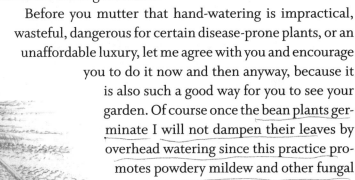

Before you mutter that hand-watering is impractical, wasteful, dangerous for certain disease-prone plants, or an unaffordable luxury, let me agree with you and encourage you to do it now and then anyway, because it is also such a good way for you to see your garden. Of course once the bean plants germinate I will not dampen their leaves by overhead watering since this practice promotes powdery mildew and other fungal disease; instead, I'll apply deep water to the surface of the soil around the roots of the plant, careful not to wet the leaves of the beans, and yes—I'll water by hand some of the time.

There are a few main principles of irrigation that I came to with a hose in my hand and that apply equally to all the ways that you choose to irrigate your garden.

- *Water the soil, not the plant.* This is a similar principle to "feed the soil, not the plant," since watering the soil ministers to that invisible web of underground microscopic life that sustains so much nutrient uptake and decomposi-

172

tion. Compost, air, and water all help to keep this network of microorganisms healthy and thriving, while they in turn nourish the plant kindom and conserve and deliver water to the roots of plants. I use this neologism "kindom" deliberately, out of a conviction that there are no "kings" in the biological order, only an allegiance of kinship and relationship. When at least two inches of the top foot of soil in your garden bed is living compost, this fertility reduces the need for irrigation by as much as 75 percent.

• *Water with a hoe, not a hose.* "Water with a *hoe*, sausage, not just with a hose!" Alan Chadwick admonished me. When the surface of a garden bed is kept stirred up and open, capillary action is increased and plants grow better. A thin stirred surface layer of soil serves as a conserving dust mulch during the growth cycle, and this fine layer of breathable mulch insulates the soil. In addition, stirred soil keeps water-thirsty weeds away from your cultivated plants.

First, water the soil and keep it in good heart as your plants grow, and then cultivate the skin of your garden with a hoe to help draw up deep water and to break up a possible "water crust" on the skin of the land. As your plants begin to get established, visit them with a hose or drip system and serve them a deep drink of water through well-cultivated ground. Hoeing when the soil is neither very wet nor very dry creates a good crumb or granular structure in the body of garden earth. This soil then has plenty of interconnected pore space available for storing air and for conducting water upward. Once you have "watered with a hoe," you can protect the skin of the earth and the web beneath by mulching.

• *Water deeply and irregularly for perennials, shallowly and steadily for annuals.* The Green Gulch garden has a rich, complex perennial garden including herbs, perennial flowers, flowering shrubs and trees, berries galore, and fruit trees. Our practice there is to water these plants deeply and infrequently in order to encourage the downward and lateral fanning out of roots that help to anchor these large-scale perennial plantings. The perennial beds are all dug to a depth of two feet and this two-foot depth is kept at field-capacity moisture during the main growing season so that the plants will reach for deep water and not send their roots up to the surface.

This deep application of water is received more readily when you do not let the soil dry out completely between waterings, as Charlie's garden demonstrated. When the top two inches of a perennial bed are dry it is probably time to deep water again. You also have to keep alert to other clues. I monitor the movement of water through garden earth by watching the plants themselves and the soil structure, and by keeping daily track of the weather. Wind, in particular, raises the water demand of plants. The life stage of the plants you are attending is also a factor. While plants are growing furiously, up until their fruiting or flowering stage, they require more water; once they are mature, their water need is less. A few hours after watering you can check the soil to see how far the water has actually penetrated into the ground.

Annual plants are not rooted as deeply as perennials, so it is wise to keep the surface of the soil moist, being sure that their roots are evenly irrigated. Usually this means watering for less time and more frequently, so this even layer of moisture can seep down into the top foot of the bed, enough to moisten the annuals' primary root system.

I check the moisture of vegetable beds by "reading the crop" to see if the plants are well watered and growing evenly. I also check moisture by using my time-honored trowel test of digging down four to six inches in a few random spots to see if the soil is uniformly moist. Although I am by nature a trusting person, I never rely on automatic watering devices. I regularly spy on them and monitor the field moisture.

♦ *Practice "one-dipper" watering.* The annual editions of *World Watch Journal* for the first years of the twenty-first century have all reported that the most severely limited resource on earth is clean, potable water. North Americans are the most lavish users of water, consuming an average of about 250 gallons of water a day, while the people of Kenya get along with a scant gallon or less each. To get even this much, some women in rural parts of Africa have to walk for almost five hours. This is consequential news, especially since no new water is being created on earth. All of the water we now consume and use for irrigation and other needs is ancient water, recycled again and again. We are living off the fossil water reserves of the ages.

When Shunryu Suzuki Roshi first came to America he taught us his "one-dipper practice" for handling and using water. When he was a monastic trainee in Japan, he ladled water for washing his hands and face, for cleaning vegetables, and for cooking. He learned always to be careful to fill his dipper half full, to pour just what he needed, and then to return the unused water to its source.

Water conservation is essential to a well-managed garden and to a well-chosen one: pick your plants with an eye to drought-resistant and low water-use plants in dry climates, and to plants that thrive with wet feet where rain is plentiful.

If your garden receives a natural excess in heavy rain or spring snowmelt, you can work with it by "sculpting your landscape for meander," as my friend Robert Kourik advises. If you have waterlogged soil, carve deep, meandering swales lower than the waterlogged area and make storage pools or small collection ponds.

You may be able to conserve and reuse household water. Even if we collected only the running tap water we waste while waiting for it to get hot we would save a huge amount of water. I know this firsthand since I do this in the summer before showering or washing dishes and then I carry this conserved water to thirsty perennials in our backyard home garden. You even may be able to set up a gray water system for your perennial, fruit, or ornamental garden. I have a verse over the kitchen sink:

> Water flows over these hands.
> May I use them skillfully
> To preserve the health of our earth.

♦ *Once you've figured out the perfect method for watering your garden, change it.* Be experimental in your gardens, and learn how to grow crops using less

175

water. If you have a bed of prize tomatoes interplanted with basil and irrigated by drip irrigation in your main garden, also choose another small site for a few of the same tomato plants and basil and try to bring them on using half the water of your main crop row. Do not rely on formulas, timers, new irrigation devices, or "foolproof" irrigation methods. Be observant of all factors as you water, and learn from your garden as you work. Experiment with water needs in your hardiest plants. Be willing to be surprised and don't generalize. Try to find an hour or so once a week to hand-water your plants, and pay attention to them as you water.

◆ *Stand out in the rain and get wet with your garden at least once a season.* Some of my best information about drainage and runoff comes from being "irrigated" by rainfall and downpour. Sometimes when I am drenched to the bone, I stand under the permeable shelter of a Monterey cypress for a moment before going inside. I follow the path of the driving rain sluicing off the dark trees, down into the heavy needle mulch at the base of the windbreaks. When I can, I set out pails to collect the nutrient-rich rainwater that is so good for making compost or horsetail tea, and while I work, I linger in the rain, getting wet along with the plants.

On these timeless rainy days the garden is alive and absorbent all around me. For a while I join the great cycle of water, being rained upon so that I may dry out, and drying out so that I can stand again, alone and empty-handed, in the softly falling rain.

Flowers Fall, Weeds Thrive

No matter how lovingly I coddle my prize Chinese delphiniums, they sulk and drop their sapphire blue petals, while the more I ignore the rank stands of tarweed and tansy just outside the gate, the more they thrive. Yet although I regret the falling of the flowers, I would be lost without the vigorous weeds of Muir Beach and their fierce teachings. For many years we kept a weather-beaten index card on the Green Gulch garden altar, inscribed with this passage from the thirteenth-century *Treasury of the True Dharma Eye* of Zen master Dogen: "Flowers fall amid our clinging, and weeds thrive amid our disdain." This has always been one of my favorite Zen aphorisms, dead accurate and true to life.

What exactly is a weed? I have never felt much resonance with the standard definition of a weed as "a plant out of place." I am irked by this parochial designation; after all, I hail from European genetic stock and my family first arrived in North America just four hundred years ago. Am I then a weedy gardener decidedly "out of place"? I do feel this way at times, especially as I stand over undisturbed native stands of thimbleberry and salal and prepare to clear them from their home place so that I can grow sleek rows of French beans and blowsy beds of Persian roses.

Weeds are powerful plants tenaciously and forthrightly *of* their place and *in* their place. They are firmly settled right where they are, and whether they are invasive exotics or native weeds, they are supremely good indicators of soil condition, climate, water flow, nutrient balance, and fertility levels in all of the many places where they grow. Weeds always indicate the history of the soil and its land use where you are gardening, so by staying close to the weeds, you can see how to work the land that you are gardening. They are made of the soil you cultivate.

In many cases, weeds are the ancestors of the garden cultivars we prize. When I hoe the long broccoli rows of our summer farm, the main weed I cultivate out is black mustard, an ancient relative of broccoli itself. I am careful to dig the mustard back into the garden, right beside its next of kin, the cultivated broccoli. Not only does black mustard indicate the particular nature of our land, it also transforms the heavy soil of the lower fields of Green Gulch into friable ground.

Where there are stands of sheep sorrel and sourgrass, yellow dock and horsetail ferns from the Carboniferous period, where there is hawkweed and knapweed, finger leaf weed and lady's thumb, wild pennyroyal and skunkweed,

I know that the soil is boggy and acidic. The weeds of this soil tell of a tight earth with little breath. Often this is lowland soil, waterlogged and poorly drained. The bottomland fields of the valley that runs directly out to the beach are populated with these acid-loving weeds and are especially rich in shepherd's purse, coastal sage, and sea plantain. These particular weeds indicate seams of salt water coursing through tight acidic soil.

If your garden is populated with acid-loving weeds, they not only indicate a soil with a low pH, they also whisper in soft, acidic tones that they themselves are valuable cultivators. In the early days of Green Gulch Farm we held digging contests to see who could harvest the longest intact yellow-dock root. I recall many contenders two feet long. This plant is an ancient cleanser of the blood and fortifier of the liver. All of the docks, associated with mighty Jupiter in ancient astrology, are plants of great strength. Dock roots are often massive. One of the highest natural sources of vitamin C and vitamin A, discernible in the lemony tang of the leaves and in the yellow-orange color of the sinewy root, dock has long been valued for its medicinal and culinary virtue. Japanese markets sell long, snaky roots of dock, but a homesick Japanese cook who dug up yellow dock and julienned it into a stir-fry had to compost her family's supper when she tasted the bitter gulf between the wild yellow dock of North America and the refined burdock cultivar *gobo*, so beloved in Japan.

Yellow dock is not only an indicator weed but also a remedy for the very conditions it thrives in. Endeavor to dig out the long, brawny roots of dock and you leave open a significant drainage channel to siphon off excess water from the field. If you leave the dock alone, its taproot opens deep channels that help to drain boggy soil. Another such remedy weed is shepherd's purse, which grows succulently on salty land. One of the most prolific collectors of salt, when tender shepherd's purse is dug back into the soil it sweetens the ground, sucking up salts and using them for organic compounds.

Other weeds clearly announce to you that your soil is sweet, or basic in its pH. Scarlet pimpernel, most clovers, chickweed, and all members of the thistle family indicate a porous, alkaline, and slightly sweet soil. These alkaline

dock

weeds make a rich compost that can be added to sour, acidic soil to raise the pH, just as acidic weeds made into compost can help drop the pH of an overly alkaline garden soil. Although the soil in one area will tend to be either sour or sweet, you may have both side by side, with the pimpernel of a California soil giving way to dock where water used to stand.

When your soil is rich, well-cultivated, and swelling with healthy crops, your land will often be populated with the weeds that Native American farmers have called "white man's footsteps." Here we find the major weeds that thrive in organic gardens like those of Green Gulch Farm, indicating a loose surface soil with ample organic matter. The weeds that follow in the "footsteps" love this rich soil: stinging nettle, chickweed, shepherd's purse, senecio, fairy scissors, Sanchez, poison hemlock, star thistle, goosefoot, mallow, and plantain. Many of these weeds are delicious to eat and some are medicine plants. When harvested for compost they build a beautiful and deep soil with their decomposing bodies.

Gardeners need to cultivate special reverence and respect for the stinging nettle, *Urtica dioica*. Like clover, nettles help to cultivate the ground where they grow. In California there is a native variety of this stinging nettle that is a potent, virile plant growing three feet high. I have felt the "sting" of the California nettle all the way through the wet pant legs of my thick canvas overalls. The nettle bears an exceedingly sharp spine arising out of a slightly swollen base on its stem. The sting delivered through the hollow, polished spine whenever the nettle plant is brushed comes from formic acid, the same material delivered by the sting of ants and bees. A natural remedy for the sting of a nettle is to rub the affected area with the crushed leaves of yellow dock. It is uncanny how dock always seems to grow in association with nettles, almost as if Divine Providence arranged a way for the nettle to be fully who it is, as long as dock is there to soothe its sting of truth.

Nettles thrive on a rich, deep soil and are one of the

highest known sources of vitamins A, C, and the B family. They are also extraordinarily high in protein. Having roughly 7 percent nitrogen in their green parts, the stinging nettle is richer in essential plant nutrients than many commercial fertilizers.

Nettles are food and they are medicine. The Tibetan saint Milarepa existed by eating only the stinging nettles that grew on his mountainside until he became "as green as the nettle itself," and in many tangka paintings where he is outside his cave meditating with his hand cupped to his ear so he can hear suffering beings calling out to him, his entire naked body glows in a delightful shade of green. And yet, valuable as this plant is for medicine and food and as a primary builder of beautiful soil, the nettle remains wild and does

The Stinging Nettle

Nettles have been prized since ancient times for their medicinal and culinary properties: they increase blood circulation, are a natural anti-asthmatic, and have been used as an old-world cure for consumption, ague, and goiter.

At Green Gulch we use the stinging nettle as a delicious soup stock base, as an ingredient in a poultice to relieve joint pain and mild arthritis, and as a simple hair rinse and stimulant for hair growth. In addition, we love to brew strong nettle tea for a quick and effective iron-rich stimulant for anemic students and pale-blooded plants. Here are some of our favorite recipes.

Nettle Soup Stock
Lou Hartman, Zen cook extraordinaire, paid steady homage to the nettle for its rich, savory broth. He called it the vegetarian's chicken soup stock and used it for rich vegetable soups and stews. To make this simple nettle soup stock, gather a few large bunches of wild nettles, being careful to wear long sleeves and thick gloves as you harvest. Rinse the nettles well and submerge them in clean, cold water brought to a quick boil

and let the broth simmer for about fifteen to twenty minutes, until your stock is as clear green and fragrant as a wild forest after late October rain. Then strain out your nettles and get to work composing your soup.

Nettle Arthritis Balm
Alan Chadwick taught us to gather young nettle greens (three or four large handfuls), two bunches of wormwood, and a handful or so of comfrey leaves and mash them all together with a large mortar and pestle then spread the poultice or paste on a clean cloth and bandage aching joints with the mixture.

Nettle Hair Rinse
Simmer one ounce of fresh nettle leaves in one cup of water for fifteen minutes. If you have dark hair, add one-half ounce of rosemary to your mix; if your hair is fair, substitute chamomile for rosemary. Then strain and let your decoction cool, and after washing your hair, rinse with this nettle brew to stimulate hair growth and to keep your hair luxurious and shiny.

not adapt well to being sown or managed by gardeners. Nettles grow from perennial underground rhizomes, and as they send up new tendrils from the underworld in the spring, the stinging nettle is a yearly reminder that it is far too ancient and dynamic a plant ever to be tamed.

❖   ❖   ❖

You can tell a lot about a garden and about its gardeners by monitoring how weeds are attended to. All the gardens I have had a hand in show clear indications of my mixed views about the place of weeds in the landscape. On the fringe of the fields at Green Gulch we have left healthy stands of stinging nettle and field mallow. These weed-ways are primary feeding stations for the year-round butterfly population that draws on these medicinal weed plants as their primary larval food. In the crop rows, between the 150-foot-long lines of black-seeded 'Simpson' and 'Rouge d'Hiver' butter lettuce, we scratch out all of these same weeds before they are three inches high, while nearer to the kitchen we harbor a little stand of these same weedy plants that we use to make a delicious soup stock or tonic tea.

Even though I prize the weeds in our gardens, I also know the damage they can do. The negative effects of weeds in the vegetable bed or cultivated flower border are clear and vivid. Weeds are often deep-rooted and tenacious. They draw up huge reservoirs of soil water and soil air and compete strongly with the often weaker cultivated crops for moisture and nutrients. Weeds also often have a matting and spreading habit that chokes preferred cultivars and leaves weaker plants susceptible to decline.

If you are beginning a garden from scratch and you are starting it on a very weedy plot of soil, there are some preliminary steps that are worth taking before you plant. Since most weeds produce a prodigious amount of seed, it is important that you contend with this reservoir of weed seed that will be present in any abandoned and weedy ground. Before you take anything out, notice what plants are growing there and let them inform you of the soil and water history of your future garden. Then you can proceed to rough-weed your plot and take the largest weeds to the compost pile unless they are in full seed.

If you are working a sizable plot of land it is advisable to cultivate the ground next, either by hand or with a small disk or rototiller. This will stir up the roots of the weeds and then the larger roots and stalks can be taken to the compost pile and the smaller can be incorporated directly into the soil. Alternatively, after rough weeding you can blanket the surface with layers of newspaper, compost, and old straw and transplant your seedlings into the decomposing weed soil of the garden below. Cultivating the soil helps you get to know your ground. After rough weeding, water it well. In a few weeks the weed seeds that were dormant in the soil will sprout. When they do, weed them into the ground, water again, and let the next generation of stirred-up seed sprout. Doing this process two or three times in succession will mean less work later on, as your choice cultivars will face far fewer weedy competitors. To condition the ground well, plant a cover crop next, turn it into the soil, let it decompose, and you are ready to plant.

Does this seem extreme? You may want to abbreviate the process for ground already in pretty good shape, but if you are planting a garden in an abandoned weed patch, this thorough preparation will make your soil more fertile and less weedy in the long run.

❖　❖　❖

Weeding is meditation that reaches down into the heart of the garden, centering body and breath on that secret garden hidden underneath a tangle of weeds. With a settled mind, weeds become a patterned veil laid over the intentional fabric of your garden, a curtain that you can lift to find the hidden brocade below. I spend hours in the spring garden hauling out wheelbarrow after wheelbarrow of wild radish, ropes of chickweed, and armloads of poor man's weatherglass intertwined with succulent pigweed seedlings. In these hours of weeding I learn to see the garden again, to notice the first pale shoots of prize ornamental oregano pulchellum appear, lime green and tender, under the weedy cress and ruddy knapweed.

I enjoy using pulled and well-wilted weeds as a top surface mulch to be tucked around established plantings already in production. In big gardens I prefer to spread a wheelbarrow of pulled pigweed and wild mustard weeds right around the purple cabbage seedlings as mulch, rather than wheel them to the faraway compost pile. If I do this I make sure that the weeds are not producing seed and that I do not leave senecio out in the row, since it is the one weed I know that can finish its life cycle when pulled and ripen its soft, buttery yellow flower heads into seed even after the plant itself has been uprooted from the earth.

Always try to pull out your garden weeds before they go to seed, since they are far less likely to spread in the garden or in the compost pile if they are young and tender. If your compost pile is hot (130 degrees or more) it should be able to handle seedy weeds, but I still try to get our beds weeded before this stage. Also, the weeds are most succulent when they are young and they make better compost and food for the microbes when they are tender.

Many weeds that grow in the garden are dynamic accumulators of trace minerals and certain elements. When foliage of wild vetch or chickweed is burned, significant traces of phosphorus remain in the retrieved ash. The weed

Pernicious Weeds

Before you begin a weed eradication program it is a good idea to know your weeds well. Certain weeds are known vectors for plant diseases like rust and mildew and other forms of fungal growth. The field mallows or cheeseweeds are often the first harbingers of fungal rust in the early summer garden. A member of the Malvaceae family, these cheeseweeds deliver rust spores to the cultivated members of their family growing in the nearby flower garden. When dealing with the infected weeds of this category it is best *not* to incorporate them into the soil or compost pile but rather to dry them out thoroughly and then bury or burn them or send them to a well-managed municipal composting program.

Other weeds are allopathic growth inhibitors, exuding chemicals that slow the growth of plants around them. One of the strongest inhibiting weeds in our gardens is poison hemlock; however, once pulled, these weeds can be incorporated into the compost pile.

Many other weeds are poisonous to human beings if they are ingested. These plants pack resounding medicine and poison power. Foxglove, the ground ivies, all of the nightshade tribe, blueweed or *Echium vulgare*, the field milkweeds, poison hemlock, and white snakeroot all come to mind when I think of weeds that are poisonous to humans. All, however, with the exception of ivy, may be added to the compost pile.

Then there is another class of perennial weeds that colonize land and make it almost impossible to grow crops in their wake. For these weeds I carry dread, loathing, and a dark respect that comes from years of direct combat: to all of the rhizomatic grasses, bindweed, kudzu weed, white onion lilies, and sheep sorrel oxalis, I tip my hat and pray that you will never enter the cool, fragrant soil of our garden or even into the cleansing fire of our hottest compost pile!

plants that are dynamic accumulators seem both to clear a phosphorus-rich soil of its reserves and also to accumulate phosphorus from other sources and consolidate it in their foliage and other plant parts.

Some of the most dynamic weeds can be harvested to make a special high-nutrient NPK compost pile. Dandelion leaves (not the root, which may survive the heat), goosefoot, stinging nettles, yarrow, and wild vetch are all mixed in with oat straw and horse manure until they heat up and decompose, making a nutrient-rich and dynamic compost.

The practice of nourishing the soil by incorporating nutrient-rich plants is as long as Methuselah's eyeteeth. Farmers collect oak leaves, wild nettles, or barrows of horsetail ferns to build silica and calcium in their soils, while nitrogen is amply accumulated by alfalfa, lamb's quarters, and all the clover and legume tribe, weedy or not. When made into compost, these dynamic

Nurse Weeds

When my good friend of more than twenty gardening years, Doug Gosling of the Occidental Arts and Ecology Center, set about establishing a thriving vegetable garden to feed the clients of a small AIDS hospice near Santa Rosa, California, he prepared the land of the new site by sowing a rich array of seed collected from his favorite weed plants growing at the OAEC mother garden. I worked with Doug that first season at the AIDS hospice, surrounded by a rich brocade of wild amaranth, Good King Henry, magenta goosefoot, and rangy mustards mixed with moth mullein and other feral herbs, all sown to culture and improve the soil of the new garden. Here are some of our other favorite "nurse" weeds, which consolidate minerals in their plant parts, open up seized ground, protect the soil from wind and water erosion, feed beneficial insects, suppress disease, prevent pest damage, and add great benefit and beauty to the ground where they are grown. Only one warning is to be heeded: don't allow these mighty nurse weeds to go to seed or *they* will become the perennial crops of your garden. Instead, while they are tender and succulent, dig them back into the soil and follow with your cultivated garden crops.

Stinging nettle
Goosefoot herb
Amaranth, or red root pigweed
Ground cherry
Chickweed
Annual smartweed
Sow thistle
Groundsel
Wild lettuce
Scarlet pimpernel
Lupine
Shepherd's purse
Pellitory-of-the-wall
Speedwell
Tender thistles
Bishop's weed
Mullein

accumulators of the wild edge deeply enhance garden fertility. Certain weeds such as low-growing chickweed, veronica, and scarlet pimpernel can also serve as "nurse weeds" for larger plants like tomatoes or newly planted roses. The nurse weeds cover the soil surface and draw up necessary elements so that once the main plants are established, the weedy nurse crop can be turned back into the soil to decompose and further "nurse" or nourish the established crops.

Since so many weeds are dynamic accumulators of deep minerals and trace elements, it follows that many are also good edible food. The stomach of a Neolithic man recently exhumed contained sixty-seven weeds. Did they kill him? No, instead he was made of these sixty-seven weeds. They were his last supper.

Weeds have a strong, wild taste that lingers and turns your tongue green when you eat them raw out in the field. As ancestors of the cultivated plants, weeds give your tongue a reminder of the familiar cultivated crops, except they are not so tame. Weeds pack a punch; they linger with you, as medicine or stimulant, as tonic or purge. I crave the taste of weeds and the hunt that brings them to the table. Suzuki Roshi used to say, "Be grateful for the weeds in your life. Eventually they will enrich your practice." In their unruly strength and rank stance, weeds fortify life. They stand, rugged and ancient, among the gleaming crops, anchoring the assembly with an old gravity, reminding all gardeners that flowers fall with our attachment and weeds thrive with our neglect.

Cutting Through

BITTER JANUARY IS MY FAVORITE MONTH IN THE GARDEN. THE storerooms are full of ripe winter squash, russet potatoes, and 'Cinderella' pumpkins, while our prissiest and most demanding annual vegetables and flowers have all blessedly frozen to death in the field. Only the hardiest plants remain: Siberian iris, cone-headed 'Jersey Wakefield' cabbages, wind-swept rows of bare-limbed apple trees, and hunch-shouldered winter beets shivering in the icy wind. It is the opening of pruning season in California and in southern gardens, while in northern climates it will be a good month or two before the sap rises and gardeners will be pulled away from their hearths and out to prune the still-frosty garden.

I love this season because there is no one to talk to and nothing to be said. My shears and long-handled loppers are sharpened and oiled, my pocket saw is ready to work, and my old leather gloves will soon be buttery and supple from the heat of my hands. My work is clear: prune the winter garden, clean up the branches and leaf debris, dress the trees with well-rotted manure and old compost, and imagine the unfurling of the spring garden that sleeps inside the naked skeleton of the trees and garden shrubs.

When I first began to garden I was more timid and afraid of pruning than of any other garden task. I worried about hurting the plants I loved so much, and I worried about making a mistake. Then I learned to pause before the plant I was going to prune and silently put my full attention on the *actual* plant before me, really seeing it and then imagining the pruning work to be done. When I see the pruned plant clearly in my mind's eye and am ready to begin, I ask the plant for permission to prune it. A rite like this helps to settle your heart and mind on your task.

When Alan Chadwick worked with us in the garden he reminded us regularly that plants are the great forgivers of the natural world. Since I know that I make mistakes all the time and that the plants I handle continue to grow and thrive in spite of me, I am less worried now about hurting plants or making mistakes. Pruning is an excellent teacher, one that forces us to recognize consequence and relationship and to build on what we observe.

186

Outside of the front door of the little house at Green Gulch Farm where my husband and I lived in 1977, we planted a floribunda crabapple tree on the placenta of our newborn son, Jesse. Now this tree is thirty years old and thriving. And so is Jesse. They've grown up together, vigorous and dynamic beings, not hindered by all the mistakes I have made with both of them. By now the framework, character, and structure of Jesse *and* the crabapple tree nourished by his birth are both clear and revealed and all who encounter them are enjoying a huge harvest of bittersweet crab-apples, as well as plenty of tart insight from our full-grown son.

All gardening is manipulation of a sort and pruning techniques are the high and con-summate art of manipulation. Pruning in the dormant season has an invigorating effect on plants, while pruning during the growing season slows your plants down. Both are necessary, and the most important consideration in any season is to take care of the "3 D's": remove damaged, diseased, and dead wood before you prune any other limbs from your plants. Often just by doing this you restore health and soundness to your garden, and certainly it is easier to see what pruning the plant needs after the 3 D's are taken care of. Be clear about what you hope to accomplish with the plants you are pruning ("I am training this dessert apple for fruit production and pruning my crabapple for spectacular flowers"). Then stay in touch with the plants you have pruned and see if your dreams are fulfilled.

A healthy plant has balanced top and root growth and this is conveyed by lively sap flow, which is strongly influenced by good pruning performed in the proper season. You need to get to know the two systems of roots and bud shoots and to study their connections through the sweet fluid sap, the "force that through the green fuse drives the flower," as Dylan Thomas called it.

Each species and each plant has its own unique habit, form, and season of growth, but certain tribes of plants have common characteristics so they are grouped together. Herbaceous perennials and herbs are soft-stemmed and grow freshly from their roots each spring, while woody flowering shrubs and trees have a basic architecture that is shaped slowly over years, and vines rely on whatever armature is at hand. Since fruit trees, nuts, and berry plants are prized for their fruit, their growth is guided to that end. And garden roses are a force of their own.

Most of the garden cultivars that we prize are descended from wild relatives that are vigorous and untame. If you can find a corner out of the way and a little wild itself, plant one or two of these ancestral plants in that marginal land. Then leave them profoundly alone and watch them grow, unpruned and glorious in their abandoned neglect.

One of my greatest gardening teachers is the formidable California native poison oak plant, related to poison ivy on the East Coast. Both plants bleed a resinous, oily sap that irritates the surface of the skin and causes boils, blisters, welts, and uncontrollable itching. Poison oak is most virulent when it is just coming out of dormancy, right before it puts forth its signature oak-like cluster of three leaves.

Every winter at Green Gulch we used to leave the garden far behind and go into the wild north-facing canyons above the Gulch to plant seedling redwood trees. One year I noticed a huge stand of poison oak growing in a perfect draw for redwoods, so my friends and I cut the poison oak back to the ground and planted the young trees. In four days' time most of us were swollen and delirious with massive cases of poison oak. And our pruning mightily invigorated the poison oak, since our dormant-season cutting stimulated the roots tremendously, causing them to shoot forth ten- to twelve-foot-long canes of fresh oil-rich poison oak by midsummer. The redwood trees planted in that thicket did quite well, probably because they were so well shielded by the rampant poison oak and protected from the nibbling of black-tailed deer.

After this experience, I experimented with pruning or cutting back poison oak in other seasons. I suited up in my rubber rain gear in August, well-gloved and masked, and hacked out another choice stand growing in a premier coastal meadow. The poison oak was in full leaf and bloom, and because the plants had pumped so much vigor up from the roots and out to the branches, my summer pruning significantly weakened them. Eventually that stand was succeeded by native coyote bush and cascades of wild monkey flower, and in a year or two we could return to that spot and plant coast live oak trees in the restored meadow. My experience with the poison oak is testimony to the importance of paying close attention to what you cannot actually see: you prune aboveground because of what is belowground.

Pruning Herbaceous Perennials and Herbs

When a plant is called "herbaceous" this generally means that it grows a multitude of stems from a strong underground root system and that these stems die back or are cut back at the end of the growing season, to be renewed again the following year. When these plants begin to grow in the spring there are several pruning techniques you can call on, all of them also essential to pruning shrubs and trees.

Pinching back is designed to create sturdier, bushier plants. In a plant that has multiple stems, pinching out the main tip just above the leaf nodes causes the plant to bush out rather than grow up. (Pinching does not work for single-stemmed perennials like lilies or bearded irises.) This is best done early in the growing season when the plant stems are still tender. Pinching back is also invigorating for annuals like stock, snapdragons, and basil.

In certain plants, like dahlias, peonies, carnations, and chrysanthemums, some gardeners rub off or disbud almost all the buds along a stem, leaving only one to three buds to grow into strong, hearty flowers. This practice is also done in orchards, where gardeners thin overly full clusters of fruit from young fruit trees for the sake of fewer and finer fruit.

Dead-heading means cutting off dead flower heads and spent branches after flowering where you want to encourage further flowers. If spent flowers are allowed to remain then the vigor of the plant goes toward setting seed rather than toward reflowering. Keep pruning the dead flowers off—with those plants that are willing to be manipulated to continue to bloom, and where you want to dissuade the plant from proceeding in its natural cycle to setting seed and fruit. Necessary as it is, this practice of dead-heading is also poignant, especially since plants continue to reproduce themselves and flower until they are exhausted.

At the end of the growing season, usually after the first frost, herbaceous perennials and hardy herbs (with the exception of rosemary and lavender, which are closer to the tender, woody shrubs) are cut back to the ground. This is an excellent time to lift and divide these plants and to give them an ample dressing of compost and manure for the next growing season. In mild climates it is best to wait until late winter, since pruning prematurely stimulates new growth vulnerable to frost.

Remember that winter pruning stimulates root and new top growth, so be sure the weather conditions are conducive to healthy growth before you prune. Certain short-lived and tender perennials, like salvias and rose geraniums, begin to grow again almost immediately following their "haircut," so where they can be grown as perennials—they are annuals in cold climates—it is best to wait and prune them just before spring so that new shoots do not encounter a hard frost and die.

Pruning Woody Flowering Shrubs and Trees

The most essential consideration with these perennials is to understand whether your plants flower on new wood or on one-year-old or older wood. Usually if your plants flower early in the spring they are flowering on one-year-old wood and need to be pruned right after flowering so the plants will have time to produce next year's flowering wood. Japanese maples, buddleia, dogwoods, and lilac are among the plants whose pruning needs to be timed this way.

Plants that flower later in the summer or in early fall are generally better cut back early in the spring, because they will bloom best on the new branches that develop after that early pruning. Spirea, hydrangeas, and red osier dogwood want to be timed this way. In addition to this primary guideline about the main annual pruning of shrubs and trees, it is important also to practice dead-heading, disbudding, and pinching to keep your plants in strong health over a longer period of time.

Since with woody perennials you have the opportunity to influence the habit of the plant by how you prune, it is respectful of the plant to know its natural habit and to follow this habit whenever possible. I saw a redwood tree recently in a small suburban garden. Redwoods grow fast and tall, often reaching well over a hundred feet, but this redwood had been pruned to be a huge, wide shrub. Seeing this noble and upright redwood tree pruned to be a fat bush was like looking at a long-limbed giraffe compressed into a tiny cage. Immediately I thought of the many other less vigorous shrubs or trees that would have fit neatly into that small garden, instead of practicing what I jokingly call "horti-torture" on the stately redwood.

How you cut woody plants influences their form. **Heading** cuts (or beheading cuts, as was the case of the redwood) are cuts that remove branches and cause plants to bush out at their next bud joint. When you make heading cuts remember that buds that face out cause upward branching while inward-facing buds cause drooping or weeping branching. Be sure to cut on the diagonal just above the bud and not to leave a stump, which becomes an easy access point for disease to enter the pruned plant.

Nonselective heading, or **shearing**, is a form of pruning for garden hedges. It is best to do this form of pruning when the tips of your hedge are young and tender. To shear is like mowing a lawn, only with a wider time margin between cuts. If you shear once, you will have to keep shearing once or twice a year—forever. Green Gulch Farm's formal hedges are sheared twice a year: in the winter and in early summer, and we strive to create a classic hedge with sides that are widest at the bottom and slope in somewhat toward the top, so the sun can reach the lowest branches and keep them green; a hedge that spreads out as it grows up will soon have a bare and scraggly bottom.

Many shrubs benefit from being opened up to let in light and air. To practice **thinning** of densely branched plants prune out whole branches at their point of origin with the main stem or trunk of the plant and make sure that you do not take out more than a third to half of the branches of a large tree or shrub each year. These cuts are excellent for reducing the weight load of plants, for cleaning up old or injured branches or for stimulating new growth and vigor in depleted plants.

Pruning Vines

Zen master Dogen likened the close relationship of teachers and their disciples to the "intertwining of vines," growing together and being pruned together to come up fresh and new from out of their vast reservoir of interwoven roots. Vines are vigorous, beautiful, and ancient plants and they have a vital place in every perennial garden. Garden vines are categorized by how they climb, the three main types being twining, tendril, and clinging vines.

Twining vines, which include wisteria, honeysuckle, certain roses, kiwis, Dutchman's pipe, star jasmine, and many others, support themselves by wrapping around a strong support system. In some gardens you can enjoy the yearly, determined drama of the Japanese wisteria only twining clockwise while the nearby Chinese wisteria faithfully twines only *counter*clockwise around the staves of their strong supports. Most twining vines are tip-growers that produce massively each season. The lightweight twiners (such as hops, *Humulus lupulus*) may be cut back to the ground each year, while the heavier woody twiners like wisteria have their newer growth pruned back during the dormant season as well as light pruning after flowering.

The **tendrils** by which vines like clematis, grapes, woodbines, passionflowers, and porcelain vine climb are actually modified leaves capable of wrapping around their support systems and pulling their plants up to great heights. Tendril climbers demand a variety of pruning techniques depending on when the vines flower. This wide range is demonstrated nicely within the *Clematis* genus. Certain vigorous clematis vines escape to the heights and bloom without needing pruning, while the more hybridized varieties require more care. Early-blooming varieties flower on last year's wood and are pruned after the plant has flowered in order to build up next year's bloom, while late-flowering varieties of tendril climbers that bloom on the current season's growth are best pruned in the early spring.

Clinging vines, those that climb straight up walls without needing to wrap stem or tendril around a post, accomplish their feats by producing aerial rootlets that adhere tenaciously to walls, fences, or other rough surfaces.

Think of woodbines, English ivy, all the creepers, and trumpet vine, and you are imagining the major clingers of the vine kindom. A real consideration before establishing these vines is determining how to protect the surfaces that these vines cling to. Choose your clingers carefully, since they are quite permanent. Clinging vines require, and permit, very little pruning once they are established.

Fruit Tree and Berry Pruning

In 1977 we created our first apple and pear orchard at Green Gulch. We planted the young trees on a beautiful, south-facing slope outside the garden to give them more room, and individually caged each tree to protect them from deer damage. But this orchard was a disaster and now, twenty-two years later, only one or two trees remain strong out of the fifteen trees we originally planted. Why? Because they were out of our sight and out of our minds. Not until we welcomed fruit trees back into the garden did they begin to grow and thrive at Green Gulch.

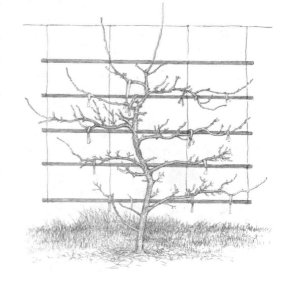

For me, pruning the fruit orchard is the most consequential and demanding of all garden tasks. Most "hard fruit" or tree fruit in the garden comes into production five to seven years after the trees are planted, and during this time it is important that a consistent pruning program be established. Having given this fair warning (often the same warning given to prospective parents), I encourage you to engage in the many delights of growing fruit trees.

Most fruiting trees in North America are members of the huge, noble rose family, bearing the timeless five-petaled flower that is the signature of the tribe. At Green Gulch we have grown many members of the rose family, including apples, pears, plums, quinces, Asian pears, sweet cherries, and crabapples, and all of these are grown in the garden, where they are lived with and noticed every day. We also grow many soft-fruit shrubs and viny members of the rose family, such as strawberries, raspberries, ollalaberries, and wild blackberries. Stone fruit like peaches and apricots, which need more heat and less fog than Muir Beach provides, are also rose-family fruits.

Most of these "rose trees" are pruned in the winter dormant season to invigorate growth, but apples and pears are also pruned in the summer to stimulate fruit buds and to train them to the espalier and cordon method developed in France during the eighteenth century. To prune your fruit trees well it is essential that you know both their fruiting habit and the rootstock on which they are grown. All reliably bearing fruit trees are grafts of a fruiting variety on a sturdy rootstock that will determine their size, vigor, and growth habit, generally categorized as dwarf (to eight feet), semi-dwarf (a substantial tree perhaps twelve feet tall when mature), and full-size.

Apples and pears are ancient trees, grafted on the rootstocks of wild crab-apples and quince trees, respectively. Many apples are planted on semi-dwarf rootstocks for ease of harvesting, and before beginning to prune the manageable semi-dwarf garden cultivars I sometimes go and sit under a huge old standard tree for inspiration and support. When I settle down and listen closely, the rose 'Gravenstein' tree exudes instructions to me through her gnarled gray bark about how to prune her stubbier cousins.

Apple, pear, and cherry trees most often produce their fruit on spurs, long-lived stubby branches that carry clusters of flower buds and take two years to begin to bear fruit. Where space is limited, apples and pears can be trained in cordon and espalier methods for maximum fruit production. These approaches create low fence-lines of trees and require early summer pruning of side branches, which forces growth back into short, packed fruit spurs.

Trees whose seeds are enclosed in pits or "stones" require considerably more pruning than their apple and pear cousins. Apricot and plum trees need heavy winter pruning for fine fruit, since most fruit is borne on short spurs formed on last year's new growth. Apricot spurs remain fruitful for about four years, and plums a little longer. Peaches and nectarines are also stone-fruit members of the rose family that only bear fruit on one-year-old wood, so they require heavy pruning every winter to generate that new wood. Stone-fruit trees bear voluptuously, so it is crucial to keep the fruiting as close to the trunk as possible by cutting back the side branches. This protects the tree from breaking under the burden of its own weight, as does a careful thinning of the fruit.

Pruning Roses

One of my greatest joys in the winter garden is to prune roses, and the huge array of roses at Green Gulch is always a special treat to prune and enjoy. I try to prune roses *after* I have worked on fruit trees because the fruit trees teach me about consequence and care, and the roses show me the freedom and wild roots of their family. Their very abundance strikes terror in many a gardener because there are so many different kinds of roses and each has different needs. They are, however, very forgiving and immensely generous.

Some roses require very little pruning, while others benefit from hard pruning. In all cases the roses are helped greatly by diligent dead-heading of spent blooms throughout the growing season. Generally, roses that flower vigorously and continuously bloom on new wood must be pruned hard in early spring to encourage renewal, while woody, old-fashioned roses that bloom once flower on old wood and need little pruning.

Always begin by removing the "3 D's": the dead, diseased, and damaged wood. This helps you see the true, healthy lines of the rose. Cut to a bud when you are doing dormant-season pruning and to a cluster of five leaves when you are dead-heading spent roses during the growing season. Do not leave stumps of dead wood, since disease finds its way into your rose plants through such stubs. And be sure to collect all damaged and diseased foliage and either burn it or bury it deep in the ground to keep down the spread of disease.

The **old roses**, species shrub roses—the moss roses, centifolias, the musk roses, the albas, and the gallicas—are not hybrids. They bloom once a year on side shoots from gracefully arching year-old or older canes. These roses are best pruned only lightly. The long canes are pruned by about one-quarter early in the new year, before growth begins, or occasionally right after flowering so they will have time to build strong new canes for next season's flowering. On strong, old plants you can completely cut out two or three old canes a year to encourage renewal from the base.

There are also re-blooming shrub roses, like the modern shrub roses from David Austin, hybrid perpetual roses, Bourbon roses, and the China roses. They bloom on both the current year's canes and on side shoots growing off old canes, and are pruned much like the single-bloomers but perhaps a little more severely.

Hybrid tea and grandiflora roses require the heaviest pruning, since they flower on new growth made in the same season. Prune them to an open center when the plants are young, choosing three or four main shoots. These shoots get cut back to about four buds, perhaps a foot aboveground in the spring in mild climates.

There are a number of different types of **climbing roses**: ramblers, free-standing climbers, and species climbers. Ramblers produce vigorously and flower on new wood, so they need to be cut back hard every winter or in the early spring, leaving only two to five canes and cutting the rest to the base. With climbing roses, canes that run horizontally produce more flowers than vertical canes, and it is true of fruiting members of the rose family also: if you weight down an apple branch so it is nearly horizontal, the branch produces more fruit buds and fewer growth buds.

The more woody and upright, or freestanding, climbers produce far fewer basal renewal shoots than the ramblers. The aim in pruning these roses is to remove old wood in proportion to new and to head many of the canes back so the plant will bloom all along the canes.

Roses have their origin in Neolithic times when prehistoric peoples roamed the earth. The beautiful, five-petaled flowering and fruiting plants have coevolved with human culture. Ethnobotanists surmise that the first cultivation of garden roses probably occurred in China almost five thousand years ago and it has continued in an unbroken line until now. Poised, pruning shears in hand, over the many flowering and fruiting roses early in the year, I can just hear their faint old music pouring out into the white winter wind. Pruned or unpruned, cultivated or left to the wind and rain, the rose garden is complete.

No Trace

EVERY SPRING IN THE YEARS THAT THE GREEN GULCH GARDEN
crew studied with Harry Roberts we made a pilgrimage in the bed of his
rattly old yellow Ford pickup truck named Buttercup. We climbed in
granny gear up Coyote Ridge, singing out the names of the parted sea of wildflowers lining the old rutted fire road snaking up to the crest of the ridge. Harry
leaned out of the passenger-side window and smoked an old Drum tobacco
cigarette with his eyes closed, listening to the music of those flower names he
knew so well and sucking in the blue-haze memory of their ephemeral beauty
as we paid slow spring homage to them all from the back of the truck.

I remember the flowers well, especially because I renew my connection
to them every year. I continue to make the pilgrimage by myself, on foot,
to greet the pale milkmaids and shooting stars, the first footsteps-of-spring,
and the pungent skunkweed and owl's clover. But even more vivid than the
flower names is what Harry was transmitting to us: he taught us to see and
to remember. He wanted us to observe the palette of the spring wildflowers,
and to name them carefully so we could observe them in greater detail and
notice how their bloom cycle linked up with the growth and bloom cycle of the
cultivated plants growing far below in the Green Gulch garden. Harry wanted
us to see and remember the links between mountain and field, and between
wild and cultivated ground, the full landscape of our practice.

Just after Harry died in the mid-1980s, and in honor of his insistence that
we do so, Green Gulch produced a farm and garden calendar. This calendar
came out of a commitment to practice land stewardship anchored in awareness of our watershed and of the cycles of the year. Working on this calendar I
had to sink down and live in the present moment of each day, to keep a broad
awareness of the season in which we were gardening, and also to follow the
seasons through the day. Both Alan Chadwick and Harry had reminded us
regularly that all four seasons of the year are present in the span of one day.
Thus, spring is the dawn of the day, full summer is high noon, autumn falls
at dusk, and father winter oversees the midnight hour.

I also thought of Varro, the encyclopedic Roman scholar who lived just before the birth of Christ. Varro wrote voluminously on all sorts of topics, but the only complete work we have is his set of three books on farming. Varro divided the growing year into the traditional four-season calendar but he wrote about a six-season cycle as well: preparing time, planting time, cultivating time, harvest time, housing or storing time, and consuming time. When you look closely, you can see that every single day is also an entire cycle of Varro's six seasons of tasks.

For our calendar, and again in honor of Harry's history as a Yurok shaman, we researched the names native people have traditionally given to the full moon times of every month. These names vary according to the regions of North America where they live, yet they reveal a common observance of the life of each month of the year:

January	Old Moon, Moon After Yule
February	Snow Moon, Hunger Moon, Wolf Moon
March	Sap Moon, Crow Moon, Lenten Moon
April	Grass Moon, Egg Moon
May	Planting Moon, Milk Moon
June	Rose Moon, Flower Moon, Strawberry Moon
July	Thunder Moon, Hay Moon
August	Green Corn Moon, Grain Moon
September	Fruit Moon, Harvest Moon (or in October)
October	Hunter's Moon
November	Frosty Moon, Beaver Moon
December	Moon Before Yule, Long Night Moon

Sometime later I began to muse about how I would name the moons that govern our months in coastal California. This naming reminded me of a passage from William James: "My experience is what I agree to tend to. Only those items I notice shape my mind." All of the names that arose for me came out of the watershed that enfolds my Muir Beach garden and the Green Gulch garden. The lunar names are the intersection of the world of my own experience and this wider world. Noting that the monarch butterflies return in September, I wait more eagerly and more observantly for them all year long, linked closely with the wild landscape and with the garden.

January	Moon of Migrating Gray Whales
February	Moon of Fetid Adder's Tongue
March	Moon of Returning Swallows
April	Moon of Wild Strawberries
May	Moon of Buckeye Bloom
June	Moon of Dusky-Footed Wood Rat
July	Moon of Long Fog
August	Moon of the Dry Grass Prairie
September	Moon of Returning Monarch Butterflies
October	Moon of Falling Redwood Seed
November	Moon of Ripe Acorns
December	Moon of Spawning Silver Salmon

It is not only with our eyes and labor that we can track the movement of the seasons: the ears can follow them, too. I like to sit still and listen to the seasons turning on the strong tin roof over our heads in the old barn zendo at Green Gulch. In the late autumn the weather grows very warm on the coast. When the temperature reaches 90 degrees, the huge Monterey pines overhanging the zendo all begin to open up their scaly seed cones. Some October evenings during the late afternoon meditation period, the crackling of the heat-pried cones sounds like corn popping overhead. Occasionally a heavy cone is released by the hot autumn wind, and it clatters down the roof while the jays explode into the air, cawing in complaint. Soon they return, however, with an uncharacteristic billing and cooing. Usually the jay has to scramble constantly for every available morsel of food, but when the pinecones release their fat load of oil-rich seeds the blue jays have more than they can eat and they signal their satisfaction with a full-belly brogue. In the winter freezing rainstorms from the Gulf of Alaska pound and fret the metal roof and tug at the stays of our hayloft meditation hall.

The time of returning swallows has always been a lively one. Around the vernal equinox (March 20 or so) the barn swallows return to Green Gulch from their southern migration. It is their particular joy to glide down onto the zendo roof and apply their considerable skill toward finding a way *into* the old barn where long ago they used to build their mud-and-wattle nests. Many hours of spring fever meditation are spent trying to keep the swallows *out* of the zendo. Every year at least one family makes it through the guard and sets up house in the meditation hall. I secretly exult at the agile swallows' moxie. I love to hear the parents coo contentedly as they take turns keeping their eggs warm and incubated. And when the chicks finally hatch out, the distinct plop of wet swallow poop is delivered from heaven down onto the floor of the meditation hall during morning sitting.

Summer meditation is heralded by the long call of foghorns along the northwest coast. Overhead the zendo cat moves soft-footed over the foggy pine needle roof, stalking summer-fattened wood rats. Occasionally she catches her prey, which sends up a high-pitched scream feverish with terror, followed by the snarl and soft weight of the cat overhead as she cracks and sucks out translucent rat bones in the long summer night.

The sounds of the seasons on the zendo roof link me to what is going on in the garden outside the zendo walls. The crackling of the Monterey pinecones opening in October goes with the first harvest of dry beans and ripe grain. The drum of rain on the tin roof in December summons me to the winter garden—to rhubarb chard in the cold wind and red Siberian kale standing in the storm rows beyond the cypress windbreak. The first planting-out of tender bok choy and pale lettuce, young burdock and the first Chinese cabbage in the spring are serenaded by the barn swallows flocking to their nests under the zendo eaves. And the sound of wood rats scurrying over the warped tin roof in late June anchors my mind in birth and death and the ripening of lavender in the summer solstice fields.

❖   ❖   ❖

For the first ten to fifteen years that I worked in the Tassajara and Green Gulch gardens I kept meticulous records of *all* plant information; in fact, I was *too* careful. Rereading my journal I find that I can't see the garden through all the overblown, ecstatic prose describing pale, new buds opening. A decade later I had settled down quite a bit, tempered by the years of very active gardening, and entered hurried notes with less fat and more meat that covered what was sown, what germinated, what was dosed with manure tea, and how the plants looked and perhaps the phase of the moon. I evolved a journal and tracking practice that I hold to today: I keep a small notebook and tiny pen in my pocket to note work to be done, and I transfer my small notebook insights to a calendar that hangs indoors alongside a moon phase calendar. I keep a detailed record of vegetable production, sowing bed preparation and planting-out, seasonal field plans that show where and when crops were planted, and at the end of the season a tally of the weight and total of the harvest. I keep a separate record of the perennial gardens, their planting and dividing, their pruning, fertilizing, and flowering. But of course food and ornamental gardens can be combined in one record, which centralizes the other essential point to track and chart: the daily weather.

The most important practice of all, and one which I am not always fastidious about, is *checking* the information gleaned and recorded from the previous growing season or seasons. In a way I am glad that I don't rely too much on the past, for without the benefit of "rising mind" I never would have sown the rare blue Tibetan poppy, *Meconopsis betonicifolia*, so faithfully season after season after season until it *finally* germinated and grew a few years ago.

I like to keep the moon phase calendar next to the date calendar because it helps me notice when in the monthly lunar cycle flowers bloom. Over the years I have noticed that plants grow more vigorously and come into their first bloom during the bright of the moon or during the waxing moon, that two-week period from new moon to full. And similarly, plants deepen their roots and strengthen their underground anchorage systems during the dark of the moon, or during the waning moon, that two-week period from full moon to new moon. Out of these observations I have set up monthly sowing schedules at all the gardens where I have worked.

There are many ways to chart the sowing and planting schedules in your garden, especially if you are growing new plant varieties that you are not familiar with. What matters most is noticing what is going on in your garden and paying attention to the principles of creating sustainable health for your green world. By tracking crops and monitoring fertility, care of your garden beds will follow naturally. Gardeners are an ingenious and iconoclastic lot; each one of us has our distinct ways of organizing the process of keeping records in alignment with our particular gardening path.

In the Zen tradition we have many collections of koans, which are public records of individual teaching exchanges that were written down and passed on from generation to generation of eager Zen practitioners. *The Blue Cliff Record*, *The Book of Serenity*, and *The Gateless Gate* are the best known of these ancient records that Zen people have pondered and plumbed for generations not just to learn about the past, but to be more alive in the present moment. Like garden records, they tell of fertile and barren efforts of our forebears and point us on the way.

When it was my turn in 1974 to manage the Tassajara garden all I had to help me besides the hurried and brief blessing of my predecessor were the journal logs and records left by previous gardeners. I immersed myself in these stories and learned that in the summer rattlesnakes often took shelter from 116-degree heat near the garden altar where the hose bib dripped onto a shady section of the stone wall, and that I could expect peach leaf curl every season unless I sprayed copper sulfate in early January when the trees were dormant and again in February when the first coral-toned peach buds began to swell.

These garden records of things heard and experienced became like the treasured Zen koan records to me. I entered the life stream of the many gardeners who had loved and known the Tassajara garden. Their questions became my questions: How does a Zen student grow sweet corn without harming hungry squirrels? When the noon heat will likely spike to over 100 degrees, do you go out at dawn to water the parched carrot beds and miss breakfast, or do you keep to the community schedule? These questions burned into my soul all the more deeply because in reading the old records I realized that I was not alone in wondering what to do.

The living garden also carries its own record. If I were curious about why the Tassajara almond trees leaned to the north, I could burrow into the weather records for the previous years and perhaps find how many days the prevailing wind gusted in a northwesterly direction. But often I just enjoyed the leaning trees and sat for a while at their roots letting the living garden reveal and remove any trace of itself in the downward drift of fragrant almond petals in the early spring wind.

When I chart the opening of blossoms, measure the rain, note what I plant, sow, and reap, I am offering tribute to the crops and soil of the garden just as I did so many years ago when we climbed Coyote Ridge in Harry Roberts's buttercup-yellow truck and chanted out the names of the wildflowers. And all the while I am aware that in the fullness of time, new gardeners will take my place and inherit all of the gardens I have tended and with them the job of keeping track of what can never be measured or recorded. What is most deeply remembered is most fully digested, leaving no trace.

GARDENING WITH ALL BEINGS

Pest or Guest?

H E WAS BENT OVER THE RED ITALIAN GARLIC BED, A PROPERLY dressed older man, shaking his head and clucking in audible disapproval. He spotted me and straightened up, striding toward me with vigor and missionary purpose. *Here it comes*, I thought, as I braced myself for my least favorite question. "How do you get rid of your gophers?" the righteous gentleman asked. "Because you know, they're taking down your entire garlic crop."

Get rid *of gophers? I thought. My garlic crop? Are you kidding?* I wanted to shout. We don't get *rid* of anything at Green Gulch, we are the universal delicatessen, open twenty-four hours a day, seven days a week, year-round, a demilitarized zone for all besieged and hungry beings. But even as I formed this thought I saw through it, because in fact I *did* want to get rid of that single, tireless pocket gopher who was wreaking havoc in the garlic bed, and while I was at it, I would also have liked to abolish all the other uninvited guests feeding on the bounty of our garden.

I feel a spreading sense of righteousness whenever I complain about all these pests and visitors who depend so mightily on the crops we raise in the Edible Schoolyard, on our Zen farm, and in all the places where gardeners plant crops and flowers. Green Gulch backs up to wild parkland that abuts the urban corridor of the San Francisco Bay Area and the suburban belt of Marin County, so pests of every stripe find their niche in our neighborhood. I know at firsthand black-tailed deer, striped skunks, raccoons, marauding dogs, feral cats, wild and escaped rabbits, pocket gophers, shrews, plush moles, Norwegian rats, mice, bats, birds by the hundreds, frogs, snakes, snails, slugs, toads, and wave after wave of insects that suck, bite, chew, spit, tear, and also keep the garden in prime organic health.

A whole other lineup of previously wild and shy native predators are now venturing into the Green Gulch garden to prey on the well-fed front-line pests that our garden has nurtured for decades. These locals include nocturnal visitors such as the gray fox, coyote, and the great horned owl, and other large native birds of prey who hunt on the farm margins in broad daylight like the Cooper's hawk, the red-tailed hawk, and the carrion-cleaning turkey vulture. There have also been bobcat sightings and even an occasional glimpse of a long-tailed mountain lion stalking the overpopulated deer that browse the Zen garden deli. It is with mixed feelings that I greet the avid birders who come specially to Green Gulch, which, they tell me excitedly, is well known to be a bird-watcher's paradise because of the ample buffet the farm provides. And these are just the stiff-spined animal pests. I haven't even mentioned the populous world of spineless insects and their arthropod kin, or the mold and fungus diseases that plague the garden every growing season.

Has Zen practice helped me be more peaceful and closely hitched to the vast mind of this pestiferous universe? Hardly. Zen practice deepens my appreciation of paradox and relationship, especially with regard to pests and problems. In the garden Zen practice helps me hold still and look at what is right in front of me without turning away. And then it helps me look again. Zen keeps me going, even when I don't like what I see, as when I encounter the well-fed gopher in the garlic bed or the indignant gentleman on the gopher's trail.

Best of all, Zen practice enlivens my sense of humor and of the ridiculous, especially when I see myself clamp down and cling to my precious notions of how the garden should be or of what exactly constitutes a "pest." Especially then. Zen practice helps me clear the field of notions and find new ground. "Just continue," Katagiri Roshi exhorted us. "Continue, under all circumstances."

✧   ✧   ✧

While my friends in the zendo ponder pithy spiritual questions, I ask myself, "What is a pest?" or "What is disease?" and more specifically, "What's the best way to deal with the gophers and rosy apple aphids in the espalier fruit tree beds?" In the safe shelter of the meditation hall I even occasionally see *myself* as a kind of pest: I plague raccoons and deer, pursue spit bugs and flea beetles, and I plot their demise. I, too, am a kind of invasive creature, an "exotic" in California. Hailing from New England, I have replaced pristine, native bogs of wild horsetail and stands of California nettles with row after row of introduced red Russian kale and clove-scented stock flowers from southern Europe. Over and over I am humbled by how quickly my insights into interbeing are burned off and vaporized by the fire of righteous indignation as one little pocket gopher surges boldly through a winter planting of red Italian garlic.

I have a hundred-year-old friend who has been a passionate fan and supporter of the Green Gulch garden for decades. One spring morning I happened upon Charlotte hovering over a newly emerged bed of spring anemones. Hundreds of crimson, dark purple, and pale cream anemone buds were lifting their heads from out of their winter reservoir of pale green fernlike foliage. Charlotte raised herself slowly, slowly, from the spell of the flowers and came to the surface of the garden for air. "This garden must be responded to," she whispered to me urgently.

Unwanted creatures are forever arriving at the garden gate and requiring response. In order to respond to an importuning visitor you must first get out of the way and drop your notions of what your garden is. The word "respond" comes from the Latin *spondere*, to pledge, to espouse, to sponsor. Pledging and promising to meet your garden and all visitors is core to every gardener's life.

When an uninvited creature comes calling, I call on my Zen training and on those lessons that every schoolchild learns early in life. I stop, look, and listen, and apply the fundamental breathing and settling techniques available to me as a meditator. Then, when I am calm and solid, I ask myself, is this creature a pest or a guest?

I understand that sometimes these categories overlap, but primarily "guests" visit certain plants briefly and then move on, like nocturnal insectivore bats or seasonal migrations of monarch butterflies. Often these visitors are beneficial to the garden and they rarely damage garden plants. We welcome these guests to the garden and depend on their visits.

Pests have a heavier tread, although of the some seventy thousand currently cataloged insects only about four hundred are pestiferous or damaging to crops and of these four hundred only about forty are serious pests. Since garden health depends on a lively balance of biological diversity, I make it my business to tell them apart. Potential garden pests come in three main flavors: vertebrates (the ones with a clear-cut inner skeletal system, mainly mammals and birds); invertebrates (spineless pests, mainly insects); and plant diseases (including fungal, bacterial, and viral infestations).

When it comes to responding to plant pests and disease there are three primary types of gardeners. The vigilant, ever-ready, and observant gardener expects and awaits pest attack and is prepared to respond directly when it comes. The gardener more like me meets all calamity with the belief that the solution lies in building better soil and root health and maintaining sustainable fertility in the garden. And the all-is-well-until-it-isn't gardener relies on blithe optimism instead of martial response.

My type of gardener often fails to notice the first wave of pests when they arrive because we're busy ministering to the soil and the plants. I have lost a lot of early-summer arugula to the infamous flea beetle by assuming that the arugula plants were weakened by lax fertility rather than by insect attack. My vigilant friends hard at work with their hand lenses notice the arrival of this minuscule pest that renders arugula into lace, but while bracing for imminent pest attack they may fail to maintain basic garden fertility, the best preventive. The blithe laissez-faire gardener is often left scurrying to catch up with a ballooning infestation.

Good pest response depends on merging these styles of gardening. If you overfertilize, your plants will be pumped and succulent, announcing themselves loudly to visiting pests or to the disease spores of mold, fungus, and other pathogens. If you underfertilize and worry about pest attack all the time, your garden will also suffer. And so will you. There is a Middle Way between these two extremes that allows relaxation and enjoyment of the garden. The key to finding, and keeping, this balance is open-minded awareness, not control. No matter how much you want to have just the right guests come to your house, uninvited pests will also arrive hungry and long-fanged at your garden gate.

Once you stop, look, and listen long enough to recognize that you have a pest or a destructive disease in your garden, sink down to ground level and notice what *exactly* is happening to your plants. There is a sensitive balance here between monitoring mindfully and waiting too long, so take Goethe's advice, "Do not hurry, do not rest," and respond in a timely fashion.

In the early 1990s the Saratoga area of northern California had a very dry winter. As the summer heat came on, the huge heritage oak that is the centerpiece of the organic Saso Herb Garden began to drop its leaves. Louis and Virginia Saso discovered that they had a full-on infestation of California oak moth caterpillars in their magnificent oak. Their neighbors complained of the same pest and immediately began to spray chemicals on their trees to kill the caterpillars of the moth before their live oaks were defoliated. Louis and Virginia elected to wait, not only out of reluctance to spray chemicals, but also because of their familiarity with the life cycle and the effects of the oak moth.

The Sasos felt sure there was a hot summer ahead. They watched and monitored every day just how much the caterpillars were eating and they noticed that there was a natural tapering off of leaf-fall as the insects began to pupate. Because they had been sprayed with pesticide, their neighbors' oak trees were covered with glossy new leaves, while the moth caterpillars had reduced the foliage of the Saso oak tree by a good third. Their once-mighty oak looked wan and ragged compared to the full-canopied oaks next door. Still, the Sasos chose not to spray.

By late August of that year many of the other grand old oaks that had been sprayed began to wither and die, because they had far too many leaves to maintain in the intense summer heat. However, the Saso oak had been stripped down just enough by the oak leaf caterpillar to survive the incandescent heat, a testimony to the patience, forbearance, and biological acumen of both the oak moth and the seventy-year-old gardeners who neither hurried nor waited in responding to their garden.

Tolerance in the garden is based on mindfulness and knowledge of your pests. Begin with noticing who is visiting your garden and continue tracking your visitor with careful monitoring, daily inspection, and written observation and description of pest damage, day by day. When you are reasonably certain of what your pest is, read about it, and learn about its biological and ecological cycle, which plants it enjoys, what damage it causes, and what natural predators it has. If you do not recognize the pest or disease in your garden, then seek local, skilled advice in identifying your visitor and always be aware of what level of damage you are actually seeing.

A key question to ask yourself before taking action is: how much damage are you willing to tolerate? I confess that a little tattered foliage and pesky nibbling in the garden actually reassure me rather than inspiring panic. I would far rather eat radishes with a little shot-hole damage on their leaves than consume pristine produce sprayed with a light veneer of chemical pesticide. And when I bend down to sniff a branch bent low with fragrant tresses of Persian 'Ispahan' roses, I prefer a little black spot mixed in with my perfume to the chemical scent of prophylactic rose herbicides.

In responding to pests and disease in your garden, keep in mind the basic teaching of the Buddha that everything changes all the time, combining that with a reminder from the modern naturalist and conservationist John Muir that everything in the universe is hitched to everything else. Follow your affection as you garden and when you meet a pest, eye to complex eye, or shoulder to thorax, consider that this very spit bug doing the backstroke through a froth of expectorated foam may have been your mother lifetimes ago, or from a more rationalist perspective is your cousin, and you share a common parentage. Fold yourself in with the lot of all the shady and noble pests and guests that also love your healthy and diverse garden. Join the party. Your very life and good fortune as a gardener depend on this integrated relationship and on giving up a measure of control in favor of responding to your garden with a playful, observant, and wide, pest-integrating mind.

Stiff-Spined Pests

ORGANIC GARDENING IS CONSEQUENTIAL BUSINESS, WITH A STING and an impact that can take life, and not just the life of a pest. Each time I accidentally mangle a snake with the blades of the lawnmower that I use to cut the grass paths in my kitchen garden, every time a field mouse gets trapped in the extensive webwork of three-inch irrigation pipeline on the farm, and whenever I deliberately crush a French snail under my boot heel in a sweep of fury after finding the Japanese gobo plants eaten to the ground and covered with telltale silver snail slime, I narrow my humanity and am diminished.

I know this is easy for the gardener to say—anything to ease our conscience as we dispatch the lives of bothersome creatures in the garden. Years ago at Green Gulch we held a special ceremony to honor the lives of the many beings who expire while we garden. I wrote the dedication that comes at the close of all Buddhist ceremonies, and I continue to ask forgiveness every gardening year, always with fresh language.

A Ceremony Asking Forgiveness from the Plants and Animals
Plants and Animals in the Garden,
We welcome you—we invite you in—we ask forgiveness and your understanding. Listen as we invoke your names:
Little sparrows, quail, robins, and house finches who have died in our strawberry nets;
Young Cooper's hawk who flew into the sweet pea trellis and broke your neck;
Numerous orange-bellied newts who have died by our shears, in our irrigation pipes, by our cars, and under our feet;
Slugs and snails whom we have pursued, feeding you to the ducks, crushing you, trapping you, picking you off and tossing you over our fences;
Gophers, moles, and raccoons, trapped and scorned by us, and also watched with love, admiration, and awe for your single-mindedness;

Rats and mice whom we have poisoned, trapped, and drowned;

Sowbugs, spitbugs, earwigs, flea beetles, woolly aphids, rose-suckers, cutworms, millipedes, and other insects whom we have lured and poisoned;

Black-tailed deer, chased at dawn and at midnight, routed by dogs and unquiet Zen students;

Manure worms and earthworms, severed by spades, and numerous microscopic compost life-forms who have been burned by sunlight;

We call up all the plants we have removed by dividing and separating you, and deciding that you no longer grow well here: colored lettuces, young broccoli, ripe strawberries, and sweet apples; all of you who have lured pests to your table; and all the plants we have shunned: hemlock, pigweed, sourgrass, bindweed, stinging nettle, bull thistle;

We invoke you and thank you and continue to learn from you. We dedicate this ceremony to you and to the endless dimension of our interconnected life.

The primary stiff-spined pests in the garden are generally deer, raccoons, gophers and moles, rats and mice, flocks of birds, and a host of other animals such as cats, dogs, skunks, rabbits, squirrels, and—sorry to say—unmonitored and overeager children. When you grow what they love, they will come, and they will inevitably become an integral part of the garden that is never really "your" garden anyway.

In many cases vertebrate "pests" have some beneficial position in the complex balance of nature in the garden. Most of them either eat insects or help to keep other pest populations in balance, or at the very least their presence indicates that some other pest has arrived. One morning in the very first years of Green Gulch Farm, our entire chicken population suddenly left their yard and swarmed all over a large iris planting in the main garden. We were stunned by this mass exodus until we saw that the hens were guzzling a whopping population of slugs and snails hiding on the underside of the strapped foliage of the irises.

Not only will they come, pests will outwit you in their drive to eat your bounty. Do not lose your sense of humor as you plot the exclusion of coveys of quail and litters of hungry rabbits. Even though it is dangerous to your credibility as the dominant upright species in the garden, every now and then the smartest thing you can do is acknowledge that you are ridiculous: you have been outmaneuvered again by a crafty masked raccoon or a persistent dusky-footed wood rat, and have stooped to vaudeville routines and Rube Goldberg devices while trying to get rid of stiff-spined garden pests. In fact, forget about "getting rid" of pests altogether. There is no getting rid of anything, because the more you focus on how good your garden would be if you could just get rid of that gopher in the garlic patch, the less you can see what is actually happening, as the Sasos did with their oak-moth infestation.

Every morning the "Heart Sutra" is chanted in meditation halls throughout the world. This line always stands out for me: "There is no old age and death and no extinction of it." I remember in the early years at Green Gulch setting up back-to-back lethal spring traps for gophers. In truth, there is no getting rid of gophers or of my need to be rid of them: "No gophers and stiff-spined pests, and no extinction of them."

Deer Park Sermon

I wish that there were some way to garden without taking life, but I do not believe there is. All life is made out of other forms of life and out of death itself, for fertility. In just one glass of clear water, thousands of microorganisms die as we quench our thirst. Now and then I muse that a full quarter of my adult life as a Zen meditator has been spent plotting the demise of other creatures. Try me on deer, fox, raccoon, gopher, mole, feral cat, skunk, Norwegian rat, or wild bunny and I am a bottomless pool of extermination or relocation advice. Unfortunately, in order to effectively plot the removal of unwanted pests, the gardener does best when she learns to take on the life of the creature itself. I remember hearing that Stephen Jay Gould once exclaimed, "Oh, to be able to spend sixty seconds in the brain of a turkey vulture!" and I shuddered from head to toe.

Why? Because once you let them in close, even in order to figure out how to get *rid* of them, the pest becomes you. Boundaries crumble and you are absorbed into and possessed by one another. Interbeing is a dangerous business when you "inter-are" with a pest. The consequence of relaxing your guard and "becoming one with the black-tailed deer" (or what I call under my breath, "having a California moment") may be precipitously dire for your garden and your overall human sovereignty.

My friend and neighbor Mayumi Oda, artist, author, peace activist, and longtime Zen meditator, had one such "California moment" a few years ago when, after a long day of meditation and painting, she went for a walk outside her garden gate, where heavy thickets of thimbleberry and red osier clog Redwood Creek. In this wild tangle, Mayumi discovered trampled patches where black-tailed deer lay down to sleep. Beyond these patches she saw her own garden, an irrigated paradise secure behind its solid fence. "It was the most ridiculous sight I have ever seen," she said, and she marveled at her inability to include the wild tangle outside the gate in her perception of paradise. The next day she took down the entire back fence of her property and opened her land to the wild river's native inhabitants. Immediately, the deer began to penetrate and claim her garden. Now, some seasons later, Mayumi shakes her head at the cost of this moment of enlightened insight. Her most precious roses have had to be individually caged to withstand the delicate browsing of the black-tailed deer, but Mayumi has not resurrected her barrier fence and I am sure she never will.

Physical protection is the first line of defense in direct pest management, and a good fence takes the lead without question, even if you have to wonder, am I fencing *in* or fencing *out*? If your large-pest population tends to be occasional guests, you might consider individual fencing for your most valuable plants, being sure to include a simple access gate for each cage. Often, though, a stout fence not only above but also dug in belowground is the only way to protect your garden from deer, raccoons, foxes, rabbits, and skunks.

An alert dog with a sense of adventure, purpose, and ownership can provide invaluable protection, especially if you site your most vulnerable plants closer to your house. Feisty raccoons can stand off even the most intrepid hound, and many dogs learn respect for skunks and porcupines the hard way, but a good watchdog does discourage predators from entering your garden.

If you resort to the alchemy of potions and amulets against deer and other predators, just remember that these concoctions have to be refreshed and monitored frequently. You can experiment and find out which are useful deterrents and which are merely sops for your fears and effective only in your imagination and as a source of humor for your friends. I have seen gardens and vineyards garlanded with flashing strips of red and silver Mylar to startle the birds and deer, and trees burdened down with baby socks stuffed with

Good Fences Make Good Gardeners

Because I prefer not to trap, bait, poison, or mutilate visitors to the garden, I fence. If there are deer in your neighborhood, you will need a high, taut fence seven to nine feet high. And while you are going to all that trouble, why not use a strong hog wire with a finer mesh at the bottom in order to exclude rabbits, dogs, cats, squirrels, skunks, and porcupines with one stout fence. If you also want the fence to keep out burrowing critters like gophers, woodchucks, rats, cats, and moles, then you have to fence underground about two feet deep. You can protect above and below-ground with one fence if you dig a two-foot-deep trench, line it with hardware cloth, and drive fence posts into the trench at eight- to ten-foot intervals, backfill the trench and stretch hog wire from the fence posts.

There are as many designs for ingenious fences as there are clever gardeners. Think of what your land and individual nature call for and get to work establishing the boundary around your garden.

If midsize mammals are pestering your garden the best physical remedy is a strong fence of tight-meshed wire, buried one foot deep and extending three feet above ground. Make sure to stake the wire up with stout metal or wooden stakes, driven

two feet into the ground and set at six- to eight-foot intervals. You might even leave the top one foot of fencing unstaked so the woodchuck, possum, or porcupine that tries to climb will fall off outside the fence, since wire curls down under the weight of these animals.

If you live in serious gopher country you may need to put your perennials and even annuals in baskets or to line your entire beds with wire. Only poisonous roots like daffodils can be safely exposed. I will always remember the young, eight-foot-high fig tree, laden with fruit, that gophers gnawed down at Tassajara. A stout, hardware-cloth cage buried around the roots of that fig would have saved it from rodent assault.

Raccoons are such good climbers that woven wire fences, even tall ones, will not stop them. Electric fences work well as long as you are vigilant about keeping the power on every night. If you have prize fruit trees that raccoons love to climb, try wrapping a three-foot-long smooth metal cylinder around your tree, two feet up the trunk to block the raccoon from climbing. Good luck. We have fenced our orchard for years, but the lure of the ripening fruit always brings out the most inventive side of our local "washing bears," as they are called in German.

blood meal to discourage other predators. These methods demand a vigilant gardener, and you must be, as the old adage says, "present to win," since the hungry creatures depend on your attention flagging so they can come in and dine.

I will long remember the night just after we had planted our double-flanking lines of 'Van Eseltine' crabapple trees down the full lower length of the Green Gulch garden road. There came a timid knock at midnight on our door. "Yes?" I called from the bottom of my burrow of sleep. "Excuse me," said a mousy little voice, "but there's a deer in the garden," and before I could bolt out of bed and nab the messenger to help, I heard her scurry away.

We had some newfangled goop that I had just purchased, auspiciously named "Not Tonight Deer," a spray made of rotten eggs and mountain lion urine. I was so intrigued by the combination of ingredients and by wondering how they extracted that much mountain lion piss, that I had bought the stuff on the spot. And so it was that I found myself in the midnight garden in my nightgown, with a flashlight tucked under my chin, tying rag strips dipped in lion piss and rotten eggs onto the endangered trees. It worked, but unfortunately I had to re-dip the rags every week all during this time, and our loyal, adoring garden dog Sierra gave me a wide berth.

What helps more than any gadget in the arsenal for responding to stiff-spined pests in the garden is to slow down enough to remember that intimate connection with our pests is a natural part of life. Shakyamuni Buddha delivered his first sermon, initiating forty years of teaching, in a deer park in Sarnath, India. In our modern "deer park" garden I continue to ponder the original teachings of the Buddha on the interconnectedness of life, the true nature of nonviolence, and the impermanent nature of all that is. Curious and ever present, stiff-spined garden pests join me in this investigation.

Living with Rodents

Every healthy garden has its population of rodents. Gardens that abut wild land like Green Gulch Farm are home and host to wild native rodents—from diminutive dusky-footed wood rats and shrews, to hearty woodchucks, porcupines, squirrels, and gophers. At semi-urban gardens like the Edible Schoolyard these are wild, eccentric beings, but the fondness I have for them does not extend to the garden-raised rodents that plague our compost and crops.

Garden rodents come for fallen grain, ripe fruit, fetid compost, and scores of vegetable and flower seeds. These creatures are in turn the favored food of an array of predators: the great horned and spotted owls, red-tailed hawks, local snakes, opossums, foxes, skunks, raccoons, feral cats, bobcats, wildcats, and coyotes.

How do you control mice and rats? The answer is you can't, not really; you live with them. A generic garden fence won't reliably deflect rodents because they can climb over or burrow under most fences. Take the rat, for example, the most dreaded of all rodent predators. The physical prowess and determination of rats is legendary: they can squeeze through any opening larger than half an inch, climb the inside of vertical pipes, dive and swim underwater, and gnaw through plastic, wallboard, wood, cinder blocks, sheet metal, and sun-baked adobe.

"A mouse," Walt Whitman said, "is miracle enough to stagger sextillions of infidels." So is a rat. Hated and pursued, rats have left a heavy, dark tread across the pages of history. Rats are dangerous. They damage structures, chew through electrical lines, eat and urinate on human and animal food, and serve as vectors of plague and other grave diseases. But rats are also a product of our communities and of our lifestyles, and they need to be engaged, monitored, and managed. It takes a village to produce and to deal with a clutch of rats.

Rodent prevention begins with monitoring: can you discriminate among the different species of mice and rats? Rats rely on their senses of smell, taste, touch, and hearing to locate food. They have poor vision so they stake out a system of pathways, which they mark with their urine and follow regularly. Incidentally, I have read, but have not confirmed personally, that both wet and dry rat urine glows under ultraviolet light, a ghoulish way to locate and track the rodent pathways around your home and garden.

Once you have identified your rodent pest and located its byways, the next step is to limit access to all rodent food sources. Mice prefer grain and seeds; rats forage in garbage and compost without hesitation.

Many people choose to set rat-traps or use glue boards to trap rodents. Rats are very clever and suspicious, so it is not easy to catch them, especially in spring traps. I have trapped a few rats in live catch or Havahart traps baited with globs of peanut butter, a rat favorite. But then I had to dispose of the frantic rat. I have driven rats many, many miles in order to release them on public land but I always feel guilty about doing this. Some people choose to drown the trapped rodent in a bucket of cold water, an experience I intend never to have.

Another option is to set out strychnine poison bait, especially if you have a rodent infestation in your garden or home. I am not in favor of using strychnine because it is so potent and dangerous. First, the bait can affect other animals who may attack and eat a poisoned rat. Second, the effects of the poison are gruesome for the animal eating the bait. I know. I have seen rats emerge from farmland hiding places, frothing at the mouth and crazed from ingesting strychnine bait.

My favorite method of rodent control is to protect the food sources and prevent rodents from establishing large populations. This means screening or boxing garbage pails; fencing your compost piles with stout, tightly woven wire; blocking all entrances to your house including chimneys, loose boards, and uneven foundations; and protecting pet food from rodent visits. It is more work for you but kinder to many sorts of beings and, ultimately, to yourself as well.

Although I am serious about curtailing rats in the garden, I also feel some strange empathy for them. When visiting my daughter's elementary school classroom I used to study their pet rat, Spotty. Without speaking I would watch her intelligent, frantic moves. Spotty's tail was a sense organ and her forelegs were both quick and hesitant at once. She would fix me with her intent, shiny eyes and I, hers, neither of us looking away.

Gophers are rodents, but as garden pests they are in a class by themselves. I understand that New England gardeners may never even see a pocket gopher, but in the places they like to live, they are a force of nature. Green Gulch Farm gophers have a sweet life and they eat well. Zen crops seem to embolden them. They thrust out of the earth, revealing their glossy pelts and rippling rings of double chins. Languidly they back into their burrows when people come near, seemingly aware that it goes against our pacifist grain to trap them. Plush moles, which, incidentally, are not rodents but insectivores, are also awesome in their determination, but pocket gophers outstrip them.

The main difference between garden moles and gophers is that gophers eat plants and moles eat insects and worms. Both animals contribute to soil health by aerating the ground as they tunnel along, and gophers also mix humus from the surface down into the soil, but both creatures are hard on plants. Moles disturb plant roots as they swim through the soil, leaving the roots hanging in the air where they easily dry out and die, so when I see mole trails I collapse the tunnels and lightly pack the earth back in place, but overall they probably do more good than harm. Gophers voraciously eat the roots of plants, including trees, shrubbery, tubers, bulbs, and tender annuals and perennials. If your garden harbors gophers and you plan to plant young trees, shrubs, and roses, planting them in wire baskets will protect them until they're grown. To figure out which underground pest you are dealing with, study the soil above their tunnels. If there is a long snaky humped trail, you have moles. If you have an occasional volcanic mound of soil and a hole, you have gophers.

I personally despise baiting and trapping, but many gardeners do choose these options. Gophers can be trapped and removed, or killed, but it is not easy to do. You may succeed in removing an individual gopher, but you are not likely to rid yourself of them for long. Prevention, in the form of underground cages, is likely to be more effective as well as less destructive.

Woodchucks, porcupines, and squirrels are usually not a severe problem in the garden, but pests they can be, especially bold squirrels like the gourmands we harbor at the Edible Schoolyard, who saunter across the garden from the compost pile with old avocados and full heads of decapitated sunflowers in their sharp little teeth.

For smaller gardens there are repellent sprays that are disagreeable to these rodent pests but not toxic. You can choose among an assortment of home-made or commercial cayenne sprays or a simple ammonium spray laced with fatty acids called "Hinder Deer and Rabbit Repellent," or purchased mixtures made of predator urine. These sprays are applied to trees, shrubs, and edible crops every two weeks and are fairly effective in shooing away rodent pests. A nice hot sauce of cayenne pepper and raw garlic, with a little bit of soap to act as a surfactant can work really well on seedlings or young transplants to protect them from rabbits, and also from birds, mice, rats, and deer, since the spray is unpleasantly piquant. This approach also has the benefit of selectivity: you can dis-courage a skunk from eating tomatoes, while leaving it all the hungrier for the insects that are its main diet.

Trapping garden rodents is not for the faint of heart. Most of us would rather remove these pests without encountering them or having to free them from brutal traps. But gardening is a life-and-death matter. My friend Christine, a serious, no-nonsense gardener, was digging a bed alone in her garden when she was eight months pregnant. She turned over a litter of newborn gophers being suckled by their mother. Gophers had been taking down a major por-tion of young fruit trees around Christine's land, trees just beginning to bear fruit. What would you have done in her place?

The Formidable Raccoon

Raccoons in the garden are another matter altogether. Smart and continuously hungry, the new-world raccoon is a member of the same family as the coatis of South America and the pandas of Asia. I've always thought of our local raccoons as runaway tropical beasts, a weird splice of mischievous monkey and unstoppable panther, although they are in fact more accurately a blend of dog and bear. We know each other in every way, and are—as Suzuki Roshi admonished Zen students to be—as intimate as water and milk. In the early days of Green Gulch raccoons ran the show: they stole freshly baked bread at night as it cooled in our carport kitchen; they overturned compost buckets and sorted our garbage for us; and they broke and entered our flimsy store-rooms and left telltale peanut-butter tracks across the dining room floor before shuffling out their pried-open exit windows.

Raccoons have gigantic, eclectic appetites: they are carnivorous and brutally effective, as we learned when we kept chickens at Green Gulch. We had to be punctual about closing the poultry house before dark, because every night the raccoons would come to shake and fret the locks. One night we arrived a little late and hastily locked up, unaware that we were enclosing a large raccoon inside a coop of dozing chickens. The next morning eight birds had been slaughtered and a fat, blood-streaked raccoon shambled past as we opened the henhouse at dawn.

In the field raccoons have a penchant for both meat and sugar. They love sweet corn, tearing it down off the stalk just as the silks get dark and the corn ripens. Raccoons are a more accurate ripeness monitor than a refractometer, the tool that measures the sugar content of plants. Once raccoons get into a crop, we know that crop is fit for harvest. In their plunder, raccoons certify the readiness of heirloom tomatoes, ripe sugar pumpkins, and heritage dessert apples.

Fortunately, because of their voracious appetite raccoons are not only pests but also excellent predators of other pests, hunting mice, rats, snakes, voles, and many insect grubs. They are excellent climbers, famous for their manual dexterity, and they have extraordinary night vision. At the back of their eyes is a tapetum that reflects light back through the retina, which is why raccoon eyes shine with a piercing red light when you aim a flashlight beam at one. I have had many night standoffs in the fruit orchard with raccoons feasting in a prize 'Newton Pippin' apple tree, plucking the sweet, yellow-green apples of autumn. No amount of arm waving and yelling fazes them as they fix me with their crimson glare and continue to stuff apples into their muzzles.

Raccoon damage control depends on blending the three control strategies of vertebrate pest management: exclusion through physical barriers, habitat management or protection to reduce food and shelter favored by the creature, and removal of nuisance individuals.

Raccoons live well by their wits. They seem to love the challenge of physical puzzles and mazes. At Green Gulch we developed elaborate exclusion systems for our kitchen compost storage bins including bungee-cord latches and many intricate handmade locks. But one night of forgetfulness and raccoons are there, without fail, sorting the garbage. Once they figure out your system, they will never forget how to work your latches and screens.

Recently a friend told me about an innovative scheme for deterring raccoons and other persistent four-legged pests. She set up a motion-sensing rotating water jet in her garden and turned it on at night. The surprise factor and the unwelcome jet of water washed her washing bears right out of her garden.

When you have been trying to outfox your raccoon population for as long as some of us have, you may develop a macabre sense of challenge and adventure. One night the raccoons of the Gulch figured out a way to jimmy the sliding lock on the farm truck and pried open the door and ate about twenty loaves of fresh bread boxed for market the next day. They scooped out all the loaves, leaving shells of bread scattered throughout the truck. Our irate head baker refused to be outdone. He concocted a tomatoey brew laced with fiery red chipotle peppers, soap, and garlic, and stuffed the goop into the scooped-out bread shells, leaving the truck door slightly ajar the next evening. Then he hid in the kitchen and waited. Around midnight two washing bears arrived, sassy, fat, and hungry. They climbed into the truck and began eating the bread. The baker heard them cough and sneeze, but they ate every last crumb of the fire-hot loaves and came back the next night for more nuclear salsa.

Bird Watch

As long as I have practiced zazen at Green Gulch Farm I have listened to the hundreds of birds surrounding the meditation hall as they wake up and begin their day. Birds have been a challenge at the Gulch, not only to concentration in the zendo but to farm crops as well. For years bird damage to tender crops was significant enough to warrant a daily "bird watch" at dawn during zazen and during the evening period of meditation. We took turns doing bird watch, actually quite a pleasant practice, walking mindfully up and down the 150-foot-long crop rows, clapping sticks together to frighten off the birds that wanted the crops for themselves.

The Green Gulch garden is on a major flyway, and migrating birds gather to feast on the large insect population of the organic farm and are a true benefit to the garden. But birds that form flocks and hang around, like grackles, crows, red-winged blackbirds, quail, starlings, and pigeons, are also formidable garden pests. Insects only whet their appetite: flocking birds gather on crops in droves to follow their insect course with fine succulent salad, finishing off their meal with a peck or two of dessert apple. I follow their unmistakable seasonal calling cards for proof of their feasting: blackberry-blue droppings in August yield to yellow, liquid stool from the wild toyon of autumn.

In addition to flocking birds, gardens also suffer from the appetites of certain common songbirds, like the American robin, the cedar waxwing, the sparrow, the oriole, the common house finch, all the jays, and a whole range of what I less-than-affectionately call "the SBBs" or "small brown birds."

There are a few basic biological controls that are effective against birds, such as a good bird dog who is experienced in flushing out flocks of birds without trampling the garden. Cayenne spray also protects seedlings from birds that like to peck succulent growth. But physical barriers are the only reliable recourse when birds pester your garden. If you ever lose a fifty-foot row of new lettuce to the frenetic pecking of hordes of courting quail, physical barriers and scare tactics for birds will suddenly become a fascinating study. You can drape plastic netting over fruit trees, berries, and grapes once the fruit begins to show color. The biggest problem with netting is that the most persistent birds fret the net and get inside. Floating row covers made of high-quality spun bonded polypropylene are light enough to be laid directly on low-to-the-ground crop rows to protect plants from birds, deer, slugs, snails, insects, and some rodent and rabbit attacks, particularly to tender seedlings. This material is porous to water and air and has good light transmittal.

In California a visit to the wine country just before harvest offers the spectacle of lines and lines of flashing red and silver Mylar tape stretched above the vines to scare away pecking birds. Scare-eye balloons bobbing over row crops and orchards can be startling and effective because birds are easily scared, but in order for scare tactics to work reliably they must be varied, since all birds soon grow accustomed to your tricks and are no longer fooled. All these scare tactics work best on high-flying flocking birds, as the flash and crackle of Mylar tape is most effective at a distance. They are not so useful in frightening solitary songbirds such as robins or jays since these pests fly closer to the ground, where they can more easily see through your ruse.

Even though I rant and rave when songbirds and flocking birds descend onto the garden, I also deeply enjoy their company. Occasionally I stay in the garden after the lunch bell has cleared the fields of hungry Zen gardeners. I love to water when everyone is gone. In this quiet zone an occasional Anna's hummingbird darts in through the slatted shutters of the glasshouse to hover above my nose, dipping her beak into the stream of water, her iridescent wings beating the hot summer air, while outside bodacious rooks tear apart the garden compost pile.

Now and then I discover a stabbed apple gouged by a hungry Steller's jay and scoured to a thin-skin balloon by the autumn wasps of the garden. I stop still for a moment, in awe of the efficiency of winged creatures. "You miss the whole point of the garden," Alan Chadwick once insisted, "if you fail to notice the birds." I also have an equally vivid memory of that Chadwick-mangled blue jay hung by a jute noose as a gruesome warning to the marauding tribe of jays scissoring to shreds Alan's prize limestone lettuce.

Dogs, Cats, and Kids in the Garden

I have an abiding fondness for all canine breeds, but an untrained dog can wreak havoc in a garden: the hunting breeds chase after all the smaller vertebrates that inhabit the garden, terriers dig caverns in your freshly cultivated carrot bed, the retrievers retrieve every dead or dying carcass within a hundred-mile radius and deliver them to you, while the quiet, lazy breeds like the bull-dogs lie down to nap on soft beds of yellow and purple pansies. Some habits will be easier to retrain than others: a bulldog will willingly sleep somewhere else, but terriers have a genetic compulsion to excavate the earth.

Being a dog person, I will never understand cats. Domestic cats often like to dig in the garden, and being cats they won't be trained out of it. To discourage this it helps to keep your beds tightly planted or covered with a rough surface mulch or with floating row covers, or you can set up one of those unpredictable water jet systems. Or get a different cat.

Cats, like dogs, have a valued place in the garden when they follow their hunting instincts, but it is impossible to have them kill unwanted gophers and field mice and then offer clemency to the songbirds trilling in the Saint John's-wort. I have seen a sleeping house cat stretched out on the garden bench in the herbal circle of the Green Gulch perennial garden lift his head at the sound of a little warbler and catch it in mid-flight as he leapt off his perch.

On Cat Manure

Remember not to handle feline feces or to try to compost cat manure. It is nasty stuff, carrying serious pathogens dangerous to children and adults and should be buried deep in the soil if you encounter it anywhere in the garden or near your soil mix and potting area. Similar dangers lurk in mouse and rat droppings, which should be swept up carefully and not touched.

As for children in the garden, much as I love them they can be a disaster if they are not monitored and entertained or, better still, put to work. Ask a child to keep a younger one out of the beds, or take the time to explain a special task to a child and give her responsibility for the harvest of the first sequoia strawberries. Their open joy and concentration is worth the forfeit of fruit and you also get a little more time to work. Never make children feel unwelcome or peripheral, or they will come to resent and resist the garden, an outright shame, and then to whom will we be able to entrust our gardens and our love for the wild and growing world?

Most of my garden life has included working with children, mine and others', and learning from them as we work. Although I do work a little more slowly when I am with children, they also help me see and appreciate the garden, both while they are next to me thinning and tasting baby carrots and, especially, when they leave, tired, dirty, and full of new life. There is no quiet like the quiet of the newly abandoned garden when happy, rambunctious children finally go home.

When I was learning to garden I worked with a Zen student who was a great gardener and a new mother. Daya's son, Kelly, was about fifteen months old, a wiry firecracker imp, shooting out random, live sparks. When he was in the garden Kelly often pulled his clothes off and scoot-crawled naked around the beds. Once we found him with a juvenile garden snake hanging out of both corners of his mouth. Daya nearly collapsed from shock. The baby saw her surprise, opened his mouth to laugh, and clapped his hands as the snake slithered away. No barrier or control stops a determined child. So just surrender. With Kelly I confess that I laid mounds of newly cut stinging nettles around my prize bed of carrots that he loved to pull up and discard, but he tanked right through the nettles, and continued until he reached and mangled the new carrots.

When children are permitted to garden not only might they develop a love and sensitivity for the life of the green world, they may also find a stomach for grief and change, a dual force at work in every dynamic garden. I have learned not to protect young people from this duality when they are in the garden, and not to interpret sorrow and death for them when they come upon it in the garden.

I learned this lesson when I was a young woman myself, first working in the Zen Center gardens, when a young doe died right next to me. The doe had gotten into the field in the early morning, at the end of the growing season when the hills were dry and barren of food. We spotted her during communal work, trotting the periphery of the deer fence, tailed by her minuscule fawn, a little flea of a deer wanting to imbed herself in her mother's hide. In our excitement at finding them in the field we chased the deer, shouting and gesturing, trying to sweep mother and fawn along the edge of the fence line, out the open gate to the coastal hills beyond the garden.

But we lost ourselves in the process and forgot the true nature of deer, and their essential wildness. Deer cannot be chased or herded. When they are cornered they explode in panic, like shattered quicksilver. We watched helplessly as the doe panicked and threw herself against the deer fence and broke her neck. Her little fawn bounded away in the rising light.

Katagiri Roshi was working with us that morning. He put down his hoe and we sat together near the foam-flecked deer. "Should I put her out of her misery?" asked Steve, who had grown up on a farm in Kansas and understood such matters. "Just sit with her," Katagiri told us quietly, and so we did.

The doe died quickly, with a black gurgle of blood in her long, elegant throat. We carried her to the compost pile and buried her in the center of the heap, covering her with mounds of manure-rich bedding straw. Her bones were picked clean and absorbed into the pile in less than three months. Only her delicate skull remained, staring out hollow-eyed from the pile when we turned that compost heap early the next spring. We never found her fawn.

I wish that there were some way to garden without harming and taking life, but I do not believe that there is. Gardener and pest are intertwined, made of each other. Practicing with this truth softens the edge between us.

Scarab Beetles and Assassin Bugs

Consider a world that up until now
you have only stepped upon.
Motto of the Sonoran Arthropod Society

INSECTS IN THE GARDEN INDUCE A GENERALIZED PANIC. THE CHEMICAL pesticide, or insecticide, industry has annual sales of more than eight hundred million dollars. And yet, the lives of insects and their offspring remain intimately hitched to our lives and to how we plant and tend our gardens and landscape plantings. Our human attitude toward arthropods, a large phyla of the animal kindom that includes insects and spiders, has not always been so combative. In ancient Egypt the scarab beetle, rolling away balls of animal dung, was seen as a sacred being, imitating the passage of the sun rolling across the heavens. At the same time, the scarab beetle was transforming manure into soil, keeping the earth fertile.

In Europe it was once traditional for the sower after planting the field to return and cover the land, imitating seed broadcasting with an empty hand, calling out, "I sow this for everything that flies and creeps, that walks and stands, that sings and springs, in the name of God the father." In recent years I have come to doubt that I garden and grow plants for hungry people; instead, I have begun to feel that, like it or not, I garden and grow plants as much for the minuscule but mighty arthropods of the animal kindom.

I am a rancher, feeding herds of multi-jointed, snap-winged insects and spiders, mites and crustaceans that inhabit not only the garden but also my mind. There are far more arthropods, or "joint-footed," beings than all other animals on earth combined. And within the arthropod phyla there are far more beetles than all of the other arthropods combined. In fact, there are more than two million species of insects in the Insecta class and most of these are beetles.

Arthropods and gardeners work side by side in the garden and form an integrated system. Such a system then widens to include the complex food webs

The Class Insecta

The class Insecta contains about thirty orders, including the familiar ones of beetles; butterflies and moths; wasps, ants, and bees; grasshoppers; flies; and mosquitoes. Gardeners often classify the array by what they eat: herbivores, who feed on plants; carnivores, who feed on blood or on other insects, worms, or slugs; scavengers, the recyclers of the insect world, who feed on decaying plants or animals; and omnivores, the insects that feed on anything they can get and populate our homes, eating soap, starch, glue, and sweet grain.

All insects grow and develop by metamorphosis, changes of body form and appearance. The damage an insect does in the garden often depends on which stage of life that insect is in, so it is important to recognize these different life stages. The most developed insects, such as bees, butterflies, wasps, moths, true flies, and beetles undergo complete metamorphosis, while more primitive insects pass through incomplete metamorphosis. During complete metamorphosis insects pass through four distinct life stages: the egg stage, a wormlike larval stage, the pupa or cocoon stage, and the adult stage. The larvae of insects that undergo complete metamorphosis live in different habitats and eat very different food from their adult form. Insects that undergo incomplete metamorphosis, like aphids, dragonflies, plant bugs, and crickets, undergo a primitive form of transformation in three stages: egg, nymph, and adult. The nymph looks similar to the adult. Adults and nymphs eat the same food and live in the same habitat.

that sustain the natural enemies of pestiferous arthropods, the plants that support the garden populations of arthropods, and all the plants, minerals, fungi, and microbes that cycle in and around these organisms. This wider world is the ecosystem that pervades and influences every healthy, open system.

Gardening with arthropods begins with knowing just who is pestering your garden. To this end, our friend and farm advisor Amigo Bob Cantisano has a tool that would strike green envy in my heart every time he visited the Gulch. It is a bug-vac, a small handheld vacuum used to collect insects for identifica-

tion purposes. One June day when Amigo was visiting we vacuumed the flat Italian parsley just to see who was there. After Amigo made one or two zippy passes over the crop he emptied out the catch net at the base of the suction tube. A vast array of stunned arthropods lay before us: tachinid flies galore, pollen-eating midges, walking sticks, numerous parasitic wasps, winged aphids, leaf hoppers, predaceous thrips, and many syrphid flies all spilled out. In addition there were lots of spiders. "Those are the wolves of the garden, gobbling up your true pests," commented Amigo. "Good sign that you have so many. Everyone eats well at Green Gulch!" he laughed.

The first insects flew through the dark coal forests that covered the earth three hundred million years ago. Fossil remains of dragonflies from this epoch have been retrieved from pressed coal seams buried 2,300 feet underground in Derbyshire, England. Their modern dragonfly descendants voraciously snapping up insect prey on a sunny afternoon in the lower garden are not greatly changed.

Insects have three distinct body parts: head, thorax, and abdomen. The head includes antennae and at least one pair of compound eyes. The head contains telltale mouth parts that reveal whether the insect bites, chews, pierces, sponges, or sucks up its food. Ancestral insects had three pairs of jaws on their heads but modern species of insects are more streamlined: these jaw parts are modified according to function. The chewing insects have strong mandibles, the first pair of jaws. The sucking insects have powerful maxillae, to help push or suck food back into the mouth. And some insects have all these mouth parts modified into piercing needles, spongelike mops, or sucking tubes according to what they eat.

Insects are essential to the well-being of the world: they help pollinate over three-quarters of the wild and cultivated crops that feed humankind, they consume their fellows who are pests and who are responsible for the destruction of 10 to 15 percent of the world's food, and they also clean up and pick clean the animal dung and rotten bodies of dead plants and animals that would otherwise pollute the world. Unfortunately, because of the spraying of toxic chemicals, the loss of agricultural land to development and erosion, and massive air and water pollution, thousands of the world's insects are also now facing extinction. When I remember that for one out of every three bites of food I take, I can thank a bee or another pollinator, I get fierce about gardening with an ecosystem approach that includes protecting arthropods rather than "offing" them.

Arthropods that live off other arthropods are classified as predators, parasites, or parasitoids, but even though there are these neat distinctions, in the garden all beings in the ten directions prey on one another. Some creatures prefer tender plant parts and succulent nectar, others choose to attack soft-bodied aphids or the translucent eggs of migrating monarch butterflies. I watch with horror and fascination but I also know that I am part of the grisly show.

Predators are free-living, general feeders. In the arthropod world, they usually chew or pierce their victims. The most effective predators among them are spiders, the other major division of garden arthropods. Spiders are distinguished from insects quite simply: they have two body segments instead of three, they have four pairs of legs instead of three, and they have no antennae.

Parasites live off their hosts while parasitoids kill their hosts. Parasitoids' finesse is fascinating and horrifying at once. Parasitoids lay their eggs in or on other insects, and when the parasitoid egg hatches, the larva of the parasitoid eats the host insect. Many insects are generalists and eat what they can find during the growing season, but most parasitoids are host-specific and some have been harnessed, so to speak, to control populations of plant-consuming pests.

Beneficial Insects

From the very first days of my gardening life I have cultivated a relationship with those insects that prey on their particularly pestiferous kin. Either predators or parasitoids, beneficial insects get their energy to track down their prey by feeding on pollen, for protein, and nectar, for carbohydrates, which is where I enter their multifaceted field of vision. My job is to grow sweet nectar treats and rich pollen banquets to keep their energy high for the hunt.

To begin with, I make a point of introducing members of the Umbelliferae and Compositae families to the garden. The flowers of both are rich in pollen and nectar that beneficials adore, and the flat-headed "umbrella"-shaped flowers of the umbellifers also provide great landing sites for beneficial insects to settle on, rest, feed, and scope out the territory.

My "good bug blend" includes coriander, Queen Anne's lace, borage, wild radish, Mexican sunflowers, and mustard, mixed in with a little vetch and buckwheat. You can plant this mixture in long rows or "friend strips" that grow and flower between crop rows, or in a home garden you can dedicate the bed ends to these beneficial insect plants. One year I grew a good-bug-blend border five feet wide and fifty-five feet long, a wild and woolly affair pulsating with a frenzy of varied insects, and one of the most beautiful flower beds in the entire garden.

Shrub and tree windbreak borders are also important habitats for beneficials. Some of the windbreaks I have cultivated are planted to California native plants as well as introduced exotics: red and blue elderberry, toyon, flowering eucalyptus, California coffeeberry — all provide good refuge and food for beneficials. By growing diverse plant guild communities for beneficial insects, you also enhance the wild and cultivated life in and beyond the garden.

Certain weeds are excellent host and larval plants for beneficial insects. Every year I notice the well-worked mallows, a favorite of the West Coast lady butterfly, and the frayed underleaves of the stinging nettle, indicating the presence of the hungry larvae of the red admiral butterfly. I allow nurse stands of these and other weeds in discrete patches throughout the garden. Once you begin to notice and appreciate your beneficial insect population you may be tempted to inoculate your garden with additional beneficials,

Major Beneficial Insects and Their Prey

The predators. These are carnivorous creatures who hunt and feed on pestiferous insects.

* *Dragonflies*: Fiercest of the fierce, the dragonfly seines the summer air for insect prey. One dragonfly can consume up to three hundred mosquitoes a day. The dragonfly depends on water for life, so if you are fortunate enough to live near a pond or a still source of water, dragonflies will work your garden.

* *Spiders*: I monitor the health of my garden by noting the presence of spiders. Spiders are among the most effective of predators, securing their prey by trapping (the web weavers are all trappers, including the funnel web, orb, and the cobweb weaving spiders), and by hunting and ambushing their prey (the wolf, crab, and jumping spiders are in this hunting subset). Spiders live in the garden year-round, consuming ants, beetles, flies, grasshoppers, snail eggs, and other unnamed residents.

* *Predaceous beetles*: This varied tribe of insects feeds voraciously on insect eggs, soft-bodied insects, and insect larvae including their own beetle clan larvae. Common beneficial beetles are the mealy bug destroyer, the ladybug beetle (predaceous in larval and adult stages of life), the ground beetle, and the soldier beetle.

* *True bugs*: Most bugs are plant feeders but a few are excellent predators, like the big-eyed bug and the minute piratebug feeding on insect eggs, tiny insects, and problematic mites. Larger bugs like the assassin bug, the damsel bug, and the spiny stinkbug feed on larger insects, caterpillars, and—sadly—all stages of other beneficial insects.

* *Lacewings*: The larvae of these beneficial insects attack thrips, mites, and insect eggs and as they grow they prey upon all soft-bodied insects. These creatures are primary beneficial predators.

* *Flies*: Although scorned and shunned by many, these insects (like the hoverfly and the long-legged midge fly) are predaceous in their larval and adult stages.

The parasitoids. This group of beneficial insects lay their eggs in or on other insects and when the eggs hatch the larvae feed on their host. Parasitoids are divided into two groups: the wasps and the flies.

* *Wasps*: Unlike the large and familiar stinging wasps such as the yellow jacket, hornet, and garden wasp, parasitoid wasps are minuscule and live by parasitizing their host prey, in particular leafhoppers, beetles, caterpillars, aphids, and certain bugs.

* *Flies*: These flies, especially the tachinid fly that looks like a large, overfed housefly, adore garden nectar and pollen and busily lay their eggs on or in caterpillars, crickets, and Japanese beetles.

especially if you develop pest problems that can best be solved or lessened by introducing host-specific beneficial insects.

Probably my most radical practice in honor of beneficial insects is planting pools of special insectory plants that will attract and host *pest* populations. I realize that Zen practitioners may be slightly off the deep end here. To cultivate a little patch of gone-by brassica plants every spring so that aphids will colonize this patch and serve as fresh meat for lacewings, ladybug beetles, and other predaceous insects is risky interbeing practice. I will long remember the year that a large garden tour visited our spring garden. The Siberian irises were glorious that year but I noticed that most of the tour members were mesmerized by the one huge, red Russian kale plant growing mid-bed, towering above the Siberians. This deliberate offering plant was covered, stem to stern, with pale gray aphids, a veritable farmers' market for beneficials. The garden club never returned to Green Gulch but their visit taught me that if you choose to grow gruesome insectory plants in your garden be sure to take them to the compost pile after a few weeks.

Garden Balance

When garden land is healthy and in good heart, insect damage is usually minimal. An infestation of pests is often a wake-up call pointing out to you that your garden is a little out of balance. I experienced this clarion cry a few seasons ago when spotted cucumber beetles took me by surprise and almost completely deformed the flowers of one of Alan Chadwick's prize yellow lotus dahlia, 'Glory of Heemestede.'

The second thing I wondered—the first was, how could I have been so unobservant that I missed the pest early in its cycle—was, how is the soil condition in the dahlia bed? When soil is in good tilth, neither too aerated nor too compacted, when it is fertile and productive and not lean or overpumped with nutrients, then the first and primary condition for plant health and pest

234

resistance is met. The key is to find the Middle Way practice and to make sure not to overfertilize, since high nitrogen content causes plants to grow succulent, yet weak, leaves, which are very attractive to sucking and piercing insects. This was the problem in the lotus dahlias—they had received too much fertilizer. A year or so after this cucumber beetle infestation I learned that yellow dahlias in particular are excellent trap crops for this insect, so since then I have planted yellow dahlias near the crops most pestered by the cucumber beetles in hopes that the insects will colonize the dahlia flowers instead of destroying the tender brassicas.

While not overdressing your plants be sure to maintain even garden fertility, since soil that is too lean causes stunted plant growth and signals pests to flock to your garden to feast. Plants are much less pest and disease prone when you follow a regular, year-round program of compost application and foliar and soil drench feeding, especially since such a program builds and sustains an enhanced microbial population that wards off insect attack and plant disease.

Pests tend to be host-specific, so rotating your crops around the garden will break the breeding cycle of some pests. I also practice "trap-cropping," a disobedient variation of crop rotation and subtly connected to growing insectory plants to feed beneficials. This practice is particularly valuable for brassica or cabbage family pests that overwinter in the soil. Brassicas need to be rotated to keep them a step ahead of their pests, but in order to trap some of these insects in the next growing season I deliberately plant a few members of the same cabbage family in the place where they were grown the previous season. These plants then lure and trap the emerging generation of pests. This practice demands vigilance and care, because you have to trap the pest population before it really takes off, and you have to deal with the infested trap plants, too. When you can pull up the host plants and compost them before the cabbage looper emerges from her chrysalis, you help reduce pest populations without having to resort to chemical pesticides.

When I notice crop damage in the garden the first thing I try to assess is how the damage happened. I have learned that you cannot assume that the damage is from arthropod pests since most serious damage to crops is caused by diseases like mildew, mold, and rust, and by bitter weather. A wry and dramatic observation of this comes from the book *Man's Plague:* "The black mount of . . . Famine rides in many guises, but he is not an arthropod."

Arthropod damage differs from plant disease. When you notice large holes in plant leaves or fruit, curled leaves wrapped in webs, leaves with raised wartlike galls on them, or tunnels burrowed into fruit, you can be sure you are seeing pest damage. Don't panic, keep looking. Insects also suck flowers, so check and see if flowers are wilted or being eaten. It is also a good idea to check the roots of plants that show signs of stress. One year at Green Gulch our larkspur seedlings began to keel over. The whole bed went into rapid decline. We discovered wireworms burrowing into the root system of the flowers. The lower plant stems were also inundated with them. We had missed their arrival and found them only at the completion of their cycle.

Managing Pests

A commonsense response to pests in organic gardens begins with indirect preventive methods and goes on to enlist direct-response tactics that intensify as need demands. The best approach I know is a refined and practical system of integrated pest management, or IPM, adopted by most organic and conventional gardeners. IPM practice begins with indirect or preventive pest management, including careful garden design, good soil culture, a diverse plant population, sound fertility management, careful design of irrigation systems, scrupulous choice of disease-free plants for the garden, and knowledge of weather and climate patterns. All indirect methods of pest suppression depend on mindful awareness of your garden and on a determination to learn about and reduce the pests' favored environment. Enhancing an environment that supports beneficial organisms goes a long way toward keeping garden pests and disease in balance.

Direct management of pests is exactly that—directing your efforts to the unwelcome visitor itself, beginning with stopping and removing pests physically. Physical and manual controls put barriers between pest and plant without directly interfering with the plants'

236

lives. This response level includes manual removal of visible pests, setting traps and putting up fences and netting to exclude pests from the garden, and using heat and cold to destroy pests and their preferred environment. Careful, timely weeding is also an important physical control of pests and disease as is the practice of digging up and removing infested plants from the garden so that disease does not spread. This physical-barrier approach is the least invasive stage of direct pest management from the plant's point of view, though obviously not from the pest's perspective.

Putting out bait is also an effective physical solution for certain pestiferous insects, especially using pheromone strips to monitor and disrupt insects' mating patterns. A pheromone is a nontoxic species-specific chemical that is produced by a female insect to attract a mate. This "scent" is duplicated in a lab and put on yellow sticky-tape traps. These traps are most effective for grain and orchard pests like codling moths, grain moths, the olive fruit fly, peach borers, and citrus red scale. Sticky traps without pheromones also trap and kill pest insects. Flypaper, yellow sticky tape, and tree-tanglefoot, a sticky salve squeezed onto tree trunks and greenhouse table legs, all snare nearby pests.

Last of all in the physical control realm is hand-picking. At Green Gulch we once paid our children a penny apiece for snails and two cents each if

Slugs and Snails

Slugs and snails (class Mollusca) are the land-dwelling kin of mussels and clams. In our moist West Coast gardens these creatures are never far away from us, enjoying almost all of our plants in almost all of their stages. All land-dwelling mollusks are formidable garden pests, rasping large holes in established foliage and mowing to the ground newly planted seedlings.

Common slugs and snails are one-eighth to one inch long, although the famed banana slug of the coastal forest may be as long as four to six inches. All these creatures travel in a silver trail of mucilaginous slime, laying their copious, clear eggs in large jellylike masses under garden debris.

If slugs and snails are an occasional problem in your garden, spread wide bands of rough cinders, wood ashes, or diatomaceous earth around your vulnerable plants. Where these mollusks are a more serious threat you can protect your plants by edging your garden beds with copper flashing or by affixing individual copper barriers around your most vulnerable plants.

I confess that I have also occasionally resorted to putting out the slug and snail's favorite bait. Filling sunken lids with fermented beer at night, inebriated slugs and snails drown in their preferred drink. Although this remedy and its mop-up is a tad gruesome, so is the tattering caused by slimy, sober garden mollusks.

they took them to the chicken yard so that the hungry poultry could feast on escargot. One dawn my son received ninety cents for his fifteen minutes of gathering snails in our prize delphinium bed.

Biological controls are a hallmark of integrated pest management. Beneficial insects are primary agents of biological control and balance, always present in diverse and healthy organic gardens. Augmenting beneficial populations by introducing a predator or parasitoid insect to your garden can be helpful, especially if you get good professional advice before doing so. Remember, beneficials must be introduced at the right season, and in the right stage of their life cycle, to be of true use.

Chemical controls are the strongest stage of direct pest management. They have a powerful impact on a pest, and an equally strong effect on the plants and the entire ecosystem of the garden. Both inorganic and organic chemicals are used as pesticides, with the inorganic ones being generally milder. Inorganic chemical compounds, those without a carbon base, such as boron, copper, and sulfur, and certain dusts, such as silica and diatomaceous earth, are among the oldest and strongest of naturally occurring chemical pesticides. Many of these inorganic pesticides come in crystal form, soluble in water and relatively easy to apply.

Naturally derived organic chemical pesticides are organic compounds with a carbon base. Though worlds apart from synthetic, usually petroleum-based, pesticides, both are organic compounds. The word "organic" has two meanings in the garden. The "organic" in "organic gardening" most simply means not using synthetic, powerful, long-lasting, and corrosive fertilizers and pesticides and relying heavily on compost-based fertility. The "organic" in "organic chemicals or compounds" means "derived from nature" and therefore having a carbon base, as for instance petroleum. Examples of natural chemical pesticides that are used in organic gardening are insecticidal soaps and horticultural oils, as well as botanically derived products like neem and pyrethrum.

Use of chemical pesticides, especially those powerful ones synthetically derived from petroleum, has resulted in pest resistance and sometimes immunity, causing even stronger chemical agents to be introduced. These pesticides tend to kill all the insects they come in contact with, often causing a resurgence in the pest problem because the beneficial insect population has been poisoned along with the pest population. Occasionally the application of chemical pesticides will lead to an outbreak of secondary pest problems. Most sobering of all, the introduction of chemical pesticides to your garden may be dangerous to your own health and to the health of your ecosystem. So use chemicals with care and only as a last response to insect pests.

Before using any pesticide on your garden, be sure that you understand what it is meant to do and that you form a good plan for monitoring and tracking the effectiveness of the pesticide. Often you can use a strong jet of water to wash off pests and not have to resort to any pesticides whatsoever. Select the least-toxic pesticide first and see if it is effective. Because of low toxicity levels, these pesticides disperse quickly and do not last a long time in the garden. Never reapply them before the recommended time. In addition, the least-toxic pesticides are often slower to get to work than more potent chemical pesticides, even though they may be just as effective against the pest in the long run. Be patient.

Give up the unrealistic goal of total removal of pests and settle instead for lowering the levels of pests in your garden. Learning to tolerate a little pest damage in exchange for the overall health and balance of your local ecosystem is essential to organic gardening. Most of all, avoid using synthetically derived chemical pesticides as they compromise human and animal health, the health of the local environment, and the overall health of the biosphere.

I divide pesticides into simple categories based on what they are made of and how they work. The application of these materials depends on knowing the life cycle of the insect I am attempting to subdue, since many of these products only work on the larval stage of an insect's life cycle. I never use synthetic pesticides since they are not certified for organic gardening.

Horticultural Oils. These kill pests by suffocating them. As early as the first century AD the Roman scholar Pliny the Elder acclaimed the use of mineral oil in controlling certain garden pests. Horticultural oils may be petroleum-based (coming from fossilized plants), vegetable-based (from living plants), botanical-based (from plant extracts or resins), or animal-based (from animal fat). They degrade rapidly and have almost no residual toxicity to humans, animals, or plants. They are best applied mixed with water and an emulsifier, such as soap, which allows oil and water to combine.

Horticultural oils are most effective against pest larvae and soft-bodied adult pests, such as aphids, scales, mealybugs, whiteflies, mosquitoes, cankerworms, mites, and leafhoppers. Organic corn growers like us are immeasurably grateful to mineral oil applied to corn silk just as the silks begin to darken and dry in order to prevent the unsightly damage of the notorious corn earworm. Oils are generally used during the dormant season to smother the eggs of pests, but recently some experimental gardening friends of mine have applied very dilute solutions of horticultural oil directly to the leaves and bark of perennial plants, particularly fruit trees and the leaves of roses to subdue summer pests. If you choose this route be sure that your plants are not water-stressed or else the oil may clog their stomata and injure the host plant.

Insecticidal Soaps. In Europe soap sprays have been used for insect control for more than three hundred years. Nontoxic to the user, insecticidal soaps are popular because they are a very effective method for controlling soft-bodied insect pests. I have used diluted insecticidal soaps for years on aphids when they colonize the spring foliage of the classic heritage roses.

Pesticidal soap works by dissolving the outer cuticle or shell of soft-bodied insects and penetrating to the inner core membranes of the insect, causing paralysis and dehydration upon contact. Modern insecticidal soaps today have their ingredients balanced so that dosages do not vary. This is important because if soaps are not balanced they can burn and dry out plant foliage as well as pesky insects. If you elect to use insecticidal soap on your garden pests be sure to check the soap first and see if it burns your plants as well as your pests. Tender, newly transplanted plants are the most susceptible, so be cautious when spraying and avoid new growth.

Botanical Sprays. Many plants contain natural compounds that discourage pests. Botanical pesticides are made from ground-up plant parts, from plant extracts or resins, or from pure chemicals extracted from pest-resistant plants.

Remember that just because a pesticide is derived from a plant does not mean that it is safe for human or animal use. Botanical substances are generally more potent than oils and soaps and must be applied with precision and care. However, like oil and soap products, organically certified botanical pesticides do tend to break down after a few days into harmless compounds. Sun and water help with this breakdown, as do microorganisms that can digest and dismantle toxic botanical substances.

Many botanical insecticides only work when they contain a synergist, or substance that helps to disarm or deactivate the enzymes in an insect's body that break down toxins. Synergists are usually blended with botanical insecticides at a ratio from two to one up to ten to one, helping to make the botanical pesticide more effective. When synergists are present, less botanical pesticide is needed.

Garlic, an allium, or a member of the lily family, contains the volatile oil alliin as well as other compounds that are effective natural insecticides. Garlic has also been used for thousands of years as a purifying herb and a plant to help strengthen the immune system and treat headaches, colds, croup, coughs, and toothaches.

Garlic is a broad-spectrum insecticide that kills beneficial insects and microbes as well as pests. Gardeners have long used homemade sprays of garlic crushed with a tiny dash of cayenne pepper, which is a lethal metabolic stimulant for soft-bodied insects. One year at Green Gulch we whizzed up the brew in our pesticidal blender and applied it in our young fruit orchard to quell an aphid infestation on our newly planted apple trees. The garlic was effective, but brutally so, and I now regret all the green lacewings and convergent lady beetles who died in that lethal dousing that would easily have routed all vampires in the ten directions from our Zen gardens.

Pyrethrums are another broad-spectrum insecticide, derived from the natural extracts of the crushed and dried flowers of the lovely *Chrysanthemum cinevariifolium*, a daisylike pyrethrum plant from Kenya. Pyrethrum extracts are stunningly effective insecticides. They are called the "knock-down" insecticide of the garden world, for once insects come in touch with pyrethrum extracts they drop down dead out of the air. In over a hundred years of documented use, insects have never developed an immunity to pyrethrums.

Pyrethrum is effective against beetles of all descriptions, ants, thrips, ticks, leaf rollers, fruit flies, caterpillars, cockroaches, mosquitoes, whiteflies, aphids, army worms, and many more insects. Unfortunately, it also stuns the good guys and knocks them as dead as the pests. Pyrethrum is generally one of the safest botanicals available for the user and may be applied even on the day of harvest. However, it quickly biodegrades in sunlight, so most growers spray pyrethrums in the evening. This fast biodegrading is what makes pyrethroid pesticides safe despite their potency. Unfortunately, new research has found that some pyrethroids last a long time in dark, muddy stream bottoms protected from sunlight. Since there is potential for these powerful compounds to enter the food chain through ground water, avoid letting any pyrethroids wash into streams.

In the Green Gulch kitchen garden we planted pyrethrum seedlings throughout the brocade of our permanent beds, on bed ends, and in random pools in our friendship rows out in the farm fields. Planting this strong insecticidal chrysanthemum in the garden connects those who handle and spray its extracts to the beauty and power of the actual living plant. It also enhances the pesticidal properties of the other border plants. In addition, pyrethrum plants provide great cut flowers.

For years **rotenone**, a ground-up powder made from the tropical cuberoot plant, was our standard organic pesticide at Green Gulch. Rotenone is no longer approved for California organic gardeners, for although it is a very effective insecticide (it poisons the insect's stomach), it is also highly irritating to the human applying it. If you live in a state where rotenone is still certified for use, you might try a liquid blend of rotenone and pyrethrum since they are very effective in combination, and the liquid form is much easier to handle. The pyrethrums rout the insect, causing it to be excited and agitated, while the rotenone serves as a stomach poison. It is a very effective combination for difficult pests like the flea beetle, scales, mites, pear psylla or pear slug, cucumber beetles, the squash bug, and leafhoppers.

Neem is a rather recent introduction to the organic pesticide market, a broad-spectrum botanical extracted as an oil from the seed and root of the tropical Indian neem tree. Long used as an effective pesticide in Africa and Asia, an extract of neem works by repelling, preventing molting, or suppressing feeding, depending on the insect and on its stage of metamorphosis. Neem oil is a broad-spectrum pesticide that is also an effective preventive fungicide and a very good insect repellent. Because neem works in multiple ways, it is most valuable sprayed at intervals against insects as they pass through the stages of complete metamorphosis.

Microbial pesticides contain microscopic living microorganisms that infect specific life stages of an insect and cause disease and eventual death. I think of microbial pesticides as a lightweight form of "germ warfare" that is relatively safe for humans, wild and domestic animals, beneficial insects, and the environment. Since microbial pesticides are quite specific in function by transmitting disease to their hosts, they must be ingested by their target species in order to be effective.

Microbial pesticides are not only host-specific but stage-specific, meaning that they only affect certain insects at specific life stages. For example, *Bacillus thuringiensis* v. *israelensis* (Bti) is often used to help control the spread of fungus gnats in greenhouses. The commercial name for this bacterial microbial spray is Gnatrol and it poisons the larval stage of the fungus gnat by infecting it with sickness. Having used this microbial pesticide in our greenhouse regularly one season when the fungus gnat was destroying many of our young seedlings, I can attest to its potent effectiveness. Plus, Gnatrol gave me a firsthand tutorial on discerning the life-cycle stages of the fungus gnat.

Currently many genetic engineering experiments are being conducted with microbial material. Unfortunately, the sensitive line between helpful research and dangerous manipulation is crossed when the toxic properties of microbials are incorporated into the gene structure of plants *themselves* so that insects die when they eat the plant rather than having the microbe kill them through causing direct internal sickness. The danger here is that this broad attack is always on, rather than targeted specifically, and eventually a super-strain of insect may evolve that is immune to what was once a very effective natural control. I can only imagine the GMDO-enhanced "Franken-gnat" that may someday darken my greenhouse door!

Finally, **hormonal pesticides** are insect growth regulators, which interfere with the natural growth cycle of insects. This "hormone therapy" relies on the use of natural hormones to speed up, slow down, or even arrest the natural growth cycle of insects. The most effective form of this IGR therapy so far has been the use of applied juvenile hormones to keep insects from maturing. Although I have no experience with IGR therapy I confess that this level of engagement, as well as some of the experiments with genetically engineered microbial pesticides, make me quite cautious and careful as I interact with well-known garden pests.

❖   ❖   ❖

I often wish that my pest response tactics were not so unilateral and brutal: Mow the mustard! Scythe the nettles! Spray the flea beetles! Yes, and miss out on that world that up until now I have only stepped on. Sometimes when I am out in the frosty fields harvesting flowers at daybreak, I find a bumblebee hunched over with cold, like a tiny crumpled knuckle in the frigid palm of ice blue delphiniums. As I breathe a long slow warm out-breath on the bee, she stirs back to life. I have a mind then, standing among the cold flowers, to practice with arthropods and poisonous weeds, and not just crush, spray, or colonize them.

The first precept the Buddha gave to his original followers was, Do not kill, do not take life. Yet my gardener's hands are stained with the bright blood of thousands of expired pests. I can set up an altar in the fields, offer incense and apologize, but when I turn around and see the white cabbage moth floating over the blue-green broccoli beds just behind my atonement altar, I strike.

Now and then I allow myself to imagine reincarnating as a carrot rustfly, looking for a crown of healthy, organically grown carrots where I can lay my eggs. Then I feel a rush of reverence and humility and ignore the stiff white maggots jutting at odd angles out of the carrots, and I rest in the wide lap of the all-inclusive garden, even if for just a few precious hours.

Medicine and Disease Subdue Each Other

WHEN I WAS NINETEEN YEARS OLD I LEFT COLLEGE FOR A YEAR to serve as a VISTA volunteer. I was sent to the coal fields of southern Appalachia, the oldest North American mountains, and lived deep in the folds of Saxon-Posey Holler, not far from Beckley, West Virginia.

I roomed with a coal-mining family that revolved around their matriarch, Grace Dickens, a feisty, outspoken woman who chewed Bulldog tobacco, put in a huge garden every year, and then canned all the food that came out of that garden to feed her kin through the lean winter months. Grace also kept the most spotlessly clean house I had ever seen.

I remember Grace down on her knees one Monday morning, swabbing her linoleum kitchen floor. "It's not the dirt I can see that bothers me," she confessed to me, "it's the dirt I *can't* see."

Plant disease in the garden is like that. It's not the insect damage that I can see on the young seedling *gypsophila* leaves that bothers me. It's the sleeping, mycelial web of pathogenic fungus that I *can't* see that makes me uneasy as I walk between tunnel rows of sweet peas underplanted with baby's breath gypsophila, all growing together in the early spring garden.

Years ago I stood with Harry Roberts at dusk, overlooking a winter field billowing with a chest-high swell of cover crop. Wave after wave of broad fava beans surged into tides of purple crown vetch laced with low bands of winter rye, the whole field suffused with a pale blue haze. Harry leaned on his wobbly aluminum crutches, inclining toward the field.

After a long time I asked him what he was doing. His eyes were almost closed, like a torpid lizard beginning to feel the warmth of day. "I'm reading the field," he murmured to me in a low reptilian voice.

Later on when we were inside Harry's house by the fireplace and he was comfortable and out of the blue spell of that huge winter field, he told me that it is possible to actually *read* health in plants. He said the silver-blue bloom on the cover crop was a clear indication of a healthy phosphorus content in the soil and in the field plants themselves, an analysis later confirmed by the results of our annual soil test.

When I stand out in the fields I want to be open not only to health and vigor but to what is at the edge of my view, to what I can't see at all and to what I am afraid of. There is a Zen koan from tenth-century China that comes to mind when I confront health and disease intertwined in the garden: Zen master Yunmen when teaching his community said, "Medicine and disease subdue each other: the whole earth is medicine—what is your self?"

I believe that the whole earth is medicine, but am I a bold enough gardener to also remember that medicine includes disease? In our modern world with pollution suffusing earth, water, air, plants, and even our own bodies, the stark truth of disease is everywhere. Death and disease lift the soft, dark skirts of every garden like a pestilent red wind. And it has ever been so. There has never been a healthy garden without a measure of disease. If medicine and disease are to subdue each other, both must be present, not just in the garden, but also in the gardener. On just this point, Alan Chadwick quoted Friar Lawrence's soliloquy to the gray-eyed dawn from *Romeo and Juliet*:

> Within the infant rind of this weak flower
> poison hath residence, and medicine power!

So it is with us also, we who pamper and pluck each tender, weak flower.

For many years I was terrified of plant disease. The very names of major plant diseases, the premier curse words of every gardener's lexicon, numbed me with terror: a blight of smut, mildew, and black spot on your house! May sooty mold darken your doorway and pustules of rust wilt your good fortune!

Although I know full well that "loathsome canker lives in the sweetest bud," it took an actual gardening disaster to help me confront the real presence of disease. For three seasons in a row we watched our sizable Green Gulch acreage of organic potatoes be torched with early and late potato blight, a virulent fungal disease that attacked the foliage of the potatoes,

246

turning the leaves grayish brown at first with rings of downy white spores appearing throughout the field. Later on, the leaves and stems of the potatoes died and the tubers themselves turned to putrid mush.

We had become careless and cavalier with our potato culture: we had failed to plant only certified organic potatoes and sometimes we planted organic seed taken from our own farm. Also, we occasionally watered overhead too late in the day, which is a clear invitation for fungal spores to settle and grow on crops, and certain sections of the potato field were not in a full and complete rotation pattern, so spores of blight remained in the soil or were hosted by the weedy nightshade relatives of the potato family that bordered the farm. And then we did not apply organic control sprays in time to arrest the blight.

This was an unforgettable lesson and a humbling one. We have the luxury and ability on our farm to attend to potato blight well, without depending on potatoes as our sole, staple food as the Irish did in the mid-1800s, when five or more consecutive years of blight caused the "Great Hunger" famine that brought death by starvation to more than one million people.

Blight on our farm made us better farmers and gardeners. Once we realized the extent of early blight disease in the potatoes, we responded. First, we purchased only organically certified seed potatoes to plant our new fields and then we rotated our potato patch to clean, unblighted soil and fallowed our blighted ground for two growing seasons.

Once the certified seed potatoes were planted we were careful to water early in the day and lightly, and to monitor every three to five days for signs of insect damage or nutrient deficiency. When the potato plants leafed out there was a trace of early blight in one patch so we pulled up and burned the infected plants and began to spray copper sulfate, an organic fungicide, at seven- to ten-day intervals throughout the remainder of the field. Then we made the hard decision to harvest the potatoes only when the foliage died back, because at this point the skin of the tubers is tougher and more impervious to disease. We sacrificed the enjoyment of new potatoes that year, but we were blessed with a disease-free potato patch all season long.

In every living garden soil, both beneficial and pathogenic microbes are hard at work. The beneficial fungi and bacteria attack decaying or dead organic matter and break it down into fertile plant food and soil nutrients. Pathogenic microbes live in this same healthy soil and colonize the roots and tops of choice garden plants. These microbial realms are inextricably linked and intertwined.

Disease Microbes

Fungi

In compost heaps beneficial fungi transform decaying organic matter into black gold, but the pathogenic fungi that attack plants and live off their succulence are formidable. Pathogenic fungi rely on specific living hosts for their food, and once fungal spores settle on their host plants the spores quickly grow through the tissue of their host plant in a threadlike network of mycelium. Next, they form a fruiting body and, fed by their host plant, they release a cloud of fresh spores that are moved to new hosts by wind, water, gardeners' boots, insects' feet and infected mouth parts, tools, and innocent pets passing through the moist, yeasty garden at dawn.

Fungi are responsible for the majority of plant diseases in the garden—root rots, early and late blight, soft rot in fruit, leaf spot disease, rusts, smuts, wilting, curled leaves, mold, mildew, and other dread disasters. Unfortunately many pathogenic fungi have the ability to overwinter in garden soil and spring back to life when their host plants or weedy relatives of the same family begin to grow.

Bacteria

Bacteria cause severe plant diseases—tree galls, soft rots, scabs, leaf spots, and blighted shoots—by feeding off the tissue and roots of garden plants. Unlike fungi, bacteria do not breed by producing spores, so they do not overwinter outside of their host. Instead, pathogenic bacteria live, feed, and breed within live plant tissue. Pest bacteria are primarily spread by water but they can also travel by insects, tools, or gardeners' shoes.

Viruses

Smaller even than bacteria, and far more deadly, viruses do not respond to any control measures. Where bacteria are single-cell organisms that live in host plants, viruses are microscopic particles that can only multiply within individual living cells of the host. Once viruses have colonized a host they upset the plant's normal metabolism and cause it to produce more virus particles. Viral disease is signaled by strange mottling and striation on plant leaves and by a change in leaf color. Growth is stunted and fruit maturation is also retarded by plant viruses such as mosaic disease, yellow bud mosaic, and cherry leaf-roll virus. Viruses are conveyed to new hosts by grafting or taking strikes off infected plants, by insect vectors, and by nematodes.

Nematodes

Nematodes are microscopic eel-like roundworms that damage crops by living in the soil and feeding off their roots. They invade the root systems of their host plants, causing a failure in moisture and nutrient uptake and eventual wilting and death of the host plant. As with the other pathogenic microbes, pest nematodes travel to new host plants along watercourses and in infected soil, as well as on tools and boots.

The first task of gardening in the presence of plant disease is to get to know more about the invisible world of disease microbes—who they are, how they move and grow, how they affect plants, soil, and the overall life of the garden. Far more plants succumb to disease pathogens than to insect or vertebrate pests. There are four groups of disease microbes—fungi, bacteria, viruses, and nematodes—microscopic in size but vast in their power and effect, the best "cure" for all of them is not to let them get established in the first place.

Practicing Pathogen Deterrance

The host specificity of pathogenic microbes can be used against them if you make an effort to choose resistant varieties for your garden. If you are planting crops that are prone to fungal disease, like potatoes, be sure that your seed or rootstock is from certified growers. Never be tempted to purchase vegetables for seed from the grocery store, even chic organic food stores or open-air farmers' markets. These crops are fine to cook and eat but they may carry dormant disease spores that can become established once they are planted in your garden.

The best prevention of plant disease in the garden depends on Middle Way gardening, cultivation, and fertilization that is neither too light nor too heavy. Every garden will require a different pattern of tillage and fertilization depending on its history and the sequence of your planting. Disease pathogens find their way to plants that are stressed by not enough nutrients, but they also select plants that are weakened by an excess of nutrients since too much nitrogen softens the cell wall of plant tissue and opens the plant to disease. Careful cultivation is not only a preventive measure, it is also helpful when you see the first signs of fungal disease in your garden. Cultivate the ground around the plants and make sure that you are not overdressing the plant with too much compost or compost tea. If your crop bed is too crowded air cannot circulate through the soil, so it is often helpful to thin out the bed, starting with removing all diseased plants and taking them to a burn pile. Sometimes it is necessary to use stronger means, like spraying with organic fungicides, as we did in our potato-blighted fields, but often deep cultivation and checking the fertility of the soil are sufficient to deter disease.

Disease pathogens in the soil travel with water, so never rely solely on overhead water, especially if you are growing disease-susceptible plants or if you live in a cool, foggy climate that is prone to fungal and bacterial disease.

Careful irrigation of the garden is an art. Harry Roberts used to remind us that it takes two years to learn to water your garden well, and this learning depends on steady observation as you water. If you must rely on overhead watering to irrigate your garden, then water early in the day since fungal spores and pathogenic bacteria usually settle on the garden in the cool of the evening and bloom at night, setting their spores during the warmth of the next day. Heavy watering can splash fungal spores up onto the undersides of susceptible plants. Drip irrigation definitely reduces fungal disease outbreaks. If you can only convert part of your garden to drip, begin with the plants most prone to disease pathogens, like roses, delphiniums, tomatoes, and garden fruit trees.

Disease will inevitably visit your garden, and when it does you can meet it with medicine, following the same IPM guidelines used for insect pests. Many of the remedies are the same, they just affect disease pathogens in different ways. Fallowing, cleanliness, and solarizing are the physical controls of IPM for diseases.

Practice clean culture in your garden. Since pathogens are delivered to plants through the movement of water, through infected soil, and by contact, be sure to keep the perimeter area around your garden clean of diseased plants and of infected plant material. If you discover fungal disease in your garden, remove the infected plants. Take them directly to a hot compost pile or, in the case of virus or nematode damage, to a burn pile, or to a toxic disposal site at your local dump, and be sure to wash your hands and tools well and even change your clothes and shoes before returning to healthy garden plants.

Once disease from microscopic pathogens gets started in the garden there are two ancient methods of resting or cleansing the soil that can be practiced as a kind of rotation: fallowing the garden bed, and opening the soil to extreme heat or cold, allowing sun and frost to clean the ground of your garden.

Fallowing land is an ancient practice of opening or tilling the earth and then leaving the ground unplanted and resting the soil from crop production for one or two seasons so that deep, abiding fertility can be restored. Fallowing can also be practiced if there is disease in the soil, in much the way that we rested our blight-infested potato field at Green Gulch. Fallowing for up to two years is an especially effective practice if pest nematodes have been detected on your land, since nematodes can live deep in the soil and reinfect host-specific plants or weedy members of the host genus plants for up to a year after infection.

Solarizing and freezing soil is another effective cleansing technique, although these practices kill beneficial organisms as well as pathogens. We solarized a section of the Green Gulch garden soil by covering it with black plastic for about three months and letting the sun heat the ground in order to treat a rampant outbreak of bindweed, or morning glory weeds. This method was effective for weeds within the top twelve inches of the soil but the deeper roots of the bindweed were not killed and they returned to claim the bed after a few years. However, since most disease pathogens live within the top foot of garden soil, solarization can be a very effective soil cleanser. And although I have never experienced a sustained hard freeze of the California earth that I garden every day, I did grow up in New England where our home ground was frozen solid from December until March. I still remember the fresh scent of the thawed spring earth as it returned to friable life.

Air Pollution

Plants are sensitive to air, water, and soil pollution and to the drift of pesticides or herbicides from the neighborhood. Air pollution caused by automobile exhaust displays itself as stippling on plant leaves and by a general yellow cast. If you live near a heavily traveled road or highway you will need to grow plants that are more tolerant of air pollution.

Herbicide drift manifests as burned-looking leaves or leaves that suddenly turn bronze, grow distorted, and die. Protect your garden with a well-built wall or fence or a strong windbreak and if your neighbor regularly sprays herbicides let this neighbor know how your garden is being affected. Suggest the possibility of using less toxic materials or spraying when there is no wind.

A Biological and Chemical Arsenal for Disease Response

In the garden there are a host of disease-specific and broad-spectrum biological controls that the home gardener can rely on and there are also many chemical aids that can be safely used. I base my biological and chemical response arsenal on the time-tested remedies that have been drawn on by generations of organic gardeners committed to strong, sustainable practices of microbial disease suppression. In addition to these traditional remedies there is an existing range of fresh products available to organic gardeners.

A new generation of biological controls has been developed that helps arrest plant disease before it gets started. These biological fungicides are beneficial microbes that protect disease-prone plants from soil-borne pathogens like fusarium wilt, botrytis, and phytophthora. These newer fungicides do not damage beneficial microbes in the soil; they only suppress the pathogens that cause disease.

An Israeli breakthrough is a parasitic fungus that attacks powdery mildew. There are other fungicides containing beneficial bacteria that attack the damping-off fungi that cause death to germinating seeds. Stay in touch with your local plant nurseries or garden centers since new biological products are always being made available.

The most effective botanical fungicides I know and use are derived from neem oil, the same botanical product that is used as an effective natural pesticide. Neem-based fungicides suppress powdery mildew, rust, leaf spot, and flower blight, but they should only be used sparingly since neem derivatives may reduce beneficial microbes as well as disease pathogens.

I am particularly fond of those home remedies that come from simple kitchen chemistry and can be surprisingly potent in their effect. These home remedies function as surfactants or antitranspirants and there are also similar products that you can purchase commercially to protect your garden from plant disease. What is important to understand in order to use these remedies effectively, is how they affect fungal and bacterial disease in the garden.

Surfactants, or surface agents, are soap-based sprays that coat plant leaves with fatty acids and disrupt the water balance inside of pathogenic microbes.

The fungi that are suppressed by surfactants thrive on new growth, so it is particularly important that you spray new growth.

Antitranspirants are natural waxes or polymers that are sprayed on the leaves of plants to reduce transpiration or water loss. These agents are effective against microbial disease pathogens because they form an impenetrable layer between the leaf and the fungal spore. Antitranspirants allow plants to breathe, but in cloudy climates they can cause problems themselves by inhibiting photosynthesis.

Your own kitchen can produce surfactant sprays that have natural fungicidal properties and are easy to make and apply. Baking soda and garlic sprays are effective against powdery mildew, black spot, and other rose diseases. Unfortunately they are somewhat indiscriminate in their potency and will affect your beneficial microbial and insect populations as well as disease microbes, so use these products carefully.

There are also many other strong remedies for plant disease that have been in circulation for hundreds of years among organic gardeners, some of them employing quite corrosive and toxic substances. Those based on sulfur and copper are the two strongest mineral agents used against fungal disease. When applying these sprays remember that they also kill beneficial microbes as well as insects, so familiarize yourself with the cycle of microbial disease in order to prevent unintended damage to your garden flora and fauna. For example, copper sulfate is an excellent control for peach leaf curl, a terrible fungal disease that crumples and destroys the new leaves of peach trees. But copper sulfate is caustic and can burn tender foliage, so it is best sprayed on peach trees while they are dormant.

I prefer harvesting autumn baskets of 'Cox's Orange Pippin' apples to spraying copper sulfate on the dormant orchard trees, but each procedure depends

Kitchen-Generated Garden Sprays

Baking Soda Delight
Dissolve 1 tablespoon of baking soda in 1 quart water.

Add 1 tablespoon of liquid soap and mix well. Spray on tops and bottoms of leaves every seven days for fungal and some bacterial disease. This spray is quite effective in the rose garden.

Vampire Vanquishing Garlic Spray
Mince 2–3 cloves of fresh garlic and soak them in 2 tablespoons of mineral oil overnight.

Strain and mix with 1 pint of water and 1 tablespoon of liquid soap.

Spray every seven days to treat and prevent fungus eruptions in the garden.

on the other. Because I dream of a strong harvest, winter spraying with a good biological and chemical arsenal is organically connected to that bounty, never separate. Remembering this, now and then I look up from my winter work and stand for a moment, alive in the stiff blue tide of health that rises and falls on the surface of the sea of cover crops surrounding our orchard. Medicine and disease subdue each other and I am immersed in their old pharmacology.

The Dung and Drool Garden

TO REALLY SEE A GARDEN AND THE LIFE INSIDE A GARDEN TAKES your whole life. This seeing can be dangerous and unsettling, as I discovered a few years ago when I visited the butterfly preserve of an old and renowned lepidopterist, Louise Hallberg. I hated that garden.

Not that you don't learn from what you dislike; you do. Electric shock teaches, and falling in wet cow manure reminds you to walk a higher path next time. I am sure Louise's garden had particular lessons especially for me even though it pressed against me like a gaunt tomcat with a broken rib. From the moment I walked through her gate, Louise's legendary butterfly garden set me on edge and made my teeth hurt. Expecting to taste a full-blown burgundy cherry of a garden, I was served a renegade, unripe green plum. And even now, many years later, I am still unable to clear the raw, metallic taste of that garden from the roof of my mouth.

The Hallberg Ranch is a butterfly sanctuary and preserve in western Sonoma County, seventy miles north of San Francisco. Louise was born on this ranch and has lived there her entire life. In 1883 her grandparents immigrated from Sweden and purchased the land, and in 1904 they built the old farmhouse where Louise lives today. In their early years, the Hallberg settlers raised bumper crops of berries, hops, woodland cherries, French prunes, table pears, and dessert apples.

Every garden I know contains contradictions and surprises, sometimes startling and dissonant. I usually enjoy this feature of gardens, but Louise Hallberg's swamped my every notion of the tolerable boundaries of dynamic dissonance in a garden. And it did so deliberately, without apology.

In the very heart of Louise's garden was an old catalpa tree, quite dead, serving as a skeleton trapeze for a thick grapevine that wound around its bleached bones. High overhead, supported by the dead tree, fat bunches of ripe green grapes swung in the open sunlight twenty-five feet above the floor of the garden. "For the birds and wasps," remarked Louise gaily, tracking my spellbound gaze. "I let them have all my grapes so they won't bother the butterfly larvae down here in the garden."

There were other dead trees throughout Louise's garden. They stood like phantom sentinels, protecting a garden vibrantly alive though pocked with death. Draped from the bony frame of a line of ghost trees on the periphery of the garden were long, thick ropes of healthy *Aristolochia californica*, Dutchman's pipevine, a native medicine plant. Although the pipevine is medicinal, it is also poisonous.

The leaves of *Aristolochia* are the primary larval food for the beautiful pipevine swallowtail butterfly, a pollinating insect for many of California's native and cultivated plants. This butterfly is increasingly endangered, as woodlands are progressively tamed and colonized by walled estate gardens and subdivisions. Yet only after feeding on the toxic pipevine does the pipevine swallowtail butterfly become toxic itself and safe from predatory birds.

All the pipevine plants in Louise's garden look as if they have been peppered with fresh, hot buckshot. They command a central spot in her garden, and are meticulously defoliated every season by the voracious caterpillars of the pipevine swallowtail. Last season alone Louise counted slightly under six hundred caterpillars just on the pipevine plants growing closest to her ranch house. She clucked with delight to report this success. She starts new plants every season although it takes seven years for the pipevine plant to become established and produce seed. *It would take me that long, too*, I thought, *if I were covered with caterpillars gnawing away at all of my vital body parts.*

Louise Hallberg celebrates dead trees, sucked-out foliage, unmown grass, leagues of rampant weeds, and deliberate disorder. All these features are mandatory if you want to garden for the preservation of butterflies. While most gardeners I know garden from the inside of their gardens to the edge, Louise gardens from the outside in, cultivating thick, impenetrable barriers of California blackberry vines and shade trees on the periphery of her paradise and welcoming ragged milk thistle, rank stinging nettle, and wild plantain. No part of her garden is ever mown, pruned, or weeded, since in the shady pools and abandoned clutches of heinous weeds, clouds of butterflies are born and bred.

Through years of observation Louise has learned that butterflies cannot exist on sweet flower nectar alone. They also require salts, nitrogen, amino acids, and certain chemicals necessary for making sexual attractants, materials that are exuded from the dark side of life. Salt-rich dung from old owl pellets dissolves in muddy puddles where the butterflies drink, and slug slime and decomposing carrion are equally treasured in Louise's sanctuary.

Before arriving at the Hallberg Ranch I had a romantic, one-dimensional notion of what it would be to design a garden for the benefit of butterflies. Banks of vermilion Mexican sunflowers would wash into wave after wave of acid-yellow lotus dahlias. Riding the crest of these tides of bloom would be the butterflies themselves, ascending into the air like spun sea foam as the Butterfly Woman herself parted the waves and passed through the drifts of her garden.

How rude, then, the blunt truth of the Hallberg place! In October, when I arrived, gardening for butterflies meant nurturing their larvae and letting plants be stripped bare by starving caterpillars. What gardener in their right mind would celebrate the almost audible crunching down of hundreds of caterpillar mandibles on tender plants? In the last light of late October a Halloween feeding frenzy was going on in Louise's garden.

This sanctuary reminded me of one secret, midnight pilgrimage that I made to the Green Gulch garden while all of my Zen friends slept. I had to see what nocturnal creature was eating the juvenile plants from Alan Chadwick's prize collection of cherry tomatoes. I crept into the greenhouse carrying a small votive candle, just enough light for me to see beneath the tomato plants piles of telltale black caterpillar frass, or insect manure.

In the dim light I saw the tomato hornworm itself, a caterpillar beautiful and terrible at once, curled in a hook around the immature fruit, chewing large pieces out of the perfect green globes. The insect was hypnotically effective and very hungry, and it was not alone. Legions of hornworms were inhaling the choicest of our prize tomatoes. The horn or sharp thorn at the rear end of the diagonally striped caterpillar glowed red and sinister in the candlelight. With a dark delight, I plucked off the hornworm multitudes, dropped them into a bucket of cold water, and blew out my light, soothing my fair-weather Buddhist conscience with a quick vow to feed the drowned caterpillars to the chickens.

But in Louise Hallberg's garden my most dreaded fear hatched. It broke out of its egg sac and crawled forth, consuming everything in sight. Louise has lost control of her garden, I realized, and even worse, she has not simply lost control, she has given it away. She has chosen to be controlled by the insects of her place, while she works around the clock gardening for them.

In the deep shade of Louise's dung and drool garden two realizations arose simultaneously in me. First was the recognition of my own unwillingness to relinquish control in the garden. And right behind this resistance was an even older fear, that not only was I not in control of my garden, I was unable to even really *see* what was happening all around me.

"You can't teach someone to see," Louise mused aloud as we walked into the heart of her place. She seemed to be channeling my anxiety and speaking directly to me. As I followed Louise around, she stooped over and lifted a bough of bridalwreath spirea from across the garden path. Minuscule egg sacs of the echo blue butterfly clung to the underside of the finely cut foliage. I could barely see these egg casings even when they were pointed out to me, I noted with discomfort. "Seeing has nothing at all to do with age or intelligence," murmured Louise. "Some see and some don't. I just point."

Later Louise drew me into the cool shadows of her hundred-year-old home. In her bathroom, just off the master bedroom, Louise was raising monarch butterflies. "It's far too cold for them in the garden now," she explained in a soothing voice. "The steam of the bathroom keeps them just warm enough until they emerge." There is no boundary between the inside and outside of her life, I realized in a rising panic. Louise's entire bathroom was hung with screened rearing cages teeming with monarch caterpillars and chrysalids. She even had some cages balanced over the bathtub itself. I leaned over the edge and peered in.

The juvenile monarch chrysalis is a startling iridescent green with a raised tiara of gold pearls encircling the crown. "A glass house hammered with golden nails," runs one nineteenth-century description of this chrysalis. As the chrysalis ages it becomes transparent, until you can see the sleeping butterfly wrapped within its pale green sheath. These chrysalids hung in all their stages, full of mystery and brooding, filling Louise's bathroom.

I saw that I want both to observe change and metamorphosis in the garden's life and also to be protected from it. I want simultaneously to manage the garden and to let go of my control and learn from that older order that incubates beneath the stretched green silk of every garden's skin.

Louise Hallberg gardens for the lepidopterous instars, the stages of life of the thirty-four distinct species of butterflies that inhabit her garden. I worship plants and garden for them, without reserve, giving my heart unconditionally to that solitary sweep of virgin's bower clematis that originates on the floor of the redwood forest and climbs a hundred feet up through cool green air to the sunlit summit of the trees. Where I am a gardener growing crops, Louise is a frontier rancher, gardening for hungry caterpillars and butterflies. She protects every fetid puddle as a potential watering hole for her beasts and delights in malodorous slime as a rich source of protein for her insect herds. The Hallberg sanctuary is their feedlot, where many of the rare and exotic plants that I protect with my life are fine fodder for Louise's six-legged beasts.

I will never outgrow my repulsion at what I saw in the Hallberg sanctuary. After all, I have my gardening standards and opinions. They are dear to me. But that Indian summer day in Louise's paradise stretched me, enough to allow me, one year later, to plant a thirty-foot-long bed of milkweed on the edge of the Green Gulch Farm kitchen garden to feed the larvae of the migrating monarch butterflies that crisscross the autumn garden every year.

Did I have a conversion experience in the Hallberg sanctuary? Are drool and slime now sacred nectar of the gods to me? Hardly! But I am able to look a little more deeply now at what I do not love and cannot control, both in myself and in the garden. I recognize that, like Louise, I garden for hungry beings, human and more-than-human, and for beauty in all of its guises and instars, from maiden to crone-whiskered hag and back again, in an unbroken circle.

RETURNING TO ORIGIN

Inward Seeds of Fire

IN BUDDHIST TEXTS, CONSCIOUSNESS IS SAID TO BE A FIELD, A PIECE of earth on which every kind of seed is planted. On this field of consciousness are sown the seeds of hope and suffering, the kernel of happiness and sorrow, anger and joy. The quality of our life depends entirely on which seeds we garden and nourish in our consciousness.

Growing a garden, like cultivating the wide field of consciousness, is original work. Each time we plant a garden we are returning to origin, to the source of every garden ever grown. The word "origin" derives from the Latin verb *oriri*, to rise, as the sun and moon rise in a cyclical pattern in the day and night sky. Originality has a still older meaning described by the upwelling of deep springwater through stony ground. Growing a garden depends on this double force of originality that is both rhythmic and permeating.

Gardeners understand the origin of the cycle and the cultivation of seeds in the field of consciousness because we know the steady work of selecting and culturing by hand the living seeds of the garden. Growing a garden from scratch is mysterious and also absolutely mundane, the secular liturgy of generations of gardeners. The continuity of the cycle is assured by propagation, for like all fundamental work, plant propagation has its origin in the ground, in the broad bottom of the world.

In an established garden of annual and perennial plants, of trees and shrubs, there are two distinct methods of propagation: sexual propagation, by seed, and asexual propagation, by cuttings, or by division of perennial plant material. In sexual propagation, a completely new individual is produced from each fertilized seed.

In asexual propagation, a part of the parent plant is removed and used to start a new plant. New plants can be started asexually from even a single cell, for all of the genetic information in a parent plant is reproduced exactly in the vegetative offspring. Yet even though a musk grape from biblical times might still be living today through continual asexual cloning, I incline toward spitting out the hard seeds found inside the Old Testament grape and planting these living seeds in the garden. The pip-sown sexual offspring from Noah's vineyard may not be genetically identical to their biblical parent, but I know that they will be full of the fire and brimstone of surprise that continues to ferment in the original fruit of the vine.

I am committed to starting plants from seed. It is not uncommon for the first spring sowing of the growing season at Green Gulch Farm to include more than seventy varieties of herb, vegetable, flower, weed, and fruit seed collected from all over the world. I do practice asexual propagation, particularly when I want to maintain the precise qualities of specific perennial garden cultivars, but I confess that growing a garden from seed, and returning to the original mystery asleep inside every seed, is my primary passion and calling.

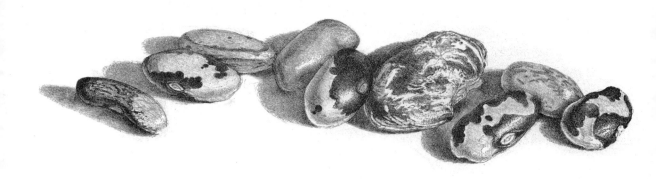

I cannot walk through the woods or traverse the coastal prairie that blows and bellows above our garden without collecting ripe seed from the multitude of native plants. Sometimes at night I wake up dreaming of the wildland roses of the coast, heavy with cerise flowers whose petals will soon fall, yielding to fat rose hips stuffed full of white seed. My hands sweat in the dark.

All the early high civilizations whose diets are known to us—the Incas, the Mayas, the ancient Egyptians, the Chinese, and the inhabitants of the Fertile Crescent of the Middle East—were sustained by seed grains. Yet at the beginning of the third millennium, 95 percent of all seed planted in agriculture over the centuries has become extinct. We deplete our genetic base and diminish our genetic inheritance by a lack of imagination and by an overdependence on too few highly specialized varieties of crops. The simple act of returning to origin and sowing a garden from seed preserves a rich heritage of diverse crops and opens the imagination of the sower to the garden of Eden.

In old fairy tales and in the myths of many world cultures, the task of separating and sorting kernels of grain is the work given to test the mettle of the heroine of the tale and to teach discernment and discipline. Here, Psyche, you long to see Cupid—then sort these mountains of millet seed from the barley, separate the poppy seed of the underworld from these grains of winter wheat. Often the fairy-tale heroine is aided by old magic or by the wild creatures of the earth who help her sort the seed, each kernel burning with the fire of a living embryo smoldering inside its husk.

At the end of a day of hard work in the garden, my hands ache. They are swollen and hot after splitting open the porcupine-like seed heads of the Mexican sunflower and threshing its spiny seed, or dividing the Michaelmas asters of late September. Wearing gloves is inconceivable. I wouldn't be able to trace the sinews of the plants. Besides, I have never been able to keep a pair of garden gloves for longer than a few days. They disappear under the heavy branches of Chinese crabapples in full fruit and become garden soil. In the evening I examine my husband's farmer hands. He also never wears gloves, claiming they slow him down. His fingers are stout and knobby, strong like the 'Rose Fir Apple' potatoes that he has grubbed out of our bottomland soil for decades.

"Each seed is coated with the DNA story," writes Kathleen Harrison of Botanical Dimensions. "Each seed is a long, winding story." This tale is told anew every season in our own backyard gardens as we work with our hands to free the harvest kernels. From the beginning of time, gardeners' hands have been selecting seeds, sometimes choosing seed plants that offer the highest yield and plumpest grain, on other occasions selecting lines that promise to resist disease or not to shatter. And then there are times when we ignore all practical considerations whatsoever and select for beauty, for that rare purple glint in the inner shell of a fava bean that appears once in a blue moon.

I am convinced that the human hand and the seeds we thresh and are nourished by have evolved together. "What sower walked over earth?" asks poet Rolf Jacobson. "Which hands sowed our inward seeds of fire?" In our hands is this original question and the old memory of when we lived in trees. Our hands know when we lifted the first stones and fashioned them into tools for the hunt and the harvest and then into primitive plows to ream open

the soil and plant the seed crops for the next season. Seeds rich in nutrition have stoked the fire of curiosity and provided us with the strength to develop, dream, and continue. Seeds have given our hands intricate and ancient puzzles to solve, since all hands crave a puzzle to turn and unlock, especially if the puzzle contains a prize, like the rich kernel of oily pecan fitted into its soft mahogany casing. Breaking open the treasure stored inside the dry husk of the autumn garden, inward seeds of fire and the work and mystery of this very moment are in our hands.

Purity and the Horsetail Fern

EARLY IN THE SPRING OF 1973 A CIRCLE OF WILD LAND IN THE LOWER fields of Green Gulch Farm was skimmed open and the first garden was planted. The earth was raw and black, bellowing with green timothy and bull thistle. Steve and John, two early Zen students, sowed seed of every imaginable crop, from beefsteak tomatoes to Chinese parsley. They even planted rows of peanuts across the fertile bottomland. They were asking the soil to show the inner lining of her dark robe in the soft-shouldered French lettuces that heaved up out of the ground, encircled by bands of scarlet radishes, wild onions, and heartsease viola from Old England.

In that first season, all of the seed was sown directly onto open ground. But by the next spring, thick stands of lowland weeds swamped the cultivated seedlings. Steve and John and a few other carpenters banged together a ramshackle greenhouse out of a mountain of discarded windows and old barn boards and in this old, swaybacked greenhouse—green with moss and coastal lichen—we began to plant seed in our first rough-hewn redwood flat boxes. Two years later I went to work in the greenhouse, and we expanded into pressure-hardened plastic flats and polystyrene cell flats called speedling trays, choosing these petroleum product flats because they can be washed clean and sterilized with a light dose of vinegar.

265

In those first years of planting we always filled our seed flats with rich bottomland soil gathered directly from the open field. We never purchased potting soil or worried about germs and disease. It was only much later, when we were cultivating acres of fresh food and flowers, that we began to purchase ingredients for potting soil and to plant the seedlings, sown by the thousands every month, in plastic pots protected by stretched polyethylene greenhouse tunnels. We had begun to accumulate nondegradable materials and to consider the mystery of purity and cleanliness in our potting area.

"When you do something," Suzuki Roshi said, "burn yourself up completely, like a good bonfire. Leave no trace of yourself." So in 1993 when we took apart our funky greenhouse and created the immaculate new propagation glasshouse of my dreams, I despaired as I surveyed the heavy trail of nonrenewable resources we had summoned to assemble this dream propagation palace. For years we had done beautifully with the bare minimum. Now we were surrounded by piles of quarried gravel, bags of concrete, and rolls of fiberglass ground cloth. I began to wonder if we had created an insatiable monster, even though now we could finally grow finicky seeds like the rare Tibetan blue poppy, *Meconopsis betonicifolia*.

Our expert advisors and experienced gardening friends all suggested that we begin making only soil-free sterile potting mixes, to avoid the plant diseases that might be carried in living, unsterile soil. They also advised us to exclusively use plastic containers that could be sterilized with every use. Keep it clean, keep it germ-free, they intoned, and use a little bleach while you're at it. Subtly, I felt pulled away from the garden as I knew it and wheeled into an antiseptic intensive care unit for at-risk newborn plants.

When we cleared the earth for the foundation of the new glasshouse we scraped away a large prehistoric forest of horsetail ferns that had long grown in that boggy site. Horsetails are mysterious plants: they only colonize areas where they are meant to be. They are impossible to establish deliberately. But we were raising a new glasshouse of concrete, glass, and steel, and the horsetails had to go.

We laid down a heavy protective ground cloth of woven fiberglass to block new weeds and to prevent the return of the horsetails. On top of this ground cloth we added an eighteen-inch-deep bed of pea gravel. Everything gleamed. For the first time in my life I wondered if I should brush off my garden boots before entering the greenhouse.

I decided to do some experiments. I rinsed out a brand-new plastic flat with a tiny dose of bleach and hot water and filled the flat with commercial potting soil called Supersoil. It seemed strange to call this planting mix "soil" since it was testifiably soil-free and irrepressibly light and bouffant. "This stuff has no soul," my conscience whispered to me, but the mix was certifiably sterile, so I planted in it.

I sowed coriander and blue flaxseed across the suspicious cloud of black fluff and watched what happened. The seeds popped up quickly. After about ten days I saw that I was overwatering them, since a telltale green slime had appeared on the surface of the Supersoil. I realized that I was caring for the seedlings as if they were growing in real earth. However, this Supersoil was much looser than real soil and was by now quite waterlogged and algae-green. A mild fear of retribution from unknown consequences began to gnaw at the edge of my confidence.

The new glasshouse also attracted an insect pest that I had never seen before, the fungus gnat. This gnat loved the warmth, and the porous, peat-rich Supersoil gave her a premier medium in which to lay her copious eggs. Upon hatching, a scant four days after being laid, the fungus gnat larvae began to eat the tender seedling roots of the rare Tibetan blue poppies. I learned that fungus gnats have a particular attraction to sprouted wheat, so I feverishly planted random pots of sweet sprouted wheat all around the greenhouse in order to trap the multiplying gnats. Immersing the wheat sprouts in boiling water, the approved organic method of killing the gnats, was a baroque step I never managed to take, despite the merry buzz of well-fed yeasty gnats. Instead, I buried pot after pot of gnat-infested wheat in a dark pit of real soil, well outside our sterile glass palace.

267

I continued to sow seeds in a variety of soil-free mixes, not daring to sacrifice the protection of a sterile environment. I even found a fine physical and completely organic control for the fungus gnat, although it was admittedly a little unwieldy. This gnat-trap was a broad roll of fifteen-inch-wide, extra-sticky, bright yellow flypaper-type tape that we stretched the full length of the glasshouse just beneath the seed flats. In no time at all, the sticky tape was covered with a shadowy snarl of black-bodied gnats. It was foolproof! And a year later, I was still scraping yellow glue residue off my favorite garden overalls.

The yellow tape trapped adult gnats, true, but the larvae living in the soil of the seed flats were vigorous and unaffected by the death of their parents. These larvae I doused every three days with an organic spray of Gnatrol. I began to feel like a cross between a mad chemist and a wanton executioner disguised as a practicing Buddhist.

After a few months of use, the glasshouse had lost some of its pristine luster. Leagues of garden arachnids, wolf spiders and orb weavers, were colonizing the propagation mansion. A veil of pale green algae was creeping up the inside of the sleek glass walls. A pair of glossy, violet-green insect-eating swallows penetrated the baffles in the ventilation system and swept into the glasshouse every night, skimming the surface of the seed flats. "Eat gnats!" I implored them, in desperate supplication.

My final liberation from sterile greenhouse practice came one day in early March. The horsetails returned, pushing up like a miniature primitive forest through the packed gravel floor of the greenhouse, piercing the fiberglass barrier to reclaim their true terrain. That dwarf forest of horsetail ferns jolted me awake. Clearly, it was no big deal for a plant that is the last remainder of the ancient carbon forests to push up through a measly modern barricade of fiberglass and an eighteen-inch-deep stratum of gravel. Horsetail ferns have been growing in riverine gravel beds for close to 350 million years. Triumphant, the vigorous horsetails beat their ancient chests in victory, shaking free a soft green cloud of ripe spores ready to germinate into new forests of ferns.

These horsetail ferns scoured away my last notions of germ-free purity. The horsetail plant is almost 80 percent silica and has been used for centuries to abrade, scour, and polish fine silver and pewter. But for me, these gritty equisetum plants scrubbed away my tenuous infatuation with purity and restored me to the bedrock nature of my gardening life. The horsetails confirmed that I am not cut out to propagate plants in a world protected from disease, failure, and the raw lash of life. Give me the muscular ancient ones that burnish away all trace of blind belief and return me, tarnished and ready, to the unpolished work of gardening that I know and love.

Propagating Mystery

IN AUTUMN AROUND THE FALL EQUINOX GREEN GULCH FARM HOSTS an apple tasting in the garden. There are almost twenty distinct heritage varieties of cooking, cider, and dessert apples growing in the fruit garden and this event is one of the most popular celebrations of the gardening year, especially with children.

Almost all these apples in the garden are grafted heritage varieties spliced or grown on the strong origin rootstock of the wild crabapple tree. It is virtually impossible to grow a decent eating apple from apple seed. All of the finest apple cultivars, like the apple trees growing in the small Green Gulch orchard, are propagated vegetatively, from growing parts of the parent apple tree and not from seed, because apple seed doesn't behave. It goes feral in an instant and returns to the wild crabapple ancestor from which all apples derive. Not 'Mrs. Bramley's' seedling apple, however.

Mrs. Bramley was a British woman who loved to garden and who also happened to be a legendary cook. She never ceased working. In contrast, her husband was a sedentary fellow, exceedingly fond of his wife's renowned homemade apple tart. How fitting, then, that Mrs. Bramley would bake her husband just such a tart for his birthday celebration.

The portly Mr. Bramley fell upon his birthday confection with rumbling snorts of delight. He devoured the pastry while his wife watched with pride from the kitchen. When Mr. Bramley retired for a long birthday snooze after finishing off almost the entire feast in one sitting, the last remnants of the pie were indecorously tossed out of the open kitchen window onto the compost pile just outside.

About two months later, in true fairy-tale fashion, there arose from the heart of the kitchen compost one strong apple tree seedling that shot out of the heap like a pumped-up missile aiming for the moon. Of course Mrs. Bramley noticed the tree immediately and pulled the compost pile away from it, protecting the young plant with ardor, grooming the seedling tree for the mystery of its imagined fruit.

When this tree began to bear a few years later the apples were as huge as the appetite of the master of the house. The fruit was flat-globed and yellow-green, splattered with crimson freckles. The flesh of the apple was grainy gold and sweet, a true cooking apple with stable, deep-bodied flavor, rich and moist. The tree bowed down, heavy with the burden of Eden, and announced its impossible truth. Behold! A seedling apple, never seen before, and grown from a random pip, has produced fruit of paradise. There is a 'Mrs. Bramley' seedling apple tree growing in the Green Gulch orchard. But ironically, this tree, like all the thousands of other Bramleys growing in orchards around the world, is now propagated vegetatively in order to replicate exactly the unique qualities and attributes of its unruly seedling ancestor.

❀   ❀   ❀

Propagating mystery and growing plants for your home garden begins with following your affection and continues with steeping yourself in the knowledge of how to propagate the plants you love. "The gardener," Alan reminded us, "puts a hand into paradise and brings down the seeds of invisible mystery."

When you hold mystery in your hand and cherish a certain plant with an old abiding love, as I love 'Mrs. Bramley's' seedling apple, you will go to all lengths to grow this plant well, according to its own particular nature.

Even though I fully agree with a good gardening buddy when he proclaims that "in general, everything is specific," there are a few basic principles to remember when engaging in plant propagation, like knowing that all annual plants have soft bodies and fast metabolism and must be started from seed so that they can return to seed in one short growing season. They do not live long enough to develop the woody parts that are essential for asexual propagation. This is true for biennial plants as well, those plants that are started from seed in summertime and come into flower the next spring or early summer, ripening their seed in the autumn of their second year.

Perennial plants, woody and flowering shrubs, small trees, and large trees as well, can be propagated by two methods: sexually, by seed propagation, and asexually, or vegetatively, by using a part of the original plant vegetation to grow out duplicates of the original. There is one graphically and horticulturally simple difference between sexual and asexual propagation: when you grow a plant by sexual propagation surprise sleeps in the seed. A whole new race or line of individuals may spring up from out of a simple seed, a whole new world "never seen before" as Alan Chadwick loved to say, because two parents' DNA is mixing and recombining. When you propagate a plant asexually you use a part of the parent plant to grow a new one, and you get an exact replica of the original plant, because it contains the same DNA as the sole parent.

Sexual propagation keeps the genetic base of diversity broad and unpredictable while asexual propagation stabilizes and strengthens your favorite lines of perennial plants. Just remember to every now and then inject a little surprise into your well-established perennial garden by letting your asexually propagated plants set seed and propagate mystery in their full ripening.

Propagation requires paying attention to the two-phase life cycle of all seed-bearing plants: growth or assimilation, and reproduction or flowering. Plants cannot be propagated either sexually or asexually until they are ripe and in their reproductive phase. Flowering is stimulated by environmental or cultural conditions. Alan Chadwick had us in stitches by mimicking this signaling of the change from juvenile life to flower production in a growing plant. He pantomimed in proper theatrical fashion the roots of a plant telephoning up to the top branches of the plant and announcing, "I say, nourishment is rather slim down here. You've received your full allotment so best to begin flowering, old chap." "Oh, is that so?" queries the hardening green stem. "Well then, right-o. It's what I've been feeling in my veins, after all. Time to make babies, off we go!" and flowering ensues, to an insistent background chorus of "Babies, babies, *babies*." The two stages of growth, vegetative and reproductive, intertwine and depend on each other and from their mutual and distinct expression the principles and practices of seed and asexual production follow.

When ripe seed is cast on moist ground germination unfolds. Sexual propagation begins as seed dormancy is broken and the embryonic plant inside the seed awakens and begins to absorb nutrients. In this first stage of new growth, protein synthesis is initiated and the embryonic plant breaks free of its layered casings.

Next enzymes appear in the new plant and begin to digest the reserve nutrients stored in the germinal tissues and organs of the seedling. These nutrients are translocated and pumped out to the growing tissues.

With this suffusion of nutrients, the primitive cells of the embryo begin to divide and expand. The radicle of the seedling drops down into the soil and branches out as roots while the stem shoot rises up from the cracked-open seed, into the light, differentiating into stem and leaf as the new plant emerges.

Many environmental factors influence the growth of seed born plant: water availability, dark and light, temperature variation and stability, soil aeration and the aeration of the actual seed coats. There are dormancy factors that influence germination as well, such as impermeability to water in the seed coats or mechanical resistance to germination in the seed coverings of certain plants, chemical inhibitors to germination, and the need in certain plants for prolonged chilling in order to break dormancy and initiate germination.

Once you fall in love with seed-born plants your passion for them will direct you, like any ardent lover, to learn more about how to tend and grow the seed in your hand. In love, no technique is too extreme: since the seed coats of coastal lupine are best cracked open by fire, you sow the seed of lupine on the soil surface of a seed flat and cover the seed lightly with fresh earth and dry straw and then light this straw afire, breaking the dormancy code and initiating a firestorm of germination.

The techniques of sexual seed propagation are fundamental and simple. When they are followed with mindfulness and attention, they include the whole world, whether you are handling quick-germinating seeds like fresh Italian parsley or the seeds of antiquity, like the handful of lotus seeds that were uncovered in the tomb of the Theban King Tutankhamen. These lotus seeds, buried fourteen centuries before the time of Christ, were found to be viable by a team of botanists, although the sprouted seeds did not have the vitality to grow into full planthood.

Since all plants are made of the potting soil they are started in, for healthy, vigorous food or beautiful flowers, it is essential to pay close attention to the fundamentals of creating a good potting soil mix. Such soil needs to be both well-aerated and to retain water and hold nutrients, while also supporting young roots and conducting warmth from the sunlight that pours into the earth.

I follow a soil mix recipe that I learned decades ago because plants develop so well in it. It is also absolutely simple. The mix is called "a third, a third, a third," which stands for equal parts by weight of sharp or silver sand, leaf mold, and soil. When I share this recipe with friends who ask us how we compose our potting soil, I remember Alice Waters's recipe for fresh pea soup. "It's absolutely simple," the founding chef of Chez Panisse restaurant claimed with a mischievous twinkle: "Fresh cream, young garden peas, and black pepper." Yet it is up to you to discern the taste of tender lucerne alfalfa in the spring cream of the Jersey cow, up to you to feel the fingers of the gardener who shelled plump English pea pods at exactly the right moment, and up to you to savor the scent of the hard, sun-blistered peppercorns of Majorca as they burst to life in the grinder held over your soup. "It's all in the ingredients," concludes

Alice. So it is with potting soil ingredients. Just remember, these even thirds are measured by weight, not by volume. So when you mix a batch of potting soil, measuring by shovelsful, or volume, the mix will come out something like four shovelsful of leaf mold, three of soil, and one of stone-heavy sand.

Sand is essential to the mix. Alan Chadwick insisted that we use only silver sand, or sharp sand, in our flat mix. This is sand that comes from pulverized granite or other hard rock. The granules of this sand are angular and jagged, and make a sharp "skrich-skrich" sound when you rub them against each other near your ear. Sharp sand transmits light into soil mix. When I first heard Alan Chadwick praise the virtues of sharp sand in soil mix and its ability to transmit light into a heavy soil, I wondered what in the world he was talking about. Sand transmitting light?

I decided to investigate on my own, with the fine-dust beach sand found a half mile from the Green Gulch garden and with river sand from Russian River gravel bars an hour or two to the north. Sadly, my special soil mixes from nearby Muir Beach locked into a solid, impenetrable cement. The silver sand granules from the Russian River, so angular and sharp-edged, transmitted light because they held the clay particles in the soil mix a good distance apart. Silver sand was fundamental to good drainage and texture in all the early seed flat mixes that I made in the beginning of my gardening life.

Leaf mold comes from well-decayed leaves and is added to potting mix to lighten the weight of sand and soil and to make the mix both water retentive and porous. Leaf mold helps maintain the two principles of healthy soil mix: it regulates the flow of air in the seed flat and also helps potting soil stay moist without causing rotting. Young seedlings do not need a nutrition-rich soil mix when they are getting started, but they do need a mixture complex in organic ingredients. To give freshly germinated plants an overly fertilized soil mix is like giving a newborn baby a sirloin steak. To grow plants well from seed demands a light and lean soil. In this mix, leaf mold is essential because it is both rich in minerals and well-decomposed nutrients and lean in nitrogen.

To add leaf mold to soil mix is to inoculate potting soil with the life and death of the forest. The best leaf mold comes from broad-leaved deciduous trees such as oaks, maples, sycamores, chestnuts, and beeches. Avoid using the fallen needles of conifers such as pines, cedars, redwoods, and firs, as these trees are acidic and their needles will cause a sharp drop in the pH of your soil. Many plants will not germinate in an acidic soil.

When you collect leaves for your potting soil, take time to consider the forest ecosystem. Throughout the year, the wastes of the forest undergo constant transformation. Leaf mingles with stem, twigs drop into deep moss littered with bark and fallen flowers and all these materials are interlaced with millions upon millions of bacteria and fungi as well as other invisible and visible animal life-forms. On the floor of the forest it is almost impossible to distinguish animal from vegetable life.

Leaf litter lies in distinct strata. The top layer is always loose, freshly decaying leaves. Just underneath this layer fermentation by molds and microbes occurs, and below this aerobic layer the final decomposition of leaf mold happens in the dark with very little circulating air. These layers of leaves teem with fungi and bacteria. When leaf mold is added to potting soil mix, these fungi and bacteria inundate the tender roots of seedlings and prepare the new plants for their eventual life in open garden soil. Thus trees serve as primary nursemaids for young plants. Trees are also invaluable cyclers of mineral wealth, for the roots of deciduous trees plunge down into the subsoil and draw up nutrients from the vast resources of dissolved minerals. These minerals are then pumped throughout the tree by its hydro-vascular circulatory system. In the autumn, when foliage decays and falls, the stored minerals contained in tree leaves drift down to the earth and reenter the soil through decaying leaves. Aware of these cycles as you collect leaf mold for your potting soil, draw back the top layer of newly fallen leaves and collect a light skimming of well-decayed leaf. Then cover up your tracks with the protective top layer of leaves so that natural decay can continue.

Another simple way to provide leaf mold for your potting mix is to rake fallen deciduous leaves in the autumn and store them in a cylindrical wire mesh cage in a corner of the garden where the leaves can decay and rot all winter long. They will be ready for use in your flat mix within half a year or so.

The core ingredient of potting soil, the heart of the matter, is soil itself, the seat of culture and the source of life. In many ways good soil is analogous

Commercial Potting Mixes

When choosing ingredients for making a good potting mix or when selecting a potting soil mix that is already made, check to make sure the ingredients of the mix you choose are organically grown so that no toxins or chemical sprays are present.

Cocopeat: This product is a reliable renewable-resource alternative to peat moss, which is mined from ancient peat bogs. Organic and biodegradable, cocopeat is made from the husk fiber of coconut plants and provides nutrients and water storage as well as disease resistance. The coconut plant annually sheds its bark, so this product is a true renewable resource.

Vermiculite: This is made from mica rock, which is puffed under pressure and 2,000-degree heat to create a soil-free product that increases aeration, as well as nutrient retention and exchange.

Perlite: This volcanic rock product is produced by heat-popping lava rock. Perlite helps in soil drainage and is an excellent medium for rooting plant cuttings.

Peat moss: This is a generic term for any plant that decayed partly underwater. Most gardeners use sphagnum peat moss gathered from Canadian peat bogs. This product is extremely retentive of water and has excellent antibiotic properties. However, peat moss is being rapidly depleted by mining the ancient peat bogs where it is found.

There are as many recipes for commercial potting mixes as there are gardeners, but here are some of my favorites. Remember these mixes are combined using equal parts *by volume* since their weight is roughly equivalent.

For Starting Seeds
1 part cocopeat or peat moss (moisten this ingredient first with warm water)
1 part perlite
1 part vermiculite
1 part potting soil (if unavailable this ingredient can be omitted)
A shake of local garden soil

For Transplanting Pricked-Out Vegetable, Herb, and Flower Seedlings (Soil Free)
2 parts aged compost mixed with a shake of garden soil
1 part sifted cocopeat
1 part sharp sand and/or perlite

For Transplanting and Hardening-Off Transplants (With Soil)
2 parts compost
1 part soil from the garden
1 part sharp sand
1 part loaf mold, if available

For plants that require a richer mix, add additional compost and some worm castings and seaweed meal or other organic fertilizers to your mix.

to yeast in the baking world because both ingredients contain local flora and fauna and both give life to their batter. Without a baseline of real soil in your potting mix, seedlings lose their tone and vigor and fall flat.

I understand that not every gardener has the range of "a third, a third, a third" ingredients that I have on hand. Then it is crucial to find good commercial potting soil ingredients, as we sometimes do with students in the King Middle School garden, where we grow beautiful plants from seed. Pay attention to where your commercial mix comes from and how it was cultured. Commercial ingredients are easy to mix and since they are roughly of equivalent weight they can be combined by volume.

Once our soil mix is cultured and ready, I scatter decayed oak leaves and a few horsetail ferns on the bottom of each slatted seed box to remind me of the ancient parent plants of these ingredients as well as to help with drainage. Next I sprinkle on the potting soil I have mixed, filling the seed boxes to within a quarter inch of the top, and sowing the seed onto the surface. I seed generously, but carefully, often sowing a few different varieties of seed into one box but separating the varieties and labeling them clearly. I sow in silence, my attention moving back and forth between the seed and the plant it promises to become.

I always lace my sowing with a vow to follow through. Especially in the first sowing of early February my commitment is hot with ardor. I haven't planted a seed for more than three months. But by late spring my zeal cools. Now the seed boxes are packed with cajoling plants. Flat after flat of young Queen Anne's lace and copper fennel, of hull-less oats and quinoa from the highlands of Central America, beg me in their distinct native tongues to follow through with them all. I understand now why April is the cruelest month. There is far too much work to do and no one to blame but my own seed-happy hands.

The seedling plants are grown in their original shallow seed flats until they have one or two sets of true leaves. Before that, germinal leaves, or seed leaves, sprout, functioning primarily to provide the new plant with reserve food until the roots and stems begin to establish. A healthy seedling is balanced, its roots and shoots equivalent in size. Once the true leaves begin to sprout and grow, the plant is ready to feed itself by photosynthesizing and it is also ready to be transplanted to deeper ground. The strongest annuals, plants like clove-scented stock and heirloom treviso radicchio, can be transplanted directly to the garden from the greenhouse at this "true leaf" stage. But most seedlings need an intermediate step known as "pricking-off" or "pricking-out." This procedure involves mixing new potting soil, now enriched with compost or well-aged manure, and then transplanting the established seedlings into this enriched soil mix in deeper boxes.

It is essential to handle young plants with awareness and care when they are transplanted. Some of the healthiest seedlings I have ever seen were raised organically at the San Bruno County Jail garden project where my husband, Peter, worked for years. The San Bruno workforce is almost entirely made up of inmates, or "crooks" as they like to call themselves. Jailhouse crops are pampered and loved. Former drug addicts and street prostitutes coo and hover over their seedlings and make sure that the plants in their care are not crowded or stressed. Plants like those at San Bruno County Jail that are grown-on steadily, without being checked, or arrested in their growth (checking can happen through inconsistent watering, poor soil culture, crowding, insufficient light and other basic cultural causes), are always the strongest and healthiest plants in the garden.

Guidelines for Purchasing Commercial Plants

If you purchase your seedling starts from a commercial nursery be sure that the top growth and root growth of the seedlings is equivalent and in balance, and try to determine when the seedlings were started. Look to see if they are rootbound or stressed. Plants that have been held too long in pots are often weak and suffer setback when they are planted out in the garden. Don't choose plants that are in bud or in flower while still small or, worse yet, in fruit. These plants will not thrive even after being pricked-out into deeper and richer soil because they have been checked and malnourished early on in their lives, and they tend to run to seed very quickly. Check their root systems to see if they are rootbound or diseased. When young plants have been held too long their leaf surface changes, and the bloom of soft health on young leaves disappears, hardening to a tough, leathery surface. The best destiny for checked, stressed plants is the compost pile, that black and fiery furnace of decay and new life.

Plants that are damaged when they are tender seedlings rarely recover their vigor. The most vulnerable part of a young seedling is that delicate region of the stem neck where the roots of the seedling meet the upper stem. When you handle a new seedling make sure you hold it by its seed leaves. Never grip the vulnerable neck of the plant, because the plant may bruise and be opened to disease by your touch.

Once you plant your seedlings in the garden, treat them to a foliar feeding of liquid seaweed mixed with a light dose of foliar fertilizer. This will help allay transplanting shock and keep early pests away. I also recommend feeding your seedlings a little later on with a simple compost tea enriched with sea minerals contained in water-soluble kelp-extract powders. Seedlings do not require a rich dose of nitrogen but do benefit from this blend of compost and mineral-rich sea powders.

Alan Chadwick had a fine way to remind us about the necessity of increasing nutrients slowly and steadily to young plants as they grow. He called the process "serving your plants breakfast, lunch, and dinner." When a seedling is first started you give it a light diet, a lean "a third, a third, a third" Continental-style soil "breakfast." Then, as the plant grows on, it is pricked-out to a richer "lunch" soil where it receives additional nutrients to aid and establish steady plant growth. Finally, the plant is ready to move to its permanent bed in the garden where it is served a fertile "dinner" soil that will nourish it throughout its entire life (with occasional "midnight snacks" served on the side to certain nutrient-hungry plants by doting gardeners).

❧   ❧   ❧

One of the greatest challenges in the garden is to be thorough with the wealth of ingredients trusted to us, and one of the most important things to do with this wealth is to give it away. An old friend and Buddhist teacher once told me of an award-winning organic corn-seed breeder and farmer who made it a point to share his prize corn seed with his neighbors every season. "Are you *crazy?"* asked one of his entrepreneurially minded friends pointedly. "You're giving away your best secrets along with your best seed!" "Not at all," retorted the corn grower, "I'm adding the complexity of this corn seed to my neighbors' fields so that *all* of our corn will be stronger."

Another way I like to take care of the crops that I preserve and grow from seed is to learn their history. By knowing that the seed of the rare stand of hand-pollinated white-flowering *Clarkia imbricata* that you are saving comes from Vine Hill in Sonoma County, California, one of the last known places where white, native clarkia still grows, and that this very spot is soon to be developed into vineyards, the history and the plant become all the more precious.

At the heart of thorough-going care, for me, is preserving the genetic integrity of certain varieties of seed that I grow out in my garden, and being careful not to let them cross- or interbreed with other varieties. This means since I chose to grow the rare white variety of clarkia from Vine Hill, I need to remember that this clarkia will readily interbreed with the more common pink clarkia varieties that are native to the coastal headlands above my garden. So I planted the rare white variety a good half mile from the dominant pink clarkia stands to keep the white strain from being cross-fertilized by wind, insects, and other visitors. For good measure I also screened the white flowers from visiting bees by making little fine-mesh screen cages over the white clarkia.

Alan Chadwick loved the wild experimentation possible in gardening from seed but he was always careful to protect the genetic integrity of particular plant strains. In early May of Alan's last year, one of his old friends brought him a glorious bouquet of fragrant flowers, a bouquet rich in sweet peas, one of Alan's favorite blooms. Alan was beginning to teach a class just as the flowers arrived. I watched in fading delight as Alan's brow and mouth puckered in displeasure as he gazed at the flowers. "Look at that mottled *Lathyrus!*" he commanded, pointing his bony, accusing finger at a single marbled, maroon-and-mauve sweet pea flower waving its bicolor banner from deep within the bouquet. "Clear evidence of V.D.," he proclaimed in disgust, averting his gaze from the flowers.

V.D.? I wondered to myself. *Really?* As if Alan were reading my inner thoughts he rotated, slowly, irrevocably, toward me, like a hungry viper sensing the meager warmth of a nearby mouse. "And *what* is V.D.?" he demanded. "Do be so kind as to tell the assembly."

I stood in mute terror before the tyranny of Alan's ire. The pea and I cowered as one body. Alan summoned me again in heightened tones of righteousness. "What, I ask you, is V.D.? Please answer, sausage!" I wondered if my revered and dangerous teacher might also be going a bit batty. Did he really just call me "sausage" in front of all these people? Could sweet peas actually contract sexually transmitted diseases? Or am I misunderstanding Alan's strong British accent? Might I feign a coughing fit and escape this V.D. trap? My mouth opened and closed, like the lips of a hooked fish flopping out of water on burning hot sand.

"It is *varietal disintegration*, of course!" the master bellowed. "V.D. is the bane of every classic garden," he proclaimed, yanking the varietally disintegrated sweet pea out of his bouquet and crushing the intruder in his massive hand.

If Alan were alive today I trust that I would dare question his standards of ethnic purity, because on another occasion when he spied a rare yellow-toned sweet pea in a bouquet I brought him from our garden he demanded of me that I forbid any further harvest from the sweet pea line in order to protect the superior yellow sweet pea plant for seed. "The sweet pea trade has waited for generations for the cream-colored pea that might produce a yellow flower or for the common lavender pea that could be the ancestor of a blue sweet pea, heretofore unseen in the trade," he whispered to me. "And this charming flower is rich in yellow potential—close the line immediately, sausage!"

Also rich in cowardly, yellow potential I did not have the courage to question why a marbled sweet pea flower showed signs of V.D. while a pale yellow pea of the same trade was a rare and anticipated treasure. The larger lesson I learned, however, was to make an effort to isolate and protect certain

plant varieties from cross-pollination and varietal disintegration and to continue to grow unusual strains of seed. I also incidentally learned that in my British teacher's rich lexicon "sausage" was a cheeky term of endearment as well as a sharp-tongued curse.

Much as I love sowing plants from seed, this very loving care sometimes has a way of turning into clinging to old and useless baggage. Last year I surveyed my bags and jars, my pouches, and all the old, well-labeled sacks of seed I have kept so faithfully for years. My stomach fell as I realized I had saved far more seed than I could ever sow in my entire lifetime, or even in the lifetime of my children or of their unborn children. I decided to make a seed compost out of all my old bags of saved seed. I lit some incense to acknowledge the religious import of what I was about to do, sorted through the bags to make sure I was not jettisoning some irreplaceably rare and precious seed, and then I dumped my vast cache into a tall mound. I mixed this old seed, some of it from 1973 and before, with hot horse manure and a little sickled grass, and watered the seedy mountain with weak compost tea. I stirred the pile daily as it decayed. To my horror, some of the seeds on the edge of my experiment sprouted, but I was not deterred and, with cool equanimity, I stirred this green life into the

decomposing rot of my seedy compost pile. After a few weeks I had a decently decayed compost to fertilize my established garden plants. Old failures and unsprouted dreams nursed the garden on.

One of the great adventures of sowing seeds and propagating mystery is that no matter how mindful and careful you are, inevitably some of your dreams will end in the failure so essential to a gardener's soul. Failure punctures pomposity and inflated dreams, and makes you lean. Every paradise garden of Eden needs a little failure to culture its true character. Not until you know devastation from the loss of prized and coddled rare seeds like the blue poppy from Tibet, and learn to continue on with empty hands and an open mind, have you begun to truly garden.

Roots and Shoots of Eden

As a young man Alan Chadwick walked through a legendary pear orchard in rural France and tasted the unforgettable fruit of paradise. The pear is closely related to the apple, since both are members of the extensive rose family renowned for that subtle fragrance and lingering sweetness that distinguishes the entire rose tribe. Alan's pear was uncommonly sweet. I imagine it now, a heavy globe, and dense, a pale green 'Comice' variety ripening, in the way of pears, from the outside in, into a rich, buttery gold interior veined with sugary seams of translucent white pear syrup.

The orchard Alan had discovered was the source orchard for a unique pear juice renowned in France for its full, sweet flavor. Alan described the trees of this orchard growing in radiating circles, widening out from the gigantic original pear tree in the center of the orchard. The branches of the parent tree had grown heavy with fruit until they lowered themselves to touch the floor of the orchard, where they had taken root over the years. When the parent tree expired pears continued to be produced on the offspring trees that grew in widening, concentric circles fanning out from the original ancestral tree.

"There will be a fire of orchards and delicious fruit spreading out from the garden of Eden," Alan proclaimed to us, remembering the French pears of his youth. "A fire, unstoppable and complete. Imagine this," he exhorted us, "and then get to work!" I never questioned for one moment whether Alan's pear orchard *actually* existed or not. It hardly mattered. The sweetness of his remembered French pears suffused my body and mind and woke up in me a hot spark of determination to grow beautiful pears, grounded in mindful attention. What fired my imagination and most inspired me about Alan's pear orchard was imagining a forest of fruit originating from a single ancestor and increasing in a burning ring of sweetness.

I began to see plants differently after Alan's tale of the French pear. I would look at the young 'King David' apple tree that we had planted in our south-facing meadow orchard and imagine it as an old and venerable apple tree, heavy with blush and tawny-skinned fruit. And when I closed my eyes and held still long enough, I could taste the lingering sweet-and-tart blood of that fruit on my tongue.

I remembered Yorky, one of Alan Chadwick's best students, who once wanted to propagate a new stand of black currants from some plants entrusted to him by Alan. These prize currants had been smuggled into the United States by Alan's brother Seddon, who hid the cuttings in the binding of a fat philosophy book and shipped the booty to Alan. "It was spring and not the time to take vegetative cuttings," Yorky recalled. "But I really wanted to increase the stand, so I just sat and looked at the plants, trying to imagine what was possible." Perhaps he was inspired by the unabashed vigor and beauty of the currants, or by the faint memory of a prolifically sweet French pear. Who knows? But all at once raw vision and the currants lined up, a spark was struck and ignited, and Yorky imagined taking a handful of the plump, about-to-burst-into-leaf buds off the lower branches of the black currant bushes and sowing these buds in a deep flat full of rich, fertile soil. And then he did just that. Did it, then watched and waited.

After about a month the buds began to grow and to send out tiny white rootlets. By the autumn equinox of that same year Yorky had a new plantation of black currants grown asexually from his original parent plants and fired by his lively, fertile imagination. "This just isn't *done* in the trade," an admiring observer noted, looking at Yorky's vigorous black currant stand. "That's why I did it," Yorky replied with pluck. "Plus, I didn't have any other choice."

Asexual or clonal propagation of plants may be as ancient an art as sexual propagation by seed. Recent archaeobotanical evidence has uncovered carbonized figs on the outskirts of Jericho that push the dawn of agriculture to 11,400 years ago. The figs were grown on sterile female trees that could only be propagated asexually, by stem cuttings. For migrating populations to carry with them a branch or rooted portion of a prized tree or fruit-bearing shrub, such as these Neolithic figs, to their next settlement and to bury that branch or root system in new earth, keeping it moist until a new plant springs up from the old clone, is a great and compelling mystery enacted throughout horticultural history.

When a clone off a parent plant is taken there are many factors that affect its appearance and growth. The actual, physical expression of a plant, its phenotype, is influenced, but not completely determined, by the inherited genetic code of the parent plant, its genotype. So, a clone of Alan's French pear grown here in the sea-bottom soil of our northern California garden, and watered with the turbid, gravel-rich backwater of Redwood Creek, will differ dramatically in habit and appearance from the same vegetatively propagated pear grown in its home soil and watered with the seasonal runoff from the French Pyrenees mountains. And yet, even though the California coastal environment may alter the flavor and appearance of the French pear, its genotype remains unaffected and constant.

The greatest danger that gardeners face when growing plants vegetatively is the danger of viral attack. Since vegetatively propagated plants all share

Chimeras

Although it is rare, occasionally mutations develop within the meristem region of a perennial plant where cell division is most active. When two or more genetically distinct tissues grow adjacent to each other you have what is vividly described in the plant world as a *chimera*. Immediately images are conjured up of the fire-breathing monster from Greek mythology with the head of a lion, the body of a goat, and the tail of a serpent. Chimeras may also be benign and beneficial to the plant world, reinvigorating it with their strangeness. What is important to remember is that if you propagate a botanical chimera vegetatively you will perpetuate its mutant genetic lineage in your garden.

the same genetic code, certain viruses may get established in your garden and infect the parent plant from which you are propagating asexually. If your parent plant is prone to virus attack it will pass this susceptibility on to every offspring, and you run the risk of losing all of your plants to disease. For this reason it is important to practice vegetative propagation from a wide and diverse spectrum of plant species, varieties, and cultivars in order to build health and resistance to disease into the plant structure of your garden. It is also wise to occasionally grow new plants from seed, in this way establishing a fresh genotype profile and once again widening the overall genetic pool.

Over my years of cultivating and propagating perennial plants I have followed a few clear principles for asexual propagation that are worth noting.

First of all, be sure that you only propagate plants that are healthy and disease-resistant. When purchasing plants, especially with an eye to propagating asexually, try to purchase only certified rootstock and licensed garden cultivars. If you are growing a plant genus that is prone to disease or infection be sure to choose the strongest species and varieties within this genus and be vigilant in your care of this sensitive plant.

Before propagating a plant vegetatively make sure that you understand all the forms of asexual propagation available to you and be clear about what the best form for your specific plant is. These forms will depend first upon what kind of plant you are working with, and then on the age, size, and habit of the plant and the season in which you are propagating it. When you propagate plants regularly by vegetative means, it is wise to use a fresh propagation medium with each new procedure. This way you limit the possibility of passing any soil-borne dormant disease on to your new clones.

Keep good records of your propagation procedures so you can keep track of what works for you and what to avoid next time. Last of all, keep your mind open and your imagination free to range. Enjoy yourself, and be ready for the mystery and excitement of learning how to propagate a plant in a new way, like Yorky establishing a fresh black currant plantation from a handful of currant buds. And always, of course, leave room in your life for irreverence and surprise, as in this favorite story of mine from John Cage. A neighbor of his had a prize iris garden that he improved each season by throwing away his more common iris varieties. One day the neighbor visited an unknown iris garden, stunning in its fineness. Jealously, Cage's neighbor inquired about this garden, only to learn that it was the delight of the man who collected his discarded garbage.

❖   ❖   ❖

Gardens are syncopated with many distinct rhythms of ripening and reproduction. The annual and biennial plants have a fast, staccato pace as they go from seed to seed; I call them the "teenagers" of the garden. The perennials, such as the regal lily and the slow-to-fruit black currants, have a slower, more "middle-aged" rhythm and beat. The stately evergreen and deciduous trees and shrubs have their own pulse and pace of propagation as well, the long steady throb of wise elders, a rhythm made of the blended hum of heartwood and ligneous fiber.

All perennial plants have the same two growth stages as their annual and biennial counterparts, the juvenile, or vegetative, stage and the mature, or reproductive, stage. In annual and food plants, vegetables are their most succulent and tasty in the juvenile stage, for once they enter their reproductive stage they grow woody, bitter, and tough as they close their growing cycle and run to seed. This is one of the simplest of the reasons gardeners faithfully remove any vegetable plants that begin to flower and go to seed, or at least prune off that precipitous chard stem that elongates and pushes into flower, because this helps keep vegetables young, tender, and savory for a longer growing season.

In perennial and woody plants the stages of growth are also clear. If you propagate from seed, you must wait until the garden plants are in their adult, reproductive stage, and if they are woody perennials, shrubs, or trees the full growth cycle is likely to take a number of years. My observation is that the woodier the plant, the longer before it ripens its seed. Our threshold oak outside the Green Gulch office took a good thirty years before forming acorns while oak leaf lettuce growing in the garden sends up a strong seed stalk after a brief three months of growth.

Asexual propagation, not needing to go to seed or grow from seed, will most often be considerably quicker. And yet stage remains important, since the stage of growth from which you propagate a new plant also influences the habit, growth, and reproduction of that new, cloned plant.

When you propagate asexually from an actively vegetative part of a perennial plant, the vegetative characteristics often dominate in the clone, although eventually the cloned plant will transition to the flowering stage in order to finish its natural life cycle. The vegetative stage is marked by elongation of the stem, vigorous leaf growth, and strong thorniness, while the flowering stage of growth is marked by the end of stem elongation and a concentration of energy and development clustered in the individual flower buds along the stem.

Likewise, when you propagate asexually from the flowering or adult stage of a plant, the properties of that life stage will dominate in the clone. Sometimes it is possible to find both a juvenile and flowering stage on one plant—as with certain apples and other tree fruit. The juvenile stage is found lower down on the plant, so an apple bud taken from this vegetative, lower part of the plant will spend quite a number of years putting on vegetative growth before it flowers and fruits. A bud taken from a more mature, close-to-flowering upper section of the same tree will always fruit before its vegetative counterpart. However, this same clone may go out of fruit before its counterpart since it is propagated from older wood.

Just as with annuals, a healthy perennial plant is one with balanced root and shoot growth. I notice that when I propagate plants by seed, such as the mourning bride scabiosa, this balance happens quite naturally, as long as I provide the proper environment for growth. However, when I propagate asexually from a section of living tissue taken from the vegetative growth of our garden scabiosa, the missing root or shoot system must be regrown. In the case of scabiosa this takes six to eight weeks, yet this time must be allowed for the new clone to develop its balance of roots or shoots before it is set out in the garden.

There are many ways to propagate a garden asexually or vegetatively. I rely on three simple methods of propagating plants from roots: natural suckering and root division; wild, undisturbed suckering; and taking root cuttings. In almost all instances the best time for root division of your favorite plants is generally autumn, after perennial garden plants have flowered and fruited.

Root Division. Root division, the favored method of asexual propagation practiced by most home gardeners, works best with herbaceous perennials. When the top parts of these plants die down or are cut down at the end of the growing season, all the energy and life force of the plant descends to the roots. In order to propagate your perennial plants asexually by root division, make sure your plants are at least a few years old and have an established root system. When this is the case the plant is lifted or dug out of the ground and split, or divided into pieces.

In order for a root division to thrive it is important that some of the crown, or top section of the dormant stem structure of the plant, be present. Sometimes just one or two dormant buds will suffice to initiate the necessary stem or shoot growth aboveground. Once the aboveground growth gets established it helps to feed the root system of the divided plant. Root division propagation offers a strong and rapid resurgence of the parent plant. Remember, not all plants can be propagated by root division, since success depends upon the ability of the roots to produce adventitious shoot buds or fresh top growth off their original root system. Adventitious buds are simple to notice since they arise casually or in unusual places all along the root system, growing into healthy, aboveground shoots.

Taking root cuttings from an established plant is the most exacting and economical method of propagating a garden, since seasonal and polarity factors influence the ability of roots to regenerate stem buds and the additional roots needed to thrive. In the early years of the Green Gulch garden I propagated many vigorous, three-foot-tall comfrey plants for our medicinal herb garden from tiny two-inch-long joints of comfrey roots. Inserted in fertile garden soil these root cuttings produced full-grown comfrey plants in one season.

Stem Division. Many plants store their nourishment in underground organs that are not roots but really modified stems. The whole tribe of bulbous, or swollen-stemmed, plants are part of this classification and all lend themselves well to vegetative division of their underground modified stems, which is where the plant stores food and can be regenerated from division. All types of these plants possess the characteristics of stems: they have a growing tip bud and the capacity to generate leaves and buds.

These underground stems are tubers like the swollen stem of the potato, rhizomes like those of bearded iris plants, corms like the short, broad swollen stem of a gladiolus, bulbs like the bright yellow scaly regal lily, offsets like a tropical pineapple, and runners like the common strawberry. All of these modified underground stems must generate aboveground leaves and buds in order to continue to grow and must also establish a strong, anchoring root system below the buried stem. With the exception of the tropical pineapple I have propagated all of these plants with great joy and ease.

Plants can also be propagated vegetatively by taking a section of aboveground stem that does not have roots and encouraging the establishment of a root system to anchor the new clone in the ground. Because a plant's capacity to root declines with age, gardeners often choose to propagate using stems from the juvenile sections of the parent plant, rather than from flowering sections. The capacity of a stem to regenerate roots is influenced as well by the season in which the stem part is taken. The stem piece may be cut from the parent plant, at the outset, or it may be left attached.

There are many ways to propagate plants from their stem parts without severing the stems from their parent plant, as in Alan Chadwick's French pear. The simplest methods involve burying a stem that is still attached to the parent plant and nourished by it. The buried plant stem generates both new stems and roots, and then the alert gardener cuts the lifeline to the parent plant and a new, rooted individual begins its distinct garden life.

Stem Cuttings. Most of the vegetative propagation practiced in perennial and shrub gardens that is not root division is from stem cuttings that are severed from the parent plant. Some cuttings such as the 'Grenadin' carnation are from softwood and some are from hardwood, like seasonal rose cuttings. The stiffer the bark and the wood of the cutting, such as that of the classic yew tree of antiquity, the longer it takes the new plant to root. We have patiently waited more than two years for cuttings from our Irish yew hedge to root and give us fresh plants.

When you take cuttings from well-established perennial plants it is crucial that these cuttings be grown in a clean and sterile medium of perlite or clean, sharp sand, to help roots get established and to prevent disease. Be sure to choose propagation wood that is disease-free, healthy, and vigorous, and to monitor the process and time it takes for a vegetatively selected cutting to root. Once a cutting is established with a decent root system, a process that can take anywhere from six weeks to six months or longer, depending on the plant, you can ease the rooted cutting into garden soil enriched in much the same manner as the breakfast, lunch, and dinner process prescribed for seedlings.

The "breakfast" menu for the cutting is a lean diet of sterile rooting medium (perlite or sharp sand). This medium offers no nutrition to the seedling since fertile soil is not required until the cutting establishes roots. Once the cutting has established roots it is transplanted into a lightly amended soil where the roots begin to receive nourishment. At this "lunchtime" feeding it is also possible to administer light doses of foliar food to the plant leaves that develop on a cutting once the roots are formed. The "dinner" meal for the established cutting is served in your garden, in the good home earth of your place, and under an open sky studded with stars and washed, by day, with clear sunlight. The new plant is watered by summer rain and dried by rising wind, encouraged in every way to take hold and thrive in the well-cultivated soil of your home garden.

With the earnest success of these simple and profound vegetative methods of root and shoot propagation from Eden you may be inspired to engage in more complex magic, such as the budding and grafting of your favorite fruit tree or rose. Since even a single cell recapitulates the entire species of plant you yearn to increase, let your imagination join with the garden as you bring forth new plants from the original mind of the green world.

As with sexual seed propagation techniques, vegetative propagation offers a wealth of plant material beyond measure. And not only plant material, but relationships beyond measure, as well. I will never forget going into the Green Gulch garden early one morning in the late 1980s to find six large burlap sacks of bearded iris plants left right inside the gate. In these sacks were more than ninety named varieties of bearded iris, all carefully propagated asexually by a wonderful, mad gardening colleague who was moving to Iowa with his family, and was unable to bring his iris collection with him. David and I had never met, but in his note he implored me to plant his irises at the Gulch and to share them with any gardeners who were drawn to them. Some of the names of these iris plants—'Dancing Beauty,' 'Mauve Mink,' 'Abyss,' and 'Pompano Peach'—and the care with which each rhizome was labeled, started to work on me as soon as I opened the sacks and began to handle the plants. By the end of the day we had dug three new iris beds and two days later all of David's irises were in the ground. I still have never met their propagator, but every spring when this tribe of ruffled and plumed plants breaks into bloom, I greet David anew, along with John Cage's neighbor and his garbage collector, all under the garish petticoats of the sumptuous bearded ladies. Bound by the roots and shoots of Eden, we are never strangers.

Sun Face Buddha, Moon Face Buddha

ONE OF MY FAVORITE JOKES IS ABOUT TWO ROARING DRUNKS WHO come reeling out of a bar late at night and collide at a corner lamppost. "Is that the sun or the moon?" the first drunk slurs to the second, pointing up at the bright lamp globe overhead. "How should I know?" the second drunk complains. "I don't live around here."

When it comes to the country of light and shadow, we all share a common neighborhood, finding our bearings and orienting ourselves again and again to the ancient cycles of the sun and the moon moving over the land. Since the beginning of time, humankind has measured the seasons and charted the quarters of day and night by watching the movements of the celestial bodies. The ancient Greeks paired off sun and moon as brother Apollo, in his fiery solar chariot, and sister Artemis, protectress of the hunt and goddess of the moonlit sky. The first Egyptians saw the heavens as the outstretched wings of a huge falcon where the sun and the moon burned as the matched eyes of the divine bird. And in the Popol Vuh, the sacred creation myth of the Quiché Maya, the present era was born when Hero Twins were transformed into the Sun and Moon to rise triumphant from the underworld of death into the living sky.

Observant gardeners since the dawn of time have followed the particular influence of the heavenly bodies on the plant world. The daily rhythm of sunlight from dawn to dusk, and moonlight from dusk to dawn, have always influenced the growth and decline of life. And their longer cycles, the moon marking the duration of a month in its phases, and the sun anchoring the arc of the year-long orbit of the earth, are of course equally critical.

Alan Chadwick taught that in response to these natural rhythms, "The entire garden is pulsation, pulsation and a huge zest for change." Gardeners respond to this swell and ebb in the natural world because our lives and our very bodies are intertwined with light and dark and with the tendrils and leaves, flower petals and ruddy roots of the plants we love and tend.

Over the years I have made it a practice to mark and celebrate the cardinal dates of the calendar year, those solar holidays that have been celebrated for millennia. The turning of the seasons coordinates intimately with the turning of night and day. So the spring equinox that occurs around March 21 is the dawn of the year; the summer solstice, on about June 21, is high noon; the fall equinox, around September 21, is the sunset of the year; while the winter solstice, on about December 21, is the long, dark night of the year. The four seasons are also echoed within the twenty-four-hour span of each day and night, the morning springlike, midday summer, dusk the autumn of the day, and nighttime a kind of long, dark winter.

Since the cardinal holidays all celebrate dark and light, I always mark these holidays with simple ceremonies held outside at their coordinate time of day. When I gardened at Green Gulch Farm the spring equinox was welcomed at dawn on March 21 by standing on the porch of the meditation hall and chanting praise to the day as we watched the mallard ducks nuzzle their ducklings on the spring pond just below us. The summer solstice was celebrated with a beach picnic at noon on June 21, the autumnal equinox with a walk up to the ridge overlooking the long coastal valley at dusk on September 21, and the winter solstice by setting candlelit lotus boats free on the surface of the dark pond outside the meditation hall in the dead of the night around December 21, or sometimes on New Year's Eve, to welcome in the fresh year. I continue to celebrate these holidays to this day, though now surrounded by naughty twelve-year-olds in a large, urban middle school garden or by setting up a simple tribute altar to light and shadow on the top of the baby grand piano in our home living room.

On each of these holidays I pay close attention to where the sun rises and sets on the horizon and then orient my gardening year to this specific information. I have noticed that the summer and winter solstice times are the two moments of the year when the sun appears to stand still (which is what the Latin word *sol-stice* actually means: sun-standstill) at either its northernmost point, on June 21, or its southernmost place, on December 21. Marking how the cardinal holidays appear on your own garden landscape extends your awareness of your land. In my garden in the bright season from March to September the sun is located slightly north of the coastal mountains, riding high in the wide saddle of Coyote Ridge, while in the opposite dark season of the year, from autumn until spring, the sun rides low in the southern sling of Coyote Ridge, closer to the broad plain of the Pacific Ocean.

Many earthbound traditions associate the seasons themselves with the four great elements, also clearly represented in the physical form of plants. Spring is expressed in moving water, or as the sap flow rising and falling in green stems; summer, in the warm air element rustling in the wind-pollinated corolla of June sunflowers; autumn, with the ripening fire encased in every seed and fruit; and winter, in the deep roots of plants that dive down into cool, dark earth. The cardinal holidays are coordinated with the tasks and cycle of the seasons: spring with planting seeds, summer with ripening crops, autumn with dividing perennial plants and bringing in the harvest, and winter with deep dormancy and invisible root growth. But particularly, these holidays are celebrations of the seasons of light and shadow and the effect of bright and dark on the garden and on the gardener.

The sun pushes and the moon pulls, and green chlorophyll is developed in the thrust of sunlight. The natural pulsation of light and shadow influences every aspect of the garden day. I try to harvest flowers and vegetables only when the garden is not in full sun. Before daybreak, or at the edge of dusk, plants are firmer and less likely to wilt than in the downward pulse of hot, pushing sunlight.

The moon pulls with its magnetic force on the waters that course within the cells of all plants, for just as the moon influences the tides of the ocean, so does it influence the water running in every green plant stem. Garden plants pump into accelerated growth in the two-week-long period of the waxing or inclining bright-of-the-moon phase that runs from new to full moon every month. In the dark of the moon, that two-week-long period of the waning moon that runs from just after the moon is full until it is new again, the pulse of growth seems to go underground and strengthen the root system of garden plants. Top growth slows in this period and root growth hastens, spreading deep and wide. I prefer to transplant garden seedlings in the dark of the moon and take advantage of this downward energy to help plants root.

In addition to its pull on the waters within soil, seed, and plants, the moon exerts gravitational force on the ground as it follows its path around the earth. Every month when the moon is at perigee—the closest point to earth in its elliptical orbit—there is additional gravitational force exerted on moist soil as well as on the waters of the earth. The highest high tides, the spring tides, and the lowest low tides of the month occur at this time. And when the sun and moon are lined up with the earth at new and full moon, the sun's gravitational force is also at its greatest, and the tidal force exerted by the path of the moon is even stronger.

The celestial push and pull of sun and moon influence how I work in the garden with plants; I sense their force pulling and pushing on my own blood as well. For the last two decades I have sown garden seeds in the bright of the moon, doing most of the seeding two days before the new moon. I have seen how quick-germinating seeds sprout most readily in that two-week-long period of waxing moonlight from new to full moon. I also sow the slower germinating seeds, those that take a month or more to sprout, just before the full moon, when there is a complete month for the seeds to experience the cycle of lunar pull.

These are simple and ancient principles: seeds sprout best during the bright of the moon, while during the dark period of the moon it is advisable to minister to the underground roots of plants, which is why many gardeners transplant seedlings in the dark of the moon. This is also a good time to prune, weed, and divide perennial garden plants.

In my early years of gardening I not only paid attention to gardening with the phases of the moon, I also followed a rigorous pattern of planting and tending the garden that was dictated by my early fascination with Western astrology and the houses of the zodiac. In this system the night sky is divided into twelve discrete constellations or "houses." These twelve constellations correspond to the four great elements that comprise all garden and plant life. Accordingly, the constellations of Taurus, Virgo, and Capricorn are earth signs and they are considered to influence the earth element or the roots of plants. The constellations of Cancer, Scorpio, and Pisces are said to govern the water element, which influences stem and leaf growth in the plant world. The air element is consolidated in the zodiac houses of Gemini, Libra, and Aquarius, influencing the growth of flowers, while the fire element is said to be concentrated in the houses of Aries, Leo, and Sagittarius, fire representing the energy of fruit and seed.

But how could the houses of the zodiac *actually* influence terrestrial plant life, I used to wonder. The answer is, through the pull of the moon. As the moon orbits in its monthly cycle through the night sky it passes through the twelve houses of the zodiac for a brief, two- to three-day-long period every month. During these days the individual houses of the zodiac represent each phase of the pull of the moon on the garden world below. So during the two-week period of the inclination of the moon, astrological gardening encourages you to sow the seed of your root crops when the moon passes through an earth sign constellation, the seed of leafy greens in a water sign constellation, the seed of flowers in an air sign, and the seed of fruit and grain crops in a fire sign constellation. Similarly, when the moon is in its two-week-long dark phase of declination, it is advisable to tend and transplant the roots of plants in an earth sign, to plant out leafy greens in a water sign, to plant flowers in an air sign, and fruiting plants in a fire sign constellation.

When I tried to follow lunar astrological rhythms in my gardening life with some regularity I became tense and fairly dogmatic. I could often be heard muttering that the moon was in the great house of Taurus, that primary earth sign of the zodiac, for only two and a half more hours. It was the ideal time to sow the seeds of all root crops *now*, before Mars entered into opposition with Pluto. Why were we hurrying to the zendo to practice wall-gazing meditation when we could join the ancient star-seers of old and sow ripe beet seed in its perfect constellation cycle? Yet even though I fervently followed every celestial rhythm for a number of growing seasons, persistent doubt nagged at me, whispering that the houses of the zodiac I attended to were a contrivance of the Western astrological mind. Would Chinese cabbage seed *really* hearken to the pull of European ideas regarding Pisces and Scorpio?

In the first years of the Green Gulch garden our lunar sowing practice was ponderous with religious awe. We prayed the first crops up out of our heavy black earth, much as in the children's story of Frog and Toad. Frog is an experienced gardener, who counsels the terrified neophyte Toad. Toad sows his garden and broods, paces, intones, chants, and recites poetry by candlelight to his underground seeds. Finally, after several sleepless days and nights of ceremony, Toad drops off in an exhausted stupor. Effortlessly, the garden comes up. In spite of Toad, all around him the seeds sprout.

It takes years of extensive Zen training and day after night after day of dedicated gardening to become as stupid, innocent, and successful as Toad.

Just as we finally believe that it is possible to learn the laws of the celestial cycles and understand the forces of light and dark on the life of the garden, it is also time to remember how to forget. Fifteenth-century Zen master and poet Ikkyu writes:

> sick of all the names
> sick of whatever it's called
> I dedicate every pore to what's here

And what is here, naturally here, rather than supernaturally imposed on what is here, is the rhythmic pull and release of the moon, the fire and ice of the cycles of the sun, and our close attention to sky and earth that is the true teaching encoded in the constellations of the zodiac. Perhaps modern poet Jack Gilbert expresses this best when he writes, "We must unlearn the constellations to see the stars."

✦   ✦   ✦

Often gardening can be overwhelming and unsettling, especially if you are swept up in the task of sorting out the overlapping influences of the various sun and moon cycles. When I lose my bearings I return to the grounded teaching of Zen master Ma, a renowned Buddhist teacher who lived in the steep mountains of China in the eighth century. Master Ma, or the Horse Master as he was called, was a huge fellow with a long, equine tongue that reached out to touch the end of his nose and to lash out at heaven and earth as well, awakening 139 enlightened Zen successors. When Master Ma was on his deathbed, his temple superintendent came to see him and asked, "How is your health, venerable teacher?" The great master answered, "Sun faced Buddha, moon faced Buddha."

According to the ancient texts, a Sun Face Buddha lives in the world for eighteen hundred years, while a Moon Face Buddha enters extinction after a day and a night. In the ephemeral and ever-changing life of the garden the distinction between slow, long time and a single, fleeting moment, and the difference between light and shadow often blur and merge into one bold harmony of difference and equality. In this timeless world the sun-face garden abides in darkness while the brief shadow world of the moon-face garden is embroidered with light. "In the light there is darkness, but don't take it as darkness," spoke a great Zen contemporary of Master Ma, and "in the dark there is light, but don't see it as light." Settling down in the garden, letting go of all distinctions and becoming as still as a toad, light and dark are made of their opposites, merging together like forward and backward steps that leave no footprints at the dragon's gate.

When I first began to garden at Green Gulch I did not yet experience the presence of light and dark intertwined in the muscle and marrow of Master Ma's Sun Face Buddha, Moon Face Buddha. Instead, I bound myself to zealous

occult speculation and forfeited my true ground. So when visible light and dark and the force of the sun and the moon sweep you away from the living garden, lie down on the earth and look up at the stars. Forget where you are in time and place. Unlearn the constellations. Drop away body and mind and become toad flax. Let the moon-face garden hold you in its fleeting black magic that is made of light, and let the sun-face garden that is always anchored in old darkness direct your gardening life, on and on, until the end of time.

Gift-Bestowing Hands

ONE OF THE LAST THINGS I DID WITH MY TEACHER HARRY ROBERTS before he died was to sow a deep wooden flat with the seeds of a tap-rooting member of the ancient redwood family, *Cryptomeria japonica*, gathered from around the Koji national preserve in Japan and sent to us by Masanobu Fukuoka Sensei, natural farmer and author of *The One-Straw Revolution*.

Fukuoka visited North America in the late 1970s and made an especially strong connection with Harry. They walked together for hours beneath the towering redwoods of Muir Woods National Monument and noted how difficult it is for new, shallow-rooted redwoods to get established on eroded soil outside of woods like those. "Perhaps a tap-rooting variety of redwood from Japan would help stabilize your soil," suggested Fukuoka to Harry. "I will send you some seed."

The redwood tribe forms a giant ring of influential elders growing all around the Pacific Rim. This noble family includes the coastal redwoods of the Pacific Northwest, *Sequoia sempervirens*, the tallest trees on earth; the stately redwoods of the lower reaches of the Sierra Nevada range, *Sequoiadendron giganteum*, the broadest in girth; the *Cryptomeria japonica*, the national tree of Japan; the prehistoric, deciduous dawn redwood of China; the Chilean pines of the South American coast; and the angular monkey puzzle tree, originating in central Chile and spreading to southeastern Australia and throughout the Southern Hemisphere.

The Japanese redwood seeds arrived two years after Fukuoka Sensei's visit. He had made a special pilgrimage walk to the edge of the Koji preserve, where the old-growth *Cryptomeria* had never been cut, and there he had gathered ripe seed for Harry.

Although Harry was extremely weak and close to death when the seeds arrived, he was determined to sow them. "Remember," he wheezed weakly to me while I prepared the seed flat, "these trees are not for your lifetime or for the lifetime of your children. They are for the next five hundred years."

That was in February of 1981. Harry was dead one month later. The *Cryptomeria* seeds sprouted like wildfire just a month after his death and three years later we transplanted these strong, tap-rooting Japanese redwoods to a badly eroded northwest-facing slope overlooking the Green Gulch reservoir, a place where Harry had always dreamed of building a small cabin and living out his days hidden in the green fur of the chaparral-covered coastal mountains.

The Japanese *Cryptomeria* trees proved to be vigorous growers, plunging their muscular roots down into our thin coastal soil and clawing into the very marrow of the land. We built a simple cage around each tree to protect them from deer and grazing cattle damage and watched as they rooted and grew in their new home.

In the mid-1980s Fukuoka Sensei returned to California and we took him to visit the young stand of *Cryptomeria*. It was early winter and the trees were wearing their new green foliage, brightened by cold winter rain. The vivid tips of new growth looked as if they had been dipped in freshly stirred chartreuse paint. Fukuoka Sensei leaned against the protective cages, fingering the new growth, and wept.

It is a daunting honor to care for a plant that will not produce viable seed for seventy-five years. Just to live with such plants in your care and consciousness drops a deep anchor down into the well of your conception of time. "In fifteen years or so you can take cuttings from the lower five feet of these *Cryptomeria*," Fukuoka Sensei explained to me, showing me carefully how and where to take the cuttings. "The trees are most vigorous then and cuttings made over the next five years or so from that same region of the tree will give you strong, healthy *Cryptomeria* for this grove."

"That will be in the autumn of the year 2000," I said to myself, marking my mind with the task, and with the round circle of that new millennium date. It seemed like ages in the future but in that appointed season a new deep flat was planted just outside the glasshouse, filled with bronze-green side-shoot cuttings of the Koji preserve *Cryptomeria*, growing amid flats of black dragon lilies, native purple needle grass, and rows of tree collards.

My life as a gardener has grown and developed in these last decades. Where I was once eager to entirely reforest the eroded Green Gulch hills with Japanese tap-rooting redwoods, now I would not dream of doing that. Instead, I work every winter with dedicated volunteers to reestablish locally grown California native plants in the eroded eye-sockets of our blind hills. But when I am tired of bushwhacking through poison oak and wild blackberry vines to plant California native plants, I drop down to the cryptomeria grove that encircles our reservoir and sit with my back against a twenty-foot-high Japanese redwood and let my mind range over unmapped terrain.

❖   ❖   ❖

On my outside garden altar not far from our home workshed I keep a small, butterfly-shaped bowl that my daughter fashioned out of local clay. The bowl holds revolving seed offerings from the harvest garden, offerings that occasionally mysteriously disappear at night thanks to our resident dusky-footed wood rat that faithfully patrols my garden altar. Next to the butterfly bowl is a small placard with the name Nicolai Vavilov inscribed on it. Vavilov was a renowned Russian biologist and botanist who lived in the first half of the twentieth century and traveled the world collecting seed and plant material to enrich the diet of hungry people. On these hunting and gathering missions Vavilov discerned several regions of extraordinary genetic and biological diversity. In these regions, he postulated, the major food crops of our world have their origins. This is important because it counters the old notion that agriculture developed on lean land to feed the hungry. In truth, agriculture has its roots deep in the rich soil of tremendously varied and distinct regions of biodiversity.

Vavilov returned to Russia with a wealth of carefully selected plant material that he had gathered from his many botanical missions and established the Vavilov Institute in an old, rundown three-story building in Leningrad, with experimental testing grounds just outside the city. Working with a small band of dedicated scientists from all parts of the world, more than 165,000 distinct samples of seed and plant material were cataloged, collected, and preserved by the Institute, including single rare strains of seeds such as a hard flint corn discovered by Vavilov in northern Siberia and found to tolerate the cold, harsh climate of the northern tundra.

Vavilov continued his collecting missions until his arrest by the Stalin regime in 1940, about one week prior to the start of the terrible siege of Leningrad, which lasted for almost nine hundred days and saw the death of almost six hundred thousand people.

During the siege of Leningrad, while Vavilov was in prison, his team of scientists protected with their lives the almost quarter of a million samples of seed stored in the Institute. Under German fire these scientists harvested the rare potato tubers growing in the experimental fields just outside of Leningrad and kept these potatoes from freezing by burning every scrap of wood they could salvage to keep the tuber collection alive.

When the siege of Leningrad ended Vavilov was dead from starvation in prison. Twenty of the scientists in the Vavilov Institute had also died of starvation while protecting their cache of rare seed varieties of rice, corn, wheat, oats, beans, and peas stored in the Institute and known to be the last living samples of their kind of seed. Of the twenty scientists who died, fourteen were the leading experts in the world for their crops. The director of the rice collection, which was at that time the largest collection of rice in the world, starved to death surrounded by hundreds of bags of unopened rice.

Today the work of the Vavilov Institute continues, and although its scope is much narrower than in Vavilov's time, this Institute is joined by other seed banks and seed-saving societies worldwide, from Seed Savers Exchange in the United States, where more than eighteen thousand varieties of crops are grown out and preserved yearly on the Exchange farm in Decorah, Iowa, to Navdanya, an Indian seed-saving movement established by the environmental activist Vandana Shiva, with sixteen community seed banks in six Indian states.

Nongovernmental agencies like these work to preserve and maintain genetic diversity alongside botanical gardens, locally based small-scale heirloom seed companies, and regional horticultural society seed exchanges. Still, the fundamental work of preserving and maintaining these rare legacies of seed remains in the hands of individual gardeners and farmers.

In the United States alone about forty-three million American families grow a portion of their own food. This means that close to one in every three families is involved in growing and harvesting some of their staple food, while an estimated two-thirds of the population of the world subsist on what they are able to grow. And yet we are witnessing in our times a precipitous erosion of genetic diversity in food crops that until now have been bred, developed, and shared freely over the long ten-thousand-year history of agriculture.

When I first began to sow flower seeds for the huge perennial garden at Green Gulch in 1975, there was a far greater range of seeds available than are currently found in the twenty-first-century seed market trade. At the turning of the millennium in the year 2000, 95 percent of all the seed sown throughout the history of agriculture was extinct. True, there are new varieties touted in garden catalogs every year, but the diversity of these modern varieties is far less than what we could draw on even as recently as twenty-five years ago.

Knowing this, and experiencing the diminished range of seed available in the modern commercial marketplace, I am committed to preserving, propagating, and sharing the diverse range of plant material that I grow myself, and that I help others grow, with eager gardeners' help.

Gardening, and growing plants for seed and for the benefit of future generations, is political as well as horticultural work. Recognizing that ten multinational corporations control one-third of the twenty-three-billion-dollar commercial seed market and 100 percent of the market for genetically engineered or transgenic seed crops, inspires me to work my hardest to avoid using the seed of these same corporations that also control the global pesticide and chemical agriculture market.

"There is life in the ground," writes plant historian Charles Warner. "It goes into the seed and when the seed is stirred up, it goes into the person who stirs it." The more I study the history and plight of falling biodiversity in seed and plant material, the more stirred up I become. And the more motivated I am to garden for the health and continuity of present and future generations.

My decision is political, of course, but it is primarily anchored in my gardener's love for genetic diversity and for growing a wide and healthy range of plants. Lack of broad-based genetic diversity in plants breeds disease and genetic weakness, a truth corroborated by the Irish potato famine of the 1840s. A million people died because the diminished biodiversity of the Irish potato fields could not fight the blight caused by the water mold fungus *Phytophthora infestans*.

Traditional hunters and gatherers, farmers, and gardeners understand the danger of relying on a narrow genetic base for staple food crops. In the Andean highlands where the potato originated, indigenous farmers have grown and bred more than three thousand distinct varieties of potatoes, each adapted to the conditions of its particular region, while in India, where rice is a staple food equated with *prana*, or the life force of breath, local farmers have cultivated and developed some 200,000 distinct varieties of rice.

Seeds are strong. They breed true to type and cultivate new land with their muscular roots. And seedy characters from all over the world nurture a singular passion to share their seed wealth and hard work with many beings. I find my companions in the coalition of more than two thousand groups of Indian gardeners who have made a pledge to preserve their native seed stocks and not comply with the patenting of life practiced by large seed conglomerates.

I also receive deep inspiration from the brave women of the Greenbelt movement in Kenya, Africa, founded by 2004 Nobel Peace Prize recipient Wangari Maathai. These tree-planting women are replanting their native land with thousands of indigenous trees raised in propagation nurseries cultivated in their own small backyard lots.

Learning how to care for and culture local strains of seed and plant materials that are adapted to the soil and climate of each particular garden endows the seed-saving or plant-breeding gardener with "gift-bestowing hands." These hands come alive stirring the seed of the next generation of life-force crops.

For gardeners who have a calling and inclination to propagate and grow plants for the next generation of gardeners, or for those of us who have a hankering to do some simple backyard plant breeding and selection, be sure to save your best plants for seed and for vegetative propagation and learn to tolerate a little wildness and seediness in the process. Remember, a garden saved for seed is never a neat garden. Far from it. A seed garden is more like an old Southern plantation that has run to wrack and ruin. Tall stems of ripening *Linaria* with the palest, shell-pink blooms overrun Crater Lake blue veronica and ragged drifts of coral *Alonsoa* that are also ripening their burden of seed under the slow, late-summer wings of nectar-heavy honeybees.

As you learn to tolerate your seedy tangle and to discern the families of rare seed ripening within the thicket, a strange freshness stirs to life among the bone-dry rattle of your seedy autumn garden. Standing still inside this tangle, the wind moves through the unsown gardens of tomorrow.

Not everyone has a garden or a lifestyle that allows fallowness to dominate while the green world dries out and runs to seed, so for those of us purchasing seed or plants grown by others it is very important to support the smaller seed houses and nurseries that protect native strains of seed and local varieties of plant material that are not offered in the commercial horticultural trade.

Whenever possible give back to the earth by purchasing your seed from companies that endeavor to grow their seed organically, since plants grown without pesticides, herbicides, or chemical fertilizers leave behind a soil that is not depleted of nutrients or stripped of biological wealth.

Even more important is the commitment to support seed houses, plant nurseries, and food sources that do not rely on multinational corporations that produce genetically modified organisms as the basis for their profitability. We live in an age where the modern field of biotechnology or genetic modification is dominant. The basis of this new technology is grounded in the ability to take DNA or code genetic material from one organism and insert it in another species, creating transgenic organisms. Normally human beings cannot share or exchange genes with crops or critters, but genetic engineering changes and dissolves some of the boundaries that have defined life as we know it. What is most dangerous right now is probably the unregulated introduction of modified crops into the wide arena of the natural world. We know precious little about the threats that transgenic modification pose to living organisms, food, or seed. At the very least I want to be informed before I purchase or ingest any genetically modified material. My reasons are fundamental and simple, grounded in biological, political, and ethical concern.

While biotechnology claims to increase biological diversity, the new organisms being engineered have not been sufficiently tested to gauge their true impact on life. Genetically modified organisms live outside of human ecosystems and yet they influence these ecosystems through biological crossbreeding and mutation. Whole new races of super-insects, super-seeds, and mutant bacterial and viral strains of disease are emerging in the field of transgenic technology. In addition, genetically engineered bacteria have been shown to suppress beneficial populations of mycorrhizal soil fungi, while in the presence of mutant microbes many plants fail to grow.

Many of the agencies responsible for developing genetically modified organisms are financed and supported by multinational corporations. Politically this is of concern when a handful of global corporations control the access to and content of a vital portion of the world's food supply, set global trade rules, own the intellectual property rights of seed production, and control national food and agricultural policy. By being an informed and engaged consumer and an alert gardener it is possible to withhold support from these global corporations and to help reverse this corporate trend.

Growing food and plants and preserving the seed and diverse genetic inheritance of those plants is an ancient human practice or moral custom. "Moral custom" or what I call "moral presence" is at the root of the word "ethics," the study of those principles that govern the conduct of human life.

Every garden is a living being, full of gifts and surprises, loneliness, longing, and untold stories. As gardeners we grow along with our gardens until it becomes ethically impossible to own or tamper with the genetic lifelines of any garden without direct consequence for both the garden and the gardener.

Gardens always exist nested in a wider context: neighborhood, ecosystem, watershed, and bioregion. In a healthy and dynamic world these nested systems influence each other and exist in relationship to each other. Each system, then, is an integrated whole with clear, semipermeable membranes and boundaries, while at the same time each system responds to every other system nested about it.

True moral presence in the garden gives room to experimentation, risk, and strong lessons from danger and failure. At the same time, gardeners are wary and alert. We deeply know that we are not only gardening for our own lifetime but for lifetime after lifetime, for generations of *Cryptomeria* forests and for clean fields of open-pollinated corn. Remembering this, and hearkening back to the old tongue of garden law, we are careful before introducing technologically altered organisms that cannot be "un-engineered" into the body of our garden or into our own bodies.

When you have successfully grown plants for seed or for vegetative increase, it is a fine practice to keep a bit of this wealth for your own garden and then to share the bounty with neighbors and green-thumbed strangers. The Zen tradition has a wonderful old expression, "Return to the marketplace with gift-bestowing hands," which describes cloud-and-water wandering practitioners returning home to the world from long transformative practice in the deep mountains of the mind and heart, to share the benefit of their awakening with all beings.

So every season keep a measure of seed and divisible plant material for your home garden and then give the rest of it, and *all* of it, away. Give with gift-bestowing hands to the lonely and the stranger, to wandering gardeners and to old friends. For the benefit of all beings, give the harvest away.

BEAUTY
COUNTS

Divinely Superfluous Beauty

YEARS AGO WHEN HARRY ROBERTS FIRST BEGAN TO WORK WITH US at Green Gulch and to teach us what he knew, we were sitting with him on a Sunday afternoon in late summer, shelling our first crop of English peas over in a shady corner of the garden.

"Before you do anything, anything at all," Harry suddenly announced to us, in the midst of our green reverie, "make sure that you have three good reasons for doing what you do." I looked up at my grisly old teacher perched on his camp stool, unzipping his pea pod with pristine care and attention. It was quiet in the garden but for the round "plink" of peas falling into our warm metal bowls. "That goes for setting up a garden, too," Harry cast down to me, eyeing me intently before picking up his next pea.

I sat there in the filtered sunlight, staring into my bowl of iridescent peas. They shone from the inside out, luminous gems chipped from the deep green mines of August. "What about beauty?" I asked Harry. "Is beauty a reason?"

"Beauty?" he queried, hovering over his mounded bowl of summer peas. There was a long pause. "Beauty counts," he finally proclaimed, letting loose a rain of peas.

✦ ✦ ✦

I am a garden dreamer, but a practical one, rooted in working the ground and sustained by pushing wheelbarrows full of growing plants. The garden will never be a metaphor for me, but always an actual place of danger and wanton beauty. When I walk into a garden I step into paradise with an address, paradise located on earth. This is just as true in an abandoned city garden with its chain-link fence ripped down and all the forgotten crops running to seed in a wild jumble of sun-gold tomatoes and old collard greens as it is in a plump, well-tended country estate garden fat with sumptuous figs and overripe white melons

I love the word "paradise," rich in meaning and association. It comes from the old Persian *pairadaeza*, or a walled enclosure, and, by horticultural extension, an enclosed garden. In biblical and classical literature, paradise is found on earth in the original garden of Eden where four great rivers meet, and in the celestial heavens where the blessed dead gather together for the final Resurrection.

Rosmarinus and *Lavendula*

In the days when humans lived in balance they were watched over and guided by the stars. And at a certain period it was observed that people were beginning to over-rely on their reason and intellect. Therefore two stars were ordered to descend to earth to enlighten humankind. It so happened that those two stars arrived on earth at the very moment that the archangel raised his sword and drove Adam and Eve out of the garden. And these two stars attempted to follow, in the endeavor to fulfill their orders. But the archangel raised his sword again and said, "None may follow these two where they must travel in the land of darkness."

And the one star raised a medallion and said, "I represent the King of Fishes and am strength." And the other raised a medallion and said, "I am the Queen of Crops and I represent comfort."

And when the archangel recognized his two siblings he lowered his sword and permitted them to pass in the form of two herbs—*Rosmarinus* for strength and *Lavendula* for comfort. In this form they traveled beside Adam and Eve throughout all the lands of darkness showing them always, when they required it, the paths that led back to where they had come from.

Spoken narrative delivered by Alan Chadwick

Curiously, in the biblical garden of Eden, Adam and Eve do not really begin to garden until they disobey God, eat from the fruit of the Tree of Knowledge of Good and Evil, and are expelled from the protection of Eden. Sent out into that wild and untamed world beyond the gates of enclosed paradise, man and woman toil by the sweat of their brow to garden a new, worldly paradise on earth. According to one of Alan Chadwick's favorite parables, Adam and Eve had two companions when they were forced to leave paradise because of their over-reliance on reason and intellect and their refusal to obey God. On their journey out and east of Eden, he said, Adam and Eve were accompanied by two archangels in the form of plants. Rosemary for strength and lavender for comfort protected them on their journey and reminded them always of the way home to the garden.

When you design and plant a garden, mystery and magic manifest in the rich brocade robe of plants you lay out on the earth of paradise. I planted rosemary and lavender just inside the garden gates at Green Gulch to welcome visitors to the Zen Center. Long borders of English lavender with formal plantings of Tuscan rosemary standing behind them flank the main road leading through Green Gulch and out to the sea. Bumblebees fumble in the lavender flowers gathering pungent nectar from the Queen of Crops and turn slow somersaults in the thick sea of lavender perfume. When guests enter the summer garden the old spell of lavender brings them to a silent standstill.

In the first years of farming and gardening at Green Gulch I dreamed of creating a self-sustaining garden that would buffer Zen practitioners from the busy-ness of everyday life. We would only eat what we grew on our own pure land and only use materials generated from our local bioregion to build and sustain the new farm and garden. I was mightily righteous in my notions of seceding, untainted, from the marketplace of society.

Over the years I shifted my stance. Instead of retreating from the world I advanced, falling in love with it as it radiated out in widening circles from the core of the garden. Nowadays I am called to help establish tiny plots of paradise in local schools, hospitals, prisons, and abandoned city lots throughout the wider Bay Area. Sometimes I wish that these urban gardens were a little more Eden-esque and a tad less demanding, but this doesn't seem to be in my horticultural cards.

Perhaps I love the garden most for this combination of engagement with the world's needs and those long hours when I find myself alone in paradise in the cool of the day. The evening light is slanted and pale green and wind moves through the gaps in the dark rosemary hedge like blue smoke over the uncut lavender. Ask me then for three good reasons to garden and I will tell you: for beauty, for the coming apart of beauty, and for the opportunity to begin again with no design in mind.

❖ ❖ ❖

Every paradise garden I know is rooted in real work and real bounty. The two beget each other. Every garden worth its salt becomes paradise by being both a safe refuge from the madness of the world and a field of action within the cacophony of this very world.

Paradise is made of grunt labor and a love for the garden far too old to bargain with, tame, or understand. The garden is different every day, made of what Robinson Jeffers calls "divinely superfluous beauty." Now you see paradise, now you don't, and this seeing and not-seeing is as intimate as spring and sea water poured together into a cut-glass bowl.

A close friend, Kay, both showed me her version of paradise in the Green Gulch garden and unsettled me deeply as we worked together in that garden. Kay first came to Green Gulch as a guest a few months after her husband died of brain cancer. She was a painter and a brilliant colorist, yet her life had gone dark. Death bore down on her with wide open raptor's wings. Kay crawled blind into Green Gulch, death perched between her shoulder blades.

At first we rarely saw Kay in the garden. She sat for hours in the zendo, bargaining listlessly with life. After a few weeks she came down to the garden. She was picked-over carrion. I sent her to work in the flowers by herself. Slowly, Kay pruned back the beauty bush, *Kolkwitzia amabilis*, standing ankle-deep in soft drifts of faded coral flower petals and lime-green leaves. Poet Tess Gallagher says, "You can't go deep until you go slow." Slowly, slowly Kay went

314

down into the flowers; she weeded the mourning-bride scabiosa, watered the black dragon lilies. On more than one occasion I happened upon her asleep in the sunshine on the grass behind waves of fragrant white-flowering myrtle.

In spite of herself Kay began to live again, breath by lonely breath. Beauty brought her back, broken and bedraggled. She was in the garden now every day. After a while I asked her to harvest and arrange some flowers for the altar. "You choose which flowers," I said, giving her my shears.

Kay's first floral arrangement broke all the rules I had in my mind, mixing vermilion tithonia with dark-purple monkshood, acid-green foliage with cobalt-blue Chinese delphinium, and dead branches intertwined with wild gooseberries, all in one vase. She was painting her way out of Hades, calling on the rainbow arc of summer flowers to be her path. I am sure that Manjusri Bodhisattva, the main figure on the Green Gulch altar, is still recovering from the heat of Kay's original floral offering and especially from her final stroke, full-blown scarlet roses that lay with curved thorns exposed across the naked midsection of the arrangement.

Kay slowed down, went deep, and came back to life in the flower garden. The flowers stepped forward, fully revealed, as Kay plucked and arranged them. Inspired and unsettled, I saw phantom beauty stand up from the wilted parings of the day, and become flesh, a living paradise on earth.

Designing paradise so that the secret garden within the garden can step forward is an art. Each garden is unique and chameleon-like, with its own unspoken rules made to be followed and, like all rules, to be broken. Divinely superfluous beauty cracks the door ajar for a brief moment, then slams it shut and the world grows opaque, covered with dark vines.

Tangible paradise depends on beginner's mind, on a broken heart, and on the living earth on which we stand. When you have a garden design made of these elements, leave this design outside overnight on a moonlit patch of chamomile lawn behind the leopard lilies. See if your design holds up after nocturnal snails ooze across your plans, sliming them with their silver trail and perforating your plans of divinely superfluous beauty with their deft mouthparts. If it does, set to work.

Plotting Paradise

IN 1975, WHEN I FIRST BEGAN WORKING IN THE GREEN GULCH garden, we plotted the design of an elaborate Herbal Circle garden not far from the garden gate, a small surprise paradise on earth to be planted in the very center of the ferocious bustle of our kitchen garden. We rolled out a sinuous, serpentine path snaking through Italian artichokes and beds of round-shouldered, oxblood beets, and uncoiling into the herbal circle in slow loops. On the seaside edge of the Herbal Circle, the snake path slithered out of paradise and disappeared into the vast order of our symmetrical, 150-foot-long lines of farm vegetables that ran for acres west to the sea.

We planted this plot of paradise "stam," smack-dab in the middle of productivity and abundance, and "dafka," in order to stop daydreamers short in their tracks and wake them up. *Stam* is a modern Hebrew word, slang for "suddenly, without warning—out of the blue," and *dafka*, also Hebrew slang, means "in your face, contrary to what you expect and without rhyme or reason." The Herbal Circle succeeded in this, far beyond our wildest dreams, evolving as an orderly and beautiful bit of flowering paradise plunked down in the middle of a bustling and productive vegetable garden. It was stunning.

In truth, the Green Gulch Herbal Circle didn't just fall stam, dafka, on the face of the garden like an erratic meteor hurtling down from the dark edges of heaven to explode on earth. Every garden grows out of long hours of secret musing, planning, and forethought, since gardens incubate in our consciousness for an abysmally long time. The centerpiece Herbal Circle garden at the Gulch had its genesis in three strong reasons for plotting paradise on Zen earth.

Beauty was first, anchoring the trinity: we wanted to increase the beauty and diversity of our vegetable garden by interplanting perennial herbs, flowers, and shrubs among the vegetables.

Our garden vision was second: we dreamed of a circular garden softening the rectilinear order of straight row crops, a garden reminiscent of old-world

maze gardens or contemplative labyrin-
thine landscapes.

Third was how the garden would be
peopled: we wanted to create a spot
where visitors would be stopped by
beauty and encouraged to sit down
and rest, meditate, talk, catch their
breath, or play tag with their children
in the heart of the garden.

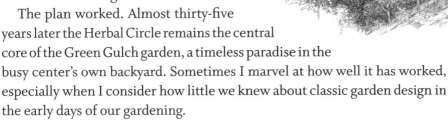

The plan worked. Almost thirty-five
years later the Herbal Circle remains the central
core of the Green Gulch garden, a timeless paradise in the
busy center's own backyard. Sometimes I marvel at how well it has worked,
especially when I consider how little we knew about classic garden design in
the early days of our gardening.

That we did not know too much was probably the greatest advantage we had
in designing the Herbal Circle garden. By following our affection and conviction that every garden belongs to the many beings passing in and out through
its semipermeable membranes, the Green Gulch garden came to life.

"*Et in Arcadia ego*" reads the classic inscription in Alan Chadwick's primary
garden, in Santa Cruz, California: *And I Am in Arcadia*, in the garden of living
paradise on earth. I scratched this sentiment in secret onto the top rung of
one of our main rose arbors leading into the Herbal Circle at Green Gulch. I
equally love the sign that welcomes visitors to Food for Thought, the thriving
food bank and garden in western Sonoma County where almost five hundred
people with AIDS receive food and garden comfort every day underneath a
gateway sign that proclaims, *Welcome—life begins the day you start a garden.*

As you compose and start a garden a certain balance of elements is always
present: shadow and light, moisture and dryness, enclosure and boundless-
ness, order and wild abandon. This balance is included throughout the history
of gardens as well: the original gardens of the Middle East, where the Persian
pairadaeza originated, were organized around a central well and marked by
the watercourses going out from the well to water the paradise garden. These

desert-born gardens were often enclosed by a substantial wall or tightly interwoven hedge. Often the watercourses divided the garden into sections, as in the garden of Eden:

> God planted a garden, eastward in Eden, and a river went out of Eden to water the garden and from thence it was parted into four heads.
>
> *Genesis II:8*

At San Francisco Zen Center I pored over the elaborate records and garden plans for European medieval monastic gardens. It was clear to me these gardens survived over the centuries because monasteries of the Old World were sanctuaries and protected places of refuge during times of war and pillage.

I studied the garden plans of the seventh-century Swiss Benedictine monastery of St. Gall closely and saw an interior skeleton of garden paradise plots within the monastic compound: the potagers garden of herbs and vegetables growing next to the monastery kitchen, the sacristy garden where flowers for the altar were tended by the sacristan, the infirmer's garden of medicinal herbs and roots, the orchard garden that included a simple cemetery for the monks, and even the ale-maker's garden planted to bitter herbs harvested for flavoring ale.

In the earliest Byzantine culture and monastic compounds the central garden of the monastery was designed in the shape of a cross, creating an inner sanctum that was often a cloistered spot reserved for prayer and meditation. Likewise, since ancient times, it has been possible to trace lost gardens by studying the cemetery plots of old churchyards, since it is a timeless practice to plant memorial gardens for the dead.

The classic four-square garden pattern has prevailed worldwide throughout horticultural history, repeated in the walled gardens of India as well as in medieval Europe, in Italian and French Renaissance gardens with their hedged parterres and knot gardens, and in the early botanic and physic gardens of the New World. And when I visit the six acres of classically inspired Conservatory Gardens in New York City's Central Park, I walk through the old and modern mind of paradise.

In these gardens the four-square pattern is often subdivided recursively into smaller patterns of four. The classic four-square design is also echoed in the patterned garden designs woven into Persian carpets and repeated in the extraordinary detail of Egyptian wall paintings dating from more than four thousand years ago.

Historians of garden design often say it was the French landscape architect André Le Nôtre who first broke down the clipped walls of enclosed paradise. At Vaux-le-Vicomte and Versailles, the eighteenth-century palace of King Louis XIV, Le Nôtre let his *allées* run out, unbound, from the central château into the surrounding French countryside. But long before the French loosened the cords of staid control, societies like England, Japan, and China, which may have felt less pressure to protect themselves from military attack, were designing their gardens following the wild, ungirdled lines of the natural world.

Paradise is evident in both enclosed gardens and gardens open to the sinuous, wild domain beyond the cultivated row. My garden teachers taught me to work both the walled and boundless worlds. They encouraged me to lay out gardens that contained the space I was working in, by planting a protective hedge on three sides of the garden, and also to let the eye and mind run free by offering a fourth view, a *clair-voyez* or unbound "clear view," into the wild world beyond enclosure.

One of my favorite garden design books, *The Poetics of Gardens*, suggests strategies for design that follow the free lines of the natural world. My strategy, based on *Poetics*, is to occupy the site or garden place of the land I am working; to shape the space of the garden; to create the climate of the garden through designs and plantings; and then to step back, take a deep breath, and forget what I have made.

Occupy the Site

Every garden "stakes a claim" to the site it occupies by engaging with its particular place. There is no such thing as gardening in general; every plot of paradise is unique and specific. Since this is so, gardeners establishing a garden would do well to heed the advice of Alexander Pope given to his eighteenth-century patron Lord Burlington:

> Consult the Genius of the Place in all;
> That tells the Waters or to rise, or fall.

Before you break ground for a new garden and occupy the site, take some time to consult the genius of the place. Sit still on the spot where you are plotting paradise, perhaps by surprising it with a midday visit, or by coming in a driving rainstorm, without even an umbrella to protect you from your garden dreams. Consider spending the night camped out on your proposed garden site, enjoying the night sky and the dawn chorus of hidden birds. Mostly, walk the land every day, pacing the open ground, no matter how small your plot is, before you occupy the site.

There are many strategies of occupation. Sometimes gardens stand out boldly on the face of creation, like a solitary circle of oaks occupying a windswept headland in Marin, while other gardens merge seamlessly with the natural landscape, tucking themselves neatly into the folds of wild meadows and crumpled hills. Occasionally, a garden "borrows" surprise, beauty, meaning, and even context from a nearby landscape, just as the formal Japanese tea garden at Green Gulch that includes not a single flowering shrub "borrows" the voluptuous down-drift of pale pink petal confetti sloughed off by the huge sweetheart rose planted outside the teahouse gate. And now and then a garden occupies its spot by enclosing a piece of landscape, like the Herbal Circle garden creating an interior, walled garden of Eden, excluding the busy commerce of black radishes ripening underneath Hopi blue corn.

The important point is simple and manifest: gardens occupy the sites where they grow, and they change their sites and themselves as they root and take their place. Additionally, gardens occupy their gardeners as well, ripening the mind, body, and imagination of all who step inside their green gates. The eighth-century poet Wang Wei observed, "Landscape softens the sharp edges of isolation," as true today as 1,300 years ago.

Shape the Space of the Garden

Almost every year I visit the garden at the University of California in Santa Cruz that Alan Chadwick started forty years ago. Once I brought along a clutch of ten farm and garden apprentices from Green Gulch. Four or five 150-foot-long beds in the lower apple orchard had just been dug and shaped for cover crop seed. They stood unadorned in the late summer sunlight, terra-cotta red and naked of plants. We visited countless plots of paradise within the walled enclosures of Santa Cruz that day, but what I remember most vividly were those unplanted garden beds: bare, soft-shaped clay beds of paradise awaiting their allotment of autumn seed.

You can shape a garden by raising the soil into lofty, double-dug beds like the ones I saw at Santa Cruz, you can shape permaculture swales to plant and help hold steep hillsides, you can sink your beds of vegetables below a natural wall and create a system of berms, vales, bands, and hollows to suit your landscape. Or you can simply follow the natural, wild contours of your land and let your garden step forth, unbidden, from its native ground.

Once you have shaped the earth of your garden the next task is to cover the ground with a growing mantle of plants, or with other materials that will protect, conserve, build, and hold your soil. Here again, let your affection guide you as you "dress" your garden. Be bold! Mughal emperors and their Persian ancestors spread priceless silk and wool carpets on their gardens to cover and shape their plots of paradise. All around the inner edge of the

Some Solid Wall and Edging Materials	Some Living Hedge Walls
Wood	Rosemary
Brick	Lavender
Mortar	Bay
Stone	Ivy
Adobe	Bougainvillea
Shaped soil	Bamboo
Steel wire	Rose
Bamboo	Yew
Paper	Cypress
Cement	Box myrtle
Cloth	Pittosporum
Cob	
Straw bale	
Rammed earth	
Old tires and recycled rubber	
Metal and recycled metal	

Herbal Circle at Green Gulch we planted a thick ground cover of tight, fragrant chamomile, the same plant that is used in northern Europe to create herbal "couches" for rolling on after enjoying a hot, steamy sauna. Our motivation was simple: chamomile is the herb of calm and contentment. We wanted that quality to infuse the plant-scape of our inner garden at Green Gulch, so that the chamomile would exude quiet through its green pores. Over the years the Zen gophers of Green Gulch Farm have assisted us by distributing tiny plugs of chamomile throughout our paradise via their underground burrows. We now have a "wall-to-wall" chamomile carpet in the original Herbal Circle.

One of the most important features of your garden is how you choose to mark and define your plot of paradise. An old friend of mine, a scholar of Greek, Latin, and most recently, the Pali scriptures, wrote me a wonderful letter years ago in which he observed this important truth about garden walls: "The enclosure around a garden serves to let me know that I am inside. . . . Yet the garden wall is also a gateway, an aperture, a passage which joins us to the transcendent particulars of coming into bloom and facing, slowly or quickly, wild or tame, inside or out."

A single wall or shaped edge can form the main organizing axis around which a garden paradise is plotted. Composed of solid or living matter, garden fences and walls not only enclose and contain but open out to include the entire sweep of the wide world. Every wall permits limited passage, whether by plant choice or by a gateway, so every plot of paradise is like a living cell, protected by a semipermeable membrane.

Some of the most memorable garden walls I know are utterly porous. The Kashmiri design of the Char Chinar is a garden simply marked by four upright trees designating the corners of the square enclosure. Now and then, in the world of Chinese painting and landscape design, the edges of paradise are raised like ethereal "dragon's veins," drawn with ambiguous lines suggesting that the garden goes on forever, in twists and turns until it is finally absorbed into the vastness of its native landscape. I also think of a wonderful canvas enclosure my gardening friend and artist Alan Gussow stretched around his upstate New York garden. Whenever a bird called out, Alan slit an opening with his razor-sharp mat knife into the taut canvas surface of his cloth wall, until within a few short days Alan's garden was lacerated, inside and out, by song.

If gates and fences, walls and marked edges enclose and open a garden, then the garden path winding through paradise is the pattern that connects inside to out. When it was time for us to lay out the main paths of the Green Gulch garden we marked their width by measuring the space needed for two adults to walk together with a child between them.

I enjoy well-ordered, clear garden paths, but I also delight in going off the marked trail and following those secret paths that deliver me to random surprise and occasional terror. These are the "less traveled" paths, like the thin, serpentine trail I discovered late one summer afternoon under a shadowy, black-leaved wild plum tree where masked raccoons had feasted on ripe fruit above the night river. Gnawed plum pits aswarm with drowsy flies marked their track. I sat there off the trail until dark, invisible and forgotten, my thoughts growing feral and immoderate. When I left that place I covered all sign of me with decayed plum leaves and never returned.

In the garden some paths behave, unraveling like thread from a spool, leading you into the core of paradise and safely out again. Others baffle, leading you away from the center of the garden and challenging you to find your own way back. When my daughter was just three years old and driving with her father at dusk far from home on a maze of unfamiliar, twisting New England roads, she asked Peter in a small voice, "Are all these roads connected?"

And they are. Somehow the wild-plum-pit cliff edge path leads back into orderly paradise in the same way that the best formal garden paths carry the scent and feel of that long-toothed wildness just beyond the dragon's gate.

Create the Climate of the Garden

Every garden conveys mood and atmosphere influenced by the natural and created climate of moisture and drought, light and shadow, and fluctuations of warmth and coolness. Gardens are rich in alternate microclimates, some inherited and others contrived. The north end of your paradise may be a shady cavern of Grecian laurels planted before you were born. Why not set a bench among the whispering trees and hide there in full summer, far away from the whining complaints of your ripe crops? If you are gardening in a hot, arid southern exposure consider planting a chorus of the three new-world sisters: teosinte, the ancestor of corn; speckled blue tepary beans from the Sonoran Desert; and warty squash from southern Guatemala. These three sisters worship the sun and weave white-hot light into staple food.

> When it is hot, eat the hot;
> When it is cold, swallow the cold

is an old piece of Zen advice given to a novice wondering how to deal with discomfort. This is also good gardening advice. By settling into the natural climate of your place and planting accordingly, you actually create a paradise of surprise and change. Suddenly, the hottest inferno garden grows cool with the rustle of arid wind running through dry corn husks while the coolest, most dank grotto is warmed by the stature of noble laurels shedding sunlight from their dark, shadowy crowns.

Always begin by working with what you have. Then play with the climate in your garden and create mood and atmosphere with your plantings. Remember that running or still water cools the air by evaporation while shade plantings reduce the radiance of the sun by absorbing heat. On the other hand, if you want to create warmth, capture the sunlight and bounce it back. A sheltered, east- or south-facing wall is a wonderful place to espalier a French pear tree and warm a blustery morning with rose-scented pear blossoms.

Never hesitate to draw on the assistance of the material world. Wood insulates, glass and metal conduct. I discover the raw truth of this in freezing January, cowering from the winter Alaskan storms in the shelter of the wood-and-glass greenhouse at Martin Luther King, Jr. Middle School, where the kids have planted pots of paperwhite narcissus just pushing into bloom, or when I hide from the scorch of Indian summer under a lichen-covered rose arbor in early October.

Work the subtle realm as you garden. Bloodred 'Altissimo' roses can warm a windy gap in your flower garden while pale lavender drifts of Serbian bellflowers cool even the warmest corners of the summer perennial border. Fragrance also creates atmosphere. Tuck a surprise urn of just-opened regal lilies behind your plantings of summer cabbages and float on a white river of perfume past the yellow halitosis of the brassicas. Don't just consider your own joy at the surprise lily fragrance: think of the delight of the ball-headed cabbages as well.

Sound in the garden also creates atmosphere, mood, and climate of a sort. Include in your paradise water dripping over black stones, bamboo wind chimes secreted behind an opaque garden wall, or a planting of hawthorn and hazel to draw down and feed the summer songbirds of your region. On the edge of the San Francisco Bay a bold gardening colleague and stonemason friend of mine created a "wave organ." He laid blocks of old granite from uncut gravestones and discarded cobblestones from the original streets of San Francisco in careful patterns near the shore so that the slap of the rising and falling tides would play a fugue of sound over his watery stone organ.

Be creative and experimental and a little naughty as you plot your garden. At the same time, be conservative and true to your given climate. If you live in the desert, please don't replumb paradise and create acres of emerald lawn and sunken water gardens on arid land. This conceit draws down the water table of your region. Settle instead for a small, secret fountain recycling clear water underneath white rocks where lizards sun themselves. Consult the genius of your place in all things and plot paradise with every breath as you garden.

Step Back and Breathe

All designed gardens, no matter how wild or ordered, are contrived, so once you are settled in your home place, allow yourself to take a backward step and undo all your garden plans. Drop your routine, follow your breathing, and

enter the unknown. Instead of marching headfirst into the garden, put down your trowel and that flat of clove-scented stock seedlings. Take a deep breath and walk backward into your garden. Literally. If you know your garden well, close your eyes and spin slowly around like an old dervish before you move. Be disoriented. Forget what you think you know and what you think you don't know. Every garden is a field far beyond form and emptiness, a paradise not only yours, not always safe, and not only gauged in human time.

Paradise is staggering, and made to be undone. When you enter blind and backward through the dragon's gate, the four-square pattern of all your hard work may dematerialize, dropping you down the plum-pit path of no coming and no going into the uncharted heart of your garden. Your only guide is your in- and out-breath.

Beauty is no longer only lovely or symmetrical. Like the ancient weavers of the best Persian carpets, beauty works an *abrash*, or inconsistent fault, into the pattern of paradise. Unsure of exactly where you are going, design with the flawed world guiding your heart and mind. Plot and erase paradise on the same breath and let long-toothed beauty count.

The Wind of the Family House

BECAUSE IT IS A UNIVERSAL TRUTH THAT IN GENERAL, EVERYTHING is specific, I have always taken great delight in seeing what distinguishes a radish from a rose, and noticing what characterizes the specific family lineages of different plants. Observing with affectionate attention their distinct particularities, the cross-shaped blossom of the 'Easter Egg' radish and the five-petaled, single dog-rose flower of antiquity present themselves, each unique beyond measure.

Zen speaks of the "wind of the family house," the incomparable breath that animates each of the five lineage families of the classic Zen tradition. There are many unique teachers in each of these houses, and numerous single-minded students, and there is also a shared and particular breeze that draws the family members together and distinguishes one lineage from another.

When it comes to gardening, I like to think in just such a family way, focusing on the plant families growing together and influencing each other in every healthy backyard garden. The more I learn about the individual families of plants and about that ineffable wind that distinguishes each plant family house, the more I also understand the wider kinship among the families of the green world. When I design the garden with kinship in mind, I begin to see connections I never knew existed between 'DeCicco' broccoli and the wild field radish, and between blackberry brambles and a shot-silk rose. My mind expands with consanguinity as does the mind of the garden that holds and contains me.

Gardeners sort. We arrange and rearrange our gardens constantly, heeding the pulse of the present moment, guided by equal measures of hubris and humility. Families of plants, like human families, never conform to rules or well-documented standards. For example, many different members of the brassica family are heavy feeders requiring ample fertility, while some are light feeders preferring a lean soil. Yet broccoli and wild radishes have a common bloodline; they share the wind of the same family house. By developing and designing your garden with a perception of individual plant families guiding your hand you may become a more relaxed and attentive gardener, deepening your innate affinity for green kinship in the garden.

✦ ✦ ✦

In her autobiography, *Blackberry Winter*, Margaret Mead describes how when she was a young child her grandmother sent her out to the forest on foraging excursions. Margaret's grandmother once gave her a sprig of cultivated strawberry from her garden and encouraged her granddaughter to "bring me three different plants similar to this one." I imagine the old woman guiding her bright grandchild, not unlike Yurok Shaman Robert Spott working with Harry Roberts and his native apprentices. A good long time later the child returned, tired, dirty, and exultant, bearing a broken cane of wild blackberry, a ragged cluster of woodland strawberries, and a branch of native dog rose that had been nibbled by shy, white-tailed deer. Keen-eyed Margaret was given a heroine's welcome for seeing and following the wind of the rose family house.

At a tender age Margaret Mead learned to see kinship and to recognize affiliation within the vast rose family and beyond. She learned by looking into the heart of flowers and noticing the distinct pattern of leaves and flower forms that indicate family lineage. The five-petaled bloom and the signature five-lobed leaf of the rose family taught Margaret detail and discrimination, qualities that endured and deepened throughout her long life.

Gardens call up such seeing in their gardeners. We learn to see out of love for the variety and sameness that animate the plant kindom. And in turn, the eye of the garden sees *us* and commands the gardener to look deeper still into the secret life of plants. Whenever I begin working with new garden students and apprentices, we commence our practical study of horticulture by looking into the core of flowers and learning to recognize plant family lineages and that distinct wind that perfumes each plant family house. I enjoy keying plant families by recognizing their flowers: the cross-bearing, four-petaled crucifix flower of the brassicas or crucifer family, the butterfly-shaped insignia blossom of the legume tribe, the simple five-petaled flower of the rose family.

In the early years of teaching apprenticeship classes I was startled into a new view of kinship and lineage while working in the familiar heart of our productive herb garden, where two very different families of cultivated herbs were intertwined.

The umbellifer family is a tap-rooting tribe of plants that are mostly biennial, sending up a single stalk topped with a wide umbrella-like panicle of bloom that can be harvested fresh or collected as dry, pungent seed. Once umbellifer seed is ripe it falls straight down from the underside of the "umbrella" like a torrent of rain on a windless day. This family includes the herbs like fennel and parsley, carrots and celery, and the lovely flowering Queen Anne's lace.

The other herb-rich family is the Labiatae or "lip-flowered labia" family. Unlike the elongated umbellifers, the labia plants arise on short stems from a dense mat of intertwined, perennial roots. This family includes such herbal treasures as mint, sage, basil, and lavender, and hosts a few rare vegetables as well, such as the Chinese artichoke, and some beautiful flowers, among them snapdragons and all the colorful salvias that hummingbirds so adore.

Investigating the flower and leaf forms of these herbal plant families I began to see the kinship within the umbellifer and Labiatae clans more clearly. This seeing engendered a curiosity about the distinguishing traits of the other major plant families growing in the garden. I wanted to feel the wind of their particular kinship and learn more about their botanical affinity, style, and habit.

The Crucifer Family

The crucifer or brassica family has deep ties to northern and seaside Europe, and parts of Asia, although the exact origin of the family is unknown. The brassica clan is a huge family of plants with some 350 members, many of which have been grown in gardens since the beginning of recorded time.

The brassica family is commonly called the cross-bearing family, since every member bears a cross-shaped, four-petaled flower as its insignia. This is a hugely versatile family, often called the family of the "archetypal plant," since every plant part of the brassica family is cultivated for food, from the roots of turnips, rutabagas, and radishes, to the stems and leaves of kohlrabi, kale, collards, and all of the Asian greens, to the flowers of broccoli, cauliflower, mustard, arugula, and radish. There are even fruits among brassica crops, particularly cabbages and Brussels sprouts, which are also signature members of the cross-bearing family.

The Cauliflower

I wanted to be a cauliflower
all brain and ears,
thinking on the origin of gardens . . .

Not like my cousins, the cabbages,
whose heads, tightly folded,
see and hear nothing of this world,
dreaming only on the yellow
and green magnificence
that is hardening within them.

John Haines

Most brassicas are heavy feeders, requiring a rich soil, heavy in nitrogen and phosphorous, in order to produce the healthiest crops. They thrive on plenty of moisture, as well. Some brassicas, notably those with edible roots like the turnip, radish, rutabaga, and daikon, can grow in a leaner soil and are often interplanted with the heavy feeders of their tribe. All members of the brassica family are rich in sulfur and produce a pungent, smooth oil from their pressed seeds.

The brassica tribe crosses and interbreeds like wildfire, so if you intend to keep seed from your cultivated brassica garden you must isolate your plant family members so they do not interbreed. To ensure seed purity in the brassica tribe an isolation distance of half a mile is recommended, which explains why most gardeners are happy to let good seed companies culture the seed of their future brassica crops. Brassicas all have beautiful and fragrant flowers, which is another reason to just allow them to go to seed. Enjoy their cross-patterned blooms, which also provide a primary, rich source of nectar for beneficial insects.

Some Brassica Family Members

VEGETABLES
Mustard
Kale
Turnip
Broccoli
Cauliflower
Brussels sprouts
Cabbage
Collards
Watercress

FLOWERS
Hesperis
Clove-scented stock
Candytuft
Sweet alyssum
Nasturtium
Wallflowers

The Legume Family

Cultivated for over six thousand years, the bean family is second only to grain in its importance as a staple food crop. This vast family includes some six hundred genera and twelve thousand species, most of them ornamental flowers and trees and only about twenty-five species commonly used for food.

Sacred in many cultures, and revered in most, the legume family has the distinct ability to take in free atmospheric nitrogen through its leaves and to fix it in the soil, with the help of specific bacteria that cover the roots of the legume host. For this reason the bean and pea tribe are considered the primary "heavy givers" of the plant kindom, although they will not give all gifts simultaneously. You can harvest when they are beginning to flower, and they will give their root-fixed nitrogen to the soil; or you can enjoy the flowers and the protein-rich peas and beans.

Legume flowers are botanically perfect, containing both a stamen and a pistil, and self-pollinating. They are also lovely beyond measure, often shaped like bicolor butterflies. There is some debate about whether or not insects cross-pollinate the legume family, but this form of cross-pollination is certainly not as common in the tight anatomy of the legume flower as it is in plants that are more easily accessible to winged visitors. If you want to guarantee purity of a legume seed variety, however, it is wise to cage or bag your legume flowers while they are ripening their pollen and opening into bloom.

Legume seeds are left on their plants to dry. These seeds are enclosed in pods that split along both sides, uncorking or shattering open when the seed is ripe. This process is very rapid and legume seeds are hurled far and wide as the seed pods twist open to dramatically distribute their wealth. Consequently, many gardeners harvest this seed when the pods begin to get dry and hard and let the uncorking, spiral dance of the legume clan happen in the safety of a well-closed, dry paper bag.

To my biased gardener's mind, there are few treasures in the plant kindom more beautiful than a full bouquet of varied sweet pea flowers or a harvest bowl brimful with dry bean seed mixed together in a celebratory offering. 'Jacob's Cattle' beans, 'Vermont Cranberry' beans, hyacinth beans, scarlet runners, tiny robin's egg blue tepary beans from the Southwest gleam and remind every gardener of the true wealth and nourishment contained within the vast legume family.

Some Legume Family Members

VEGETABLES
Peas
Beans, including fresh green beans and dry
    beans such as lima, pinto, and soybean
Peanuts

FLOWERS
Sweet peas
Flowering vetch and cloves
Lupine

TREES AND VINES
Acacia
Black locust
Redbud
Wisteria
Ceratonia

The Umbellifer Family

Most members of the umbellifer tribe are considered root crops because of their deep, tap-rooting nature. Umbellifers function as light feeders in garden soil and are excellent plants to follow the heavy feeding crops. All umbellifers cultivate and aerate the ground, consolidate vitamins and minerals, and leave the soil in good heart for your next rotation of garden crops.

The umbellifer family originated in the Far East and Persia, where carrots came in an odd assortment of colors: burgundy-red, dark-purple, violet, and black, all from the pigment anthocyanin that dominated the family until the sixteenth century, when a pale, yellowish-orange albino carrot appeared in Western Europe, a sport from which eager Dutch botanists bred the warm orange carrot of modern times.

Umbellifer flowers are perfect flowers; however, they cannot self-pollinate since umbellifer pollen often ripens and is shed before the female stigma is ready to receive this pollen. Because of this, members of the umbellifer family rely on bees and other insects to move their pollen from one flower to another. The umbellifer clan also produces a sweet nectar and their curved umbrella crown of flowers provides a fine landing surface for insects, making the entire tribe of plants quite attractive to the very insects upon which the life and continuity of the clan depend.

Some Umbellifer Family Members

VEGETABLES
Carrot
Parsnip
Celery
Bulb fennel

HERBS
Dill
Parsley
Anise
Coriander
Cumin

FLOWERS
Queen Anne's lace
Cow parsnip
Bishop's weed

The Labiatae or Mint Family

The highly significant mint tribe is composed of 160 genera and close to 3,000 species of plants. Believed to have originated in the Mediterranean area of Europe and the Near East, the mint family is prized for its volatile oils and bitter extracts as well as for its wide range of garden plants. In this labia family there is no clear separation between working and ornamental members, or where would you put the peerless lavender?

Most mint family plants grow as annuals or short-lived perennials, appreciating a deep, fertile soil, and a warm, sunny climate. These lip-flowered plants all appreciate rich soil with minimal water and, with the exception of peppermint, which is a shade-loving plant that thrives in bog conditions, labia family members grow best in long days of sunny heat. The labia family spreads itself by underground runners or by

seed, and may easily be divided into small root clumps that readily establish new plant crowns.

The stems of mint family members are square, with opposite or whorled leaves growing along the stem, which is topped with the lovely, two-lipped flowers that invite and appreciate insect pollination.

Some Labia Family Members

Basil
Mint, including spearmint and peppermint varieties
Lavender
Rosemary
Marjoram and oregano
Savory
Thyme
Sage
Snapdragon
Salvia
Germander
Ajuga
Catmint
Catnip

In addition to the crucifer, legume, umbellifer, and Labiatae families there are numerous other plant families in the wide clan of garden cultivars grown for food, ornament, and potent medicine. Each family house has its signature genius and style, expressed assertively in a diverse kinship of related cousins. The Gramineae, or grain, family houses forty-five hundred known species of grass and grain, the major food plants of the ancient and modern world, while the vast Compositae family is home to twenty thousand species, from lettuce to artichokes to sunflowers, some members having their origin in Egypt more than four thousand years BCE.

If you want to cultivate an awareness of the wind of each plant family

Herb
Circle

house, you might set up a family circle or wheel garden, divided into four quadrants with each quadrant hosting a different plant family. If you ha[ve] ground and inclination to try this form of garden design it is an excelle[nt] to both welcome a diversity of plants and to learn about different b[otanical] families. For variety of form and function, it is important to choose plant families that include vegetable, herbal, flowering, and fruiting members as well as annual and perennial plants, although if you want to renew your family garden every year or so, it is wise to choose the shorter-lived annual and biennial family members.

To really appreciate and become familiar with the full nature of the different plant families you are studying, be sure to let your different family members go full cycle and run to seed. This decision means that you are not growing these particular plants for utilitarian purposes. Your edible broccoli patch will be elsewhere, but in your family circle garden two or three broccoli plants could be invited to complete their cycle of growth, flowering and running to seed, a luxury and privilege most cultivated vegetables are never allowed.

Designing a Family Circle Garden

- Orient yourself to the four directions and clear a section of your garden, laying out the dimensions of a circle in scale with your land. I advise a circle with a diameter of fourteen feet and beds six feet long with one-foot-wide paths.
- Drive a stake in the center of your garden plot and stretch a rope seven feet long to the stake. Then walk in a circle around the stake, marking the ground with pulverized clay, chalk, flour, or white sand to show the circumference of the circle. Next, mark out your pathways.
- Dig the pie-shaped beds to a depth of one foot, adding compost and soil amendments to these beds.
- Mark the pathways around and between beds with sawdust or chipped bark. Avoid gravel unless you want a more permanent garden.
- Plant your beds and enjoy the wind of the plant family houses as your garden grows.

Many plant families lend themselves well to cultivated family circle gardens, among them the umbellifer clan, the labia tribe (although these are mostly perennials), the brassicas, cucurbits (the squash and gourd family), the legume lineage, the solanum or nightshade tribe, the Compositae or sunflower and salad family, the members of the Gramineae or grain family, and the goosefoot chenopodium, or spinach family clan.

As you shape your family circle garden remember to let surprise and whimsy guide your hand as much as careful botanical research. Let your garden make and remake you as you garden. Trust the old wind of the family house to perfume the air you breathe as you work and let your circle garden be a tribute to that mysterious spirit of kinship uniting and liberating all life.

Tales of Eden

> Draw your chair close to the precipice and I'll
> tell you a story.
>
> *F. Scott Fitzgerald*

WHEN SHE FIRST VISITED THE LOUVRE IN PARIS IN THE EARLY twentieth century, Gertrude Stein surveyed the collection of paintings with a trained eye and an artist's mind. "Each one is one," she commented in characteristic fashion, upon completing her tour. "There are many of them." And so it is also with gardens.

Every designed garden holds at least three good reasons for its existence and then, beneath these reasons, runs the older story of the garden. And in what every garden is *not* there is also a story, the shadow voice of what is told aboveground in green stems and woven light.

Pull your chair close to the precipice and listen to the story of a meditation garden of shrubs, trees, and subtle herbaceous plantings, the creation myth of a productive fruit garden growing on a little less than a quarter acre of land, a chronicle of a tiny backyard home garden, the tale of a wild public school garden, and the saga of creating a memorial garden hidden in the heart of Green Gulch Farm.

In the stories of these gardens, things are not what they seem, nor are they otherwise, an insight gleaned from the almost two-thousand-year-old "Lankavatara Sutra." Because each garden is unique, each one is one. Their stories belong to all beings in the ten directions.

Black Bamboo, Green Wind

In 1982 we began the present Green Gulch gardens. I worked with my friend and colleague Skip Kimura, a longtime student of Alan Chadwick's, and a fanatic gardener. Skip was not a Zen student: he came to Green Gulch the year after Alan died to help us design and lay out a new garden, a garden dedicated in spirit and form to Alan and to what we had learned with Alan.

Skip's sole practice was organic gardening and I was his sole apprentice and accomplice in the garden. He plotted the garden methodically and incessantly. We were very different beings and we had a few colossal fights, usually over the conflicting tones and hues of lavender mixed with soft peach in the designed color palette of the garden, or about whether or not to interplant short-lived perennials or herbs among the august shrubs of the grand herbaceous border. Curiously, the garden only got stronger when Skip and I locked horns. Our wrangling was a kind of fertilizer. The garden clearly benefited from opinionated, artistic strife.

Since Green Gulch is a meditation center we designed two complementary gardens, both dedicated to contemplation, repose, and resounding emptiness. The Herbal Circle is a round garden within a square and is planted with all the colors of the rainbow and beyond and the Altar or Peace Garden is a quiet and subtle world of liquid shadow with muted plantings of white mist, soft cream, and green wind. These two gardens took their place in the central core of the first field of the farm, just across the road from each other.

From the first I was drawn to the Herbal Circle, like a hummingbird pulled down into the long, red throat of dorisiana sage. Entranced by the tucked bustles of the French roses and rinsed by the faint, lingering perfume of

339

'Palibin' Korean lilac, I was held hostage to this fickle, well-rouged garden throughout her prolonged year of gestation.

Skip sought refuge from the throbbing horticultural heat of the Herbal Circle by working in the cool green shade of the Altar Garden. He immersed himself in the subtle world of bark texture and naked branch, of well-rolled lawn and rough outcroppings of stone, as he drew that garden out of his complex internal palette of plants and foliage color. Skip painted with pale gray-green fading into smoke green and accented with points of pitch-dark forest green, squeezed from the dripping needle tips of fog-bound Alaskan fir. Occasionally, a surprise meteor of wild chartreuse plant material would sizzle down, searing the cool façade of the Peace Garden, and an unblinking tropical iguana would step out of a molten pool of green sunlight.

Each of these gardens had to be contained. They were distinct worlds, not meant to mingle. To anchor the Herbal Circle we planted a formal hedge of classic yew around it, a perfect foil for the overdressed hussy plants of the inner circle. This yew hedge became the stern chaperone of the Herbal Circle, gathering all of the chattering exotics into the somber fold of its dark, clipped embrace.

Because the Altar Garden was a more formal world it called for a softer border to balance its rigor, a semipermeable membrane of undulating green. We chose bamboo, Skip's delight. He had recently returned from a gardener's pilgrimage to Savannah, Georgia, where a USDA bamboo testing station set up in the 1920s was being disbanded. The government was giving this bamboo collection away. Skip brought home a rolling truckload full of rare bamboos from China and beyond: Arundínaria, crookstem, timber, and sass were among the twenty-six varieties he dug up and rescued. "Did you bring back any black bamboo?" I asked Skip as he unloaded the overburdened truck. "I wish," he muttered, under his breath.

I am not a fan of bamboo. I share the common prejudice that bamboo takes over, can't be controlled, and eventually invades every corner of the civilized world. But black bamboo is different. Elegant and mysterious with its slender, polished ebony canes that rise thirty feet aboveground, I had encountered black bamboo waving its banners of pale green foliage in the center of Suzuki

Roshi's private garden at Tassajara in my first years of practice. I thought it was the most strikingly beautiful plant I had ever laid eyes on.

Suzuki Roshi had been dead for two years when I first saw his garden. No one was allowed to work in this inner sanctum but Roshi's *anja* or attendant, but somehow I was assigned to help in Suzuki Roshi's inner garden one windy autumn day. I worked on my hands and knees, collecting fallen sycamore leaves from the floor of the garden. It was a thankless task, since twice as many more leaves blew down on me as I worked, though perhaps for that reason it was good for my practice. During one particularly blustery gust I looked up to see the black bamboo, startling against the inner dome of Tassajara's lapis lazuli sky. An unquenchable fire of black bamboo lust and greed was ignited in my heart that day.

When we planted the Altar Garden at Green Gulch some years later we dedicated it to the "three friends" of Japanese folklore, *sho, chiku, bai*. These three friends are three plants that represent primary virtues worthy of human as well as of garden cultivation: pine, for strength; bamboo, for flexibility; and cherry, for beauty and its transitory nature. When we planted the Altar Garden borders we made sure that the three friends were woven deeply into the fabric of the garden design.

Flexible bamboo was the designated guardian hedge of the Altar Garden. After two years the young bamboo hedge filled in and the Altar Garden took root, darkening to a deeper shade of green. We set a wooden altar cabinet deep into the thicket of bamboo and placed in it a weathered granite figure of Jizo Bodhisattva, the patron saint of children and travelers. Overhead the bamboo billowed and rolled, and every spring a pair of Swainson thrushes made their nest in the flexible hedge, washing us at daybreak with their liquid song.

A longtime benefactor of San Francisco Zen Center and writer on Buddhism died just as we were completing the Altar Garden. Nancy Wilson Ross, a friend of the Green Gulch garden, willed us a beautifully carved stone figure of a Buddhist *arhat*, a fully enlightened person according to the earliest Buddhist scriptures. This noble arhat had practiced diligently for years in Nancy's elegant Long Island home. Arhats are not afraid of hard practice: they sit in meditation day and night. Our rock arhat was no slouch. He had a fearsome scowl of determination etched into his stone features. Even naughty children fell to hushed silence in his presence and tiptoed past the arhat's new perch at the base of the bamboo border, not far from the garden altar. Arhats practice by themselves, off in a corner, so we complied with our arhat's secret wish to practice in solitude. I set him on a lovely, low sycamore stump and left him profoundly alone under the bamboo.

A month or so later, in early summer, I came down to the Altar Garden just at daybreak. The arhat had been upended and was lying facedown on the wet lawn, looking quite undignified. I called Skip over and together we righted the poor heavy fellow, marveling that not only his repose but also his meditation platform had been split asunder. A blast of sudden enlightenment? No, only a vigorous sprout of wild bamboo rooting around under the bamboo litter and poking up beneath the arhat's perch. Apparently this sharp-nosed shoot had surfaced just below the grumpy meditator, split his stump in two, and goosed the noble one on his rocky bottom, sending him ass-over-teakettle into the world of foolish, common people. We brushed the arhat off, and settled him on the floor of the bamboo forest where hopefully his practice has grown somewhat more flexible. In any case, he sits there in stony silence to this day.

Not long after this seismic event, Skip found a dried-up knuckle of bamboo buried in the compost buckets from our sister meditation center on Page Street in San Francisco. I heard him whoop from all the way across the garden. "I think it's black bamboo," he whispered excitedly, scraping old oatmeal and coffee grounds off his treasure. *It must be from Suzuki Roshi's garden at Tassajara*, I thought to myself, noticing that the remnants of this bamboo plant looked quite dead. But Skip took his find to the glasshouse and planted it in loamy, compost-rich soil and ministered to it lovingly all winter long. While the Zen students were sitting in the zendo, Skip willed a dead bamboo clump back to life.

By early March a small red shoot with black whiskers poked up out of Skip's folly, unfurling its first living flag. Skip moved the revived bamboo to a deeper pot and then to a deeper one still, and the bamboo flourished. By midsummer when it was planted out in the Altar Garden, this black bamboo was as vigorous as a well-nourished mountain gorilla. It pounded its chest, gave a loud roar, and took hold.

Now more than twenty years have passed since that planting. Skip moved on long ago to found a thriving two-acre garden for disabled people. "I couldn't have done it without my training at Green Gulch," he commented wickedly. Later this garden passed on to a local elementary school, and it is still pumping out voluptuous pumpkins and rich, dark kale seedlings for kindergarten to fifth graders.

I think of Skip every time I walk past the Altar Garden with its fifteen-foot-long waving patch of black satin bamboo growing just across the road from the north gateway into the Herbal Circle. "Don't say dead, don't say alive," whispered an old Zen master centuries ago, holding up a bleached white skull against the empty sky. Gardeners follow this same code, persevering and not being fooled by appearances. We just continue, under all circumstances, not taking no for an answer, and designing paradise gardens from a handful of dust blowing across a solitary pine tree, from the beauty of shattered cherry blossoms floating on a muddy puddle, and from the flexibility of black bamboo moving slowly in the green wind.

The Apples of Eden

Our children were born twelve years apart in the frontier days of Green Gulch and we dug their birth placentas into the earth and planted a strong, flowering crabapple tree, *Malus floribunda*, for each of them. Did we perceive our children's true bittersweet, wild natures before we chose their totem trees, or did they grow into their "crabapple" selves as their trees took root and began to blossom and set fruit? This, of course, is a mystery as old as the origin of the first wild crabapple tree of antiquity.

We chose the crabapple tree for our kids because this untamable member of the rose family is presumed to be the ancestral parent of the modern apple of today. Believed to have originated high on the slopes of the Tien Shan, or Heavenly Mountains, which form the boundary range between China and the former Soviet Union, the wild crabapple of the forests of Transcaucasia inspired Russian plant geneticist Nicolai Vavilov, when he surveyed the region in the early 1920s, to call the fruit forests of the present-day republics of Armenia and Georgia a true "Garden of Paradise."

Although the precise botanical origin of the apple is lost in antiquity, we know from apple remains discovered in the Jordan River Valley at Jericho that this orchard fruit was being enjoyed by residents of the Fertile Crescent of Mesopotamia as early as 6,500 BCE.

Each apple holds a religious mystery at its core as well as a puzzle of botanical lineage. How is it that cultures as diverse as Judeo-Christian monotheists from Palestine to Philadelphia, and Eastern Indian Vedantics as well as Aryan, Germanic, and Celtic ancestors all share a common conviction that the apple is the sacred tree of life and knowledge? Perhaps the answer lies in the very accessibility so many cultures have had to the apple and in the tangy, abidingly sweet taste of the fruit itself.

In the early years of the Green Gulch garden we dreamed of establishing a section of land dedicated to growing rose family fruit, particularly the apple. We inquired of local commercial fruit sellers which apple varieties would do best on the coast and to our surprise they wrote back advising that *no* apples be grown in our coastal region due to cool summers of salty wind and low-lying fog, and warm winters without the requisite six hundred hours of below 40 degree chill that helps apple trees develop taste and texture in their fruit.

This was the perfect challenge for us. How could we grow a paradise garden without the fruit of Eden? We decided to disregard our advisors and plant a fruit garden dedicated to heritage varieties of fruit, laid out to baffle the stiff coastal winds by alternating upright fruit trees with rows of low-growing fruit vines, bushes, and shrubs. Enthusiastically, we set to work.

Braided into our first garden design was the sharp expectation of failure. We knew that not all of the apple varieties would thrive in our capital city of fog and mold. But we decided to try to grow them anyway, giving them ample bed depth and fertility, undersowing them with a carpet of Dutch white clover to fix and offer rich atmospheric nitrogen to their roots, and following a careful schedule of disease-protection spraying, pruning, foliar feedings, and deep irrigation, as well as meticulous fruit harvest.

The early years of this Green Gulch Eden were turbulent ones. During the second winter of the orchard's life a freezing cold storm from the Gulf of Alaska lifted off one of our heavy glass coldframe panels and carried it across the garden until it dropped down onto a new seedling apple, decapitating the young plant and covering the ground with shards of broken glass that continued to be dug out of that plagued apple tree bed for a decade. We removed the beheaded apple and replaced it with a prize dessert apple, 'Cox's Orange Pippin,' which grew to yield a huge ten-bushel-basket fruit harvest two years later.

The next summer a freak twister ripped through our garden, and while I cowered in our rickety garden toolshed hiding behind the English digging forks I saw the small, Wizard-of-Oz-type mini-tornado pick up a heavy table from the Herbal Circle garden like a dollhouse toy and toss it into the ill-starred Eden fruit area, slicing out a healthy, three-year-old cider apple tree. Muttering the enigmatic and difficult-to-heed Zen adage, "Don't say good, don't say bad," we dug out the cyclone-mangled tree and planted a newly grafted 'Mrs. Bramley's' seedling apple in its place. Tornado and twister-free since that freak summer, 'Mrs. Bramley's' apple tree is pumping out huge cooking apples and erasing the checkered history of her domain with steady fruitfulness.

We had three good reasons for planting the orchard: first of all, to celebrate the apple of Eden; second, to experiment with old heritage varieties of fruit and see if they would grow on the foggy coast; and last of all, to grow this fruit intensively, in a small area, and then share the results of this culture with anyone who was hungry.

Rose-Family Fruit
    Apple
    Crabapple
    Pear
    Quince

Plum
Apricot
Peach
Red, black, and white currants
Gooseberries
Raspberries
Strawberries
Boysenberries

Once the fruit orchard began to bear in earnest we held a blind taste test of the apples of Eden in late autumn. We waited until Indian summer in the October garden, the burnished season of true ripening. The apple trees bent down under the weight of their fruit. All of our apple trees are grafted on rootstocks originating from the wild crabapples of the Heavenly Mountains of Transcaucasia: the dessert apples and the cider apples, the cooking apples and the tart apples for eating out of hand received their strength and vigor from their wild crabapple ancestors.

At our last apple tasting we gathered in the orchard in late afternoon to drink a brief toast to the apples—a sip of freshly pressed Snow White apple juice from our 'Fameuse' apples, a French Canadian cider variety and a heavy bearer in the Green Gulch garden. Then the kids took baskets to harvest just a few ripe apples from each of our twenty or so varieties of apple trees and brought the fruit back to our gathering circle so that we could all sample it, blindfolded, slice by slice. This year, like every year, 'Ashmead's Kernal,' 'Mutsu,' and 'Cox's Orange Pippin' won the taste test. We should have known this by now since these are the varieties of apples that the birds prefer as well, along with the sugar-starved yellow jackets of late summer.

At the end of the raw apple taste test we sampled hot apple crisp made of 'Mrs. Bramley's' seedling apples mixed with some 'Roxbury Russets' from heritage New England stock and drizzled with fresh cream. The kids gathered windfall apples while the grownups talked. Cutting these apples through their central equator, a star pattern of apple pips marks the core of each piece of fruit. The kids dipped their bisected apples in bright tempera paint and made star-centered apple prints on rough farm paper until the orchard grew dark and the chill of autumn sent us out of the garden of Eden and home again, with the taste of paradise in our mouths.

Slate Moon Refuge

Many years ago I came upon Herb Arnold for the first time as he sorted through a mountain of rusty old metal junk in an abandoned corner of Green Gulch. He was a shaggy bear of a man with a stubby gray beard that covered most of an animated face topped with high-voltage electric-blue eyes. This ursine man nearly crushed my hand as he introduced himself: "Hi—I'm Herbie. I live downstairs at Martha's and I'm here to make art out of your junk," and with that he returned to excavating his Zen middens.

It was no surprise that someone like Herbie lived in the lower rooms of Martha's Muir Beach house. Ever since the 1970s when local friends helped Martha complete her house perched on a sea meadow overlooking the beach, this home and garden have sheltered many beings, the more creative the better. Authors have finished their books at Martha's place, paintings have been painted there, and more than one lively baby has been born in the shelter of Martha's home.

I have known Martha for more than twenty-five years, so I know her long, wild roots full of hidden fire. We have practiced together as lay teachers at Green Gulch and beyond, and served in the Zen Hospice Project, which Martha helped found in the 1980s. She now works a few days a week with her Zen priest husband, Lee, teaching meditation and mindfulness in local Bay Area prisons.

As well as I know and treasure Martha, it was not until I visited her home garden to see Herbie's first sculpture that our friendship found its true depths, anchored by her garden. Herbie had welded a gigantic auger to a metal post and

347

mounted the spiral blade above a vast metal funnel. "Pennies from Heaven," he called it, an iron masterpiece designed to catch and collect celestial wealth and funnel it down into Martha's garden soil.

While Martha and Lee are engaged activists, wry and understated, they are also deeply private people. Their garden is a refuge for them in the oldest sense of the word, where refugia were places left unscoured by the glaciers, and where seed caches that had been swept into those untouched places of refuge could spring back to life to grow again after the glaciers receded. Martha's garden is just such a fertile sanctuary within the expandable borders of her life.

Although I am most at home in chaotically abundant public gardens that pump out a steady green flood of choice organic crops, this garden is a resting spot for me, a place of repose and deep familiarity, probably because most of the plants Martha grows were originally started at Green Gulch or purchased from Las Baulines Nursery, one of my favorite plant havens.

Sited on a steep, south-facing hillside above the Pacific Ocean, Martha's Garden is really a series of small green-jewel gardens set in leveled terraces dug out of the thick coastal grassland of her place, and strung together with a cord of pathways all lined with soft strips of fragrant catmint and silver wormwood.

At the top of Martha's land is a small enclosed garden of herbs and flowers surrounded by a low wooden fence covered with fragrant, white-flowering jasmine. At the back of this garden, behind pungent waves of Mexican marigold washing over lime-green *Helichrysum*, a painted giraffe stands sentry. This garden with its muted plantings of English lavender and pastel yarrows surrounded by a year-round sweep of forget-me-nots is a quiet sitting zone that not even the rambunctious grandchildren penetrate. It was a favored place of repose for Gail, Martha's best friend of forty years, who died in 2004. Gail was also a mad gardener; passionate about roses, she loved to flee her raucous Berkeley garden and take refuge at Martha's place, where they read Wallace Stevens together above the ocean.

Martha buried some of Gail's ashes in this garden that Gail loved so well, between the Buddha and the birdbath and not far from a memorial site for Herbie that we dedicated ten years ago near a fig tree he loved just off the path leading downslope to Martha's tiny zendo.

This zendo has a beautiful slate roof. Now and then I come to sit with Martha in the morning, delighting in the sound of wild apples falling on the stone roof. I suggested that Martha call her elegant meditation hut Slate Moon, a name that has somehow held ever since. Just outside, not far from Herbie's tree, hangs an old metal acetylene canister that is the temple bell of Martha's place. She rings this gong every morning on the way to meditation.

Just last season Peter helped Martha put in a small vegetable garden, a two-hundred-square-foot plot below the zendo on level ground fenced with stout wire painted dark hunter green. Nearby is a communal compost pile

for Martha's garden and for her neighbors to contribute to and gather from as they like. We supplied Martha with her first vegetable starts—Italian kale, bok choy, and Florence fennel with sweet cherry tomatoes and soft-leaved lettuces. Martha's broccoli plants were so huge this season that they could have won a blue ribbon at the state fair except that they fed Lee and Martha and one ravenous gopher (now excluded by underground wire) instead.

Peter and I have been astonished by the productivity of this small Slate Moon garden. Martha spends hours weeding and thinning and harvesting an abundance of crops that she shares with her Muir Beach neighbors and friends. Upon returning home from meditating with felons in prison she disappears under the green canopy of her vegetables. Not only that, Martha has become a walking encyclopedia of inventive kale and chard recipes.

Just before Lee's seventieth birthday I dropped by unannounced early one morning to bring Martha a book. She and Lee were sitting together at the breakfast table lost in conversation, sharing a common plate of scrambled eggs and tofu stir-fried with some of their voluptuous garden greens. Near their front door was a lavender string bag stuffed with bright red, orange, blue, and green blocks for their grandchildren to play with later that day. A harvest basket brimful of rhubarb chard and broccoli for their neighbors was on the porch while all around their sanctuary the scent of winter violets and freshly cut chives diffused the salty November air.

I crept away, leaving my friends alone in their refuge, grateful for the many gifts their plot of paradise has given me—its abiding stillness and sumptuous productivity, its understated beauty. In many ways this refuge garden is a deep mirror, reflecting back the quiet way of my friend Martha, and the force of her invisible root system that urges open the uncultured ground. At the top of the garden I paused to overlook this coastal refuge. Early winter light shone on the slate roof of the meditation hut, reminding me of one of Martha's favorite poems by Issa:

> Full moon
> My ramshackle hut
> Is what it is.

Children of Paradise

One of the primary places for which I regularly abandon the well-ordered calm of established Zen windbell gardens is a new Eden growing at Martin Luther King, Jr. Middle School in north Berkeley, a huge and diverse public school where over nine hundred students speak a mixture of twenty-nine languages in the corridors. I work with a rowdy, rotating population of eleven- to fourteen-year-olds whose lives are often quite challenging, and with their dedicated teachers, cultivating a one-acre Edible Schoolyard plot in the heart of a huge public school.

In late summer when this twelve-year-old garden is in full cry, it is not possible to see across the green and gold tangle of food to the far side of the school campus. You step into a thicket of paradise designed by rambunctious children and disappear from view.

"A school garden carries the life of the community," proclaims a 1909 pamphlet on suggestions for garden work in California schools. This has certainly been true for the Edible Schoolyard since its conception in 1995 when Alice Waters, founder of Chez Panisse restaurant and a local Berkeley resident, met with the school principal to found not only a garden within the school community but a *school* with a lively continuum of garden and kitchen classrooms.

In his 1577 book, *The Gardener's Labyrinth*, Thomas Hill describes the garden as a "ground plot for the mind." The Edible Schoolyard, then, is a ground plot for the wild and experimental mind of curious young people working with community residents, teachers, and parents as well as a savory medley of chefs and food service folks, all coming together to nourish the creation of a ground plot of the mind flavored by hands-on learning.

I vividly remember our first communal investigation about how to set up an edible schoolyard. A motley crew of us—kids, parents, cooks, gardeners, community activists, local funders, restaurateurs, teachers, and administrators—stood on the deserted eastern bluff of the schoolyard where only a few ragged warty ox-tongue weeds pushed up through the cracked asphalt. It was a site from hell, but what better place for paradise to root? We all felt the faint green wind of whispered fertility blowing across the plot.

Not long after, the asphalt was jack-hammered open and a mixed cover crop was ceremoniously planted on the sallow, ashen soil while an Aztec dance group prayed and blessed the land. Six months later, eager kids dug this somewhat stunted but nutritious cover crop into the parched ground and the hollow-cheeked earth began to hum with new life.

From the beginning there have always been at least three good reasons for the Edible Schoolyard garden and kitchen classrooms on the campus of King middle school: to inspire the curiosity of children and teachers and to encourage them to learn from the real world; to help grow and savor nutritious homegrown food; and to bring wanton beauty to a derelict corner of a public school campus. These three reasons for being have spawned a fourth: that this robust school garden and kitchen campus inspire and support many other such plots of paradise in the public domain. In 2006, one year after Hurricane Katrina ravaged the city of New Orleans, the Edible Schoolyard helped to establish a sister program there at the Samuel J. Green Middle School.

The Edible Schoolyard is not a neat garden. Kid designed, it growls with feral fertility and quirky imagination. Certain stable features anchor the garden—an outdoor, wood-fired oven for baking fresh bread and pizza, a back border of espaliered fruit trees planted in the third season of the garden, a compost yard on the northeast border where kitchen and garden waste is transformed by spirited adolescents and billions of swarming bacteria into mounds of black gold compost, and a beautiful toolshed put together by a local builder working with the kids. A few seasons ago a large chicken coop was added to the backside of the toolshed to house the beloved pet chickens of the schoolyard.

Inside the body of the garden is the ramada meeting place, a shade structure created by the kids and a group of visiting college students, constructed from acacia trunks and limbs harvested from the shaggy outback behind the schoolyard, nailed together and covered over with succulent, growing vines of kiwi, chayote, and random sweet melons. In the

352

shelter of this outdoor structure the students meet every day, sitting on stout straw bales, to volunteer for garden work. Later they break into small groups and set out to harvest collards and red romaine lettuce for the kitchen along with a bucket or two of purple-podded peas, to turn the compost pile, to build trellis fences woven out of supple cotoneaster wands, or to sow the first seeds of 'Golden' beets on their freshly dug, valentine-shaped "heartbeat" bed.

The kitchen, with a view of the ramada, is the hearth of the Edible Schoolyard program. Raw food from the garden growing just outside its door is transformed into tasty 'Red Kuri' winter squash frittatas or brown rice sautéed with chopped garden vegetables and wrapped up, burrito style, in rainbow chard leaves tied together with tender red scallions. Following a demonstration by the kitchen staff about how to prepare the dish of the day, the children take over at several well-stocked workstations, washing, chopping, cooking, and seasoning fresh, organically grown food. Next, they clear their sturdy worktables and set them with red-and-white checkered tablecloths, silverware and napkins and festive metal plates. There is always a garden flower arrangement on each table as the students sit down together to enjoy their food. Then they clean up and put everything away for the next class. All this happens in one whirlwind, ninety-minute-long work period.

After school, small clutches of students congregate in the garden and kitchen, which are clearly their second home. Roughhousing and laughing, they wander between the seventy-foot-long beds of dark red and golden raspberries, eating their way through paradise as they gossip in the row. These delectable fruits are planted solely for the young foragers. In the six years that I have worked at the Edible Schoolyard I have never tasted a ripe raspberry. The kids get them all, and no raspberry has ever been shipped to the kitchen, either, not even to enhance a special dessert, which is just as it should be, since a shippable raspberry is a blasphemy under heaven.

In the back of the kitchen on the shining eggplant-colored linoleum floor, groups of spunky middle-school girls practice their moves, singing and dancing to boom-box tunes. Some of the kids participate in an after-school cooking program called the "Literary Chefs" where together they choose, improvise, and prepare dishes mentioned in their favorite books, like watershrimp and hotroot soup from the Redwall book series by Brian Jacques. Of course, all of the vegetables for this hotroot soup come from the organic garden growing just outside the kitchen door while the elusive watershrimp spice the soup with their absence. As school lets out the community comes in: babies in buggies, joggers, friends walking together, and roving homeless people of north Berkeley.

These urban children of paradise are part of a wider food security policy called the School Lunch Initiative, which mandates that no student in Berkeley go hungry. While the details of this policy were being worked out, a volunteer group of parents, teachers, Edible Schoolyard staff, and friends came together during National Achievement Test Week at six o'clock in the morning to make hot breakfasts of oatmeal, spicy hash browns, and fresh organic apple slices for the hundreds of middle-school students who showed up before their tests to eat in the schoolyard kitchen.

Gardens take lifetimes to evolve even though their original character and design show up the moment you walk through the gate. The Edible Schoolyard is a ground plot of the mind of lively, puckish children—a kids' garden, through and through, designed by students for students, yet open to all beings. Beauty counts here, but not always in an orderly, sequential fashion. Zigzag loops of round-shouldered carrots double back on green pools of butter lettuce, a sun-shaped bed of winter wheat with ten long rays of ripening grain grows in the blue haze of Hopi corn, and bloodred 'Empress' tulips push up through wet ground at the edge of the known world. When the students of the Edible Schoolyard leave their garden at the end of the day the land expels a long exhalation of relief and then waits all night long, with one eye half open, for the children of paradise to return.

Hotroot Soup

3 carrots	2 garlic cloves
5 potatoes	1 teaspoon chili flakes
2 beets, with greens	2 cups milk
2 leeks	Salt and pepper
2 tablespoons olive oil	Watershrimp
5 cups stock	

Slice the leeks. Peel and chop the carrots, potatoes, and beets. Chop the beet greens. Sauté the leeks in the olive oil. Add roots and stock. Simmer until tender. Mash garlic and chilies with mortar and pestle. Add spicy paste, milk, and salt and pepper to taste to the vegetables.

Serves 4–6 hungry readers.

Paradise Lost

In the late 1980s a young woman visited the Green Gulch garden with her two small children and her mother at her side. They lived just north of the Gulch, connected by the same coastal road but facing the open ocean. They sought me out, compelling me with their story. More than five years before, when her youngest son was a baby and her daughter was just two years old, this young woman's husband had gone out on the ocean on his surfboard to the deep seawater that breaks just beyond the bar. This was his love and passion, but his surfboard washed up on the shore that same evening and the young man was lost at sea, never to return.

They searched for him for weeks, combing the ragged coastline, but he was gone from their lives. They waited for word of him for years, before deciding that after a half-decade of mourning they were ready to release him to the sea and begin to live again.

The family members were observant Jews and their faith gave them solace and forbearance. But grief remained, bottomless and long of tooth. Unable to turn away from sorrow, this family wanted instead to dig into grief's cold ground and plant a tree for the lost young man. "I'd rather face my broken heart than try to bargain with it anymore," said the young mother. "And I'd like to do it here, in this garden, with my family around me."

Although I had not known it, this family had been coming down into the Green Gulch garden over the past few years to sit and walk, to be alone, to speak to their lost surfer, and to rest. It was their garden as well now, through an old unwritten contract signed with dashed hope and tears. Without hesitation we agreed to do a memorial planting.

My neighbor, a Zen priest of almost fifty years, led the service. No-nonsense and solid, this woman doesn't flirt or flounder with grief. She grabs it by the collar and looks it in the eye. Our service was stark, truthful, and complete. I found the perfect tree for the family, a rare cherry, *Prunus serrula*, known for its stunning dark mahogany bark and supple, red limbs—a clear plant version of the young mother herself.

The family laid out pictures of their beloved surfer on the open ground and also a few of his favorite things—his journal, an old navy blue watch cap, a dried rose his wife had kept from their first date. We summoned him to join us in spirit, and each family member spoke to him and released him. Together we dug a large, deep hole in the center of the Green Gulch Peace Garden. Then, without ponderous ceremony, metaphor, or explanation, we planted the tree in the garden, chanted the twenty-five-hundred-year-old Buddhist prayer of loving-kindness, and stood in silence as the water that the children offered to their father's tree seeped into the thirsty ground.

> May I be happy,
> May I be safe,
> May I be peaceful and at ease.

May you be happy,
May you be safe,
May you be peaceful and at ease.

May all beings be happy,
May all beings be safe,
May all beings be peaceful and at ease.

Today this cherry tree is twenty feet tall and breathtakingly beautiful. There is no memorial plaque anywhere near it, no sign, no notice. And yet visitors to the garden always gravitate to this particular cherry, touching the silky bark and looking up into the crown where bright blue sky and the sound of the ocean breaking on the beach are caught in its willowy branches.

There are many such secret memorial sites within the Green Gulch garden. Although no physical remains or mementos are included in any of these spots, the dead are present in their plantings. Each memorial site is a kind of garden unto itself, never seen before. Each one is one and there are many of them. The founder of the AIDS interfaith network lives on in his memorial bloodred 'Will Scarlet' rose, just as fifteen-year-old Timmy breathes again in the memorial planting dedicated by his brokenhearted family and friends. And when I walk past the pool of fragrant regal lilies in the southwest corner of the Herbal Circle, I can hear Stella's loud horse laugh and remember tales of her estranged father making peace with his daughter after so many forgotten years, and eating bagels at her Zen hospice bedside while he smoothed back her runaway hair.

If paradise is an enclosed garden within the wider world, then a memorial garden breaks open enclosure and grows as a solitary reminder of paradise lost and new paradise found. One plant, grown with love and intention, includes the entire field. A single red-barked cherry tree stands in the brisk ocean breeze of early April. The north branch owns the entire spring, the south branch owns the entire spring.

357

HARVESTING FIELDS OF GREENS

No Anonymous Food

W HEN I WAS A NEW ZEN STUDENT LIVING AT TASSAJARA WE
practiced zazen meditation in an old stone building that had been
a rough-and-tumble bar before San Francisco Zen Center purchased
Tassajara Hot Springs Resort. I sat in that stone zendo for hours, sometimes
just by myself. Now and then Ed Brown, a young Zen priest and author of *The
Tassajara Bread Book* and *Tomato Blessings and Radish Teachings*, would join
me, sitting in meditation nearby and never saying a word. That year Ed was
the head monk, or *shuso*, for the three-month practice period at Tassajara and
he was the person responsible for watching over new students. He saw right

away that I was wrestling with the burly demons of self-doubt and loathing, so he kept me company.

Every few weeks or so during our practice period the shuso gave a lecture, a Zen talk that came out of his own practice experience. I remember Ed's raw and personal talks. They startled me. Instead of screaming "Kwatz!" and flashing the blade of some unsheathed and esoteric Zen sword, Ed spoke about turnips pushing up out of the ground and about 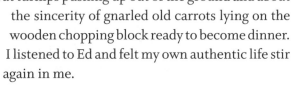 the sincerity of gnarled old carrots lying on the wooden chopping block ready to become dinner. I listened to Ed and felt my own authentic life stir again in me.

During the two years I lived at Tassajara the seventy or so of us gathered for the practice period ate all of our meals in the meditation hall, enjoying food grown in the Tassajara garden: salads of ripe 'Marmande' tomatoes mixed with odd-shaped burgundy string beans, and simple soups made from pureed butternut squash grown in the lower garden near the stone wall where squirrels hid their caches of black walnuts.

For the first three months, when I wasn't sitting zazen I dug ditches and hauled firewood; for the next nine months I worked in the kitchen; during my second year at Tassajara I met Peter and fell in love, and I worked in the garden growing food. Peter and I left Tassajara for Green Gulch in the autumn of 1975, just as the late-summer garden crops of Tassajara were beginning to ripen.

At Green Gulch I was assigned to work in the kitchen, where I pined for the Tassajara garden. About six weeks later a huge lug box of fresh produce arrived in the Green Gulch kitchen with my name written on top of the box. *Especially for Wendy to enjoy*, the greeting read, and I recognized the handwriting of the fellow Zen student I had worked with in the Tassajara garden. I opened the box slowly and found row after gleaming opal row of miniature Japanese eggplants, neatly packed and nestled together. I had started these eggplants from seed six months before and nursed them through their lavender flower-set to their juvenile fruiting stage. I put my head down in the box, drank deeply of the dusky spell of the nightshades, and wailed. About a week later I was removed from kitchen detail and reassigned to the Green Gulch Farm garden, where I worked for the next twenty-plus years.

In the mid-1990s Ed Brown came to Green Gulch to cook a special West Marin County growers' dinner to be created only out of what was in season in local Marin organic farms. It was early spring, and the leanest season for fresh crops. Ed and I went down to the fields together in mid-afternoon to harvest enough Swiss chard to feed the assembly. It was a good crop, vigorous and yet still tender, even after being in the field all winter. "Bone-chilling cold builds character and taste in chard," I observed to Ed.

Ed was quiet and thoughtful while we harvested the rainbow chard. The spring wind gusted around us as we worked. When the harvest was complete Ed began to muse about a good friend of his from India who expressed astonishment at the volume of "anonymous" food consumed daily by North Americans. Most people do not know who grew the food they are buying and eating, or where and how the food was grown. "This chard is *not* anonymous," proclaimed Ed, wiring closed his bulging crate of greens.

About sixty or seventy organic farmers gathered that evening to celebrate the hard work that we all do with dedication and spirit. Each guest came to dinner bearing a seasonal homegrown contribution: fresh cream and butter from the Straus family dairy, amber clover honey harvested in Marshall, tiny snow peas from Gospel Flat farm in Bolinas. Even the salt we used in our meal was air-dried sea salt from the foggy Tomales Bay coast.

During supper I remembered a comment made by a thirteen-year-old child visiting Green Gulch a few years before with his Zen-teacher mother. Hans had been eating slices of fresh-baked bread in the Green Gulch kitchen, bread still warm and baked from a simple recipe worked out by Ed decades ago. "This bread is real," Hans announced with gusto. "Real bread, not a ghost!"

This all-Marin meal that Ed cooked in the Green Gulch kitchen fifteen years ago continues to nourish my fierce commitment to savor and serve food that is grown locally and served seasonally. There is a strong and growing movement today in many places around the world to eat this way, and one of the newest ways is the "locavore challenge," taking a vow to eat for a week or a month, preferably at the height of the growing season, only foods that are grown and produced within a hundred-mile radius of home. People are stepping up to do this because it is fun, taxes your ingenuity, tastes good, and raises your awareness of the distances food travels and of the abundance and scarcity of your home place. Eating this way reminds me of where I live and where I don't live—it reminds me of my regional "food-shed" from which I am nourished and inspired.

✦ ✦ ✦

I am used to gardening in large communal plots, so when I go to pull Detroit dark red beets out of the heavy bottomland soil of Green Gulch Farm the beets get loaded into a whole fleet of funky wheelbarrows where they are hosed off and the muddy water from this initial cleaning is poured off to irrigate the thirsty raspberries. Then we scrub the beets clean in old iron bathtubs that once watered Black Angus cattle in the Green Gulch hills before the tubs were moved to the garden. Elbow deep in cold, muddy water, I scrub and rinse beets until my mind settles and grows clear. But for a few days after the harvest I carry the red stain of fresh beets on the palms of my hands.

After almost thirty-five years of organic gardening I am still grateful for each harvest of plenty that is gathered from the garden. I also keep sight of the darker side of this bounty, for even while the garden pumps out its abundant harvest, the population and economy of the world expands. In autumn of 2006 in the United States the population reached 300,000,000 people. The natural systems and resources of farmland are strained by this growth and by global climate change.

I witness with alarm the drop in plant and animal species in my own watershed as well as in the wider community, and the increase in temperatures and the drying up of the great and lesser river arteries of our time. Worldwide, ancient and modern forests are being diminished, topsoil is eroding, water tables are dropping, wetlands are disappearing, the world's fisheries are fast being depleted, grain consumption has tripled in the last fifty years, while air and water pollutants have increased dramatically in my lifetime. But so has my love of and commitment to organic gardening. Not only is hunger endemic in industrialized nations as well as rampant in the developing world, but fewer and fewer small farmers are able to keep producing food, due to the proliferation of global corporate markets and the ascendancy of industrial, large-scale agribusiness. Most food travels an average of fifteen hundred miles to reach the family table, and in the last twenty years or so in North America alone we have seen the loss of almost 650,000 small family farms.

Despite the critical loss of arable land nationwide, people are reclaiming vacant lots and growing gardens throughout the neighborhoods and alleyways of this country, from El Barrio in New York City to the Hunters Point neighborhood of the San Francisco Bay Area. The greening of our cities is perceptible and in this green tide people are finding community and culture as well as nutritious, locally grown food.

Years ago in the early 1980s Wendell Berry visited us at San Francisco Zen Center and gave a talk on food and farming. "How do we simplify our lives and stay connected to each other, living here in the city?" asked a sincere urban Zen student. The poet thought a good long time before answering. "Why not let food be your connection?" Berry suggested. "Real food, grown in your own backyard and on the fringe of your city."

Perhaps we put too much emphasis on simplicity and not enough on supporting a complex and diverse network of small farms and gardens surrounding our urban areas and nourishing us with local, organically grown food. In northern California alone there are numerous nonprofit projects designed to connect urban people to land, food, and revitalized community involvement. These projects are echoed throughout the United States and around the world, reflect-

363

ing Wendell Berry's keen enthusiasm for urban farms and food connecting people to the land around our cities.

Peter serves as farm manager for one such urban project, a collaborative AgPark Farm on public utilities land thirty miles east of Oakland, California, with the clear purpose of making public land available to low-income people who want to grow food for their home neighborhoods. In its founding 2006 season this Sunol Water Temple Agricultural Park was immensely successful.

Seventy miles north of San Francisco another local nonprofit, the Occidental Arts and Ecology Center, with whom I have been involved for twenty years, established a beautiful organic garden at the collaborative food bank Food for Thought, providing a huge array of fresh food for the food bank's more than five hundred members. Cooking, gardening, and nutrition classes are held year-round at the food bank, which is clearly a place of refuge and community for all who participate. Each autumn Food for Thought hosts a calabash festival, celebrating gourds grown and decorated by local artists who gather at the food bank and help to raise enough funds to keep the project turning year-round.

At Green Gulch Farm we grow as much food as possible for "hand to mouth"

Sunol AgPark

The Sunol AgPark is an eighteen-acre parcel situated on prime agricultural land owned by the San Francisco Public Utilities Commission. The model for the AgPark—part organic agriculture, part managed parkland—makes possible direct marketing opportunities for small farmers, fresh food for underserved Bay Area communities, and an environmental and educational component for young people. In the founding season of the project, four East Bay nonprofits each committed to farming one to two acres.

* *The Mien Farming Collaborative* is a project to help immigrant Asian farmers revive their agricultural traditions through affordable farmland near their Oakland homes. In the first season they cultivated three acres of traditional Mien crops.

* *People's Grocery*, an Oakland nonprofit working to build a local food system through agriculture, enterprise, and education to improve the health and economy of their East Bay neighborhood, grew two acres of productive summer crops at Sunol.

* *Baia Nicchia*, a small business focusing on growing heirloom tomatoes for seed specifically developed for Bay Area climates, grew a half acre of heritage tomatoes.

* *SAGE (Sustainable Agriculture Education)*, an educational nonprofit, grew a quarter acre of sunflowers in the founding year for beauty, pollination on the farm, and for market.

or "garden to plate" consumption. We also make the harvest available to Bay Area residents by selling at local direct markets, by running a small produce delivery program for our Muir Beach neighbors, and by donating surplus food and fresh organically grown vegetable starts to other nonprofits, soup kitchens, and local food banks.

The farmers' market is a teeming world inside a world, and it is a challenge: it is wonderful to grow good food to donate, but it is a far different thing to have a viable farm production program and be responsible purveyors of produce. At Green Gulch, since farming is woven into a program of apprenticeship and Zen practice, it is not as difficult to have a break-even harvest as it is in a farm dedicated solely to growing honest, no-ghost food. Direct marketing supports a complex network of local organic farming and creates community. It keeps the links alive. The Green Gulch farmers' market stand also teaches dreamy, well-intentioned Zen students how to come down to earth *fast*, making change while weighing fingerling potatoes and bagging fresh blonde beans for hungry customers, all at the same time.

Growing food and distributing the harvest is always personal, never anonymous. At the Green Gulch farmers' market stand we offer recipes to help customers expand both the ways they cook vegetables and the ones they choose to cook, recipes developed over the years in the kitchens of San Francisco Zen Center and at Greens Restaurant at Fort Mason, the popular vegetarian epicure restaurant just a mile or so away from the open-air market, which is affiliated with San Francisco Zen Center.

After the market closes growers often have time to visit with one another. This is my favorite time of all, when farmers trade and barter among ourselves: "Hey, I'll give you this box of Treviso radicchio for that half lug of muscat grapes." We are good at this business. It's our lifeline, after all, and we'd much rather come home bearing the jewels of exotic bartering than with empty trucks. What farmers don't trade with one another is given to the organizations and individuals who show up every week at the close of market to collect surplus produce for the hungry.

Green Gulch Farm is one of the oldest organic farms in the Bay Area, and it has always combined growing beautiful food with a commitment to cooking this food with love and attention. In the early 1980s a longtime Zen Center friend and colleague, Sibella Kraus, founding director of the San Francisco Ferry Plaza farmers' market, had the brilliant idea to bring Bay Area chefs and growers together for a tasting of summer produce hosted at Greens Restaurant. More than a hundred friends, chefs, growers, and marketers came together for this historic event that included a small farmers' market in the entryway to the restaurant, a sumptuous dinner prepared from our shared farm produce by a collective of great Bay Area chefs working together in the Greens kitchen, and the opportunity for all of us to sit down together and enjoy the fruits of our labor.

Farmers' markets are proliferating like ripe zucchini in high summer these days, bringing local color and fine organic food even into the core arteries of busy urban streets. The same pioneer spirit that brought those Bay Area farmers and cooks together in 1983 for a tasting of summer produce pervades every open-air farmers' market I have ever visited, from Burlington, Vermont, to Kona, Hawai'i, to Santa Fe, New Mexico. In these markets we exchange more than good food and farming advice; we create fresh culture and community on common ground, meeting face-to-face over local produce: at a sampling of the different first-run maple syrups of northern Vermont, to savor the white pineapples and non-GMO papayas of Ginger Hill Farm in Hawai'i, and at the annual chile festival held in northern New Mexico in late September, when farmers roast truckloads of green chiles in large rotating wire drums suspended over open fires.

In the mid-1990s there were about

A Tasting of Summer Produce

Greens at Fort Mason   *August 29, 1983*

Puff Pastry Tarts with grilled eggplant, grilled peppers, basil, and sun-dried tomatoes
Salad of Red and Yellow Tomatoes with Moraga mozzarella
Garden Vegetables: beans, potatoes, beets, baked onions, grilled squash with aioli
Deep-Fried Squash Blossoms stuffed with Moraga mozzarella and herbs
Sweet Corn with roasted chile butters
Garden Salad with herbs and flowers
Peaches and Strawberries with crème anglaise
Assorted Melons: ambrosia, Crane, Charentais

1,700 farmers' markets in the United States, while by the year 2000 the number of fresh-air farmers' markets numbered close to 3,000, and they are expanding every day. Several autumns ago, on a rainy October morning I experienced this proliferation firsthand while visiting my family in Manhattan. After dropping my young nephew off at school, I spotted a familiar-looking cluster of funky farm trucks negotiating around honking yellow cabs, unloading produce on the edge of Eightieth Street and Lexington Avenue. Ecstatic, I began to trot toward the trucks and was soon buried deep in the street-side thickets of Migliorelli Farms from Tivoli, New York, sorting through wooden boxes of Cortland, Empire, McIntosh, and Macoun apples. At the Oriental farm display the next stand down, I gathered immodest bunches of broccoli raab and Asian greens for stir-fry, while admiring bushel baskets loaded with the seasonal first 'Red Kuri' and kabocha winter squash, grown from seed that hails from Japan.

Among a throng of hungry New Yorkers, I pushed through the swollen crowd to taste thick slabs of late-season Jersey tomatoes before buying a bunch of farm dahlias, plucked from a rainbow selection of peach, pearl-white, hot-coral, custard-yellow, and wine-colored blossoms tied loosely in huge five-dollar bunches that lined the city streets below the groaning vegetable tables.

The open-air markets of New York City are painting the streets and avenues of the Big Apple red, gold, green, and bronze with farm-grown local wealth. Making my way home to my sister's, I caught sight of my reflection in the rain-glazed opaque windows of Starbucks and Citibank, carrying the wealth and culture of numerous organic farms. Behind me, brightening the dark sheen

Yes, We Have No Lemons

There are street-side farmers' markets held every day throughout Manhattan and the other four boroughs of New York City, more than forty of them at last count. New Yorkers can find the nearest one by going online to the New York City Coalition Against Hunger's NYC Farmer's Market finder at www.nyccah.org/maps/farmers.php or to www.cenyc.org.

These markets dedicated to selling locally grown produce among the skyscrapers and subways induce a kind of culture shock. As I was tasting my way through the vendors' stands parked along Lexington Avenue, I heard a well-dressed woman complaining with noisy disbelief to her companion. Wasn't it ridiculous that with all these stands *not one* was selling the lemons she needed?

of corporate America, unrolled the named and unnamed farms of rural New York and New Jersey, a living patchwork quilt of fresh food and tradition, spread out under the low October sky. Grateful for the bounty of gifts that are beyond measure, I walked home in the rain to cook dinner.

❖   ❖   ❖

Along with buying at local farmers' markets, many people choose to support community supported agriculture programs, or CSAs, most of which are organized by organic farmers in an elegantly simple and mutually beneficial way for farmers and supporters: customers contribute to a farm's annual production expense in exchange for a weekly share of the farm's harvest.

The first CSA farm was developed in Japan in 1965 by a group of dedicated women concerned about the escalating presence of pesticides in their food and the corresponding decrease in local farm production. These women approached a local farmer and set up a cooperative partnership. Their movement was called *Teikei*, literally translated as "food with the farmer's face on it." The CSA idea spread to the United States soon thereafter and to Europe, where it has become very popular in the last twenty years or so.

My good friends at Full Belly Farm in the Capay Valley of north-central California started their CSA about fifteen years ago in order to expand the web of connection and support for their farm, and now they serve more than eight hundred families with a full range of harvest from their thriving organic farm. In the summer Halie Muller—born and bred at Full Belly and the daughter of Dru and Paul, two of the founders of the farm—organizes Camp Full Belly, a very popular weekly sleepover farm camp for kids that fills up every year. In addition to this camp, school groups visit Full Belly for three day overnights throughout the school year. In October at Full Belly there is an all-day-long harvest celebration called the Hoe's Down Harvest Festival for friends, CSA supporters of the farm, and the general public, where people can shear sheep; make yarn out of raw wool; watch sheepdog trials; taste scores of heritage tomatoes and fresh basil; thresh, winnow, grind, and bake hot wheat flatbread in the outdoor wood-fired oven; make necklaces out of Indian corn; and swim in Cache Creek, which runs by the farm. A few years ago more than four thousand people attended this festival, which was staffed with the volunteer help of CSA members and scores of local organic growers and friends from the Capay Valley.

CSA projects provide more than a weekly box of farm-fresh organic produce harvested for their members. "Food with a farmer's face on it" encourages CSA members to be involved in the complex life pattern of the farm they are connected to. Elizabeth Henderson of Rose Valley Farm in upstate New York told me one year about late spring flooding on her farm that had made their regular weekly CSA harvest impossible. To her amazement, rather than complaining, scores of CSA subscribers showed up for days on end to help Rose Valley Farm with cleanup and tardy planting work.

Many CSA projects publish a weekly newsletter to distribute along with their produce as well as a lively description of the crops included in the harvest and a few reliable recipes as well. This can come in handy when your membership farm grows a diverse range of wild and cultivated crops like those grown at Harmony Valley Farm in Wisconsin, which cultivates close to seventy-five acres of one hundred distinct crops, from ramps to radicchio.

Growing food well and sharing it with others is a joy and a privilege, and it is also a deeply political act of good citizenship and support for local farms and good food. Independent small-scale family farmers and organic gardeners who tend their land over the generations with a deep commitment to sustainable agriculture are the frontline growers that I am proud to support and stand next to, shoulder to shoulder. Together we work for the highest standards of quality and safety for food, land, and people. We are all partners in a vast soil-food-life web. It is essential to support independent organic farmers, especially in these times of industrialization of both commercial and large-scale organic agriculture. We are all consumers and every choice we make, no matter how small, is consequential.

❖　　❖　　❖

One year at Green Gulch we hosted a big potato harvest party at the end of the growing season called This Spud's for You. We invited neighbors, Park Service friends, kids galore, Zen folks, volunteers, and local teachers to join in grubbing out the last 'Ruby Crescent' potatoes from the autumn fields. A good portion of these well-cured potatoes were for the Marin City Food Bank and for our favorite soup kitchen in San Francisco. Everyone also took home a big bag of spuds at the end of the harvest. Then we walked down to the beach where some had gone ahead to make a giant bonfire set at the edge of the ocean. The coals of the fire were red-hot and banked when we arrived. We roasted potatoes mixed with Green Gulch garlic, made fresh garden salad by firelight, and enjoyed home-baked apple pie made the night before from our first harvest of 'Mrs. Bramley's' seedling apples. Fully satisfied, we lay back on the sand and watched the October stars mix with the last hot sparks from the fire, pledging allegiance to the gift of good land and to the abiding taste of no anonymous food.

The Mamadella's Garden

I GREW UP IN THE EARLY 1950S IN THE SMALL SUBURBAN TOWN OF Westport, Connecticut, about forty-five miles east of New York City. We lived in a rambling old two-story house with crooked brick fireplaces on land surrounded by uncut woods of shagbark hickory and white oak. Dark hemlock and fir trees grew by mossy stone cliffs of granite that stood as silent sentries behind our well-lit home.

Westport was a stony town. Not far from our house was a small quarry where my sisters and I would play after school on the mountains of crushed rock. The stones seemed to push up out of the ground like slick gray seals surfacing for air from the cold bottom of the Atlantic Ocean where it ran into the inlet of Long Island Sound only a few miles away. I am pleased to hail from stony land. I know how to coax young daffodils up between rocky fissures in the ground and how to gather handfuls of tender lily of the valley flowers from between the rising rocks of frosty April.

Our land was bordered by a low stone wall that surrounded the property, marking the western edge of a small apple orchard not far from the house. This orchard was planted in a soft, fan-shaped arc, radiating out from a deep stone well from which we drew our drinking water.

This stone well always frightened me. It was covered with a heavy slate lid but I knew how to inch the slate aside and peer down into the well. Sometimes in the late-summer evening when my parents were drinking cocktails with friends, their voices growing louder with every swallow, I would escape from the house and hide in the orchard eating ripe windfall apples, and dropping the cores down the thirty-foot-deep stone well shaft to where black fossil water bubbled up out of the rock-cold ground.

Our family knew nothing about growing food; we were suburban "hunters and gatherers," shopping at Gregory's Market and eating Chinese food from the West Lake Diner when Mom was too tired to cook. But a little more than five miles from our home, in the Italian neighborhood of Saugatuck, my sister's future husband, Dick, was helping his *mamadella*, grandmother Angela Maria Caccavella, to cook and can traditional tomato sauce prepared over an open wood fire.

In the days before Westport became an upscale bedroom suburb of Manhattan, Saugatuck was good dairy country. The Italian community that settled there was a thriving, self-sustaining village that continues today. Dick's mother, Mickey, the fourth of Angela's six daughters, still grows tomatoes just a few miles from her childhood home.

Angela Maria Caccavella came to the New World from her Italian home village of Bari as a young bride at the turn of the twentieth century. She and her husband, Angelo, settled in Saugatuck, where the thick marshland tracts were still affordable, living alongside other old-world family members. Angelo worked as a mason until his accidental death in the early 1930s, when Angela was left to provide for their six young daughters.

Angela was a survivor. She had no money and she earned no wages, but she knew how to barter and trade and she lived in a community knit together by family, food, and the Catholic Church. Every year Angela planted a huge two-acre production garden and grew a vast amount of food to eat fresh and to put by. She planted old-world Concord grapes for wine-making and in her ample root cellar she put away all of the crops that she could not can, the carrots, turnips, cabbages, potatoes by the bushel, beets, and huge, sweet onions. They were buried under layers of clean newspaper and fresh sawdust to be excavated throughout the winter for rich stews that she brewed in a blackened stew pot on the back of her cookstove.

Angela kept one milk cow and scores of rabbits, goats, and chickens to feed her family. Once a year a hog was slaughtered in the community and Angela made sausages. She also grew tobacco and rows and rows of red garlic as well as rhubarb, strawberries, fresh peaches, and soft pears, to can and make into fruit pies, cobblers, and sweet preserves.

Angela was an adept haggler. When her neighbor's cow trampled her garden one growing season, the scolded dairyman delivered truckload after guilty truckload of cured cow manure for Angela's next-season garden. She also bartered for flour, oil, and salt, and once a week she and the other mamadellas of the village made fresh pasta. They enlisted eager children like Dick to help them hang the golden ropes of fragrant noodles on the backs of chairs and tables and from tree and shrub limbs where the fresh pasta air-dried in the sunny wind.

Occasionally the mamadellas made a pilgrimage into the forest behind their village and emerged balancing huge fallen logs on top of their heads. They wore a thickly wound circlet of rags called a *mapine* on the crown of their heads to balance their loads of wood. With these logs the mamadellas set "push-wood" fires—just pushing a log farther in as it burns—in the clearing behind their homes. Not far from the suburban sprawl where Dairy Queen and golden-arched McDonald's franchises were colonizing the old cow corridors of the Saugatuck countryside and freeway overpasses bent like cocked scorpions above the sweet, arable farmland, the mamadellas turned their strong backs to this noise and excitement, stoked their open fires, and baked crusty bread and hot pizza behind their homes while the world hurried by.

This was not so long ago, perhaps less than a generation or so from today.

I was in my early twenties and traveling around northern California, getting up well before dawn to practice Zen meditation in our drafty hay-barn zendo and spending my days learning to grow organic lettuce and long rows of russet potatoes, while in my own hometown three thousand miles to the east the mamadellas of old Saugatuck were stirring their cast-iron cauldrons of fresh tomato sauce over push-wood fires.

After World War I about 30 percent of the people of North America were involved in agriculture. By the end of World War II this number had fallen to 14 percent of the population, and by 1973, around the time that ninety-three-year-old Angela Maria Caccavella noticed a distinct and unmistakable pain in the core of her body and cleaned her house, paid all her bills, and sat down to comb her cats before she died peacefully in her sleep, a scant 4.5 percent of the people of this nation were responsible for growing all the food consumed in our country, doing the hard and satisfying work that the old Italian mamadellas of my hometown had been doing all the days of their lives.

❖　❖　❖

In the year when Alan Chadwick was dying at Green Gulch and giving his last teachings, his students elsewhere were sending their teacher gifts of rare seeds and exotic crops that they had grown together over the years. Among these gifts was a small box of treasured 'Rose Fir Apple' fingerling potato starts from Alan's final garden project at Carmel-in-the-Valley in Virginia. "Won't you grow these prize potatoes and preserve their lineage?" Alan implored me in a weak and dramatic whisper, full of portentous gravity.

Alan Chadwick had given us detailed instructions that year for preparing an underground potato clamp, a simple root cellar for storing and preserving the seed crop of the best of the season's potatoes. The idea of the clamp intrigued me. Here was an old and old-world way of preserving a crop throughout the winter, a method that worked with the natural dormant cycle of ripe potatoes. Even though the advent of modern refrigeration has rendered the old-fashioned root cellar obsolete, there was something about the technique and practice of the clamp that attracted me: ingenuity and simplicity of design, a hearkening back to the practice of the mamadellas of my hometown, perhaps a dormant homesteading urge of my own. As I listened to Alan describe the potato clamp, I vowed to someday excavate our own garden clamp and fill it with choice seed potatoes.

To create a potato clamp you tunnel a cave or chamber into the side of a north-facing hillside and clear the earth out of your horizontal vault. When we finally created our clamp we hollowed out just such a chamber at a slight angle to help with water drainage. It was about three feet deep and two feet wide and high. The reason the clamp is dug horizontally into the side of a hill rather than vertically and underground is to provide optimal air circulation and to allow for proper moisture drainage during the storage period. A horizontal clamp is less likely to be inundated by rising groundwater.

The next step in clamp construction is to line the vault with dry, clean organic matter. We chose dry bracken fern collected from the mountains of Tassajara since bracken fern has antiseptic properties and had been a preferred clamp-lining material for years.

Next you place your crop into the clamp. It is important to store crops that are undamaged and fully cured or ripe. I have been trained not to clean a crop before storing it since washing a storage crop removes the natural protection of the soil and may cause bruising or removal of the protective outer cell wall on the skin of the crop.

As we stored the potatoes in the clamp, we carefully packed fresh bracken between the potato layers to cushion the weight of the harvest. In the colder regions of the country, the organic padding is intended also to protect the crop from freezing. It is important to store the crop deep in the clamp, leaving the front eight inches or so clear, so that when the clamp is filled, that space can be packed with more organic insulation material and sealed with a light capping membrane of garden soil. In our clamp we simply tucked the potatoes in with lots of bracken and sealed the opening in the hillside with a stout wooden trapdoor that we then covered over with even more bracken. If you want to construct an underground clamp and you live in a heavy snowfall zone, be sure to chart your earthen clamp on a good garden map or mark it with a bright flag so you can find it again after snowmelt.

When Alan died in late May, the 'Rose Fir Apple' potatoes were just showing their first aboveground leaf growth. We nurtured these potatoes with a loving reverence only slightly encumbered by grief and sentimentality, and harvested a phenomenal yield of fingerling potatoes that year. In the autumn we excavated our old-world potato clamp, and filled it with perfectly formed 'Rose Fir Apple' potatoes to save for next year's seed crop. The clamp was a sort of memorial potato crypt and I am embarrassed to say that I acted as if this simple spud cave was the sanctified tomb of King Tut himself, especially as I walked by the burrow in mournful silence all winter.

On the anniversary of Alan's death late the next May, I unsealed the potato crypt and prepared to excavate the clamped seed potatoes. I knew we were a little tardy in the season to be unbuttoning the clamp, but the anniversary of Alan's death seemed such an auspicious date to exhume the 'Rose Fir' potatoes. As we pried the lid off the earthen tomb a cascade of translucent, pink, fleshy potato sprouts uncoiled into the light, the uncombed serpent tresses of Medusa herself. The other gardeners working with me dropped their solemn piety and retreated in horror, overwhelmed by the hissing nightshade sprouts and the foul stench of gassy flatulence from hundreds of pounds of rotting prize fingerling potatoes.

Failure is a marvelous teacher: stern, accurate, and irrevocable. I tried to unsnarl the potato kink, of course; and I failed, of course. I gave up trying to untangle my error and sat down on the ground. I laughed until I wept, and I cried until it was funny again, and then I remembered my last, thin strand of unsentimental good sense. I had kept some of the precious 'Rose Fir Apple' potato seed in our modern walk-in cooler, and these potatoes had all been planted out on time and were growing famously. For my penance I cleaned out the fetid potato sepulcher by myself and backfilled the hole with good soil.

375

It is obvious what happened, isn't it? The soil warmed up as all soil must and the potatoes broke out of dormancy and began to grow, as all potatoes must, searching mightily for the light. While we were offering incense to the ghost of Alan Chadwick, his prize potatoes were speaking in tongues and clamoring to testify aboveground.

In my potato-clamping effort, nostalgia and superstition had overtaken common sense. In my desire to honor Alan Chadwick, and to follow his classic directions for building an earthen clamp, I failed to consider that California has a relatively warm climate with a very short and rainy winter season that never experiences a deep freeze. Clamps work best during the colder months of the year and in regions of the country where there is some frost, like in my hometown where seasoned mamadellas know in their bones that potatoes have a natural dormancy period of three to four months, after which time they begin to sprout and grow. Most important of all, I learned that crops that are out of sight are also out of mind, especially when it is possible to eat fresh, in-season organically grown food year-round.

I am happy to report that over the last twenty-five years since this spud fiasco, Green Gulch has grown splendid 'Rose Fir Apple' potatoes season after season, sharing the wealth with numerous garden friends, a practice just as time-honored and revered as excavating an old-world potato clamp, a task which I shall not soon endeavor to repeat.

Zen practice teaches that life is one continuous mistake, full of learning and growth especially when you cultivate a sense of humor and balance, refusing to hide from your mishaps. Then if schmaltz or melodrama threaten to overtake you, remember the mamadellas' gardens of old and the unsentimental sincerity of 'Rose Fir Apple' potatoes lying on the open ground ready to be planted, and come back to your true self.

Keep the Links Alive

ONE AUTUMN DAY A NUMBER OF YEARS AGO I WENT DOWN TO THE garden to count the almost-ripe 'Rouge d'Estampes' 'Cinderella' pumpkins just before their harvest. To my surprise, all of the largest pumpkins had been gored repeatedly. Viscous pumpkin sap oozed thickly onto the field. The only clue I could extract from my discreet, nontattling garden colleagues was that Sean, a new child who had moved to Green Gulch from San Francisco just a few weeks before, had been playing by himself in the garden, shouting, "*En garde!*" at top volume and brandishing a sharp irrigation-spike sword above his head.

Sean confessed easily to the stabbing of the pumpkins, guileless and thoroughly unrepentant. "Do you know that these pumpkins are food?" I asked the wiry musketeer, not particularly proud of my tactics. *Even if they weren't food, why would you go around spearing bright vermilion beings that are almost as big as you are, you little twerp*, was what I was really wondering to myself.

Sean was grinding down a fresh gopher mound with the toe of his sneaker, avoiding my penetrating, righteous glare. Yes, he knew that pumpkins were food. "Well, where does food come from, Sean?" I asked him in condescending exasperation. "From the Safeway," he mumbled, under his breath. That got to me. *OK, drop down a notch*, I coached myself, remembering that this kid had lived his entire life in the city. "And where does the Safeway get food from?" I probed. "From another Safeway," Sean answered.

Sean was not just being a wiseacre; he was telling me his precise experience of where food comes from. And he was painfully accurate, especially in his designation of the vast industrial distribution network that both connects and separates us from the food we eat.

What was missing in Sean's world system was a garden that he was linked to, a piece of land that he knew inside out and depended on for health and well-being. "Keep the links alive!" is the motto of the Ecological Farming Association that I have been a member of for three decades. Stabbed 'Cinderella' pumpkins and self-righteous preachy gardeners sever the links. What is forfeited is consequential relationship and fresh connections.

Sean was not further harangued or punished for his pumpkin stabbing spree. Instead, he was invited to work in the garden and the kitchen for one day with those of us involved in growing and cooking food at Green Gulch. He was assigned, naturally, to the pumpkin harvest. He enjoyed collecting the speared 'Cinderella' pumpkins from their vines, washing them, and bringing them to the kitchen in several trips with his own wheelbarrow.

In the kitchen Sean cut the pumpkins open and scooped out their seed, which he rinsed and spread out on baking sheets to dry. While the seed was drying, he cut the pumpkins into wedges to be baked for soup, a job he enjoyed immensely since it involved karate chops with a sharp Japanese cleaver. Tasting the soup at lunchtime was less popular. "Nasty!" was Sean's sole descriptive comment about the velvety-rich pumpkin soup.

I managed to lure Sean into my net again about six months later, when it was time to sow the seed he had saved from the 'Cinderella' pumpkins. That plucky kid settled down out of warrior mode in a flash, walking the 150-foot-long rows and planting pumpkin seed at careful three-foot intervals in the dark spring soil. The pumpkin harvest that season was stellar.

✦ ✦ ✦

When I work with young people in the People's Grocery back lot gardens of West Oakland clearing rubble and planting beds of winter peas and red onions, or when I harvest crates of fresh collards and dry Guatemalan black beans with sixth graders in the Edible Schoolyard, I often think of Sean and the 'Cinderella' pumpkins. I also think of all the children I meet these days who do not have access to healthy food and who suffer from asthma, diabetes, and obesity. Since the 1970s the obesity rate has doubled or even tripled for children ages six to twelve, so much so that in 2005 the *New England Journal of Medicine* reported that due to obesity and type 2 diabetes this generation of young people may be the first to die at a younger age than their parents.

This is unacceptable to me in every way. All children deserve to be fed well and to know where their food comes from and how it gets to their table. This is not a privilege but a basic right and a necessity. For urban children to learn from the real world, and to be involved in every way possible, requires encouraging them to recognize and honor their own food heritage. When food and culture and the enjoyment of gardening are all connected, learning is a pleasure that does not fade and is not forgotten. This pleasure has a lingering flavor that creates and strengthens more than the bodies and minds of our children; it creates and strengthens civil society.

One day last summer in our "Food and Justice" summer camp at King middle school, ten of the twenty-three students in the program, all ages twelve to fourteen, were fanned out harvesting lunch ingredients from the King garden that they and other young people had planted and tended during their middle-school years. Esther and Nicole, beloved kitchen teachers, were harvesting alongside the kids. After about half an hour they all disappeared into the kitchen to make lunch for us. I stayed outside with the other garden teachers and students as we worked, tying up 'Sungold' tomatoes, thinning purple cabbage, and dead-heading spent larkspur stems from our glorious summer flower border.

We were plenty hungry when the kitchen team called us to lunch at the long plank table set out under the acacia trees. They had made a summer favorite with all of our garden vegetables, "Beautiful Soup," piping hot and served with fresh cornbread ground up from our Hopi blue corn. Vanessa, a particularly active thirteen-year-old, had been assigned to dance as fast as she could for eight minutes without stopping, with a jar of Straus Family Farm cream held in each hand, churning up gorgeous rock-and-roll butter for our bread. We took our time eating, telling stories, and commenting on the soup. For dessert we had ripe Persian mulberries and fresh strawberries from the garden, served on perfect garden "plates" made out of raspberry leaves. Nobody wanted to ever move again or to leave that boundless summer table following this meal.

✦　✦　✦

When my life goes flat and I forget to heed the real voice of the garden, working with children brings me back to life. I remember coming home from the beach one spring evening when my daughter was small. Night fell earlier than I expected and I was hurrying Alisa through the spring fields, oblivious to the gathering spell of the March night all around us. "Mama," my daughter called out in the descending darkness, "let's count the newts walking home on the path. They know where to go, even when it's dark."

I stopped and looked down. Orange-bellied newts were crossing the muddy path that ran through the shadows of red fescue and purple needle grass. The Tibetan saint Milarepa's terse advice came to mind: hasten slowly. I stopped rushing and joined the spring night. In complete darkness, thirty-one newts delivered us home.

Beautiful Soup

You will need:
- Onions
- Carrots
- Celery
- Assorted vegetables, green and fresh herbs
- Olive oil
- Garlic
- Vegetable stock
- Salt and pepper

Wash all vegetables and herbs. Chop up onions, carrots, and celery. Heat ¼ cup olive oil in a heavy pot and add onions, carrots, and celery. Sauté for three to five minutes. Chop up other vegetables (some ideas: peppers, kale, leeks, cabbage, broccoli, potatoes) and herbs—don't forget the garlic! Add all chopped vegetables and herbs to pot and sauté for another five minutes. Pour in vegetable stock, season with salt and pepper. If you want, you can add a little soy sauce. Simmer for a bit, then serve. (This is a favorite recipe from the kitchen of the students of the Edible Schoolyard.)

Following newts home is a kind of harvest, a gathering in of real wealth and nourishment. So is marking out an abandoned city lot for a vegetable garden or noticing exactly when the barn swallows return to nest under the March eaves of your toolshed. Real time is told by linked events in the garden, and every garden season has its own particular rhythm and distinct flavor. "All the lives this place has had, I have," writes farmer and poet Wendell Berry. "I eat my history day by day."

At Green Gulch Farm after a long winter's diet of savory tofu stew and roasted root vegetables, I crave the first weedy greens of spring. I love to go out with kids of all ages to the woods bordering the muddy spring fields. The sky is low, alive with the scent of rain. We gather wild onions, round-capped miner's lettuce, green necklaces of chickweed, and the tender mallow growing among stands of yellow mustard and pastel radish flowers.

Big-leaved maples flower along Redwood Creek in this season, and we harvest five or six tender flowers from each tree we can reach. On the homeward trek hidden garden treasures are uncovered: tender side-shoots of winter broccoli, milk-white cauliflower curds underneath leathery wrapping leaves, handfuls of snow peas, and occasional spears of new asparagus pushing up out of the cold ground like newborn dragons.

By the time we get back to the Green Gulch kitchen it has begun to rain. We heat up oil in the huge wok and make a simple tempura batter. The kids dip maple blossoms in the batter, one by one, and broccoli, cauliflower, peas, and asparagus. These spring offerings sizzle and puff up in the hot oil.

Lukas and Olivia, the smallest children, help compose the spring weed salad. We are cagey parents: if they make it, they will eat it, a lesson I know well from urban school gardens. Last of all, we steep a lime-green wild mint tea and sit down to eat. Black rain pelts the dark windows. Our wet raincoats and muddy boots are drying by the stove as we sit and feast on timeless spring.

381

✦ ✦ ✦

Summer is wild berry season on the California coast, the time when the Green Gulch kids migrate to the edge of the high summer garden to build secret blackberry forts. While the "growns," as they call us, work harvesting butter lettuce and the last lavender of the season, Zen rascals guzzle ripe berries deep in the maze of summer.

The kids do come up out of their blackberry thicket for high tea in the late afternoon. Hot, dirty, scratched, and indigo blue with blackberry juice, they are hosed off and served iced lemon verbena tea afloat with sprigs of black mint and anise hyssop blossoms. The garden crew bribes the kids into coming to tea: if they gather us a few baskets of wild blackberries early in the day, we'll make fruit tarts for teatime, we cajole them. No surprise, they agree.

High tea is good at the end of a long day of making forts and living outside of Zen law. We all spoil our appetites for dinner with tiny fruit tarts made from wild blackberries mixed with dead-ripe gooseberries and the last white currants of the season.

After tea we lie back on the grass and watch the evening clouds mount in the west, out over the ocean. The hills darken, russet and amber, and all the garden cranberry bean plants sag with the weight of August. The kids' parents are probably worried about where they are but we are too lazy to move or be mildly responsible. Even when the first owls settle on the dark cypress limbs, we fail to budge. Young and old together, we are sated with full summer.

✦ ✦ ✦

In autumn the ground is thirsty for rain, and by late October Redwood Creek has dropped underground. Outside of the garden, the coast live oaks and huge tan oaks of the watershed ripen their acorns. The blue jays collect the first acorns of November, drilling them into the dry ground with their sharp beaks. Watching the jays work I know it is time to begin my own harvest of acorns from oaks on the lower flanks of Mount Tamalpais that have been harvested for generations by the native Costanoan tribes of the California Bay Area.

As recently as 250 years ago the Ohlone people who lived in the Redwood Creek watershed were hunter-gatherers who also "farmed" the land, cultivating the wild oaks. Particular oak trees were in the care of individual family groups for generations, in an era when time itself was linked to the seasons of the oak. The autumn harvest, when tribes came together to celebrate by gleaning, gathering, and preparing food harvested from the oaks, marked the New Year. Winter was measured in moon phases from the time of the acorn harvest; spring was told by the flowering of the oaks; and summer was marked by the progression toward the ripening of the acorn harvest. Ten thousand native people inhabited the 150 miles from the San Francisco Bay south to the Esselen nation of Big Sur.

The native people tended their trees faithfully. The first drop of acorns was usually riddled with acorn moth larvae. The Ohlone people covered these wormy acorns with dry grass and set the grass afire, destroying the primary larval phase of the oak pest. Then, when the healthy main season acorn drop occurred in early November, the fruit fell on a clean understory of savannah-like parkland beneath the huge oaks.

There is an old story told by the Karuk people of northern California about how the different species of oak came to earth. In the old days, acorns were sky maidens living in the heavens. Once when there was famine on the earth, the sky maidens took pity and came down to be food. Valley Oak girl dove down first, clapping her small gathering basket on her long, slender head. Her sister, Black Oak maiden, wore her large burden basket, which is to this day her signature acorn cap. Next came tiny Coast Live Oak girl with her small basket cap, and last of all, wearing her messy, rough burden basket cap, Tan Oak maiden descended, becoming the richest food of all.

Gathering acorns was a favorite autumn practice for my daughter and me for many years. I still gather acorns every autumn and, miraculously, my teenage daughter often helps. We take the acorns home and spread the good ones to dry behind our wood-burning stove. After a few days we crack the acorns using a prized stone pestle—though a mallet or hand pruners are equally effective—and pry the acorn meat out of its shell. Every season we begin pounding the acorn meat by hand, but soon move to a modern food processor that whizzes the remainder of the acorn meat into golden meal.

Acorns are bitter in taste and rich in tannin and oil. Native people leached their acorn meal in slow-running river water to wash away the tannic acid. My modern adaptation is simple: I hang the acorn meal in cheesecloth pouches under a slow-dripping cold-water tap overnight. Dark ocher tannin colors our old enamel sink a rich butternut gold every November.

After it is leached, the acorn meal is laid to dry on clean towels before I toast it slowly in our oven until the kitchen smells like the inner kernel of the sunny oak forest. I mix the roasted meal with honey and fold in some fresh pumpkin pulp, adding whole wheat flour and a little baking soda to raise the bread. Every season the acorn bread is a little different, depending on whim and fancy and on what is at hand.

Thanksgiving Acorn-Pumpkin Bread

This seasonal bread comes out of a yearly tradition of walking the coastal hills of Marin and gathering acorns of the coast live oak.

Dry Ingredients
1 cup whole wheat or white flour
¾ cup acorn meal
1 teaspoon salt
1¼ cups brown sugar
2 teaspoons baking soda
Spices to taste (cinnamon, nutmeg, mace, etc.)

Wet Ingredients
1 cup pumpkin pulp (simply bake a small pumpkin until it is cooked, cut it open, scoop out the seeds, and blend the pulp with a little water)
⅓ cup vegetable oil
¼ cup water
2 eggs, beaten

Combine the dry ingredients. Mix together the wet ingredients separately and then fold them in together. Pour into a well-oiled baking tin and bake at 350°F for fifty to sixty minutes. Enjoy!

I do not bake acorn bread on hot slabs of rock as the Ohlone people did. I am a modern kind of native to this earth, baking in a Wolf oven as I keep the links to our watershed alive season after season.

❖   ❖   ❖

In early December when winter unravels the organized garden, I want all work wound up, but winter's skein of ragged tasks lengthens as the days shorten. By the evening of the winter solstice, darkness drops well before five p.m., like iron shears cutting the last threads of the lit year.

Yet every December, cold, wet soil calls me out of my warm house. I like to climb Coyote Ridge with a small clutch of kids and plant one-year-old fir and redwood seedlings in the shelter of shadowy, north-facing canyons. From here the willows down in the creek float in a copper haze against the steel-blue Coastal Range and the sea and fields are one dark wash of green.

When we finally come down from the headlands we are cold and mean with hunger. We raid the winter garden for abandoned vegetables to make into soup. The forgotten rhubarb chard is still quite tender, its roots running bloodred and tangled underground. At the back of the field the rain-beaten remnants of my favorite 'Bleu de Solaise' leeks are still wearing clean white silk stockings under their mud-spattered wrapping leaves. We carry our treasures to the Zen Center kitchen and sauté the leeks with red garlic and cook the chard with tender yellow-flecked potatoes in a rich vegetable stock. Next, we purée the steaming winter vegetables into a thick, hearty soup and feast on the bounty of winter. The kids eagerly slurp down every last drop of soup, cleaning their bowls with slabs of freshly baked Norwegian rye bread spread with sweet butter.

It is almost dark when we finish this winter feast. We have worked hard and the headlands are anchored by more than a hundred new trees this evening. As night falls outside the cold windows, I remember hidden treasure. Reaching into my coat pocket I pull out a bright green bouquet of fir tips collected that afternoon from young Douglas firs that we planted two seasons ago. Delight ripples through the throng. A fresh reason to stay together! Water is boiled, and the fir tips are tossed into a teapot to steep—for two minutes only—into fragrant forest tea rich in vitamin C. Chocolate chip cookies materialize as if by magic from the locked cookie cabinet that only thirteen-year-old Davy knows how to open with an unfaltering sleight-of-hand. Everyone looks the other way as Davy opens the forbidden door. Triumphant, he serves us cookies while Alisa helps Sabrina pour hot fir-tip tea. We lift our steaming cups to the cold night and warm company. "Love winter," wrote Thomas Merton, "when the plant says nothing," and all the links that bind us to one another, to real food and the sleeping land, are alive and intertwined.

Dragon Greens

WHEN I PRACTICED AT THE TASSAJARA ZEN MOUNTAIN CENTER monastery in the early 1970s, it was my responsibility as head gardener to make a survey of the garden once a week with my dharma sister, who was serving as head cook, or *tenzo*, of the monastery. Our task was simple—to plan nourishing meals to feed the monastic community out of the bounty of the Tassajara garden.

I loved our slow walks through the dawn garden as the chill of the night rose in cold columns from the razor-sharp mountains surrounding Tassajara. These planning sessions were as much a part of my monastic training as the rigorous periods of formal meditation that ordered our practice life. "No grumbling about ingredients" was our common sworn pledge, drawn from the thirteenth-century *Instructions for the Zen Cook* written by Zen master Eihei Dogen and passed on, warm hand to warm hand, through generations of monastery cooks and gardeners, to our modern Zen place.

386

Green Gulch Farm Thanksgiving Harvest Report

Every Thanksgiving Day at Green Gulch we bring a sampling of our harvest (including noxious weeds and a range of flowers and herbs) into the meditation hall, where the community can appreciate the bounty of the crops. Then just before Thanksgiving dinner the farm manager chants aloud this litany of harvest for the full year. Shown here is the tally of our 2003 growing season, both in the farm and in the garden.

Farm Harvest
1,156 cases lettuce
421 cases baby lettuce
428 pounds raddichio
86 cases curly endive
39.5 cases escarole
1,051 cases chard
408 cases kale
840 pounds red cabbage
2,501 pounds green cabbage
2,227 pounds broccoli
1,102 pounds and 444 bunches spinach
1,465 bunches red beets
333 bunches Chioggia beets
384 bunches 'Bull's Blood' beets
816 pounds topped beets
141 bunches golden beets
694 pounds and 185 bunches green garlic
32 pounds dry garlic
403 bunches leeks
5,027 pounds zucchini
1,461 bulbs fennel
1,990 pounds salad mix
449 pounds arugula
104 pounds burdock
686 bunches radishes
67 pounds snap peas
1,811 pounds 'Red Kuri' squash
1,579 pounds pie pumpkins
26 'Cinderella' pumpkins
72 pounds green beans
9 cases collards

142 bunches 'Mei Quing Choi'
71 pounds baby beet greens
57 dozen bunches red dandelion
55 pounds fava beans
119 artichokes
552 bunches scallions
258 bunches 'Purplette' onions
156 bunches dill
248 bunches cilantro
232 bunches parsley
76 bunches chives
97 bunches baby carrots
32 pounds baby chard
69 pounds Napa cabbage
126 pounds 'Joi Choi'
11,143 pounds potatoes

Garden Harvest
1,200 flower bouquets for market
33 fresh herbal wreaths
2,250 flower arrangements
64 herbal bouquets
55 one-gallon cans of tea mix
80 cans of rosemary
90 cans of spearmint, peppermint, orange
   bergamot mint
100 cans of rose geranium
11 cans of marjoram
26 cans of edible flowers
15 cans of lemon verbena
173 pounds plums
1,023 pounds apples
115 pounds pears
60 pounds quince
30 pounds Green Gulch Farm honey
10 loaves of acorn bread
And innumerable strawberries, raspberries,
   apples, plums, and pears picked hand to
   mouth with our delight
And one eight-pound baby girl, Lyla, born on
   May 4, 2003, to Garden Manager Leslie Thiele
   and her husband, Michael

In the formal monastic system of China and Japan the tenzo was also known as the Head of the Rice Pot, since it was the chief responsibility of the tenzo to sort, clean, and cook the rice that fed the monastic community. I asked my Tassajara tenzo friend what she imagined would be a good title for the garden manager at Tassajara. "How about Head of the Cabbages?" she suggested with a sly smile.

This title proved prophetic for me, especially during my first winter growing season in the Tassajara garden, when cabbages ruled my life. I had inherited scores of tiny packages of Asian vegetable seed in the autumn and, loath to waste a single seed, had dutifully planted out more than twenty garden beds with hundreds of mysterious seedlings grown from indecipherable Japanese seed packets. By midwinter when all of the plump heritage tomatoes and succulent French butter lettuces of the summer garden had expired from cold, I was marooned in an ocean of ice-capped cabbages without end.

"From a single leaf of greens create a sixteen-foot golden body," admonished Dogen in his *Instructions for the Zen Cook*. "And from a sixteen-foot golden body, create a single leaf of greens." This became our secret Zen challenge as we negotiated the high seas of Tassajara cabbage and planned our daily menus to nourish a Zen population of almost eighty hungry meditators.

Every evening at Tassajara we were served a grain casserole or gruel composed of delicious leftovers all blended together into one substantially dense offering, accompanied by a side dish of fresh greens harvested from the garden. That winter we ate an unaltered diet of cabbage in its many guises: Napa cabbage, bok choy, 'Joi Choy,' 'Kyona Mizuna,' 'Han Tsai Tai' greens, Osaka purple mustard, 'Komatsuma' cabbage, 'Tokyo Bekama' greens, along with a long green swell, with no apparent end, of Chinese cabbage.

These cabbages thrived at Tassajara. They lacked all subtlety and overflowed with an embarrassment of vigor. The colder and wetter the winter weather became, the nastier the pelting hail and frozen mud of the monastery, the stronger the cabbages grew. Now and then I stood alone among them, my cropping knife resting at my side, and looked out over the cold field, some cabbages elongated with frosty-green cone heads, some squat and dimpled with raised icy warts like old bullfrogs suspended in frozen animation in the cold soil. These chilly guardians of the winter garden seemed to incline selflessly toward the warmth of their final, fiery destiny awaiting them on the monastery kitchen stovetop.

Sadly, I was well aware that my reverence for the cabbages was not always shared by my monastic colleagues. Some evenings when the zendo doors swung open to admit the supper servers with their heavy casseroles of gruel and their unmistakable vats of steaming, sulfurous-fumed cabbage, a thin but unmistakable groan rose from the hungry assembly.

Concerned, the Head of the Rice Pot and I intensified our menu-planning sessions. We began to walk the garden twice a week now, admiring the multitude of cabbages and proposing braised, baked, boiled, broiled, stir-fried, seared, sautéed, and even *fresh* Chinese cabbage salad tossed in a rich tahini dressing and accented with baby mandarin oranges. Still, that winter practice period was one of the longest forced cabbage feeds on record, ending not a moment too soon in mid-April, when the cabbages finally succumbed to spring temperatures, narrowly averting a monastic mutiny.

❖   ❖   ❖

It has been over thirty years since I served as Head of the Cabbages in the Tassajara garden, yet the lessons of that season continue to guide my life and practice. My tenzo friend and the endless fields of sincere garden cabbages showed me what it is to be resolute and respectful of all ingredients, whether coarse or fine. Even when harvesting or making a broth out of the most rumpled of cabbage greens, I learned to handle each leaf with attention and care, without stirring up too much preference or distaste. Likewise, I observed that when my kitchen compatriots were composing a cream soup, they wasted no time crowing with delight over the fancy, rich ingredients. Instead, they extended the same attention and care to cream as to cabbage, acknowledging both as equally precious.

In his *Instructions for the Zen Cook* Dogen reminds each practitioner to maintain "joyful mind," "grandmotherly or nurturing mind," and "magnanimous or big mind." Joyful mind is the mind that delights in the fundamental and ordinary crafts of cooking and gardening in this very lifetime with all of its possibilities and challenges, working with a pleasure that does not tire or fade. Grandmotherly or nurturing mind is the mind that offers the benefit and bounty of a simple meal or of a day of work in the garden to all beings in the ten directions, without discrimination. This nurturing mind is equally well sustained by cabbage and by quiche when they are both prepared with love and wholehearted attention. Magnanimous or big mind is boundless and enduring, like the steep mountains of Tassajara or the vast ocean stirred by the dragon's tail at the bottom of the Green Gulch Valley. Magnanimous mind is inclusive, never halted by discouragement or lost in ecstasy. Magnanimous mind sees the entire world revealed in one, round cabbage seed and finds abiding nourishment in a single grain of rice.

✦ ✦ ✦

For the last ten years every spring or summer, and often again in the late autumn, Annie Somerville, executive chef of Greens Restaurant and my good friend, and I have offered an all-day workshop at Green Gulch on cooking and gardening, combining our shared experience and enthusiasm to present principles and guidelines that keep kitchen and garden practice fresh and connected.

Usually at least twenty-five people join us for these "Fields of Greens" days of meditation, gardening, and cooking. We begin the morning sitting zazen and then walk through the farm appreciating the crops, a luxury that we are all too often denied in our busy work lives. After wandering, struck by how vivid and abundant the garden always is, we get ready to harvest and to set in motion the round of preparing and cooking and—best of all—eating together.

Before we enter the garden we stop at the toolshed, a cob and straw bale structure brimful with the well-used tools of our trade, oiled and gleaming with age and hard work. Each person chooses the tool they want to work with—a Scottish manure fork, a battered Bulldog digging spade, a carmine-red pair of Felco hand pruners from Switzerland. We learn as much about each other from the tools we choose as from the work we will soon engage in. I am convinced that the tool chooses the worker as much as the worker the tool.

There is always plenty of food in these Zen fields, so it is well to remember that millions of people go to bed hungry every night, and to pledge for this one day to harvest with special care and attention. A farmer friend from Allstar Organics farm says that as a nation we waste about a quarter of our food—in the field and garden, from the table, and from uneaten "science experiments" that spoil in our refrigerators. With this in mind, we pledge to enjoy and eat everything that we harvest.

It is a rare gift of a day when we can garden and cook in mindfulness all day long. We are all held in the spell of the garden bounty and the creativity of a kitchen where many are nourished. How we live and practice on this day together matters and somehow influences our cooking and gardening lives at home.

The garden has trained me to always deliver well-cared-for produce to the kitchen, absolutely clean and trimmed and ready to be cooked. This takes time to do well, we discover, as we pluck off all of the yellow or flea-beetle-chewed leaves of Napa cabbage and red scallions for our winter salad. It is good to work together—some picking through the salad mix, some scrubbing shallots, some harvesting English black peppermint for hot tea, all gardening together under the low coastal sky with the ocean at our backs.

At the end of the morning we survey our harvested wealth, now boxed, bagged, and loaded into farm carts, and ready to be hauled to the kitchen. We pause at the compost pile on our way up, to offer our discarded stems and roots to the furnace of transformation. We always harvest a few extra boxes of chard or potatoes to send to the local food bank, where fresh organic food is received like medicine.

While we have been in the garden the tenzo and the Green Gulch kitchen crew have been making lunch. We come into the warmth of the dining room and sit down to a simple vegetarian meal of soup, salad, and bread. Then while our guests are relaxing after lunch, a few of us help Annie set up the afternoon cooking class with all of the garden produce we've just delivered. Despite the vow not to waste, I always harvest too much, but nothing goes unused during this workshop. Happy for the excess, our guests take every last leaf of greens home at the end of the day.

By early afternoon we cross a new threshold, into the world of the kitchen. I delight in Annie Somerville, trim and ready to work in her immaculate white chef's coat. The kitchen has become a new world for me, full of mystery and surprise and alive with the fragrance of newly pressed olive oil, zesty Meyer lemons, and freshly chopped basil.

For two hours we cook and sample the gifts of the morning harvest, rendering young red onions even more sweet by scalding them in boiling water and then soaking them in balsamic vinegar, making a delicious soup stock out of stinging nettles and fresh comfrey leaves, learning the latest roll-cut with a sharp chef's knife. Sometimes we fire up the homemade Green Gulch grill, fashioned out of a clean split-open fifty-five-gallon barrel filled with slow-burning charcoal, and roast a medley of seasonal vegetables.

Miraculously, by the end of this long afternoon of tasting while absorbing Annie's wealth of cooking knowledge we are still hungry for the grand finale dinner that caps our day's work. We pile up the vegetables on huge platters, dress the salad, serve the soup, set out dessert, and clean up the kitchen. Before we eat, we stand in a circle around the harvest table and bless our good fortune with silent gratitude. We have served a new and original dish at every sitting of our "Fields of Greens" event, yet much remains constant. The true taste of camaraderie, happy exhaustion, and abiding intimacy flavors each of these unique days of cooking from the garden.

✦ ✦ ✦ ✦ ✦ ✦ ✦ ✦ ✦ ✦ ✦ ✦ ✦ ✦ ✦

Annie Somerville's Spring Menu

Dragon greens, a spicy Asian slaw of green cabbage, scallions,
chilies, ginger, and Thai basil
Grilled vegetable and tofu brochettes
Coconut and jasmine rice
Spicy peanut sauce
Strawberry/mango compote with lime

DRAGON GREENS

This crunchy Asian slaw gives a refreshing twist to our grilled vegetable and tofu brochettes with spicy peanut sauce. If you don't have Thai basil in your garden, use cilantro and mint or another variety of basil instead.

Serves six.

1 medium head green cabbage, thinly sliced, about 8 cups
3 scallions, white and green parts, sliced on the diagonal
2 jalapeño chilies, cut in half, seeded, and thinly sliced
20 to 30 Thai basil leaves, bundled and
    thinly sliced, about ½ cup
Juice of 1 lime
1 tablespoon sugar
½ teaspoon salt
Rice vinegar

Combine the cabbage, scallions, chilies, and basil in a bowl and toss with the lime juice, sugar, and salt. Set aside to marinate for thirty minutes. Season to taste with a splash of vinegar if needed.

✦ ✦ ✦

❖ ❖ ❖ ❖ ❖ ❖ ❖ ❖ ❖ ❖ ❖ ❖ ❖ ❖ ❖

Annie Somerville's Summer Menu

Three-potato salad with triple treasure beans, capers,
and fines herbes
Open-face sandwiches of grilled hearth bread with Cowgirl Creamery
fromage blanc, *garden tomatoes, and opal basil*
Summer berries (black and red currants, alpine strawberries, golden raspberries,
and poorman gooseberries) with rose geranium crème anglaise

THREE-POTATO SALAD WITH TRIPLE TREASURE BEANS, CAPERS, AND FINES HERBES

This favorite summer salad features the cream of the potato crop—'Red Chieftain,' 'Rose Fir Apple,' and blue Peruvians. Just be sure to toss the warm potatoes gently with the vinaigrette, so they keep their shape. The cooking time for the beans will vary, so cook them separately if you're using different varieties.

Serves four to six.

> 2 pounds small potatoes
> Olive oil
> Salt and pepper
> Red wine mustard vinaigrette (recipe follows)
> ½ medium red onion, diced, about ½ cup
> Red wine vinegar
> ½ pound fresh summer beans: any combination,
>   stem ends trimmed and cut on the diagonal
> 1½ tablespoons capers, drained and rinsed
> 1 tablespoon chopped fines herbes—fresh
>   tarragon, parsley, chives, and chervil

✦　✦　✦　✦　✦　✦　✦　✦　✦　✦　✦　✦　✦　✦　✦　✦

Preheat the oven to 400°F.

Toss the potatoes in a baking dish with a little olive oil and sprinkle with salt and pepper. Cover and roast until tender, thirty-five to forty minutes. Set aside.

Make the vinaigrette.

Bring a pot of water to a boil and salt lightly. Place the onions in a small bowl and scoop a little water out of the pot, just enough to cover them. Let the onions soak for thirty seconds, drain, and toss with ½ tablespoon of the vinegar. Drop the beans into the boiling water and cook until just tender—one to two minutes for young green beans, up to six minutes for larger beans. Drain and rinse under cold water to keep them crisp.

When the potatoes are cool enough to handle, cut them into halves or quarters. Toss the warm potatoes in a large bowl with the beans, onions, capers, fines herbes, and the vinaigrette. Adjust the seasoning with salt, pepper, and a splash of vinegar, if needed.

RED WINE MUSTARD VINAIGRETTE
Makes about ½ cup.

3 tablespoons red wine vinegar
½ tablespoon Dijon or stone-ground mustard
½ teaspoon minced garlic
½ teaspoon salt
6 tablespoons extra-virgin olive oil

Whisk everything but the oil together in a small bowl. Slowly pour in the oil, whisking until emulsified.

✦　　✦　　✦

✦ ✦ ✦ ✦ ✦ ✦ ✦ ✦ ✦ ✦ ✦ ✦ ✦ ✦ ✦

Annie Somerville's Late-Autumn, Early-Winter Menu

Kabocha winter squash, 'Bleu de Solaize' leek, and apple soup with Cider Crème Fraîche
Bitter greens salad with 'Fuyu' persimmons, pomegranates, pistachios, and citrus honey vinaigrette
Warm herb bread with Bellwether Farms sheep's-milk ricotta
'Roxbury Russet' apple and sour cherry crisp with whipped cream from Straus Family Creamery

WINTER SQUASH, LEEK, AND APPLE SOUP
WITH CIDER CRÈME FRAÎCHE

This hearty roasted winter squash soup is deeply satisfying. We suggest kabocha or 'Red Kuri' if available, or butternut, or any other winter squash. We roast the squash to bring out the best of its flavor and texture.

Makes about two quarts.

6 cups vegetable stock (recipe follows)
1 large winter squash, about 4½ pounds,
    cut in half, seeds removed
1 tart apple, peeled, cored, and cut into quarters
1 tablespoon olive oil
2 leeks, white parts only, cut in half lengthwise,
    sliced, and washed, about 2 cups
Salt and pepper
½ tablespoon minced garlic
½ cup white wine
1 bay leaf
½ cup heavy cream
Cider Crème Fraîche (recipe follows)

396

❖ ❖ ❖ ❖ ❖ ❖ ❖ ❖ ❖ ❖ ❖ ❖ ❖ ❖ ❖

Preheat the oven to 400°F.

Make the stock and keep it warm over low heat.

Place the squash, cut side down, and the apples in a baking dish with a little water. Cover and roast until tender, thirty-five to forty minutes. When the squash is cool enough to handle, scoop it out of the skin. You should have about 6 cups.

Heat the oil in a soup pot and add the leeks, ½ teaspoon salt, and a pinch of pepper and cook until they begin to soften, about three minutes. Add the garlic and the wine and cook until the pot is nearly dry, about three minutes. Add the squash, the apples, the stock, ½ teaspoon salt, a pinch of pepper, and the bay leaf, and bring to a boil. Lower the heat and simmer, uncovered, about twenty minutes. Remove the bay leaf and purée the soup in a blender until smooth. Return to the pot, stir in the cream, and cook over low heat for fifteen minutes. Adjust the seasoning with salt and pepper.

Make the Cider Crème Fraîche and swirl a spoonful of it into each serving.

CIDER CRÈME FRAÎCHE
Makes about ⅓ cup.

⅓ cup crème fraîche
2 tablespoons apple juice

Whisk together in a small bowl.

VEGETABLE STOCK

This versatile stock is surprisingly rich, adding tremendous depth to many of our favorite dishes. It is just right for risotto and all kinds of soups and stews, both delicate and hearty. It's great for thinning leftover soups, ragouts, and pasta dishes, so double the recipe and freeze half of it for later. It keeps nearly indefinitely in the freezer, but only a day or two in the refrigerator.

Makes about two quarts.

1 large yellow onion, sliced

2 to 3 leek tops, chopped and washed

3 celery ribs, sliced

2 large carrots, sliced

½ pound white mushrooms, sliced

1 large potato, sliced

6 garlic cloves, smashed with the flat side
   of a knife, skins left on

1 teaspoon salt

½ teaspoon peppercorns

6 parsley sprigs

3 to 4 fresh thyme sprigs

2 fresh oregano or marjoram sprigs

5 fresh sage leaves

1 bay leaf

10 cups cold water

Combine all the ingredients in a stockpot and bring to a boil. Lower the heat and simmer, uncovered, for about forty-five minutes, stirring as needed. Pour the stock through a strainer, pressing as much liquid from the vegetables as possible, then discard them.

✦ ✦ ✦ ✦ ✦ ✦ ✦ ✦ ✦ ✦ ✦ ✦ ✦ ✦ ✦ ✦

The last time we were together, Annie surprised me by creating a savory dish she called "Dragon Greens," in honor of the spring cabbages that populate the Green Gulch fields with almost the same ferocious presence as their Tassajara relatives. I watched her as she composed this piquant Asian dish, surrounded by the harvested bounty of the Zen fields and by the lively group who had spent the day together. It was a little cold outside; a March wind licked closed the warm seams of the kitchen windows while fragrant steam rose from our old stovetop all the way up to the roof of the world.

I stood in the back of the kitchen, still wearing my garden overalls with an old blue denim apron over the top. I closed my eyes and let the tangy scent of the freshly cut cabbage carry me back to my first year of gardening so many years ago, in the Tassajara mountains. To my surprise the end of that infamous cabbage-season practice period came back to me. When the last Chinese cabbage of our winter lifeline was finally cut in early May of that year, a respected Tassajara monk suggested that we hold a special ceremony to honor the cabbage.

This ceremony was simple and intimate, convened after hours in the quiet of the Tassajara kitchen, and attended only by the cooking and gardening crews. My friend who had suggested the ceremony officiated; he was a newly ordained Zen priest, wrapped in reverence and wearing his best ceremonial robes. We entered the sanctuary of the kitchen solemnly bearing the sacrificial cabbage. Well-trained, I dropped my gaze, followed my breathing, and focused my eyes on the worn tiles of the Tassajara floor.

On the kitchen altar the last Chinese cabbage reclined ceremoniously on its right side, its green wrapper leaves tucked demurely beneath its ample carcass. It was a large cabbage, slightly limp, and clearly had expired of heat prostration. We gathered around the plump offering, chanted and bowed and offered incense to the cabbage while the altar candle flickered in the spring wind. From the core of the ceremony the celebrated cabbage expelled a long, world-weary sigh of farewell.

I had not thought of this ceremony for three decades, until Annie picked up a handful of cabbage leaves from our present-day garden and staccato-chopped them into fiery dragon greens. Then every cabbage throughout space and time gathered in the warmth of the Green Gulch kitchen as all beings in the ten directions entered the tangle at the dragon's gate and were fed.

RESOURCES

(For additional and updated resources, please visit www. gardeningatthedragonsgate.com.)

CHAPTER 1: VALLEY OF THE ANCESTORS

BOOKS

The Immense Journey: An Imaginative Naturalist Explores the Mysteries of Man and Nature, Loren Eiseley. New York: Vintage, 1959.
This beloved classic comes from a scientist who examines the natural world with reverence, curiosity, and enduring depth.

Assembling California, John McPhee. New York: Farrar, Straus and Giroux, 1993.
This excellent book investigates a cross-section of geologic and human time, unfolding with the suspense of an unsolvable mystery.

The Practice of the Wild, Gary Snyder. New York: Farrar, Straus and Giroux, 1990.
Like all of Snyder's works, this book is infused with animal sense and bare, poetic truth. The chapter "The Place, the Region and the Commons" is one of my favorites.

Gardening with a Wild Heart, Judith Larner Lowry. Berkeley: University of California Press, 1999.
This book pulses with life and is written by a colleague and local friend who gardens with the native plants and is the founder of Larner Seeds (see page 425).

Holdfast: At Home in the Natural World, Kathleen Dean Moore. Guilford, CT: The Lyons Press (an imprint of The Globe Pequot Press), 1999.
This collection of lyrical essays by a naturalist and philosopher examines our connections to home and our response to loss of anchorage in our lives.

Planetwalker: How to Change Your World One Step at a Time, John Francis. Point Reyes, CA: Elephant Mountain Press, 2005.
In this inspirational book, environmental activist and friend John Francis tells of his twenty-two years of walking across America, seventeen years in silence.

Home Ground: Language for an American Landscape, Barry Lopez, ed. San Antonio, TX: Trinity University Press, 2006.
A lexicon of American geography, literature, and natural history, this book is a tribute to people and their home landscapes.

Reading the Forested Landscape, Tom Wessels. Woodstock, VT: The Countryman Press, 1997.

This unforgettable book, written by my friend and mentor, ecologist Tom Wessels, is a deeply original portrait of the forests of New England. Tom teaches how to read a landscape from the outside in.

Garlic Is Life: A Memoir with Recipes, Chester Aaron. Berkeley: Ten Speed Press, 1996.
Written by a California neighbor who had a religious conversion experience brought on by fiery garlic, *Garlic Is Life* is a well-written delight.

For clear information about Zen practice these three books from the tradition of my root teachers have been invaluable:

Endless Vow: The Zen Path of Soen Nakagawa, Kaz Tanahashi and Sherry Chayat. Boston: Shambhala Publications, 1996.
A beautiful, spare introduction to the teaching of Zen master Soen Nakagawa, this is a collection of his poetry and journals.

Zen Mind, Beginner's Mind: Informal Talks on Zen Meditation and Practice, Shunryu Suzuki. Tokyo and New York: Weatherhill, 1972.
A classic introduction to the heart and mind of Zen, this book is from the spiritual founder of San Francisco Zen Center.

The Miracle of Mindfulness, Thich Nhat Hanh. Boston: Beacon Press, 1975.
A concise and inspired description of the basics of Zen mindfulness practice, this is a book for daily life.

ORGANIZATIONS, PUBLICATIONS, AND INFORMATION

The Orion Society
187 Main Street
Great Barrington, MA 01230-1601
413-528-4422
www.orionsociety.org
Orion, my favorite journal, comes from The Orion Society. The work of The Orion Society is rich in science, poetry, provocative writing, and raw truth.

Native Seeds/SEARCH
526 N. Fourth Avenue
Tucson, AZ 85705-8450
520-622-5561; 866-622-5561
www.nativeseeds.org
I am a dedicated member of this organization and a strong supporter of their work to preserve a diverse range of agricultural seed from the Southwest. The scope and scale of Native Seeds/SEARCH is vast — check them out.

CHAPTER 2: THE GARDEN MAKES THE GARDENER

BOOKS

Enduring Seeds, Gary Paul Nabham. Berkeley: North Point Press, 1989.

   In one of my favorite books of all time, Gary Paul Nabham brings botany alive through the stories of Native American agriculture and wild plant conservation.

Some Flowers, Vita Sackville-West (illustrated by Graham Rust). New York: Harry N. Abrams, 1993.

   Originally published by the author in 1937, this book describes twenty-four flowers in startling and erudite prose.

The Metamorphosis of Flowers, Claude Nuridsany and Marie Pérennou. New York: Harry N. Abrams, 1997.

   One of the most beautiful and beloved books in my library; the authors include the photographs of twenty species of flowers accompanied by a detailed and poetic text. This team also produced the classic text and film *Microcosmos*, on the life cycle of insects.

The Vegetable Garden, M. M. Vilmorin-Andrieux. Originally published in Paris, 1885; reissued by Berkeley: Ten Speed Press, 1981.

   This gardener's classic is a treasure store of information on fine vegetable cultivars and culture.

The Attentive Heart: Conversations with Trees, Stephanie Kaza (illustrated by Davis Te Selle). Boston: Shambhala Publications, 1996.

   Written and illustrated by two lifelong friends, this beautiful book opens a door of vision and delight into the world of trees, and beyond.

Green Thoughts: A Writer in the Garden, Eleanor Perrényi. New York: Random House, 1981.

   Highly useful and intimately personal, this book is an encyclopedia of inspiration from the green world of plants.

Botany for Gardeners, Brian Capon. Portland, OR: Timber Press, 1990.

   An excellent introduction and guide to basic horticultural botany, this book is well illustrated with clear photographs and drawings.

How Plants Grow: A Simple Introduction to Structural Botany, Asa Gray. (Out of print; used copies available.)

   This classic text on botany is one of my most beloved books and one of Harry Roberts's favorites. Complete with beautifully drawn diagrams of the parts of plants, the book opens new insight on each rereading.

The Complete Book of Fruits and Vegetables, Francesco Bianchini, Francesco Corbetta, and Marilena Pistoia. New York: Crown Publishers, 1976.

   This elegant book describes in detail the origins and uses of about 400 plants, accompanied by 110 superb watercolors.

The Secret Garden, by Frances Hodgson Burnett; *The Princess and the Goblin*, by George
   MacDonald (many editions); and *Tistou of the Green Thumbs*, by Maurice Druon. New
   York: Charles Scribner's Sons, 1957.
   These are my favorite garden-related children's books. Find them at all costs.
The Gift of Good Land, Wendell Berry. San Francisco: North Point Press, 1981.
   Gratitude to my special women friends at the Center for Ecoliteracy who directed my
   attention to Wendell Berry's essay, "Solving for Pattern," in this book. This essay has
   deepened my appreciation of the challenge of true garden design.
I Opened the Gate Laughing, Mayumi Oda. San Francisco: Chronicle Books, 2002.
   This is the story of the creation of a diverse garden of plants from all around the world,
   a garden which brought strength and clarity to artist and activist Mayumi Oda. The
   book is lavishly illustrated with the artist's paintings.
A Zen Wave, Robert Aitken. New York and Tokyo: Weatherhill, 1982.
   Haiku and Zen teaching both evoke the plant world in this wonderful text.
Crow With No Mouth: Ikkyū, Fifteenth Century Zen Master, Stephen Berg. Port Townsend,
   WA: Copper Canyon Press, 1995.
   One of my favorite Zen books, alive with the power of the raw world, conveyed in
   bare, brash poetry.

PERENNIAL NURSERIES
Every gardener has a unique style and personal involvement with plants. I prefer to
make my perennial plant selection by looking at the *actual* plants and how they are
grown, although there are a few mail-order houses I can recommend from positive,
direct experience.

For Fruit Trees and Fruit Plants
Trees of Antiquity
   20 Wellsona Road
   Paso Robles, CA 93446
   805-467-9909
   www.treesofantiquity.com
Southmeadow Fruit Gardens
   P.O. Box 211
   Baroda, MI 49101
   269-422-2411
   www.southmeadowfruitgardens.com

Roses
Pickering Nurseries
   3034 County Road #2, RR1
   Port Hope, Ontario L1A 3V5
   866-269-9282
   www.pickeringnurseries.com
Antique Rose Emporium
   10,000 Hwy. 50
   Brenham, TX 77833
   800-441-0002
   www.antiqueroseemporium.com

Greenmantle Nursery
   (roses and rare fruit trees)
   3010 Ettersburg Road
   Garberville, CA 95542
   707-986-7504
   www.greenmantlenursery.com
   $5 per catalog (this is my favorite
   of all plant mail-order catalogs)

Bulbs and Perennials
Ednie Flower Bulb
   37 Fredon-Marksboro Road
   Fredon, NJ 07860-5014
   1-800-24-EDNIE
   www.ednieflowerbulb.com
John Scheepers, Inc.
   23 Tulip Drive
   P.O. Box 638
   Bantam, CT 06750-0638
   860-567-8734
   www.johnscheepers.com

Unique Trees and Plants
Forestfarms
   900 Tetherow Road
   Williams, OR 97544-9599
   541-846-7269
   www.forestfarm.com

Mountain Maples
   P.O. Box 220
   Potter Valley, CA 95469
   888-707-6522
   www.mountainmaples.com
Wildwood Farm
   10300 Sonoma Highway
   Kenwood, CA 95452
   888-833-4181
   www.wildwoodmaples.com
Rare Conifer Nursery
   P.O. Box 100
   Potter Valley, CA 95469
   707-463-1245
Bear Creek Nursery
   P.O. Box 411
   Northport, WA 99157
   509-732-6219
   www.bearcreeknursery.com
Digging Dog Nursery
   P.O. Box 471
   Albion, CA 95410
   707-937-1130
   www.diggingdog.com
Raintree Nursery
   391 Butts Road
   Morton, WA 98356
   360-496-6400
   www.raintreenursery.com

CHAPTER 3: THE LIVING SOIL

BOOKS

The Soul of Soil, Grace Gershuny and Joseph Smillie. White River Junction, VT: Chelsea
Green Publishing Co., 1999.
This guide to ecological soil cultivation is clear, comprehensive, and based in organic
soil management procedures.

Dirt: The Ecstatic Skin of the Earth, William Bryant Logan. New York: Riverhead Books, 1995.
A profound natural history of the soil combining science, philosophy, and history
conveyed in elegant, quirky prose, this is one of my favorite books.

The Nature and Properties of Soils, H. O. Buckman and N. C. Brady. New York: Macmillan, 1974.
This is a classic textbook for the curious student of soil.

Soil Science Simplified, Helmut Kohnke and D. P. Franzmeier. Prospect Heights, IL: Wave-
land Press, 1995.
This guide to understanding the physical, chemical, and biological composition of
living soil is comprehensive and deeply scientific in its expression.

Altars of Unhewn Stone, Wes Jackson. Berkeley: Northpoint Press, 1987.
Calling for an agriculture that knows its oldest roots and does not destroy or sup-
plant human or biological communities, Wes Jackson is unrelenting in his love and
knowledge of the land.

Soil Biology Primer, Clive Edwards. Ankeny, IA: Soil Quality Institute with the USDA and
NRCS, 1999.
This excellent introduction to the vast living component of soil and how it contributes
to the health of countless beings is terse and richly informative.

Guide to Planet Earth, Art Sussman. White River Junction, VT: Chelsea Green Publishing
Co., 2000.
This is the excellent ecology textbook, short, sweet, and deep, that we use to teach
sixth-grade science and ecology at the Edible Schoolyard.

The Unsettling of America, Wendell Berry. San Francisco: Sierra Club Books, 1997.

Citizenship Papers, Wendell Berry. Washington, DC: Shoemaker & Hoard, 2003.
These books, and many others by the same author, span a twenty-five-year-deep river
of thought and commitment to sane farming. Berry's ideas are grounded in practical
knowledge, clear and passionate writing, and the joy of sustained work.

The Heart of Buddhist Meditation, Nyanaponika Thera. York Beach, ME: Samuel Weiser,
1965.

When I want to turn to a fundamental book on meditation, this book is my bedrock guide.

The Georgics of Virgil, translated by C. Day Lewis. New York: Oxford University Press, 1947. More than two thousand years old, this timeless pastoral poem elucidates the techniques and beauty of agriculture.

ORGANIZATIONS AND PUBLICATIONS

Ane Carla Rovetta

P.O. Box 155

Petaluma, CA 94953

707-762-5239

I have known Ane Carla for more than thirty years. A naturalist, artist, storyteller, and educator, she draws all of the materials for her craft from the natural world. To learn more, contact her directly.

Peaceful Valley Farm & Garden Supply

P.O. Box 2209

125 Clydesdale Court

Grass Valley, CA 95945

888-784-1722

www.groworganic.com

Founded by our lifelong friend and farm advisor Amigo Bob Cantisano, Peaceful Valley Farm Garden Supply produces a comprehensive catalog of tools, seeds, soil amendments, and sound organic philosophy. I read the Peaceful Valley catalog cover to cover every year and I always learn something new. In particular, I recommend *Know Your Soil*, a fifteen-page pamphlet that helps you read and understand your soil analysis. For more information on Amigo's work, and the rich organic teaching offered by Kalita Todd, Amigo's partner and wife, contact them at:

Organic Ag Advisors

Heaven and Earth Farm

P.O. Box 942

North San Juan, CA 95960

530-292-3619

www.aeoliaorganics.com

UCSC Farm and Garden Apprentice Program

    The Center for Agroecology and Sustainable Food Systems (CASFS)

    University of California at Santa Cruz

    1156 High Street

    Santa Cruz, CA 95064

    831-459-3240

    www.casfs.ucsc.edu/training/index.html

       This wonderful 6-month-long apprenticeship program was established with Alan Chadwick's original garden on the UCSC campus in 1967. Now in its fortieth year, the 27-acre farm and garden project welcomes 35 apprentices to the farm for intensive training from April to October.

Soil Association and Organic Farming Quarterly

    Soil Association

    South Plaza, Marlborough Street

    Bristol BS1 3NX, United Kingdom

    0117 314 5000

    www.soilassociation.org

Organic Materials Review Institute

    P.O. Box 11558

    Eugene, OR 97440-3758

    541-343-7600

    www.omri.org

       For a rich array of practices and principles connected to organic farming and gardening, please see their Web site.

California Certified Organic Farmers (CCOF)

    2155 Delaware Avenue, #150

    Santa Cruz, CA 95060

    831-423-2263

    www.ccof.org

       Green Gulch Farm has been CCOF certified for three decades and we are proud of this lineage. We also are certified by Marin Organic (P.O. Box 962, Pt. Reyes Station, CA 94956, 415-663-9667, www.marinorganic.org) since our farm is in Marin County and we want to support local organic standards that are of concern in our specific county.

Northeast Organic Farming Association (NOFA)

    Box 135

    Stevenson, CT 06491

    203-888-5146

    www.nofa.org

This organization certifies farms in Connecticut, Massachusetts, New Hampshire, New Jersey, New York, Rhode Island, and Vermont.

Maine Organic Farmers and Gardeners Association (MOFGA)

P.O. Box 170

294 Crosby Brook Road

Unity, ME 04988

207-568-4142

www.mofga.org

This organization publishes an excellent quarterly newsletter. For more information, visit their Web site.

CHAPTER 4: LIFE INTO DEATH INTO LIFE

BOOKS

An Agricultural Testament, Sir Albert Howard. London: Oxford University Press, 1940; and *Soil and Health*, Sir Albert Howard. New York: Schocken Books, 1947.

These two classic books on the source of fertility arising from the decay and life of the forest both offer a clear, early articulation of ecological composting based in the preservation and formation of humus.

Culture and Horticulture: A Philosophy of Gardening, Wolf Storl. Available through the Biodynamic Farming and Gardening Association (see Resources for chapter 5).

I refer to this book steadily—it is an old friend, a clear and inspiring text on biodynamic methods to conserve and build fertility in the home garden and beyond.

Worms Eat My Garbage, Mary Appelhof and Mary F. Fenton. Kalamazoo, MI: Flower Press, revised edition, 1997.

This is a classic manual on introducing and cultivating worm colonies to enhance garden fertility.

Feed the Soil, Edwin McLeod. Graton, CA: Organic Agriculture Research Institute, 1982. Available through Peaceful Valley catalog and Harmony Farm catalog (see Resources listings for chapters 3 and 6).

A definitive text on the art and use of cover crops to build fertility in the home garden, the book outlines and discusses over a hundred crop mixes.

Compost Tea Brewing Manual, Dr. Elaine Ingram. Available at Peaceful Valley Farm Web site: www.groworganic.com.

This is a comprehensive pamphlet about making, applying, and assessing compost tea for the home garden.

Lovingkindness: The Revolutionary Art of Happiness, Sharon Salzberg. New York: Random House, 2002.

Loving-kindness is taught and conveyed by a teacher deeply seasoned in the practice. This attitude and activity are the abiding source of a fertile, well-grounded life.

Taking Our Places: The Buddhist Path of Truly Growing Up, Norman Fischer. New York: HarperCollins, 2003.

Written by my friend and Zen colleague of three decades, this is a simple and profound book on maturation.

ORGANIZATIONS AND PUBLICATIONS

Ecology Action/Bountiful Gardens

18001 Shafer Ranch Road

Willits, CA 95490

707-459-6410

www.bountifulgardens.org

www.ecoact.org

Begun in 1970, this organization has a thriving research garden, food-growing projects in many countries, an active apprenticeship program, a fine seed and resource catalog, as well as numerous teaching pamphlets outlining the thirty-plus years of research by John Jeavons and others.

For excellent information on the soil-food web of microorganisms at work in your compost pile and garden here are a few contacts that I find inspiring:

A recent publication entitled *Indigenous Microorganisms Revisited*, by Gil A. Carandang at Herbana Farms, Burol, Calamba City, Laguna, Philippines (gil_carandang@hotmail.com) has us all astir in the organic farming network. This is fresh research on culturing beneficial indigenous microorganisms and bionutrients through natural, backyard recipes and farming practices.

The research and development of Professor Elaine Ingham, who teaches at Oregon State University, is available through the Soil Foodweb Institute: Soil Foodweb Oregon, LLC, 1750 SW 3rd St., Suite K, Corvallis OR 97333-1796. Web site: www.soilfoodweb.com.

Necessary Organics

P.O. Box 603

One Nature's Way

New Castle, VA 94127-0605

800-447-5354

This organization is an excellent source of organic fertilizers and amendments.

Intervale Center

    180 Intervale Road

    Burlington, VT 05401

    802-660-0440

    www.intervale.org

    I have visited the working farm of the Intervale Center in Burlington, Vermont, with its gigantic compost operation, sustainable businesses, and fuel and fiber production. They also host a thriving farmers' market and CSA operation. The founding organization, Gardener's Supply Company, is also on the Intervale site.

CHAPTER 5: TENDING THE GARDEN

BOOKS

Rodale's All-New Encyclopedia of Organic Gardening, Bradley and Ellis, eds. Emmaus, PA: Rodale Press, 1993.

    In publication since 1959, this practical volume offers newly updated material and research on gardening organically. The definitive resource book!

How to Grow More Vegetables, John Jeavons. Berkeley, CA: Ten Speed Press, seventh edition, 2006. Available in many languages through Ecology Action Network (listed in Resources for chapter 4).

    From the teaching lineage of Alan Chadwick, this is a classic on the biointensive method of growing and maintaining a productive organic garden at home.

Designing and Maintaining Your Edible Landscape Naturally, Robert Kourik. Santa Rosa, CA: Metamorphic Press, 1986.

    I always feel that I am visiting a lifelong friend when I open this highly original and valuable book for the home gardener.

Golden Gate Gardening, Pam Pierce and Pam Dardick. Seattle: Sasquatch Books, revised edition, 1998.

    This is a complete guide to year-round food production and to organic garden culture for the Bay Area, although Pam's research and organization makes her book widely relevant to long-season growing climates around the country.

The New Organic Grower, Elliot Coleman. White River Junction, VT: Chelsea Green Publishing Co., 1989.

    Written by a pioneer in the organic movement, this is a clear and creative guide to setting up a productive organic operation. Elliot's more recent book, *Four-Season Harvest*, shows North American gardeners how to grow fresh produce throughout the year.

The Organic Method Primer, Bargyla Glyrer Rateaver. San Diego, CA: Rateavers Press, 1993.
An excellent guide to organic gardening with a new section on plant absorption of nutrients, this book is well worth finding and adding to your library.

Step by Step Organic Vegetable Gardening, Shepard Ogden. New York: HarperCollins, 1992.
Building on the work of his grandfather, Shep has added his own considerable research, experience, and love to produce a clear, relevant, and inspiring book.

Weeds and What They Tell, E. E. Pfeiffer. Wyoming, RI: Bio-Dynamic Farming and Gardening Association, Inc., 1981.
With scientific rigor and clarity Dr. Pfeiffer shares his research and observations on the importance of weeds in garden ecosystems.

Weeds: Guardians of the Soil, Joseph A. Cocannover. New York: The Devin-Adair Co., 1950.
In praise of weeds for their vital function in building, maintaining, and protecting fertility, this classic book is radical in its reach.

Pruning and Training, Christopher Brickell and David Joyce. New York: DK Publishing, 1996.
A fully illustrated plant-by-plant manual to over 800 garden plants. In addition to this book, Brickell is editor-in-chief of the Simon and Schuster step-by-step encyclopedia of practical gardening, a fine series published in cooperation with the Royal Horticultural Society.

Sensitive Chaos, Theodore Schwenk. London: Rudolph Steiner Press, 1971.
Water is life, and this book is a tribute to the movement and mystery of water.

Water and the Cycle of Life, Joseph A. Cocannover. New York: The Devin-Adair Company, 1962.
This simple, elegant book traces the natural cycle of water from ocean, to air, to land, to plant and back again to air and ocean. It includes an excellent glossary of water terms.

Drip Irrigation for Every Landscape and All Climates, Robert Kounk. Santa Rosa, CA: Metamorphic Press, 1992.
A classic volume about the principles of water conservation and irrigation design.

ORGANIZATIONS AND PUBLICATIONS

Rodale Institute
611 Siegfriedale Rd.
Kutztown, PA 19530-9320
610-683-1400
www. rodaleinstitute.org

One of the oldest and finest American sources of organic gardening information, this nonprofit educational organization publishes a wealth of books as well as a monthly magazine, *Organic Gardening*.

Biodynamic Farming and Gardening Association, Inc.

25844 Butler Road

Junction City, OR 97448

541-998-0105

888-516-7797

www.biodynamics.com

This membership organization has a wealth of teaching and learning materials, including an excellent press, catalog, and biodynamic supply inventory. I particularly love using their planting calendar, "Stella Natura."

Gardener's Supply Company

128 Intervale Road

Burlington, VT 05401

888-833-1412

www.gardeners.com

Connected to the Intervale Center, this tool and supply store also offers seeds and plants and garden furniture. They have a mail-order catalog.

Mellingers, Inc.

2310 W. South Range Road

North Lima, OH 44452

800-321-7444

www.mellingers.com

This heritage company offers an extensive range of home garden and nursery supplies.

Raindrip, Inc.

337 West Bedford Ave.

Fresno, CA 93711

800-FOR-DRIP

www.raindrip.com

This is a good source of drip irrigation systems and supplies.

Bullfrog Films

P.O. Box 149

Oley, PA 19547

800-543-3764

www.bullfrogfilms.com

This organization has an excellent inventory of educational and entertaining films about ecology, the environment, politics, and social and environmental justice.

Educational and Training Video Catalog

P.O. Box 6715

Los Osos, CA 93412

805-528-8322

This organization also offers excellent audiovisual teaching aids for agricultural, botanical, horticultural, ecological, and environmental justice interests.

CHAPTER 6: GARDENING WITH ALL BEINGS

BOOKS

The Gardener's Guide to Common-Sense Pest Control, William and Helga Olkowski and Sheila Daar. Newtown, CT: Taunton Press, 1996.

The definitive text on integrated pest management for the home and garden.

Pests of the Garden and Small Farm, Mary Louise Flint. Berkeley: University of California Press, 1999.

For gardeners interested in nontoxic management of pesky insects, slugs, and snails, plant disease, and weeds, this book is essential, with its 250 large, clear photographs that help with accurate definition of your problem.

Controlling Pests and Diseases, Patricia S. Michalak and Linda A. Gilkeson. Emmaus, PA: Rodale Press, 1994.

This book offers a succinct description of pest and disease symptoms and provides a wealth of organic solutions.

The Forgotten Pollinators, Gary Paul Nabham and Stephan Buchmann. Washington, DC: Island Press, 1996.

When this book first came out I attended an unforgettable slide show about the authors' research. They explore the vital relationship between plants and their pollinators, offering vivid examples of the connection between endangered species and their threatened habitats.

The Voice of the Infinite in the Small, Joanne E. Lauck. Boston: Shambhala Publications, 2002.

This compilation of information and perspectives from science, mythology, history, and indigenous traditions helps us reenvision the insect-human connection.

Broadsides from the Other Orders, Sue Hubbell. New York: Random House, 1993.

Did you know that for every pound of human life in the world there is estimated to be three hundred pounds of insect life? This wonderful and scientific book highlights the rich brocade of interwoven life within thirteen selected orders of insects.

Borne on the Wind, Stephen Dalton. New York: Readers' Digest Press of E. P. Dutton & Co., Inc., 1975 (out of print but available used).

The message of this book is conveyed in extraordinary photographs that show insects on the wing and in association with their preferred plants.

Thinking Like a Mountain: Towards a Council of All Beings, Joanna Macy and John Seed. Philadelphia: New Society Publishers, 1988.

This slim volume contains a wealth of creative exercises for seeing and summoning the more-than-human world that we so influence by the way we live on earth.

ORGANIZATIONS AND PUBLICATIONS

I recommend that every serious gardener find a trained guide to help them understand and see the vast world of insects. Kate Burroughs is such a guide for me. Trained entomologist and dedicated organic farmer, Kate and her husband, David Henry, are the founders of Harmony Farm.

Harmony Farm Supply and Nursery
    3244 Hwy. 116 North
    Sebastopol, CA 95472
    707-823-9125
    www.harmonyfarm.com
        Committed to organic farming and gardening, this organization maintains a full inventory of seeds, books, plants, tools, IPM supplies and experience, and much more. They also produce a wonderful mail-order catalog.

BioQuip Products
    2321 Gladwick Street
    Rancho Dominguez, CA 90220
    310-667-8800
    www.bioquip.com
        This company offers equipment, supplies, audiovisual aids, and books for entomological and related services.

Bio-Integral Resource Center
    P.O. Box 7414
    Berkeley, CA 94707
    510-524-2567
    www.birc.org

BIRC specializes in finding nontoxic and least-toxic, integrated pest management (IPM) solutions to urban and agricultural pest problems. Years ago the folks at BIRC helped develop IPM programs for the city of Berkeley. What great teachers!

Digger's Product Development Company

Box 1551

Soquel, CA 95073

831-462-6095

www.califdir.com/digger-s-p-soquel-biz472689.htm

Go to this great source of underground, wire-mesh baskets for help with gophers. Be sure to order galvanized cages, which last best in the soil.

Planet Natural

1612 Gold Avenue

Bozeman, MT 59715

www.planetnatural.com

Beneficial insects, pheromone traps, botanical pesticides, and more are available here.

CHAPTER 7: RETURNING TO ORIGIN

BOOKS

Gardening for the Future of the Earth, Howard Yana Shapiro and John Harrison. New York: Bantam Books, 2000.
This book brings together the ecological gardening techniques of strong pioneers in the organic movement with a special emphasis on kinship gardening and preserving genetic heritage through maintaining a diverse seed bank.

The Sacred Balance: Rediscovering Our Place in Nature, David Suzuki, with Amanda McConnell. New York: Prometheus Books, 1998.
A complex and fascinating expression of an environmental ethic, this book combines conservation biology, theology, poetry, and engaged ecological activism.

Opening the Hand of Thought, Kosho Uchiyama. Boston: Wisdom Publications, 2004.
A Zen classic on the fundamental practice of deep sitting, the seed of awareness in the garden of meditation.

The One-Straw Revolution, Masanobu Fukuoka. Emmaus, PA: Rodale Press, 1978.
A classic in the organic growing network, Fukuoka Sensei's book outlines the methods of natural farming he developed in his Japanese homeland. We were fortunate to work with Fukuoka Sensei at Green Gulch in the 1970s.

Hartmann and Kester's Plant Propagation: Principles and Practices, H. T. Hartmann, D. E. Kester, et al. Upper Saddle River, NJ: Pearson Education, 2001.

This excellent textbook covers all aspects of scientific plant propagation from both the theoretical and applied points of view. Indispensable.

Hortus Third: A Concise Dictionary of Plants Cultivated in the USA and Canada, Bailey Hortorium. New York: John Wiley & Sons, 1976.

A vast list of plants in a clear and usable format.

Secrets of Plant Propagation, Lewis Hill. North Adams, MA: Storey Books, 1984.

A delight to read, this practical guide to plant propagation is written by a seasoned plantsman and deeply experienced propagator.

Monocultures of the Mind, Vandana Shiva. London: Zed Books, 1995.

Along with her more recent books, *Bio Piracy: The Plunder of Nature and Knowledge* and *Stolen Harvest*, environmental thinker and activist Vandana Shiva presents a sound critique of the dangers of global ownership of nature's harvest of seed and food.

Seed to Seed, Suzanne Ashworth. Decorah, IA: Seed Savers Exchange, Inc., 1991.

The best seed-saving resource book I know, this text includes all of the major families of vegetables with their requirements for careful seed preservation.

Faith in a Seed, Henry David Thoreau. Washington, DC: Island Press, 1993.

In addition to several of Thoreau's late natural history writings, this book contains his hitherto unpublished work "The Dispersion of Seed."

Cloning the Buddha, Richard Heinberg. Wheaton, IL: Quest Books, 1999.

Using research and examples from plant and animal research, the author offers a provocative consideration of the moral impact of biotechnology.

Seeds of Change, Kenny Ausubel. HarperSanFrancisco, 1994.

This clear and well-documented book from the founder of Seeds of Change Seed Company tells the dramatic story of the growing movement to preserve biodiversity.

Biodynamic Greenhouse Management, Heinz Grotzke, 1998. Available through the Biodynamic Farming and Gardening Association (see Resources for chapter 5).

A wonderfully simple and profound book about the art and practice of raising plants under glass.

ORGANIZATIONS AND PUBLICATIONS

Seed Savers Exchange

Rt. 3, Box 239

3094 North Winn Road

Decorah, IA 52101

563-382-5990

www.seedsavers.org

This worldwide nonprofit membership-based organization is dedicated to the preservation and distribution of heritage seed. It offers an excellent newsletter, seed bank, and seed catalog. This is one of the most important organizations you can support.

Worldwatch Institute

1776 Massachusetts Avenue NW

Washington, DC 20036

563-382-5990

www.worldwatch.org

This nonprofit membership organization provides comprehensive summaries on the current health of the global environment. Publishers of the annual "State of the World," the Worldwatch Institute has been educating the public for more than twenty-five years.

Trust for Public Land (TPL)

116 New Montgomery Street

4th Floor

San Francisco, CA 94105

1-800-714-LAND

www.tpl.org

Since they were founded in the 1970s, TPL has saved more than 2 million acres of land for people throughout the United States. The founder of TPL, Huey Johnson, an internationally distinguished environmentalist, introduced SFZC to George Wheelwright and made possible the establishment of Green Gulch Farm Zen Center.

Bioneers

Collective Heritage Institute

6 Carro Circle

Lamy, NM 87540

www.bioneers.org

In 1990 Kenny Ausabel and Nina Simons created the Bioneers organization to honor the interdependence of all life on Earth. Each year a huge conference is held to bring together innovative leaders and learners in the field of ecology and the environment, indigenous knowledge, food and farming, science, medicine, and the arts.

CHAPTER 8: BEAUTY COUNTS

BOOKS

In the Eye of the Garden, Mirabel Osler. New York: Macmillan Publishing Co., 1993.
Whimsical, yet rooted in the earth, this book combines rich horticultural experience with imagination and a love of rough and refined beauty.

Gardening from the Heart: Why Gardeners Garden, Carol Olwell. Berkeley: Antelope Island Press, 1990.
> Twenty-one intimate interviews with gardeners from all over the world.

Epitaph for a Peach: Four Seasons on My Family Farm, David Mas Masumoto. San Francisco, CA: HarperCollins, 1995.
> This beautiful book follows Masumoto's yearlong attempt to keep his Sun Crest peaches alive. The writing is strong and eloquent, alive with the flavor of summer peaches.

The Poetics of the Garden, Charles Moore, William Mitchell, and William Turnbull, Jr. Cambridge, MA: MIT Press, 1995.
> In this pattern book a score of landscapes and gardens are drawn following the "dragon-veins" of their home terrain. This is one of my favorite books on garden design.

Ecological Design, Sim Van Der Ryn and Stuart Cowan. Washington, DC: Island Press, 1996.
> A book not of things but of natural and designed systems in deep, ecological conversation, this coherent text is permeated with vision and inspiration.

Farming with the Wild, Daniel Imhoff. San Francisco: Watershed Media Books/Sierra Club Books, 2003.
> Featuring profiles from more than twenty North American states, this compelling book shows a future where farming, gardening, and ranching are integrated into their natural landscapes and designed with the genius of place foremost in mind.

The Medicine Wheel Garden, E. Barrie Kavasch. New York: Bantam Books, 2002.
> This book draws on the ancient pattern of the Native American medicine wheel to design sacred space for healing, celebration, and reflection.

Gardens of Illusion, Sara Maitland and Peter Matthews. New York: Sterling Publishing Company, 2002.
> Living gardens do not behave—they disappear and enchant, amuse and infect with their elusiveness. This book pays tribute to such ephemeral gardens.

Moon in a Dewdrop: Writings of Zen Master Dogen, Kazuaki Tanahashi, ed. San Francisco: North Point Press, 1985.
> Dogen's thought runs counter to conventional logic, a quality absolutely necessary in creating true gardens.

Wild Mind: Living the Writer's Life, Natalie Goldberg. New York: Bantam Books, 1996.
> The author of eleven fine books anchored in the old terrain of original meditation and the writing life, Natalie Goldberg writes with compassion and deep authenticity. *Wild Mind* is one of my favorite zen books.

Traces of Time: The Beauty of Change in Nature, Pat Murphy and Paul Doherty. San Francisco: Chronicle Books, 2000.

Physicist and photographer collaborate in this strong book that tracks the passage of time through events that last a fraction of a second as well as those that reveal themselves over millions of years.

Adventures of a Gardener, Peter Smithers. London: The Havrill Press with The Royal Horticultural Society, 1995.

This exquisite and classic book begins with the author's twelve principles for his garden, fair warning, and strong inspiration for any who contemplate embarking upon these adventures.

PUBLICATIONS AND ORGANIZATIONS

Occidental Arts and Ecology Center

15290 Coleman Valley Road

Occidental, CA 95465

707-874-1557

www.oaec.org

This nonprofit organization and education center includes beautiful, organically grown gardens both at the center and at the nearby AIDS food bank, Food for Thought. Much of the center's work addresses the challenge of creating communities that are ecologically, economically, and culturally sustainable and renewed by the active presence of art and creativity. See the website for a complete list of programs.

Center for Ecoliteracy

2528 San Pablo Avenue

Berkeley, CA 94702

510-845-4595

www.ecoliteracy.org

This nonprofit organization supports ecoliteracy in public school programs for grades K–12. I have been privileged to be part of the ecoliteracy team for many years, learning and growing together in the real world. Be sure to check out their wellness guide and information on rethinking school lunch.

Vallecitos Mountain Refuge

P.O. Box 3160

Taos, NM 87571

505-751-3160

www.vallecitos.org

The Vallecitos Mountain Refuge is a 132-acre wildlife refuge and wilderness ranch high in the Rocky Mountains of northern New Mexico. Surrounded by thousands of acres of old-growth forest, Vallecitos is a contemplative retreat center seeking to strengthen and support nonprofit leaders, environmental activists, and advocacy organizations working for social change. I have been teaching meditation and mindfulness practice at Vallecitos every year since 1998, a privilege I look forward to all year.

Center for Whole Communities
Knoll Farm
700 Bragg Hill Road
Fayston, VT 05673
802-496-5690
www.wholecommunities.org

This organization aims to create a more just, balanced, and healthy society by exploring, honoring, and deepening the connections between land, people, and communities. The CWC offers trainings and teachings for activists working in a new land movement that integrates a commitment to diversity, conservation, health, justice, spirit, and relationship. I have the honor and pleasure to teach meditation and gardening at Knoll Farm during their summer programs.

SEED COMPANIES

Here is an abbreviated list of my favorite seed companies. As much as possible, I support small seed companies that offer organically grown seeds.

Abundant Life Seeds
P.O. Box 157
Saginaw, OR 97472-0157
541-767-9606
www.abundantlifeseeds.com

Larner Seeds: Seeds of California
Native Plants
P.O. Box 407
Bolinas, CA 94924
415-868-9407
www.larnerseeds.com

Bountiful Gardens
18001 Shafer Ranch Road
Willits, CA 95490-9626
707-459-6410
www.bountifulgardens.org

Garden City Seeds
778 Highway 93N
Hamilton, MT 59840-9448
406-961-4837
www.gardencityseeds.net

Native Seeds/SEARCH
526 N. Fourth Avenue
Tucson, AZ 85705
520-622-5561
www.nativeseeds.org

Seed Savers Exchange
3094 North Winn Road
Decorah, IA 52101
563-382-5990
www.seedsavers.org

Inside Passage
P.O. Box 639
Port Townsend, WA 98368
800-361-9657
www.insidepassageseeds.com

Territorial Seed Company
P.O. Box 157
Cottage Grove, OR 97424
800-626-0866
www.territorial-seed.com

Wild Garden Seed
Shoulder to Shoulder Farm
P.O. Box 1509
Philometh, OR 97370
541-929-4068
www.wildgardenseed.com

High Mowing Seeds
76 Quarry Road
Wolcott, VT 05680
802-472-6174
www.highmowingseeds.com

The Cooks Garden Seed
P.O. Box 535
Londonderry, VT 05148
802-824-3400

Baker Creek Heirloom Seeds
2278 Baker Creek Road
Mansfield, MO 65704
417-924-8917
www.rareseeds.com

DeGiorgi Seed Company
6011 N. Street
Omaha, NE 68117-1634
402-731-3901

Johnny's Selected Seeds
955 Benton Avenue

Winslow, ME 04901
www.johnnyseeds.com
877-564-6697

Turtle Tree Seed: Bio Dynamic Seeds
Camphill Village
Copake, NY 12516
888-516-7797
www.turtletreeseeds.com

Southern Exposure Seed Exchange
P.O. Box 460
Mineral, VA 23117
540-894-9480
www.southernexposure.com

Stokes Seed Co., Inc.
P.O. Box 548
Buffalo, NY 14240
416-688-4300
www.stokeseeds.com

Thompson and Morgan
P.O. Box 1308
Jackson, NJ 08527
800-274-7333 or 201-363-2225
www.thompson-morgan.com

Nichol's Garden Nursery
190 Old Salem Road NE
Albany, OR 97321-4580
800-422-3985
www.nicholsgardennursery.com

J. L. Hudson, Seedsman
Box 337
La Honda, CA 94020-0337
www.jlhudsonseeds.net

Kitazawa Seed Company
P.O. Box 13220
Oakland, CA 94661-3220
510-595-1188

Plants of the Southwest
   3095 Agua Fria Road
   Santa Fe, NM 87507
   505-438-8888
   www.plantsofthesouthwest.com
Renée's Garden Seeds
   6116 Highway 9
   Felton, CA 95018
   888-880-7228
   www.reneesgarden.com

Hawai'i SEED
   P.O. Box 2353
   Kealakekua, HI 96750
   808-331-1211
   www.hawaiiseed.org

CHAPTER 9: HARVESTING FIELDS OF GREENS

BOOKS

Fields of Plenty: A Farmer's Journey in Search of Real Food and the People Who Grow It, Michael Ableman. San Francisco: Chronicle Books, 2005.
   Michael Ableman is a front-line farmer and champion of organic agriculture. I have followed Michael's work for fifteen years, through his farms and his beautiful books, *From the Good Earth, On Good Land*, and now *Fields of Plenty*.

Sharing the Harvest: A Guide to Community-Supported Agriculture, Elizabeth Henderson and Robyn Van En. White River Junction, VT: Chelsea Green Publishing Co., 1999.
   This practical and inspiring volume about gardeners sharing the harvest of their hands and hearts was written by two lifelong friends and farmers.

The Gardener's Table, Richard Merrill and Joe Ortiz. Berkeley: Ten Speed Press, 2000.
   This guide to natural vegetable growing and cooking is rich in flavor and information. Richard Merrill is one of my most valued garden mentors.

Seed to Civilization, Charles Heiser, Jr. Cambridge, MA: Harvard University Press, 1990.
   A staple book in the field of agriculture and the unfolding of civilization, this story of food is told in clear, scientific, and inspiring language.

The Healing Fields: Working with Psychotherapy and Nature to Rebuild Shattered Lives, Jenny Grut and Sonja Linden. London: Frances Lincoln, 2007.
   Meeting Jenny Grut and reading her book about gardens healing the lives of torture victims has made me a fiercer and more dedicated gardener.

Already Home, Barbara Gates. Boston: Shambhala Publications, 2003.
   This is a strong story of strong roots growing deeper into neighborhood soil, written

by a close friend and colleague.

Blue Corn and Square Tomatoes, Rebecca Rupp. Pownal, VT: A Garden Way Publishing Book, 1987.

For the sheer joy of comic relief and wild amazement, especially if you have ever wondered why chili peppers are hot or some corn is steel blue, read this book.

Seedfolks, Paul Fleischman. New York: HarperCollins, 1997.

I should have known it when I picked up this slim volume of unfathomable depth by the author of one of my very favorite poetry books for children, *Joyful Noise*, but still I was unprepared for the raw wisdom of *Seedfolks*. Just read it.

How to Cook Your Life: From the Zen Kitchen to Enlightenment, Kosho Uchiyama. Boston: Shambhala Publications, 2005.

You can taste the depth of Zen master Dogen's thirteenth-century text, *Instructions for the Zen Cook*, in this classic of the Zen world. Uchiyama Roshi's essays and commentary on the text are big-minded and large-hearted.

Coming Back to Life, Joanna Macy and Molly Brown. Gabriola Island, B.C.: New Society Publishers, 1998.

This wonderful book contains decades of original thought and practical exercises to help restore the spirit of activists working on behalf of our world.

An Inconvenient Truth, Al Gore. Emmaus, PA: Rodale Press, 2006.

In conjunction with the 2007 Academy Award–winning documentary film of the same name and by the same author, co-recipient of the 2007 Nobel Peace Prize, this book brings the current reality of global climate change into stark and clear relief. Bill McKibben first alerted readers to climate change in his 1980s classic, *The End of Nature*. Al Gore continues to examine the inconvenient truth of human impact on the health of planet earth.

Here are my very favorite food-related books, including the work of my three closest cooking colleagues from San Francisco Zen Center.

Chez Panisse Vegetables, Alice Waters (illustrated by Patricia Curtain). New York: Harper-Collins, 1996.

All of the savory books written by Alice Waters have been a primary inspiration in my life, and I particularly love this volume on vegetables with its beautiful letterpress block prints by artist Patricia Curtain. Alice Waters is the founder of Chez Panisse restaurant and the Edible Schoolyard program in Berkeley, California.

Cooking from the Garden, Rosalind Creasy. San Francisco: Sierra Club Books, 1988.

This book came out the year our daughter was born, and I remember poring over the recipes and beautiful photographs with a sense of joy and well-being, which does not fade.

Grub: Ideas for an Urban Organic Kitchen, Anna Lappé and Bryant Terry. New York: Jeremy Tarcher/Penguin Group, 2006.

This book is full of nourishing recipes and information from its two young authors about independent organic farming bringing "fair food" to the table. Hungry for some inspiring and nourishing grub? Try the "Straight Edge Punk Brunch".

Fast Food Nation, Eric Schlosser. New York: Houghton Mifflin, 2001.

This important exposé of the nutritional, environmental, and cultural damage caused by corporate fast food is essential reading. Eric Schlosser has spoken and taught with us at Martin Luther King, Jr. Middle School, where he presented *Chew on This*, his 2005 sequel to *Fast Food Nation* written especially for young people.

The Omnivore's Dilemma, Michael Pollan. New York: The Penguin Press, 2006.

In this excellent and elegant book the author traces the natural history of four meals and four food chains—industrial food; organic or alternative food; and foraged food—from their sources to the table. Essential nourishment.

The Tassajara Bread Book and *The Tassajara Recipe Book*, Edward Espe Brown. Boston: Shambhala, 1995 and 2000, respectively.

These books are splattered with dough, hot oil, and earnest effort to produce good food guided by the love and attention that Ed shares with all of us.

Local Flavors: Cooking and Eating from America's Farmers' Markets, Deborah Madison. New York: Broadway Books, 2002.

This most recent of Deborah's many wonderful cooking books evokes her creative spirit and passionate talent as well as her deep involvement and support of local farmers' markets. We spent many hours together at Green Gulch and the taste of our relationship lingers on for me in Deborah's cookbooks.

Everyday Greens: How to Cook 200 of the Most Popular Dishes from Greens, America's Celebrated Vegetarian Restaurant, Annie Somerville. New York: Scribner Press, 2003.

Annie Somerville is my cooking sister. We have worked shoulder to shoulder for close to fifteen years, and every time I am with Annie in the kitchen she opens a new world for me. I love this latest book from the hearth of Greens Restaurant, so beautifully illustrated with Mayumi Oda's paintings of rambunctious vegetables.

ORGANIZATIONS AND PUBLICATIONS

The Garden Project

P.O. Box 24292

Pier 28

San Francisco, CA 94124

650-266-9513

www.gardenproject.org

Our family has been intimately connected for almost twenty years with this extraordinary gardening project designed for prisoners at the San Francisco County Jail, for ex-offenders and their families, and for hungry people throughout the greater San Francisco Bay Area. Founder and close friend Catherine Sneed says quite simply, "Gardens save lives," and the Garden Project proves this every day.

The Edible Schoolyard

Martin Luther King, Jr. Middle School

1781 Rose Street

Berkeley, CA 94703

510-558-1335

www.edibleschoolyard.org

A nonprofit within a public school? With an acre-plus garden and thriving kitchen classroom as well? Yes indeed! The Edible Schoolyard is a tribute to learning in the real world and to the power of nine hundred creative middle-schoolers and their teachers and community who make this extraordinary project a reality, day by day. It is my privilege and honor to be a mentor and guide in this fine program supported by the Chez Panisse Foundation (www.chezpanisse.com/pgcpfoundation).

Slow Food USA

20 Jay Street, Suite 313

Brooklyn, NY 11201

718-260-8000

www.slowfoodusa.org

This organization founded in 1986 in Italy now is active worldwide with over eighty thousand members. They host a biennial gathering, Terra Madre, that convenes farmers, chefs, and producers of beautiful food from more than 150 countries.

Sustainable Agriculture Education (SAGE)

1417 Josephine Street

Berkeley, CA 94703

510-526-1793

www.sagecenter.org

SAGE was begun by Peter's and my friend Sibella Kraus in 2001. The dual mission of SAGE is to develop urban-edge agriculture as a vital urban-rural interface and to engage California's diverse population in regional food and agricultural systems. SAGE provides services in four main areas: agricultural parks, urban-edge agriculture and new ruralism, public and farmers' markets, and agricultural education.

The Ecological Farming Association

    406 Main Street, Suite 313

    Watsonville, CA 95076

    831-763-2111

    www.eco-farm.org

    Peter and I have been active members of the EFA for more than twenty-five years. Not only does this fine outfit of friends and colleagues support all aspects of ecological agriculture, they also host the nationally attended Eco-Farm conference held every January in Asilomar, California.

Community Food Security Coalition

    P.O. Box 209

    Venice, CA 90294

    310-822-5410

    www.foodsecurity.org

    The Community Food Security Coalition (CFSC) is a non-profit organization dedicated to building strong, sustainable, local and regional food systems that ensure access to affordable, nutritious, and culturally appropriate food for all people at all times. They seek to develop self-reliance among all communities in obtaining their food and to create a system of growing, manufacturing, processing, making available, and selling food that is regionally based and grounded in the principles of justice, democracy, and sustainability. This is a wonderful organization, worthy of support.

Gardening With Kids

    National Gardening Association

    1100 Dorset Street

    South Burlington, VT 05403

    800-538-7476

    www.kidsgardening.com

    This catalog, along with the newsletter *Growing Ideas*, offers a wealth of ideas as well as materials from aquatic plants to worm bins to help kids learn to garden.

Locavores

    www.locavores.com

    This lively, very local Bay Area group is a joy, reminding me that those of us trying to eat locally grown food in season are part of a wider national and international network of shared commitment.

PERMISSIONS

ACKNOWLEDGMENTS

This book begins and ends with gratitude to the garden and to the many beings, human and more-than-human, that compose a garden, all cultivating the gift of good land and growing real food for a hungry world. I have enduring gratitude for Green Gulch Farm and my fellow practitioners affiliated with the San Francisco Zen Center who believed in and supported this book over the sustained twelve-year period of its coming into print. I wish to thank Dairyu Michael Wenger; senior dharma teachers and former abbots Jiko Linda Cutts and Zoketsu Norman Fischer; and Annie Somerville, executive chef of Greens Restaurant. I greatly appreciate all the lively gardeners with whom I have worked shoulder to shoulder on the land through all the seasons of writing this book.

In the Zen world patch-robed meditators continue to practice under all circumstances. This dragon book would not exist without the extraordinary effort and support of two essential dharma sisters: Jisho Warner, guiding teacher of northern California's Stone Creek Zen Center, returned to editing to indefatigably encourage and show me the way through deep thickets of words as the red-pen roshi of this text. Layla Smith, with whom I lived and practiced at Green Gulch Zen Center for more than fifteen years, held the physical body of this book, taking reams of handwritten pages and rendering them into a coherent typed manuscript. Abiding gratitude to Jisho and Layla.

Toni Burbank, my keen and dedicated editor at Bantam Books, believed in this work from the first and brought it forth with the agency of Michael Katz and the clarity and skill of designer David Bullen. The original drawings by Davis Te Selle illustrate the text in the old sense of the word: by making bright and illuminating the garden. Deep gratitude to Davis and to Stephanie Kaza, his wife, both longtime colleagues and friends.

It has been a great pleasure and honor to be associated for almost three decades with the inspired Bay Area chef and activist Alice Waters. For the past eight years I have served as a mentor and senior garden consultant to the Edible Schoolyard, a project of the Chez Panisse Foundation, where I work with hundreds of young people every school year. Special gratitude to Alice Waters, to the garden at Martin Luther King, Jr. Middle School, and to Kelsey Siegel, Marsha Guerrero, Esther Cook, and the dedicated teachers, staff, Americorps members, and students, who give this important project life.

Gratitude to my mentor Diane Rockloff, and to Joanna Macy and Barbara Gates, with whom I wrote in the formative years of this book. Author Natalie Goldberg has been a powerful support and guide from the beginning, as have many teaching colleagues and

Dharma friends. Gratitude to Mayumi Oda, Therese Fitzgerald and Arnie Kotler, Martha DeBarros, Huey Johnson, members of the Wheelwright and Richardson families, Grove Burnett and Jenny Parks, Helen Whybrow and Peter Forbes, Will Rogers, Cynthia Jurs, Deborah Madison, Yvonne Rand and Bill Sterling, Donald Moyer, Myogen Steve Stucky, Zenobia Barlow and Janet Brown, Harriet Hope and Susannah Mallarkey, Margot Koch, Barbara Wenger, Arlene Lueck, Kathie Fischer, Leslie and Michael Thiele, Nancy Petrin, Gary Friedman and Trish McCall, Marion Weber, Paul Cassot, Jasper Eiler and Brook Jensen, Bea Thornberg and Ellie Maggiora, and Joni Goldsmith.

Primary green-thumbed friends have helped me uncover the core of this book. Special gratitude to Skip Kimura, Virginia Baker and the extended Baker family, Amigo Bob Cantisano and Kalita Todd, Beth Benjamin and Jim Nelson, Kate Burroughs, Liz Milazzo, and Mia Monroe for their deep perception of the natural world. I am also deeply grateful to many close farming colleagues and to their inspiring organic farms. A deep bow to Dennis and Lori of Blue Heron Farm; to Dru, Paul, Judith, and Andrew and all the team at Full Belly Farm; to Annie and Jeff Main of Good Humus Produce; to Mark Cain of Dripping Springs Garden; to Carl and Gina of Woodleaf Farm; to Doug-o and friends at the Occidental Arts and Ecology Center; to the UCSC Farm and Garden program; and to all the unnamed gardeners at work in the wild and cultivated world.

The steady love and support of my family has been essential to the life of this book. Abiding gratitude to my parents, Sallie B. Johnson and William Johnson, for their belief in me and in this work, and to my author-stepmother Sandy Johnson, for encouraging me through grave times. Special gratitude to my husband and farming partner for more than thirty years, Peter Rudnick, and to our children, Jesse and Alisa, for their endless support and forbearance. Gratitude to my sisters, Sally Johnson and her husband Dick Aulenti, Deborah Johnson and her sons William and Christopher, and to my brothers Mark, Bill, and Anthony Johnson and their families. Finally, gratitude to Peter's parents, Charlie and Kate Rudnick, and to Peter's siblings, Charles, Michael, and Kathie and their families.

During the twelve-year gestation of this book, indisputable evidence has traced the accelerated warming of the earth's climate to human activity, in particular to the burning of fossil fuels and the resulting buildup of greenhouse gases in the atmosphere. My fiercest mentors remind me that this is the best and worst time to be alive. Gardening at the dragon's gate, at the edge of consequential danger and pivotal opportunity, may we acknowledge the truth of our times and work together for the benefit of all beings.

I N D E X

431

ABOUT THE AUTHOR

WENDY JOHNSON is a Buddhist meditation teacher and organic gardening mentor who lives in the San Francisco Bay Area.

Wendy has been practicing Zen meditation for thirty-five years and has led meditation retreats nationwide since 1992 as an ordained lay dharma teacher in the traditions of Vietnamese teacher Thich Nhat Hanh and the San Francisco Zen Center. Wendy is one of the founders of the organic Farm and Garden Program at Green Gulch Farm Zen Center in Marin County, where she lived with her family from 1975 to 2000. She has been teaching gardening and environmental education to the public since the early 1980s, helping to establish many garden programs in public schools, local communities, and hospice centers throughout the Bay Area. In 2000 Wendy and her husband, Peter Rudnick, received the annual Sustainable Agriculture Award from the National Ecological Farming Association. Since 1995 Wendy has written a quarterly column, "On Gardening," for *Tricycle Magazine, a Buddhist Review*. She was honored in *The Best Science and Nature Writing 2000*, published by Houghton Mifflin. Wendy is a mentor and advisor to the Edible Schoolyard program of the Chez Panisse Foundation, a project that she has been involved in since its inception in 1995. This is her first book.

ABOUT THE ILLUSTRATOR

DAVIS TE SELLE holds an M.F.A. in printmaking from San Francisco Art Institute and received the 2003 James D. Phelan Award for printmaking in California. He has shown his work in group and solo exhibitions on both East and West Coasts. His illustrations have been published in *Wild Earth, Orion, Turning Wheel, Inquiring Mind*, and *Wild Duck Review*; his lithographs also appeared in *The Attentive Heart: Conversations with Trees*. He teaches nature drawing with the Environmental Program at University of Vermont and maintains a printmaking studio in Burlington, Vermont.

ABOUT THE WEBSITE

FOR SEASONAL UPDATES, additional resources, a schedule of Wendy Johnson's local appearances, and a photo gallery of the Green Gulch gardens and the Edible Schoolyard, please visit www.gardeningatthedragonsgate.com.

ABOUT SAN FRANCISCO ZEN CENTER

SAN FRANCISCO ZEN CENTER was established in 1962 by the Soto Zen master Shunryu Suzuki Roshi (1904-1971), author of the modern spiritual classic *Zen Mind, Beginner's Mind*. San Francisco Zen Center has three complementary practice centers that offer daily meditation, regular retreats and practice periods, classes, lectures, and workshops. The purpose of Zen Center is to make accessible and embody the wisdom and compassion of the Buddha for a diverse population of students, visitors, laypeople, priests, and monks guided by teachers who follow in Suzuki Roshi's "beginners' mind" way.

TASSAJARA ZEN MOUNTAIN CENTER, established in 1966, was the first Soto Zen monastery outside of Asia. Located in the Ventana Wilderness inland from Big Sur, Tassajara, with its natural hot springs, has been a place of renewal and healing for over a century. During the summer, guests are offered a schedule of Zen-related workshops, retreats, and relaxation. The guest program is also famous for its gourmet vegetarian food, a tradition begun by Zen teacher Edward Espe Brown, author of *The Tassajara Bread Book, Tassajara Cooking, The Tassajara Recipe Book*, and *Tomato Blessings and Radish Teachings*.

Located in San Francisco's Hayes Valley, Beginner's Mind Temple, also known as CITY CENTER, was established in 1969 by Suzuki Roshi as a training center open to the general public. Offerings include daily meditation and services, semi-weekly talks, classes, workshops, retreats, and residential student programs. City Center also provides a number of community outreach programs that bring Zen practice to prisoners, the homeless, and those in recovery.

GREEN GULCH FARM ZEN CENTER, also known as Green Dragon Temple, was founded in 1972. Green Gulch is a residential community and organic farm located in Marin County, just north of San Francisco. It provides wholesome produce for the renowned Greens Restaurant, the San Francisco Ferry Plaza Farmer's Market, Rainbow Grocery, and the Zen Center kitchens. For over a decade, Green Gulch has offered an apprenticeship program in organic gardening and farming that emphasizes hands-on work experience and instruction in organic methods, together with meditation practice and study of Buddhist teachings. Many schoolchildren participate in the Green Gulch Farm Environmental Education Program to learn about sustainable food systems.

Since its establishment, San Francisco Zen Center has helped shape the cultural landscape of the Bay Area and beyond, especially in the organic farming and culinary worlds. GREENS, San Francisco Zen Center's pioneering vegetarian restaurant, was opened by

Edward Espe Brown and founding chef Deborah Madison in 1979. Ms. Madison's cookbooks include *Vegetarian Cooking for Everyone, Local Flavors*, and, with Edward Espe Brown, *The Greens Cook Book*. The culinary heritage of Greens continues under executive chef Annie Somerville, whose books include *Everyday Greens* and *Fields of Greens*.

More about the life and work of Suzuki Roshi is available in David Chadwick's *Crooked Cucumber: The Life and Teachings of Shunryu Suzuki*. Suzuki Roshi's teachings are also collected in the books *Branching Streams Flow in the Darkness: Zen Talks on the Sandokai* and *Not Always So: Practicing the True Spirit of Zen*.